Alfred Barbou

Victor Hugo and His Time

Illustrated by Émile Bayard

Alfred Barbou

Victor Hugo and His Time
Illustrated by Émile Bayard

ISBN/EAN: 9783337188351

Printed in Europe, USA, Canada, Australia, Japan

Cover: Foto ©Thomas Meinert / pixelio.de

More available books at **www.hansebooks.com**

VICTOR HUGO

AND HIS TIME

F.MEAULLE

VICTOR HUGO.

ICTOR HUGO

AND

HIS TIME

BY ALFRED BARBOU

ILLUSTRATED WITH 120 DRAWINGS

BY

MM. ÉMILE BAYARD, CLERGET, FICHEL, JULES GARNIER, GERVEX, GIACOMELLI
CH. GOSSELIN, JEAN-PAUL LAURENS, LIX, OLIVIER MERSON, R. MEYER
ED MORIN, SCOTT, VOGEL, ZIER, Etc.

AND

A GREAT NUMBER OF DRAWINGS BY VICTOR HUGO

ENGRAVED BY MÉAULLE

TRANSLATED FROM THE FRENCH BY

ELLEN E. FREWER

Monsieur,

Je ne lirai pas manuscrit le livre que vous publiez. J'ai toujours agi ainsi envers les diverses publications dont j'ai été le sujet; je n'ai lu en manuscrit aucun de ces livres, pas même l'ouvrage de Madame Victor Hugo. Il me semble qu'en cette matière-là, comme en toute autre, je dois être du public.

S'il y a des erreurs, car il y en a, même dans le livre si noble et si touchant de Madame Victor Hugo, elles pourront toujours être corrigées. Ce que le public demande et veut, c'est la vérité, la sincérité, la loyauté parfaite et profonde.

Ces qualités, Monsieur, il les trouvera dans votre ouvrage. Vous avez un talent que j'honore, un esprit que j'aime, des convictions que je partage. Tous mes dons, vous me les offrez, dans cette œuvre où vous parlez de moi; je vous remercie.

Quel que soit le jugement qu'on porte sur moi, je suis tranquille. Ma tentative littéraire, ma tentation politique, ma tentative sociale, sont trois efforts vers le bien. je n'ai jamais eu de côté que contre le mal.

Humanisons l'homme. Soyons avec tous ceux qui ont en eux le désir de voir décroître la souffrance humaine. si diverses que soient les surfaces, le fond, le progrès, est toujours le même. ce qu'a voulu Socrate, est voulu par Molière; ce qu'a voulu Jésus, est voulu par Voltaire.

je presse vos mains cordiales

Victor Hugo

CONTENTS.

CHAPTER XV.

CHAPTER XVI.

CHAPTER XVII.

CHAPTER XVIII.

CHAPTER XIX.

CHAPTER XX.

CHAPTER XXI.

CHAPTER XXII.

CHAPTER XXIII.

CHAPTER XXIV.

CHAPTER XXV.

CHAPTER XXVI.

CHAPTER XXVII.

CHAPTER XXVIII.

CHAPTER XXIX.

CHAPTER XXX.

CHAPTER XXXI.

LIST OF ILLUSTRATIONS.

2

VICTOR HUGO'S BIRTHPLACE AT BESANÇON.

INTRODUCTION.

THE 27th of December, 1880, was a *fête* day at Besançon. The houses in the picturesque old town, which dates further back than the Roman conquest, were hung with flags, and the echoes of music came back from the surrounding hills. On the banks of the river, in the streets, and in the squares, a well-dressed crowd was awaiting a ceremonial of honor. One name was upon every lip—that name was Victor Hugo.

A torch-light procession had opened the rejoicings on the **evening of** the preceding day, which was **Sunday.** Rain was now falling steadily, but no unfavorableness of weather seemed **to damp** the ardor **of** the citizens.

At half-past twelve the principal people of the **town,** and the visitors—many of whom had come from Paris—assembled at the *mairie*, thence to proceed to the Place St. Quentin.

The cortége was headed by the town bands, and escorted by a detachment of soldiers.

M. Oudet, the Mayor, had on his right M. Rambaud, the chief secretary to the Minister of Public Instruction, and on his left General Wolff, commander of the *Corps d'Armée*. After them came deputations from the Senate and the Chamber of Deputies, generals, university dons, the nephew of the President of the Republic, the Rector of the Academy, the Prefect, the Municipal Councillors, and members of the press.

Victor Hugo himself was represented by M. Paul Meurice.

With the exception of a few residences of **the aristocracy,** well-nigh every house along **the route was** gayly decorated.

The deputations halted in front of a house **in the** street facing the Place St. Quentin. **Here a** large platform had been erected, covered with evergreens and flags that bore the initials V. **H.** worked in gold. The adjoining windows were all decorated with camellias in full bloom, and surmounted with escutcheons that were inscribed with the names of "Hernani," "Ruy Blas," and other writings of the poet.

As soon as the audience had taken **their** places, the Mayor introduced the name of the great author in whose honor they had met, and whose birth they were about to celebrate. His speech was interrupted by long and loud applause, and at the close of it a curtain of crimson velvet was removed from between the two first-floor windows, uncovering a memorial plate which henceforth will claim the attention of every passer-by.

This plate, or rather medallion, which is attached to the front of the house, is of bronze. It represents a five-stringed lyre with two laurel branches of gold, and bearing an inscription which, according to the poet's express desire, consists simply of his name and the date of his birth—

VICTOR HUGO:

26TH OF FEBRUARY, 1802.

The lyre is surmounted by a head, typical of the Republic, surrounded by rays.*

Before the acclamations died away, a little girl, the daughter of the proprietor of the house, came forward with a splendid bouquet for Victor Hugo, which was handed by the mayor to M. Paul Meurice.

Leaving the Place St. Quentin, the cortége adjourned to the stage of the Besançon Theatre, on the centre of which had been placed a fine bust of Victor Hugo, executed by David. The boxes, balcony, and orchestra were already occupied by such as had been admitted by tickets; but immediately on the arrival of the procession, the doors of the house

* A wood-cut of the medallion is given on the first page of this volume.

were thrown open, and the general public crowded in and filled the place to overflowing. When quietness was obtained, the Mayor, in a short speech, related what had just taken place in front of the now famous house, and called upon M. Rambaud to address the assembly.

M. Rambaud spoke not merely as the representative of the Minister of Public Instruction, but likewise as a native of Besançon. He made a vigorous sketch of the career of the great man they had met to honor. He told of the struggles which we are about to record; he dwelt upon his great literary battles, his gradual attainment of victory over thought and intellect, his ever-increasing influence, his development as a politician, his internal conflicts, and his final triumph; he depicted his eighteen years' duel with the Empire and his ultimate success; he touched upon the leading characteristics of all his lyrical, dramatic, and historical writings; and concluded by describing how, after a life fraught with conflicts, trials, and sorrows, he found his recompense in the revival of his country, in the progress of democracy, and, not least, in the peaceful joys of home and in the society of his grandchildren.

In the name of Victor Hugo, M. Paul Meurice returned his cordial thanks.

A concert followed, of which the words that were set to music were all extracts from Victor Hugo's poetry. Various selections from his works were likewise recited. M. Paul Meurice next read a letter from the hero of the day himself.

" December, 1880.

" It is with deep emotion that I tender my thanks to my compatriots.

" I am a stone on the road that is trodden by humanity; but that road is a good one; Man is master neither of his life nor of his death. He can but offer to his fellow-citizens his efforts to diminish human suffering. he can but offer to God his indomitable faith in the growth of liberty.

" Victor Hugo."

In the midst of a perfect hurricane of cheers, the marble bust was crowned with a wreath of golden laurel, and one hundred and fifty musicians performed the " Marseillaise," the whole audience standing. The crowd then left the theatre, all shouting vociferously, " Vive Victor Hugo!" Vive la République!"

In the evening the town was illuminated, and over a hundred guests sat down to a banquet in the fine dining-room of the Palais Granvelle, where many more speeches were delivered.

The fête was unique of its kind.

It is our object in the following pages, which are dedicated to Victor Hugo and his century (for the century must ever be associated with his name), to testify our admiration for a man whose every action commands our respect; for the writer who has infused new life into the antiquated diction of our language; for the poet whose verses purify while they fascinate the soul; for the dramatist whose plays exhibit his sympathy with the unendowed classes; for the historian who has branded with ignominy the tyranny of oppressors; for the satirist who has avenged the outrages of conscience; for the orator who has defended every noble and righteous cause; for the exile who has stood up undaunted to vindicate justice; and, finally, for the master-mind whose genius has shed a halo of glory over France.

The task before us is not an easy one; but, aided by many who have given their own personal reminiscences, and having enjoyed various opportunities of conversation with Victor Hugo himself, in which we have gathered not a few unpublished anecdotes, we shall trust to fulfil our undertaking not unworthily. It is the small coin of a great history that we have been collecting, and which in its aggregate is offered to the acceptance of our readers. If the contemporaries of Homer or Dante were alive, with what interest we should learn from their lips any fresh details of the doings of those giants of literature! And something of the same kind of eagerness, we would believe, will be felt even now in following the career of the great genius of our own age.

We have described the enthusiasm and pride that reigned in the streets of Besançon on the memorable fête day in December, 1880; that enthusiasm will still be felt everywhere, and that pride will never diminish. Renown will not fail to attend the name of Victor Hugo.

BUST OF VICTOR HUGO.

VICTOR HUGO AND HIS TIME.

CHAPTER I.

THE Hugo family, whose members have in
latter times become illustrious both in literature and in arms, were originally natives of
Lorraine. In the course of last century
their genealogical tree was carefully drawn
up by D'Hozier in the fourth registry of the
French peerage.

Georges Hugo, the son of Jean Hugo, a
captain in the army of René II., Duke of
Lorraine, resided at Rouvroi-sur-Meuse, and,
on the 14th of April, 1535, obtained letters-
patent of nobility for himself and his descendants from Cardinal Jean de Lorraine,
Archbishop of Rheims. These letters dated
from Lillebonne in Normandy, and the en-
noblement was afterwards confirmed on October 16, 1537, by Antoine, Duke of Lorraine, brother of the cardinal, by other let-
ters-patent dated from Nancy. They testify
that although Georges Hugo was quite
young when he obtained his warrant of nobility, he had already seen much active service; also that he had married a lady of Bla-
mont of noble birth.

The arms of the ancient Hugo family are:
Azure; on a chief argent two martlets sable;
on the escutcheon a vol banneret azure bearing a fesse argent. In the arms of the house
of Lorraine itself there are three martlets argent, so that the duke could scarcely have
conferred higher dignity on his captain.

Charles Hyacinthe Hugo, the fifth descend-
ant from Georges, obtained fresh letters-pat-
ent; and his grandson, Sigisbert Hugo, commenced service in 1788.

Although the authenticity of this descent
has been questioned by certain genealogists,
who assert that Victor Hugo's grandfather
was engaged in trade, it appears to admit of
no question. It is, indeed, quite likely that
the statement is true, inasmuch as many of
the most illustrious families have had to submit to reverses; but it does not leave it the
less certain that Victor Hugo, who would
never blush to own himself of humble ex-
traction if he were so, and who estimates
men solely by their merits, is nevertheless a
scion of that ancient nobility that earned its
venerable titles by services rendered to the
commonwealth.

The roll of the poet's celebrated ancestors
includes Charles Louis Hugo, the French historian, who died in 1739. After graduating
as doctor in theology, he devoted himself for
some time to tuition, and subsequently established a printing-press in the monastery of the
order of the Premonstrants, to which he had
attached himself for the purpose of advancing
learned studies. The result of a long dispute which he had with the Bishop of Toul
was that Pope Benedict III. gave judgment
in his favor, and, moreover, bestowed upon
him the title of Bishop of Ptolemaïde. He
was equally well known as Abbé of Estival.
He was the author of several books, one,
among others, published under the *nom de
plume* of Baleicourt, being a critical and historical treatise on the "Origin and Genealogy of the House of Lorraine;" it appeared
at Nancy in 1711. Another of his works,
comprising the history of Lorraine, was issued under the *nom de plume* of Jean Pierre
Louis, P.P.

Our poet's father, having obtained the rank
of general under the first Empire, had really
the right to assume the title of count, and to

transmit it as hereditary; but he never avail- ed himself of the privilege, although Louis XVIII., in an order dated November 14, 1814, confirmed him in his rank of major- general from September 11, 1813. A son of the Revolution, he resigned his sword in 1815. More than one of his associates re- mained in the service until 1830, and some even until 1848; but he was not a man to make any compromise with his conscience.

Brief as this sketch of his genealogy may be, it will suffice to exhibit how the blood of Lorraine flows in Victor Hugo's veins; his forefathers "avaient donjon sur roche et fief dans la campagne."

Any notice of this kind, however, would be altogether incomplete without mention of his descent by his mother's side. She was the daughter of a wealthy ship-owner at Nantes, and granddaughter of one of the leaders of the *bourgeoisie* of the province that was so long and faithfully the valiant defence of Catholic loyalty. She was also a cousin of Constantine François, Count de Chassebœuf, universally known as Volney, the author of "Les Ruines," a book which, although anti- quated, and apparently on the way to be for- gotten, yet contains many eloquent and strik- ing passages upon the fate of empires. Anoth- er cousin was Count Cornet, who played no inconsiderable part in political affairs, both during the first Empire and before its time.

A few words must be said about the per- sonal history of the poet's parents.

Joseph Léopold Sigisbert Hugo was born in Nancy, and at the age of fourteen was en- rolled as a military cadet. His family may, without exaggeration, be described as a race of heroes: five of his brothers were killed during the wars of the Revolution; the sixth became a major in the infantry, while he himself, the father of the illustrious son whose name will ever be associated with the nineteenth century, rose to the rank of gen- eral.

After being appointed aide-de-camp and secretary to General Alexandre Beauharnais, Joseph Hugo left him almost immediately, in order to follow his intimate friend, Gen- eral Muscar, into La Vendée. It was the company under the command of this officer which captured Charette in the woods of Chabotière in 1795. In the course of the campaign, young Hugo had many opportu- nities of exhibiting his courage and good- nature, and earned his captain's epaulets.

His duties very frequently took him into Nantes, where he became acquainted with a ship-owner named Trébuchet, who had three daughters, one of whom, Sophie, soon stole the captain's heart and subsequently became his wife.

There is no need here to recapitulate all the details of the union; they have already been recounted in Madame Victor Hugo's book. The marriage took place in Paris, whither the bridegroom had been summoned as reporter to the first council of war on the Seine. Two sons, Abel and Eugène, were born in succession; and shortly after the birth of the latter the father had to start off on the Rhine campaign, being appointed attaché to General Moreau, the chief of whose staff was Adjutant-general Victor Lahorie and his aide-de-camp Brigadier Jacques Delelée, of Besançon. With both of these officers Major Hugo formed an intimate acquaint- ance.

His character is described in the "Biogra- phie des Contemporains" as a happy mixt- ure of candor, honesty, and benevolence. He was intelligent in his conversation, which was ever full of interesting reminiscences equal- ly amusing and instructive. As an author he has left some important military works, which we shall subsequently have occasion to notice. He set his children a fine exam- ple of duty, being ever their instructor in the paths of honor.

On his return from the Rhine he had at- tained commander's rank; and in the begin- ning of 1801 he was appointed to the com- mand of the fourth battalion of the twentieth half-brigade, then quartered at Besançon.

At that time Jacques Delelée, Moreau's aide-de-camp, had recently returned to Besan- çon, and was residing with his young wife, Marie Anne Dessirier, in a house in the Rue des Granges. This lady, who died in 1850, used often to relate the story of Victor Hu- go's birth.

On his arrival at the town, Major Hugo took up his residence with his old friend De- lelée, partaking of his hospitality for a period of three months. At the end of that time he sent for his wife and two children, and rent- ed the first floor of a house in the Place du Capitole.

Though the wife of a soldier of the Revo- lution and of the Empire—a man personally attached to Desaix, Jourdan, and Joseph Bonaparte—Madame Hugo was herself the friend of Madame La Rochejaquelein. A true Vendean, she was intelligent, brave, and

gentle, and a sincere, though by no means bigoted, Catholic. She was a model mother.

Within a year after she had rejoined her husband, the birth of a third child was anticipated. Major Hugo, having already two sons, expressed a hope that it would be a girl, and announced his intention of naming her Victorine. A godmother was already determined on in the person of Madame Delelée, but a godfather had still to be sought, and it occurred to the parents to ask General Lahorie, who was then in Paris, to undertake the sponsorship. Madame Hugo submitted her request in such a charming letter that the general did not hesitate to acquiesce in her desire.

In due time the child was born, but it proved another boy—a miserable little creature, more dead than alive. Its decrepit condition made it indispensable that the infant should be baptized at once; a hurried visit, however, to the *mairie* was previously made, where the register subjoined was entered:

On the opening page of the "Feuilles d'Automne," Victor Hugo has written some well-known lines, which form a sort of poetical paraphrase of the above register of his birth. They run somewhat to this effect:

> "This century two years had rolled along,
> When in Besançon, citadelled and strong,
> A little babe was born, the heir of pain,
> A scion both of Bretagne and Lorraine;
> A little babe, so fragile and so weak,
> It seemed to come to life its death to seek;
> So delicate, its like 'twere rare to find,
> A tiny seed blown helpless by the wind;
> A mere chimera—yea, a thing of naught—
> To rear it must exceed a mother's thought:
> Asleep, its head bent down upon its breast,
> It looked to take upon its bier its rest.
> That little babe myself! And ah! how well
> I might the story of my progress tell!
> How, all-responsive to my mother's prayer,
> How, all-succeeding to my mother's care,
> I gain'd new life, found day by day new pow'r,
> And through her love survive to see this hour;
> A guardian dear, a very angel she
> To all her sons, but most of all to me!"

The verses in the original are very fine; but we may leave them without further

EXTRAIT DE NAISSANCE

It will be observed that Madame Delelée figures as a witness, women at that time having the right to act in such a capacity. Madame Hugo recovered so quickly from her confinement that twenty-two days later she appeared as witness to the birth-register of the son of one of her husband's fellow-officers, which bears her signature. She was at that date twenty-five years of age, her husband being twenty-eight.

comment, to inquire into the significance of their author's illustrious name.

In Old German the word "Hugo" is the equivalent of the Latin "spiritus," betokening breath or life. To this cognomen were prefixed the names Victor Marie, being those of the two sponsors, General Victor Fanneau de Lahorie and Madame Delelée, and not inaptly has it been remarked that "the northern appellation was mellowed by the south-

GENERAL HUGO, VICTOR HUGO'S FATHER.

ern, the Roman came in to give completeness to the Teuton." As Alexandre Dumas the elder has finely rendered it, "the name of Victor Hugo stands forth as the conquering spirit, the triumphant soul, the breath of victory!"

And it is indeed no exaggeration to maintain that his is eminently a triumphant soul of this our century, so that the men of Besançon may fitly glory in the master-mind that, as it were by chance, first saw the light of day among them. The people of the place declare that, although it was the blood of Brittany and Lorraine that circulated in his veins, it was not solely to his mother's care, but to the salubrity of the climate, that he owed his life; they boast that the pure air of Franche-Comté, the air which makes sound bodies and sound minds, rendered him absolutely one of themselves. They further maintain that Besançon was never a truly Spanish town, but that for centuries before it belonged to France it had had an independent existence, preserving its municipal institutions intact; and that, with the pure air of its mountains, it had handed down to its children from generation to generation those principles of liberty and equality which Victor Hugo imbibed with his mother's milk.

An impartial historian cannot ignore the fact that Victor Hugo was born with a thoroughly sound constitution. Sickly and feeble though he looked, he had a good broad chest and pair of shoulders, and was what is generally termed stoutly built. To this, as well as to the untiring care and attention that he received from his mother, he was indebted for his life.

Entered in the register as a soldier's son, Victor Hugo left Besançon while still an infant in long clothes, and has never since visited his birthplace. Not even in December, 1880, was he able to proceed thither; and although more than once he has formed the project of undertaking the journey, his incessant labors have always interfered to hinder him from carrying out his purpose.

Unlike Lamartine, who makes frequent mention of the scenes of his childhood, and speaks again and again of Milly and Saint-Point, Victor Hugo would appear never to have introduced the name of his birthplace except in the verses already referred to. He knew no particulars about the house in which he first saw the light, and the regard which has recently been bestowed upon the building, under the presidency of the mayor of the town, has made him acquainted with various particulars which have now become matters of history.

CHAPTER II.

Infancy.—From Besançon to Marseilles.—From Marseilles to Elba.—First Stay in Paris.—The House in the Rue de Clichy.—The Well in the Court-yard.—Departure for Italy.—Reminiscences of the Journey.—Early Impressions.—Victor Hugo's own Account of Youthful Travels.—The Marble Palace of Avellino.—Colonel Hugo in Spain with Joseph Bonaparte.—Return of the Family to Paris.

THE new-born infant, the third son of Major Hugo, was unlike either of his elder brothers.

Abel, the oldest of the three, exhibited that healthy robustness which ever charms the eye. Eugène's constitution was such as to give no anxiety, but Victor remained so sickly that for fifteen months after his birth his shoulders seemed incapable of supporting the weight of his head, of which it has been said that, "as if already containing the germs of mighty thought that were awaiting their development, it could not be prevented from falling prone upon his breast."

With the perseverance characteristic of a true mother, Madame Hugo succeeded in rescuing her child from the very jaws of death, and not only did he grow up himself to enjoy a life of health and vigor, but he has imparted life to an entire nation by his books, his sentiments, his intellect, and his example. The generations of the present are animated by his spirit; the generations of the future will not cease to feel its influence still.

While it was as yet quite uncertain whether the sinister forebodings of the accoucheur who had assisted at his birth would not be realized, Victor Hugo, at the age of six weeks, was taken from Besançon and carried off on a toilsome journey to Marseilles. Here, before long, his mother was obliged to leave him, having to go to Paris to endeavor to obtain a change of brigade for her husband. The little infant suffered very keenly from the separation, and it is said shed floods of tears over the bonbons with which his father tried to console him for his loss.

It was some months before Madame Hugo rejoined her family. Her application had not been attended with the success she anticipated. The reward that her husband obtained for his services was little better than exile, for he received orders to take command of a garrison in the Isle of Elba. Thus it fell out, as Alexandre Dumas has remarked

in his "Mémoires," that the author of the "Ode à la Colonne" *devait commencer à vivre* in the very island where the great Napoleon *devait commencer à mourir.*

The first language, therefore, spoken by Victor was Italian—the Italian of the Isles; and the first word he was known to speak after the articulation of papa, mamma, which is common to children of every tongue, was the term *cattiva* (naughty), which he applied to his nurse.

Moving from island to island, the family proceeded from Porto Ferrajo to Bastia; but of these various peregrinations the child's mind did not retain a shadow of remembrance, and the first intercourse which he had with the world on the threshold of his existence would appear to have left no trace upon his memory.

Nevertheless, it has been written that "the first scene upon which his eye fell with any intelligence was the rugged outline of the obscure spot since so famous. Already fortuitous circumstances were bringing his young life into harmony with the great destiny that lay before him; the thread, frail and all but invisible, was already being mingled with the splendid woof, and was running, hidden though it might be for a time, beneath the new-made purple of which he was to dignify the last shred." [*]

After a year marked by many vicissitudes, Victor Hugo's father was summoned to join the army in Italy. Joseph Bonaparte, hitherto plenipotentiary, had just been nominated King of Naples; and retaining a kind remembrance of his friend the major at Luneville and Besançon, he invited him to join his fortunes and to assist him in establishing his throne in that goodly city of which it has been said that "a man should see Naples and die." The officer had recently been promoted to the rank of lieutenant-colonel, or, as it

---

[*] "Biographie Rabbe et Boisjolin" (1834).

was at that period more generally designated, gros-major.

Napoleon, having long treated this faithful soldier with much injustice, now deigned to signify his assent to his change of service, adding that he was pleased to see the French element among his brother's forces, which were the wings of his own army.

Accordingly the lieutenant-colonel joined King Joseph, but, concerned for his family, and aware that they could hardly fail to suffer from a continuation of their wandering life, he determined to send them to Paris, where they arrived at the end of 1805 or early in the following year.

Madame Hugo, with her three young children, took up her abode at 24 Rue de Clichy. The house, like most of those in which the poet spent his early days, has been entirely destroyed, and its site is now occupied by the square surrounding the Church of the Holy Trinity.

This is the first place of residence of which Victor Hugo has any distinct recollection. As he has himself informed us, there was a goat in the court-yard, and a well overhung

·THE WELL IN THE GARDEN.

by a weeping willow, and not far from the well stood a cattle-trough.

Round this well he used to play, having for his companion young Delon, who was subsequently condemned on account of the Saumur affair, and died in Greece while commanding Lord Byron's artillery. Victor was sent to school in the Rue de Mont-Blanc, where he was treated with special care on account of his remaining so delicate; he was habitually so low-spirited that no one except his mother could ever make him smile.

Meanwhile the gros-major was commissioned to capture Fra Diavolo, the bandit-patriot who was disputing Joseph Bonaparte's accession to the throne of Naples; and in spite of its difficulty and danger, he accomplished his task, and succeeded afterwards in reducing the bands of La Puglia. In acknowledgment of these services the king made him colonel of royal Corsica and governor of Avellino.

As soon as peace was restored in Italy, the lieutenant-colonel again sent for his wife and children; and thus in October, 1807, Victor Hugo recommenced the series of travels which began before he could walk, and have continued throughout his life. It was during this sojourn in Italy that his powers of observation began to develop themselves, and he received his first artistic impressions. Many a time must he have been thrilled with his father's stories of the romantic exploits of Fra Diavolo; and although he was only five years old at the time, it is certain that he never forgot this journey.

Wearisome as was the route from Paris to Naples, it was not devoid of interesting incidents. A number of these have been related in Madame Victor Hugo's book, and others were recounted by the poet himself to Dumas, one of his best of friends.

Dumas writes: "Often on my return from Italy, whither I have been some fifteen or twenty times, Hugo, who had merely once traversed the country, would speak to me of the grand aspects of that beautiful land which appeared as fresh in his memory as if he had been my companion in all my journeys. But he always spoke of objects not so much as they really were, but in association with some accidental circumstance that for the time had diverted his attention from their normal character. For instance, Parma was to him always in the midst of floods; the volcanic rock of Aquapendente was being rent by the lightning, and Trajan's Column never ceased to be surrounded by excavations at its base. Of other places, such as Florence, with its battlemented hostels, its massive places and granite fortresses; of Rome, with its fountains, its Egyptian-like obelisks, and its Bernese colonnade, sister to the Louvre; of Naples, with its promenades, its Posilippo, its Strada di Toledo, its bay and its islands; of Mount Vesuvius — his ideas were all as correct as possible.

*   *   *   *

"It was not at Naples that accommodation was provided for Madame Hugo and her children, but at Avellino, the capital of the province of which her husband had been appointed governor. The palace in which they were quartered, like most of the structures in the country where marble is more plentiful than stone, was a palace of marble. It had one peculiarity that could hardly fail to strike the eye of a child, or to make a lasting impression on his memory. One of the earthquakes so common in the Italian peninsula had recently shaken Calabria from end to end. Like other buildings, the palace at Avellino had oscillated in the shock, but being substantially based on its foundation, after tottering till it threatened to fall, it had stood its ground, though ominously damaged from top to bottom, and diagonally across the wall of Victor's room there was a crack through which he could see the surrounding country almost as well as through his window.

"The palace was built upon a kind of precipice covered with large nut-trees, producing the huge filberts called 'avelines' after the district in which they grow. During the season when the nuts were ripe the children spent much of their time in gathering the clusters, many of which quite overhung the precipice; and then doubtless it was that Hugo had his first experience in climbing, and gained that indifference to crags and precipices which to me, giddy as I always am on a first-floor balcony, has always been a matter of admiration."[*]

To some readers these details may seem too trivial to merit any record; but, as the brilliant writer above quoted has remarked, in treating of an incomparable genius like Victor Hugo, who has played so grand a part in the literary and political history of his country, it is the duty of one who has known him to lay before the eyes alike of his contemporaries and of posterity every possible touch of light and shade which has contributed to the character of the man and of the poet.

Madame Hugo and her children did not remain in Italy more than a year. In 1808, when Napoleon had decided that the Spanish Bourbons were no longer to reign, Joseph Bonaparte was transferred from Naples to be King of Spain. Lieutenant-colonel Hugo followed him to Madrid; but as he was well aware of the hazard involved in settling in a country where war was going on, and as his wife's health and his children's education had already suffered much from their long journeyings, he made up his mind to part with them for a time, and sent them to Paris.

Arrived at the capital, Madame Hugo was fully resolved to devote herself assiduously to the education of her family. Her residence in the capacious palace at Avellino had made her appreciate the advantages of having airy and ample space for the boys to play, and she exerted herself to find a house with a flower-garden, which at the same time should be in the neighborhood of the schools.

At first, and with scarcely due consideration, she took up her abode in a house near the Church of St. Jacques du Haut-Pas. Victor Hugo does not recollect the precise spot, and does not even know whether the place is still in existence; he only remembers that the ground-floor on which he lived was approached by a passage from the street.

But although the garden was large enough for the children's play, the apartments were much too small for domestic convenience, and had to be given up almost immediately. The young family was removed to another abode not far distant, which, as it became to them a more permanent place of residence, demands more particular mention.

[*] "Mémoires de Dumas."

CHAPTER III.

AT the end of a kind of *cul-de-sac* called the Impasse des Feuillantines stood No. 12, the house to which reference has just been made. In his own writings Victor Hugo has several times referred to the place in terms that we shall presently quote; but he has also given the writer of the present biography a verbal description of some of the leading features of the dwelling where he passed a certain period of his early years. He can still picture the handsome grilled gateway that had to be passed before entering the court-yard leading to the front door. On the right hand of the door, and on the same level, was an apartment that served as a play-room in rainy weather. Immediately facing the door was a short staircase that led up to the *salon,* through which, on the left, there was access to Madame Hugo's own room, which, in its turn, opened into another room assigned to the children. By the side of these were two more apartments, one of them the dining-room, the other reserved as a spare bedroom.

The *salon* was both spacious and lofty. At the farther end of it was a flight of steps leading down to the garden. Beneath the windows were beds of the flowers to which Madame Hugo was partial, and to the left of the flower-beds was a piece of waste land, full of holes and excavations, in the middle of which was a *puisard,* a kind of shallow basin, but not containing any water. Here young Victor daily set snares, each in its turn more ingenious than the last, to catch a salamander, that marvellous creature that exists only in juvenile imaginations.

At a little distance farther on, shadowed by spreading trees, was a long walk leading to a patch of wood, the remains of a park once attached to the ancient convent of the Feuillantines, and quite at the extreme was a ruined chapel, and under the chestnut-trees hung a swing. Almost close to the front door of the house, on the left, was a narrow passage reserved for the gardener's use.

The poet has thus immortalized the scene:

"Large was the garden, weird its pathways all,
From curious eyes concealed by upreared wall;
The flowers, like opening eyelids, peered around,
Vermillion insects paced the stony ground.
Mysterious buzzings filled the sultry air;
Here a mere field, a sombre thicket there."

Again, as late as 1875, Victor Hugo wrote some additional touching reminiscences of his early years:

"At the beginning of this century, in the most deserted quarter of Paris, in a large house, surrounded and shut in by a spacious garden, dwelt a little child. The house, before the Revolution, had been called the Convent of the Feuillantines. With that child lived his mother and two brothers. Another resident in that household was an aged priest, formerly a member of the Oratory, still smarting from the persecutions of '93, but now a kind and indulgent tutor, from whom the boys learned a good deal of Latin, a smattering of Greek, but the barest outlines of history. Concealed by the wide-branching trees at the end of the garden stood a ruined chapel, to which the children were forbidden to go. House, chapel, trees, have now all disappeared. The embellishments so profusely added to the garden of the Luxembourg have been extended to the Val de Grâce, demolishing our humble oasis in their progress. A new street, equally grand and useless, now passes over its site, and of the venerable Convent of the Feuillantines no vestige remains beyond a plot of grass and the fragment of an ancient wall visible between the walls of two pretentious modern buildings—a mere fragment, not worth the trouble of glancing at, except with the eye that recognizes it as a souvenir of the past. In January, 1871, there was a continuation of the work of embellishment; a Prussian bomb made choice of this partic-

THE GARDEN OF THE FEUILLANTINES.

3

ular spot for its descent, so that Bismarck completed what Haussmann had begun.

"Here, in the time of the first Empire, grew up the three brothers. Together in their work and in their play, rough-hewing their lives regardless of destiny, they passed their time as children of the spring, mindful only of their books, of the trees, and of the clouds, listening to the tumultuous chorus of the birds, but watched over incessantly by one sweet and loving smile. Blessings on thee, O my mother!

"Upon the walls, half hidden among the cankered and unnailed espaliers, every here and there, were niches for Madonnas and fragments of crucifixes, while occasionally a notice-board might be observed bearing the inscription 'National Property.'

"To the youngest of those three brothers the house of the Feuillantines is now a dear and hallowed memory. For him it is invested with a kind of glamour. There, amid sunshine and roses, was mysteriously wrought the development of his soul. Nothing could be more peaceful than that old ruin, covered with the beauty of flowers; once a convent, now a solitude, ever an asylum; and yet the tumult of the Empire awakened an echo even there. Within those spacious abbey chambers, amid those monastery ruins, beneath those dismantled cloister vaults, in the interval between two wars, the sound of which had reached his ears, the child beheld the arrival from the army, and the return to the army again, of two soldiers — a young general and a colonel, his father and his uncle. The excitement of the paternal home-coming had a charm that was merely momentary: a trumpet-call, and all at once the apparition of plumes and sabres vanished away, and again there was silence and solitude in the lonely ruin.

"And thus, already thoughtful, sixty years ago I lived a child! Only with deep emotion can I recall those days.

"My life glided on amid the flowers. In the garden of the Feuillantines I rambled as a child, I wandered as a youth, watching butterflies, culling buttercups, seeing no one but my mother and my two brothers and the good old priest who perambulated the place, his book continually beneath his arm.

"Occasionally I would venture through the garden to the gloomy thicket at the end: in its dim recesses there would seem no motion but the winds; the solitary sound came from the birds' nests; no life was manifest except in the trees. Gazing through the branches, I could espy the crumbling fabric of the ancient chapel, and the shattered panes enabled me to perceive the sea-shells fantastically embedded on the inner wall. The birds flew in and out of the unprotected windows; for the birds the ruin was a home. God and the birds were there together."

Such are Victor Hugo's own reflections.

Madame Hugo lived a most retired life, entertaining none but a few intimate friends, and devoting herself to her children. Strict yet tender, grave yet gentle, conscientious, well informed, vigilant, and thoroughly impressed with the importance of her maternal duties, she was a woman of superior intellect, having, however, much of that masculine disposition which Plato would have described as "royal." She fulfilled her mission nobly. Tenderness, not unaccompanied by reserve, discipline that was systematic and not to be disputed, the slightest of all approaches to familiarity, and grave discourses replete with instruction, were the principal features of the training which her deep affection prompted her to bestow upon her children in general—upon Victor in particular. Altogether, her teaching was vigorous and wholesome, without a touch of mysticism or of doubt, and she did her part to make her sons worthy of the name of men. Happy are those who are nurtured with such devotion; the remembrance of its example becomes an abiding safeguard!

Every word of Madame Hugo's was listened to with respect, and every direction obeyed without a murmur. Though there were many fruit-trees in the garden, the boys were forbidden to touch the fruit.

"But what if it falls?" asked Victor.

"Leave it on the ground."

"And what if it is getting rotten?"

"Let it get rotten."

And, as far as the children were concerned, the fruit on the ground would lie and rot.

The owner of Madame Hugo's house was Lalande, the astronomer. He lived next door, and his garden was separated from that of the Feuillantines only by some light trellis-work. Fearing that he should be annoyed by the children, he proposed to put up a more substantial partition.

"You need not be afraid," said the mother; "my boys will not trespass upon your property. I have forbidden them."

No barrier of any kind was erected, yet

neither of the three brothers was ever known to set foot upon the landlord's ground.

At the beginning of their residence in the Feuillantines, and before the arrival of General Lahorie, Abel, the eldest boy, was placed at college, the other two, up to the time of their departure to Spain, going daily to a school in the Rue Saint Jacques, where a worthy man, le Père Larivière, who, in spite of his humble circumstances, was well informed, instructed the young people of the neighborhood in reading, writing, and elementary arithmetic.

Every time the two children returned from school they had to pass through groups of street-boys that were always playing in the *cul-de-sac*. These were chiefly the sons of the cotton-workers, who were very numerous in the neighborhood, as there was a factory close by, just opposite the Deaf and Dumb Asylum. No doubt both Victor and his brother, left to themselves, would have been ready enough to accept the invitation to join in the open-air sports; but their mother had forbidden it, and accordingly it was not to be thought of for an instant. It was not without an effort that young Victor turned his eye away from the games that were going on, and fixed it resolutely on the great blank wall on the other side that extended half-way along the Impasse of the Feuillantines, being the side of an old ecclesiastical structure of the seventeenth century.

Regularly at the same time, day after day, an old woman used to pass along the street carrying brooms for sale, and Victor Hugo can still distinctly call to mind the melancholy tone with which she repeated her cry, "Brooms! birch brooms! who'll buy my birch brooms?"

Many similar circumstances of this time are plainly impressed upon his memory, and he recollects how he learned his letters all alone by looking at them, and, having acquired the knowledge of their form, how quickly he learned to spell.

One remarkable incident, not likely to be ever forgotten, was associated with this period of convent-like existence. Long ago Victor Hugo promised to communicate its details, and he has been as good as his word. His godfather, General Lahorie, who had been implicated in Moreau's affair in 1804, had contrived to elude pursuit by taking refuge with a friend. There he fell ill, but his sense of honor would not allow him to be an object of danger to his benefactor. Having on one occasion caught sight of an expression of alarm on the countenance of his host, he felt so convinced that his fever would only be aggravated by the feeling that he was compromising the safety of his friend, that he insisted on being removed in a litter that very day, and was carried to the house in the Rue de Clichy where Madame Hugo was residing. With her characteristic fearlessness and generosity, she at once admitted the friend of her youth; but he was so agitated by the fear of exposing her and her children to any risk that at the end of three days, when his fever had abated, he sought another retreat. In 1809, however, worn out with adventures, weary of being pursued, and having been driven to every stratagem of disguise, he once again presented himself at the door of Madame Hugo, now settled in the Impasse of the Feuillantines.

Here for a while he found a secure refuge, the seclusion was complete, and during two years he continued to reside in the place. What he was, and how he lived throughout that period, may be described in the words of his illustrious godson:

"Victor Fanneau de Lahorie was a gentleman of Brittany who had thrown in his lot with the Republic. He was a friend of Moreau, who was a Breton like himself. In La Vendée, Lahorie made acquaintance with my father, his junior by five-and-twenty years. Subsequently they were brothers-in-arms in the army of the Rhine, and their friendship became of that intimate nature that one would well-nigh have been ready to die to save the other. In 1801, Lahorie was implicated in Moreau's plot against Bonaparte. A price was set upon his head. No place of asylum was to be found, when my father's doors were opened to him, and the ruined chapel of the Feuillantines was proposed as a safe retreat for the ruined man. The offer was accepted as simply as it was made, and there, in the shadow of obscurity, the refugee passed his time.

"None but my father and mother knew precisely who he was. To us children his arrival was a mysterious surprise; but to the old père, who had experienced proscription enough during his life to take away astonishment at anything, a refugee was merely a sign of the times, and to be lurking in a hiding-place was a matter of course.

"My mother enjoined upon us boys a silence which we most scrupulously kept, and after a short time the stranger ceased to be a mystery, for what satisfaction could there be in making a mystery about an ordinary member of a household? He soon began to share the family meals; he walked about the garden, sometimes handling a spade to help the the air, he would suddenly let me descend to within a little of the ground.

"Of his real name I was in ignorance. My mother always called him the general: to me he was my godfather.

"Continuing to occupy the ruin at the bottom of the garden, he bivouacked there,

GENERAL LAHORIE.

gardener; he gave us good advice, and occasionally supplemented the lessons of our tutor with lectures of his own. He had a way of lifting me in his arms that amused me, while it caused me some sensation of alarm; after having raised me up high in regardless of the rain and snow that in winter were driven in through the paneless window-frames. His camp-bed was under the shelter of the altar, and in a corner were his pistols, and a Tacitus, which he used to like to explain to me.

"'Child,' he would say to me, while expatiating on the Roman Republic—'child, everything must yield to liberty.'"

In this way has the poet sketched one great figure that never disappeared from his horizon, and of which distance only magnified the proportions. Thanks to his teacher, he disdained the dead level of the university, and rose to a free method of his own!

As the result of an odious machination, Lahorie was discovered and arrested at the Feuillantines in 1811, and was cast into a prison, which he left only to die.

Subsequently to the journey to Spain, which we are about to describe, and when Madame Hugo had returned to the Feuillantines with her two youngest children, she was one evening walking past the Church of St. Jacques du Haut Pas, Victor's hand was in his mother's, when she paused, her eye being attracted by a great white placard posted against one of the pillars. The passers-by seemed to throw but a hurried and unwilling glance upon it, and to hasten on their way. Madame Hugo, pointing to the placard with her finger, said to Victor·

"Read that!"

The child repeated aloud, "Empire Fran-

çais! By sentence of court-martial, for conspiracy against the Empire and the Emperor, the three ex-generals Malet, Guidal, and Lahorie have been shot on the plain of Grenelle."

This was the way in which Victor Hugo first became acquainted with his godfather's name, and it may readily be imagined how bitter and how lasting was the impression made by the execution on the ardent mind of the child.

While Lahorie was reaping the reward of his high principles in the dungeon of La Force, his two young friends received a visit from their uncle, General Louis Hugo, who came on behalf of his brother to accelerate the departure of his family to Spain, where the government of the new king seemed to be establishing its hold.

Madame Hugo told her children that they would have to know Spanish in three months' time. They could speak it at the end of six weeks.

The day before they started, Paris was gay with illuminations in honor of the birth of the King of Rome, and this was Victor Hugo's last vision of the city before his departure for Madrid.

CHAPTER IV.

A JOURNEY to Madrid at that date was an enterprise attended by no inconsiderable danger. First of all, there was the entire transit of France from Paris to Bayonne, which, though now to be accomplished in a comparatively few hours, in 1811 occupied about nine days. Madame Hugo engaged the whole of the diligence, which, like all those of the period, was painted green, the imperial color, and held six passengers inside and three in the coupé in front.

Victor begged to be allowed to make the journey in the coupé, and from Poitiers he had the company of two strangers, who, having represented that they were urgently pressed for time, were permitted to have seats. One of them, named Isnel, through his kind and flattering attentions left a lasting impression upon the poet's memory.

On reaching Bayonne the travellers were informed that they must wait there a month until the arrival of what was called "the convoy," being the treasure for King Joseph that had to be conveyed through Spain under the protection of a large escort.

That stay at Bayonne Victor Hugo has never forgotten. He still remembers the theatre to which his mother took him to see the same piece several times over.

Bayonne, too, was the scene of Victor's first romance in life, as he here met with a little girl with whom he fell deeply in love, and was absorbed for the moment in his passion; but he had quickly to part from the little maiden who had inspired it, never to see her again.

In due time the start was made for Madrid. As Madame Victor Hugo has recounted the principal details of the long journey, it will be needful only to insert a few particulars to which she has not referred.

Although Joseph Bonaparte had been proclaimed King of Spain, his authority was practically limited to Madrid and to the places occupied by the French army. All the rest of the country was in a state of revolt; and though the passage of an army corps might occasionally make a gap in the insurrection, the anarchy would immediately again break out in the rear.

To levy any contributions was an utter impossibility. Joseph might declare himself King of Spain and of the Indies, though in fact he had no possession of either the one or the other; but not simply would he have been unable to maintain the dignity of a court, he would literally have died of starvation at Madrid, if Napoleon had not regularly sent him his quarterly stipend as a prefect of the Empire.

The sum allotted every year to a prefect was 48,000,000 francs; consequently every three months there was an instalment of 12,000,000 francs to be forwarded to Spain. This was known as "le trésor," and was most eagerly coveted by the Spanish guerilleros, who more than once succeeded in capturing it, in spite of the strong escort that was sent to protect it on its transit.

Travellers on their way to Madrid were glad to make their journey under the protection of these royal convoys.

Before leaving Bayonne, Madame Hugo, to enable her to travel with this safeguard, had purchased the only vehicle that was to be obtained. It was one of those great lumbering carriages that are now to be seen only in Piranesi's drawings, or perchance at some pontifical *fête* in the streets of Rome. It may be described as a huge box, slung between two shafts by means of enormous braces, the steps being placed in such a way that, in order to get inside, the traveller has to climb right over the shaft. It had, however, one advantage; its sides were ball-proof, not to be penetrated by bullets or ordinary grape-shot; consequently, on an emergency, it might be converted into a fortress.

Following behind the treasure came a line of nearly three hundred vehicles, some drawn by four mules, others by six; altogether form ing a cavalcade more than two miles in length. Madame Hugo's carriage was at the head of all the rest, immediately in the rear of the treasure, which was guarded by five hundred men with their muskets loaded. A file of soldiers kept the line, and five hundred more, with a large cannon, completed the procession, which, as Alexandre Dumas expresses

an indelible impression upon the mind of the child, who afterwards depicted his experience in such vivid colors:

" Before my wondering eye did Spain unfold
Her prisons, convents, structures new and old.
Grand Burgos' minster reared in Gothic style,
Irun's strange roofs, Vittoria's lofty pile ;
Nor were thy courts, Valladolid, forgot
Where ancient chains in pride were left to rot !"

THE JOURNEY TO SPAIN.

it, moved forward " like a great reptile that could bite with its head, and sting with its tail." *

After a wearisome journey lasting nearly three months, and marked by diversified incidents, the convoy reached Madrid in June, 1811. The slow progress through Spain made

Madame Hugo's husband was absent from Madrid when she arrived. He had risen to the rank of general with the title of count, and had been made majordomo of the palace and governor of two provinces. He had just left the capital for his government of Guadalajara, and was now carrying on the same species of warfare against Juan Martin, known as the " Empecinado," on the banks of the

* Alexandre Dumas' "Mémoires."

Tagus, as he had waged against Charette in
La Vendée and against Fra Diavolo in Calabria. He has himself modestly related the
strategy of the expedition which ended suc-
cessfully in the capture and execution of the
guerilla chief.

The general's family took up their residence in the quarters prepared for them in
the Masserano palace, a handsome building
of the seventeenth century, furnished mag-
nificently, but in which the foreign guests
were kept fully alive to the hatred which the
Spaniards bore their conquerors. Throughout the country Napoleon was universally
spoken of as Napo-ladron—Napo the robber.

The gilding of the palace, the sculpture,
the splendid specimens of Bohemian glass,
all took a lively hold of young Victor's imagination; and the verses in which he subsequently recounted their magnificence may
occur to the minds of many.

Not for long, however, did the children
enjoy their sumptuous home. When their
father came back, he entered Abel, the eldest,
as one of King Joseph's pages; and as he contemplated doing the same with the two others, he soon sent them to the "séminaire des
nobles" along with the sons of some of the
Spanish gentry. The school is now a hospital.

Eugène and Victor were intensely bored
while at this seminary, learning next to nothing. Boys older than themselves were in the
merest rudiments of Latin, and they were,
moreover, under the superintendence of a
hypocritical monk whose mode of dealing
with them was in the highest degree irritating.

The only breaks in the monotony of that
year of imprisonment were some schoolboy
fights. The young Spaniards hated the young
Frenchmen, and there ensued, in consequence,
several small duels, in one of which Eugène
received a wound in his face. Somewhere
in his writings, the poet alludes to these
childish fights for "the Great Emperor;" and
years afterwards, in mentioning them to a
friend, he observed:

"But the Spaniards were in the right. They
were contending for their country. Children,
however, do not understand these things."

At the end of 1812 and the beginning of
the following year, affairs assumed a threatening aspect. As a result of the disasters in
Russia, the thrones erected in the various European capitals began to totter to their fall.

It was deemed prudent for Madame Hugo
to quit Madrid. Her eldest son, now a sub-
lieutenant, remained behind with the general;

YOUNG PATRIOTS.

but the two schoolboys, delighted to regain
their liberty, accompanied their mother to
Paris, and, after another journey similar to the
last, they all took up their abode in their old
quarters in the Rue des Feuillantines, which
they had retained throughout their absence.

Everything was as they had left it; the
same lights and shadows rested on the home,
and the flowers were opening to the sun-
beams. Good old Larivière, in his long
frock-coat, came just as before to give the
young lads their daily lessons.

Of Larivière wrote Victor Hugo, years after:
" His was a name that should ever be mentioned with respect. That a child has received his education from a priest is a circumstance to be taken into account with
much consideration; it is an accident over
which neither the priest nor the child has
any control; nevertheless, it is an unhealthy
union of two intellects, one of them unde-
veloped, the other shrunken; the one expanding, the other getting cramped by age. On
the whole, the advantage would seem to be
on the side of old-age. In time, the mind of
a child can free itself from the errors that it
has contracted from that of an elderly man.

" The melancholy part of instruction so
derived is that all it does for the child is for
the child's disadvantage; slowly and inap-
preciably it gives its turn to the intellect; it
is orthopedy inverted; it makes crooked
what nature has made straight, and ultimately produces as its masterpieces distorted souls
like Torquemada, unintelligent intelligences
like Joseph de Maistre, and other victims of

the system, who in their turn become its advocates and exponents. Teaching of this character can hardly fail to inoculate young intellects with the prejudices of old-age."

Certain it is that the brains of children imbibe the ideas of those that bring them up. Parents and tutors have a fertile soil wherein to sow the seeds of prejudice, which, devel-

Any dangerous tendency of the teaching of Père Larivière was happily counteracted by the gentle and loving good-sense of the mother. The basis of her teaching, as one of her contemporaries has remarked, was Voltairianism; but, with a woman's positivism, she did not concern herself to instil into her sons the doctrines of any special creed

TUTOR AND PUPIL.

oped by education and matured by love, become the giant plants of which the man, full-grown and reasonable, will have unbounded trouble to dislodge the roots.

"To break away from one's education is not an easy task; that a clerical training, however, is not always irremediable is proved by the case of Voltaire."

Besides a practical knowledge of the noble language, and the attainment of its genuine guttural accent, both the boys, but particularly Victor, had acquired in Spain something of the Castilian bearing, a certain gravity of deportment, a stability of mind, and a firmness of sentiment that boded well for future greatness. The sun of the Sierra had bronzed their characters and gilded their imagination.

Not content with tending the mental and moral education of her children, Madame Hugo took much pains to develop their muscular powers, insisting upon their doing a certain amount of gardening work in spite of its being by no means to their taste. But, while they were thus rejoicing in their comparative freedom from restraint, they were alarmed at the prospect of being again immured within the restraint of a college. This

At dingy desks they toil by day; at night
To gloomy chambers go uncheered by light,
Where pillars rudely graved by rusty nail
Of ennui'd hours reveal the weary tale:
Where spiteful ushers grin, all pleased to make
The scribbled lines the price of each mistake.
By four unpitying walls environed there,
The homesick students pace the pavement bare."

On the other hand, the sweetness of the flowers, the chestnuts, and the breezes, all seemed to plead with the mother, and to whisper in her ears the entreaty "Leave us the children," so that she finally decided on

RECREATION.

attempt upon their liberty was made by the representations of the head-master of the Lycée Napoléon, whom twenty-six years later the poet stigmatized in "Les Rayons et les Ombres" as the "terrible man bald and black," who held it necessary to shut up young people in order to make them work. He seemed inclined to believe that it was

"Good for the young to leave maternal care,
And for a while a harsher yoke to bear;
Surrender all the careless ease of home,
And be forbid from school-yard bounds to roam:
For this with blandest smiles he softly asks
That they with him will prosecute their tasks;
Receives them in his solemn séminaire,
The rigid lot of discipline to share.

keeping her sons at home. But she never allowed them to be idle; she had them taught to use their hands, and they learned to do some carpentering and to paper their own rooms. Literature is a pursuit that does not always enrich her followers, and many of her devotees must have been doomed to die of hunger unless, upon emergency, they had been able to maintain themselves by manual labor.

Except to gardening, Victor had no dislike to work, but seemed ever ready to put his hands to anything. His recreations, to say the truth, were very few; his mother saw no one, and probably would not have cared for companionship. Occasionally a little girl of thirteen or fourteen came to play in the garden, and on those days the boy's heart beat more rapidly than was its wont, for then commenced his earnest, tender, deep regard for the lady who afterwards became his wife.

The story of this most pure and exquisite love has been related by Victor Hugo himself in the most thrilling of all his works, "Le Dernier Jour d'un Condamné." He imagines himself in that book to be a child again. In depicting the agonies of a man awaiting the guillotine, he has probably conceived what would have been his own best happiness and worse regrets if brought, as he might have been, to a similar fate, since as late as the year 1848 politics have brought men to the scaffold as easily as crimes. He makes a retrospect of the joys of life, and fancies himself once more a schoolboy; he recalls the appearance in the solitary garden of the little Andalusian girl, Pepita; he sees her in all her charms, just fourteen years of age, with large lustrous eyes and luxuriant hair, with rich gold-brown skin and crimson lips; he dwells on the proud emotion which he felt as she leaned upon his arm; he recounts how they wandered, talking softly, along the shady walks; he tells how he picked up the handkerchief she had dropped, and was conscious of her hands trembling as they touched his own; and he recollects how they talked about the birds, the stars, and the golden sunset; sometimes, too, about her schoolfellows, her dresses, and her ribbons, they blushed together over the most innocent of thoughts.

It was a time he never forgot.

The home in the Feuillantines holds a large place in his affections, and, with a melancholy not unnatural, he has poured forth a plaintive lay over the old garden that became the scene of others' sports and the shelter of others' loves.

No inconsiderable part of his youth was spent with his mother and his tutor beneath those shady trees where he played with his young *fiancée*. She was the original of the Pepita so tenderly described. Her real name was Adèle Foucher.

CHAPTER V.

THE second period of residence in the Feuillantines was unfortunately destined to be only of short duration. The latter portion of the time was very merry. Madame Hugo had offered hospitality to the wife of General Lucotte, whom she had known in Spain, and who, like herself, had been obliged to come away with her children. The younger members of the two families became inseparable companions, and the last games played in the old garden were far from being the least boisterous and gay.

But the improvement of Paris now required the house of the Feuillantines in order to lengthen the Rue d'Ulm; and on the 31st of December, 1813, Madame Hugo, with her party, moved to the Rue du Cherche-Midi, almost opposite the hôtel of the War Office, the residence of M. Foucher. The new home was an old structure of the Louis XV. style. According to her wont, Madame Hugo took up her quarters in rooms on the ground-floor overlooking the garden, which was much smaller and far less beautiful than what they had quitted. The boys were obliged to sleep on the second story.

Joyous games soon began again. The young folks were joined by Victor Foucher and other companions until the Rue du Cherche-Midi became the scene of noisy romps such as are the very terror of mothers. The lads clambered on to the roof, they played at soldiers, piling up boxes and trunks of all dimensions into barricades, which were assaulted and taken only after a vigorous interchange of blows.

The frolicsome band was further reinforced by the arrival of the eldest of the Hugo boys. The general did not remain in Spain long after his wife's departure, and Abel, after serving as his father's aide-de-camp in the battles of Salamanca and Vittoria, in the last victory and final defeat, now found himself a lieutenant at fifteen, by force of circumstances unattached.

He had been sharing in the terrible contest in which France could not claim justice on her side. In order to resist a conqueror flushed with victory and inflated with pride —a conqueror who shed the blood of his subjects for the mere purpose of subjugating the powers of Europe and augmenting his own renown—who held the doctrine that right may ever be oppressed by might—Spain made those splendid and heroic efforts by which she maintained her independence. The women and children took up arms. From every bush projected the muzzle of a gun, charged with the death of an invader; every pass concealed an ambush, every height was defended by a patriot.

It was a fine example, and one that has seldom been matched for the self-devotion of the victims; yet, magnificent as was their defence, it did not deteriorate from the bravery of the soldiers of the first Empire, who had no choice but to obey their master's bidding.

To General Hugo it fell to conduct the terrible retreat. The soldiers under his command had to protect the lives of twenty thousand of the French fugitives who were hurrying with their property from Madrid—a terror-stricken multitude whom the enemy would not hesitate to massacre if only they could get the chance, and whose ranks meanwhile were being decimated by poison and dysentery.

The general, ever on the alert, performed his duty nobly. As soon as he had assured himself that the unfortunates committed to his protection were in a position of safety, he took his son to Paris, and very shortly afterwards received orders to take the command at Thionville, which was on the point of being besieged.

He made a gallant defence of the fortress, which was one of the last over which the tricolor floated. The citadel surrendered, not to the enemy, but to the Bourbons—that is, to the allies—and the French general, as the reward of defending himself against the Hessians, found himself accused of treason against those who then, as now, styled themselves the legitimate sovereigns of France.

Throughout these critical struggles the children continued at their daily work and at their daily play. Their mother was anxious for them to learn as much as possible, and had subscribed for Victor to a reading-room. There he greedily devoured everything that came in his way—romances, books of science, and even "Les Contemporaines" of Rétif de la Bretonne.

Then came the invasion reinstating the monarchs "by right divine." Even children became infected with the fever of politics, and the youngsters of the Rue du Cherche-Midi were fain to put aside their picture-books and to consult their atlases. His desire to make himself acquainted with the movements of the allied forces had the effect of making Victor, who had all General Lucotte's elaborate collection of plans at his disposal, learn his geography very thoroughly and by a very practical method.

To Madame Hugo the fall of the Empire was a satisfaction to which she did not hesitate to give expression. Although it was an assent that seriously affected her husband's fortunes, as a Vendean she was so loyally devoted to her prince that all other interests were held to be secondary.

While with a terrible crash was falling the throne of the man who had squandered the blood of France on a thousand battle-fields, but who as the result of all his exploits had left the gates of Paris open to the armies of the foreigner, Victor Hugo was wearing lilies in his button-hole. His mother approved of this; consequently he was sure he was right, although he had no little difficulty in looking with a friendly eye upon the Cossacks who encamped with their horses in the court-yard of the Cherche-Midi.

In the view of a lad of twelve, it seemed at first as if France must have sustained a humiliation in coming down from an emperor to a king. He had always felt a certain amount of admiration for the great Bonaparte; but his mother's training, combined with that of the priest, had prepared him to love royalty, and accordingly he was ready now to love it with all his heart. Subsequently it would be his father who, as a veteran, in his turn would influence his mind.

After attending the festivities in honor of the restoration, Madame Hugo went to Thionville. She did not, however, remain there long. The proud spirits of husband and wife allowed neither of them to compromise their political principles, and the recent events aggravated their differences of opinion to such a degree that at length they caused a separation between them. But on these domestic discords it is not our place to dwell.

Napoleon returned from Elba. During the period of the Hundred Days, General Hugo, who recovered his position, insisted upon placing his two sons at a boarding-school, a proceeding on his part which by no means mitigated the hostility with which they regarded the imperial government. Victor was deprived of his great delight—the evenings spent in her father's *salon* with Adèle Foucher, the object of his secret love. Moreover, for the very day when he was again to become an imprisoned schoolboy he had schemed that his marionnettes should perform a piece of his own composing, "Le Palais Enchanté." It was consequently with the greatest difficulty that he restrained his tears when, in company with Eugène, he crossed the threshold of the college Cordier et Decotte in the Rue Ste. Marguerite.

The young, however, soon forget their troubles, and the school-days seem to have been happy enough.

Eugène was now nearly fifteen, and Victor thirteen. It was not long before the two boys were elevated into two "kings" at the pension Decotte, their schoolfellows being divided into two detachments—those under Eugène styling themselves the "calves," those under Victor being called the "dogs." The result of this division was some furious fighting; but, whether they were at peace or at war, no one ever for a moment thought of disputing the authority of the leaders.

Victor Hugo still remembers with much amusement that he was a terrible despot. He never allowed the smallest act of disobedience, and went so far as to inflict personal chastisement upon any one who failed to execute his orders.

Among the most devoted of his subjects was Léon Gatayes, the celebrated harpist, who died in Paris in 1877. Besides being a musician, he was a man of taste and of considerable attainments, a journalist and a critic, and of untainted loyalty. At the time of which we are speaking he was a day boarder, and King Victor was in the habit of intrusting him with various commissions out of doors, every day confiding to him the sum of two sous to be spent upon Italian cheese, of which one half was to be dry and the other half moist. When it arrived, the monarch would survey the dainty morsel with a critical eye; if it were "all moist," a hailstorm of thumps would descend upon the unlucky shoulders of the blundering emissary; if it were "all dry," a perfect avalanche of kicks would assail his shins.

Fifty years afterwards the artist inquired of the poet:

"Do you remember those days? My legs are sore still!"

"But you were a head taller than I was," the poet replied; "why did you not pitch into me?"

"Oh, I dared not," answered the other; "you told me I should not have any more of your commissions to execute, and the mere threat took away all thought of revenge."

In spite of his tyranny, the king of the "dogs" was altogether a favorite, and certainly set his subjects a fine example of industry.

General Hugo intended that his boys should ultimately go to the École Polytechnique. In addition to their ordinary lessons, they attended courses of lectures in physics, philosophy, and mathematics at the college Louis-le-Grand. Their talent for mathematics brought them under the notice of the masters, and they both obtained honorable mention at the general examination by the professors of the university.

Victor had a way of solving problems that was peculiar to himself. He would not follow in the beaten tracks, and would not be content to obtain his results by the ordinary methods, always arriving at the conclusion by some indirect and unrecognized means; as it were, inventing his solution rather than deducing it. It would be fair to describe him as "a romantic mathematician," and the licenses he took were often far from pleasing to the professors, who could not look with favor upon any deviations from the old routine. But it was not in the mysteries of any algebraic symbols that the lad found his chief delight; poetry rather than mathematics occupied his thoughts, and at the age of thirteen he wrote his first verses about Roland and the age of chivalry. Not having learned his prosody, he invented his laws of rhythm for himself.

All the world at that time was trying to write poetry. Even Larivière tried his hand at verse; Decotte the schoolmaster, Eugène,

and twenty of his schoolfellows, as well as Victor, became worshippers of the muse.

But the young students did not limit themselves to odes and fugitive pieces; they composed grand military dramas which were performed in the great class-room. The tables were all pushed together to form a stage, and underneath these the actors dressed, crouching down in their novel greenroom until summoned to perform their parts.

The schoolboy king took Molière for his model, and wrote plays of which he had to take the principal character himself. For these performances the most elaborate costumes were held to be indispensable, and Victor Hugo, who wears no decorations now, would make his appearance covered with them in all varieties. Grand crosses of every hue, manufactured of paper; grand orders, and collars composed of strings of marbles; grand plumes, grand accoutrements, completed the attire of monarchs, commanders-in-chief, and other conspicuous characters. Never, surely, before or since, did genius devise costumes comparable to these!

Not satisfied with devoting his play-hours to these dramatic pursuits, the young author would spend a portion of his nights in translating into French verse the odes of Horace and various fragments of Virgil that he had learned. At a later page we will give examples of the early lispings of one who may fairly claim to be reckoned in the register of the precocious.

Already a change was coming over him; his hair, which hitherto had been fair, like that of a true son of the north, was assuming a darker shade; his features were getting more marked, and his eyes were gaining an expression of thought. The poet was awakening within him.

A moment may be spared to take a cursory glance at some of his earliest lyrical essays, which, owing to an accident, he had the opportunity of multiplying at will.

In the course of one of the battles that occurred between the "calves" and the "dogs" during a walk near the pond at Auteuil, Victor was so seriously injured in the knee that it was feared at first that his leg would have to be amputated. He refused to betray the name of the "soldier" who in the heat of the fray had taken a stone and made a sling of his pocket-handkerchief, thus inflicting so serious an injury upon the hostile "general."

The respite from mathematics that the lamed boy gained through his accident was

THEATRICAL PERFORMANCE AT THE PENSION DECOTTE.

most welcome to him, and the hours of his freedom were pleasantly occupied in composing odes, satires, epistles, and poems in whatever style might chime in with his fancy, amorous, chivalrous, languishing, or terrible.

In after-years Madame Victor Hugo came across ten old exercise-books full of verses dated 1815 and 1816. These first efforts of art are very curious. On the fly-leaf of the last, which contains many scraps of interest, is inscribed, in the lad's own handwriting, "The nonsense that I wrote before I was born;" and below this the rough drawing of an egg, inside which is sketched a bird, as is explained by the word "oiseau" underneath.

"THE NONSENSE THAT I WROTE BEFORE I WAS BORN."

The apprentice poet would appear not to have been always satisfied with his productions. To one of the pieces is appended the note "An honest man may read all of this which is not cancelled," the pen having been drawn through the whole composition. A few pages further on is a piece without a title, and at the bottom the remark "Let him who can, find a title; I have yet to discover what I have been writing about."

Notwithstanding his modesty, his genius was not invariably at fault. In some notes that have all the tokens of being conscientious he asserts that although he is aware that some of his verses are bad, some miserably weak, and some only barely passable, yet he believes that he has written some that are really good.

And it is to be observed how he does not by any means limit himself to petty subjects;

his imagination will not content itself with trifles. After the second restoration he wrote a tragedy upon the return of Louis XVIII., entitled "Irtamène," with Egyptian names to the characters. His perusal of Voltaire's plays had given him a predilection for this particular style. A few months later he was writing a second tragedy, which he called "Athélie, ou les Scandinaves;" but his taste had so much developed that he desisted at the end of the third act and never completed it.

But tragedies alone did not suffice; he composed elegies, idyls, fables, romances, conundrums, madrigals, and even puns in verse. He sang of bards and fair Canadians; he translated Ausonius, and perpetrated a comic opera!

Several of his translations have been reproduced, and specimens of them may be found in "Victor Hugo Raconté," and in "Littérature et Philosophie Mêlées."

A few lines of an unpublished translation of a passage in the "Æneid" may be here introduced. It will serve as a sample of the translator's power. It is the description of Cacus—

"Vois sur ce mont désert ces rochers entassés,
Vois ces blocs suspendus, ces débris disperses;
Là, dans un antre immense au jour inaccessible,
Vivait l'affreux Cacus, noir géant, monstre horrible.
À ses portes pendaient des crânes entr'ouverts,
Pâles, souillés de sang et de fange couverts.
Ses meurtres chaque jour faisaient fumer la terre,
De ce monstre hideux Vulcain était le père;
Sa gorge vomissait des tourbillons de feux
Et son énorme masse épouvantait nos yeux."
　　　　　　　　　　　　VIRG. Æn. viii. 190–200.

It is quite open to question whether this terrible Cacus is at all comparable as a romantic type to Han d'Islande; but in those days Victor Hugo thought of nothing beyond the classics, and in his original early pieces the undercurrent of sentiment that tinges them all is his love of the Bourbons. He was but fourteen years old, and he believed in them with all sincerity.

To a certain extent, all these youthful productions are the echoes of his mother's teaching and the outcome of a veneration for her, who, like a muse, though she might not actually dictate his rhymes, yet inspired all his ideas.

The child had neither the right nor the power to argue with his mother; he yielded to her with all reverence, not supposing that she could teach him other than the truth. He did not reason, he conformed; his mind was but the reflex of the mind of the counsellors who had instructed him.

CHAPTER VI.

A Pamphleteer at Thirteen.—First Connection with the Académie Française.—"L'enfant sublime."—Châteaubriand or Soumet the Author of the *Mot.*—A Romance Written in a Fortnight.—"Bug-Jargal."—Studies for Future Works.—Revision and Publication.—Subject of Play Performed 1880.

THUS regarding the world only through the medium of his mother's vision, and receiving his inspiration solely from her, Victor Hugo was incapable of breaking through the bounds of the circle that enclosed him. His passions were simply those of his instructors; but, like a sonorous echo, he intensified what he repeated. A drum touched even by an infant's hand among the mountains will reverberate like the roll of thunder.

It had been told him, and with justice, that Napoleon Bonaparte was a tyrant usurper; instantly he avowed his hatred of the despot, and within a few days after the battle of Waterloo, though he was but thirteen years old, he came out as a pamphleteer, issuing a cry of indignation against the now-defeated emperor, the general tone of which may be judged from the following version of its opening lines:

"Tremble, thou despot! the avenging hand of fate
　Down to its doom thine odious empire shakes;
Thy bitter day of dark remorse hath dawned—
　Remorse, that cruel tyrant sure o'ertakes.
Tremble! for though thy lustful, cursèd pride
　Covets to conquer, burns to vanquish all,
Yet thy delirium hath outrun itself,
　And all thy schemes of selfish glory fall.
But now, alas! thy very fall for France
　Still costs her blood, still makes her tears to flow;
For, Waterloo, the victory on thy field
　Is but a mingled cup of joy and woe."

　＊　＊　＊　＊　＊　＊

His political opinions, as we have said, were only a reflex of others, sure to be modified as he grew older; but at that time, owing to his education, they might be summed up in that line of wonderful logic

"Who hates a tyrant, he must love a king."

Such, at least, was Madame Hugo's conviction; she firmly believed that the Bourbons, whom the invasion had brought back, would restore to France her liberty by relieving the land of imperial oppression. She was, moreover, an enthusiastic admirer of Voltaire; and her son, through sympathy with her, reverenced Louis XVIII., respected the charter, and satirized the worthy monks, who, under the pretext of saving men from eternal flames, consigned them to perdition for eating meat on forbidden days. It was a contradiction of things which did not cease to haunt Victor Hugo's mind; and we shall soon see how, ceasing to be a Catholic, he became a freethinker, always, however, notwithstanding that the ecclesiastical authorities denounced him as an atheist, remaining a sincere deist. His philosophical work, lately published, comprises the impressions of his boyhood. He believes in God in spite of the priests, and in liberty in spite of everything!

But though his professions of faith were under the control of those with whom he associated, his poetical talent took an independent flight that was solely and entirely his own. Without communicating his intention to any one, he made up his mind to compete for the poetical prize that was annually offered by the Académie Française. It was not without considerable timidity that the young student of the college Decotte handed in his composition at the secretary's office. For the year 1817, when the Restoration was complete, the subject proposed was "The advantages of study in every situation of life."

The literary class might beguile themselves into the belief that "advantages of study" were an excuse for the Restoration; it was well that the mass of the people did not share their persuasion.

According to the established custom, the young competitor had to write his name inside a paper, folded and sealed, and bearing a motto corresponding with what was subscribed to the poem. The verses were remarkable for more than the title. The commencing strain was somewhat to this effect:

"When the fresh dewdrops earliest rest
Laving the tender lily's trembling breast—
When the glad song-birds chant their morning lay,
And to the orient sun their tribute pay,

4

"Ye peaceful shades, where boughs o'erhanging meet
I seek, I happy seek your calm retreat.
Yes, then I love my Virgil's page to take,
And feel my heart for Dido's sorrow ache;
E'en then, inebriate with studious joys,
My soul the peaceful solitude employs
To learn the lesson useful to the end,
How with life's anxious evils to contend."

Unfortunately, in the course of the poem, the juvenile author introduced the couplet

"And though the thronging scenes of life I shun,
For me three lustrums scarce their course have run."

It was with a charming simplicity that the future philosopher boasted at once that he had fled from the cities and haunts of princes and of men, and yet acknowledged in academic phrase that he was hardly fifteen years old. The avowal raised the suspicion of the judges, and the Academicians took the lines as an affront to their dignity. Accordingly, the first prize was divided equally between Saintine and Lebrun; the second was awarded to Casimir Delavigne; a "proxime accessit" was assigned to Loyson; and an "honorable mention" accorded to Victor Hugo, in spite of his presumed attempt to mystify, although there was little doubt that his was the most meritorious of all the compositions that had been sent in.

Saintine, Lebrun, and Casimir Delavigne are all well-known names, and will reappear in the course of this record. Loyson is not so well remembered, but his clique entered a protest against the Académie for having adjudged him only an "accessit." He died young, and it has been said of him that he held a place between Millevoye and Lamartine, approaching nearer the latter in the spirituality of his ideas.

Altogether the competition had been of a brilliant character; but when the verses were read in public, the decision of the judges did not avail to prevent Victor Hugo's production from being received with the loudest applause.

The laureate of "three lustrums" first heard of his success from his brother, who brought him the news while he was playing at prisoner's base with General Lecourbe's son, Victor Jacquemont, and some other boys. So interested was he in his game that he did not allow it to be interrupted by his brother's communication.

In the report that was published there appeared a paragraph to the effect that if M. Hugo were really only as old as he represented, he deserved some encouragement from the Académie. This at once aroused Madame Hugo's indignation. She sent a categorical statement to M. Raynouard, the secretary, who had drawn up the report, and he acknowledged her communication by saying that if the author of the poem had really spoken the truth, he should be very pleased to make his acquaintance.

More indignant than ever, Madame Hugo hurried off to her son at the college.

"Come with me," she said; "come and let me show you to these unbelievers who assert that you are a man. I have the register of your birth in my pocket!"

Together they hastened to the secretary, who was manifestly somewhat abashed, and could only stammer out the explanation that "he could never have supposed it possible."

Poor M. Raynouard was a poet who had been brought forward under the patronage of Napoleon I. He was a worthy and a learned man. This is about the limit of the tribute that can be paid to his memory. By the emperor's command he brought out several tragedies, of which the fortunate fate has been that they are forgotten; certainly he was not the man to discern the marks of a rising genius.

Some of his associates were more quick-sighted. First, there was François de Neufchâteau, who had himself been a precocious boy, and had received from Voltaire, by way of encouragement for his essays, the lines

"The womb of time must my successor bear;
Yet thee, thee would I choose to be my heir!" *

Neufchâteau became rather a questionable poet and a sceptical politician, but still made himself a name. Notwithstanding his advanced age, he took an interest in all that was going on, and addressed the young aspirant in this wise:

"Friend of the Muses! come to my embrace;
In thee the tender love of poesy I trace!" †

At a later date, when the lad Victor had grown into manhood, the worthy Neufchâteau, it must be owned, became somewhat startled at his prodigious triumphs, and, after reading the "Odes et Ballades," broke out into the exclamation "Unfortunate! he will ruin himself! He is failing to fulfil his early promise!"

---

*   "Il faut bien que l'on me succède,
      Et j'aime en vous mon héritier."

† "Tendre ami des neuf sœurs, mes bras vous sont
    ouverts;
    Venez, j'aime toujours les vers."

Another member of the Académie, Campenon, who was Delille's successor, and a fervent admirer of Bernardin de Saint-Pierre, subsequently notorious for his hatred of romanticism, likewise made some reference to Victor Hugo's poem, and indirectly expressed his admiration of it.

"O'erdone with wit and surfeited are we;
  Men's hearts are ice, for whom no verse can make
The sense of pleasure, though it teem with charms
  That Malfilatre's envy might awake."*

But Châteaubriand, the most illustrious of

cently appeared in a curious publication entitled "L'Intermédiaire," and are not unworthy of repetition.

"Many a time," writes the author of the notice, "have I heard this celebrated verdict assigned to Châteaubriand. All Victor Hugo's biographers, one after another, have adored this word 'sublime,' and it matters little to the poet who it was that thus, for the first time, depicted his youthful glory. But, though Châteaubriand has the credit of it, the expression was not originally his.

CHÂTEAUBRIAND.

all the Academicians of 1817, went further than any other; he exclaimed, "The child is sublime!"

Perpetually quoted as this expression has been, it has been questioned whether it really ought to be originally attributed to Châteaubriand. The details of this debate have re-

"One Sunday, long years ago, I was breakfasting with Alexandre Soumet, the author of the 'Divine Épopée.' . . . Émile and Antony Deschamps were present. In the course of conversation, I referred to the phrase always attributed to Châteaubriand.

"'Stop,' said Soumet, 'I must not allow that observation of yours to go uncorrected. It was I who first wrote to Châteaubriand and called his attention to Hugo as *l'enfant sublime*, and I appeal to Émile and Antony to say whether it was not so.'

* " L'esprit et le bon goat nous ont rassaslée;
   J'ai rencontré des cœurs de glace
Pour des vers pleins de charme et de verve et de grâce
   Que Malfilatre eut envies !''

"Both the Deschamps confirmed what he said.

"This conversation was reported in the Abbaye-aux-Bois, the residence of Madame Récamier, who repeated it to Châteaubriand.

"'The words express so decided a truth,' was the reply of the author of the 'Génie du Christianisme,' 'that any one might naturally have used them; and if Soumet has the advantage of me, he is quite entitled to the recognition that he claims.'"

At least the discussion demonstrates one thing: it proves that whether or no Châteaubriand was the first to apply the epithet, at any rate, in his own mind, he considered Victor entitled to be designated "l'enfant sublime." He never ceased to regard him with affection and admiration, and was among the number of those who gave him substantial proofs of their friendship.

After Châteaubriand had spoken of him in this way in a notice in the *Conservatoire,* Victor Hugo was taken to him by M. Agier to thank him for his favorable criticism, and there was established between them a union, full of kindness on the one hand and enthusiasm on the other, which was cordially maintained for four or five years. On the margin of one of his commonplace-books Victor Hugo wrote, "I would be Châteaubriand or nothing," so that it may be well understood how much he appreciated the praise of one whom he deemed his master.

To obtain an "honorable mention" in a *concours* of the French Academy was an event that was always published in the newspapers; accordingly, in 1817, Victor Hugo's name became to a certain extent known, if not renowned. His poem on "The Advantages of Study" was printed separately, and is now a rare bibliographical curiosity. In one copy there is a dedication of six verses to M. D. L. R. (M. de la Rivière), signed V. M. H.

This was not the only literary success that he made at this period; before leaving the college Decotte he wrote his first essay in prose, and composed his romance of "Bug-Jargal."

He had promised some of his schoolfellows not to take more than a fortnight in the composition of this romance, so that it might be ready in time for a kind of literary banquet that they used to hold once a month. He kept his word, and had his manuscript duly prepared by the appointed day.

Although this book was remodelled, and in great measure rewritten by the author in 1825, it was, nevertheless, his first work of the kind. It relates a dramatic episode of the revolt of the negroes of St. Domingo in 1791. Bug-Jargal, the hero of the story, is the slave of one of the colonists of the island and bears a secret love for his master's daughter, a fascinating child, betrothed to her cousin Leopold d'Auverney. Having once been rescued by this cousin, after being condemned to death for an act of rebellion, Bug-Jargal, at the outbreak of the insurrection in which the whites were being massacred, first rushes in and saves the life of the girl he loves, and next saves the life of her cousin, whom he hates. It is solely to his exertions that the young couple escape the vengeance that had been prepared for them by Jean Biassou, the leader of the revolt, and by a deformed and hideous wretch called Habibrah. At the end, after having thus heroically sacrificed his feelings, Bug-Jargal sacrifices his life, being shot down by the colonists.

It seems almost a pity that this work was ever retouched. The feature in it that is now most worthy of remark is that it contains the first rough sketches of some of Victor Hugo's immortal characters, being, as it were, the study for some of his finest pictures.

Like Ruy Blas, Bug-Jargal is an earthworm enamoured of a star, and, like Hernani, he dies for a point of honor. Habibrah, the dwarf, is the foreshadow of the hideousness of Quasimodo and the spitefulness of Triboulet; while the description of the "obi" clutching at the root of a tree in his frightful fall to the bottom of the Gulf of St. Domingo prefigures the archdeacon Claude Frollo clinging to a gutter-pipe when precipitated by the bell-ringer from the tower of Notre Dame.

These crude sketches of the master-hand are worthy of careful study; they serve in a degree to illustrate the gradual development of his *chefs-d'œuvre,* and are curious as well as interesting. "Bug-Jargal" may be considered as an early stage in the literary revolution of 1830; and this, the first note of the romance-writer, in the sixteenth year of his age, is a cry in favor of the oppressed, a defence of the suffering, an exaltation of self-devotion, and a plea for liberty.

This remarkable production did not appear in print until 1825, after it had been revised and corrected, and, consequently, not until after the public mind had been thrilled by the terrible character of "Han d'Islande."

"A BLACK FLAG WAS HOISTED ON THE MOUNTAIN."

The work, by comparison, seemed tamer than it was in reality, and contained some remarkable passages that were speedily inserted in collections of extracts from the most striking compositions of the day, and which, by their vivacity of expression and harmony of execution, have become models of style.

One passage selected from Sergeant Thadée's narrative may be introduced to serve as an illustration of the style of the touching story:

"As you wish it, captain, I must tell you that although the great negro Bug-Jargal, or Pierrot, as he was most generally called, was both bold and gentle, and the bravest man in the land—yourself, of course, my dear captain, always excepted—I was, nevertheless, extremely ill-disposed towards him; so much so that, when I heard that the next evening but one had been fixed on for your murder, I went to him in a furious rage and vowed that, if you were killed, either he or (failing him) ten of his followers should be shot in revenge. He did not exhibit the slightest emotion at what I said, but an hour afterwards he had dug a great hole and was gone."

We may break his narrative just to explain that Bug-Jargal had made his escape in order to avert the intended murder of Captain d'Auverney; if he were not back when a black flag was hoisted on the mountain, his ten associates would forthwith be executed.

Thadée goes on:

"When the flag was hoisted, Bug-Jargal had not returned. A cannon was fired as a signal, and I proceeded to take the ten negroes to the place of execution, known as the Great Devil's Mouth. You may be sure enough, captain, that I had not the least intention of letting the fellows off; I had them all bound in the usual way, and was just arranging my platoons, when suddenly Bug-Jargal emerged from the forest. I lowered my gun immediately. He came bounding towards me, quite out of breath, and said,

"'Good evening, Thadée; I am just in time.'

"Without another word he at once set about liberating his countrymen from their fetters."

The story ends with the execution of the hero, who could not and would not survive his love.

In a preface bearing the date of 1832, Victor Hugo observes that he was like a traveller pausing on his road to look back to his starting-point among the mists that clouded the horizon; and, in re-editing this work, it was his wish to publish a reminiscence of the boldness with which, at a period when all was serene, he had dealt with that weighty subject, the revolt of the blacks in St. Domingo in 1791. It was truly a battle of giants; three worlds interested in the issue: Europe and Africa the combatants, America providing the battle-plain!

The first edition of "Bug-Jargal" had a second title appended, describing it as one of the "Contes sous la Tente." These stories never appeared, neither did "La Quinquengrogne," a romance that was advertised for a considerable time in the booksellers' catalogues.

Long before the issue of the book itself, the original story was published in the *Conservateur Littéraire*, a magazine to which we shall have to refer hereafter. Captain d'Auverney is there called Delmar. The name of D'Auverney, subsequently introduced, was one which General Hugo was entitled, if he had chosen, to assume.

"Bug-Jargal," then, was the first work of any considerable length that Victor Hugo wrote. It was translated into English in 1826.

In November, 1880, Richard Lesclide and Pierre Elzéar brought out a drama, at the Théâtre Château-d'Eau, founded on the romance, which proved very successful. It had the prime merit that the original subject was not over-mutilated in the adaptation.

Since revising the proofs, the author has not read the book, being in this respect unlike the Arab shepherd who, when he had risen to be a vizier, used to contemplate his coarse vest and his reed pipe.

Nevertheless, this early essay is one that Victor Hugo might fairly reperuse with pride; it contains the germs of his mighty genius.

CHAPTER VII.

The Jeux Floraux at Toulouse.—"Les Vierges de Verdun."—Filial Affection.—Letter from M. Soumet.—Reluctance to Go to the École Polytechnique.—Allowance Withdrawn.—Numerous Changes of Residence.—Publication of Odes.—*Le Conservateur Littéraire.*—Description of the Magazine.—Victor Hugo a Critic.—His Articles and *Noms de Plume.*—Opinion of Lamartine's first "Méditations Poétiques."—First Interview of the Two Poets.

AT the time when the schoolboy of sixteen was writing "Bug-Jargal," he was not only a laureate of the Académie, but became also a prize-winner in the Jeux Floraux—celebrated games that had been established in Toulouse in the fourteenth century, and which have been reorganized under the patronage of Clémence Isaure. The subject of the poem for which he obtained the wreath was historical, being founded on the story of the "Vierges de Verdun," three young sisters—Henriette, Hélène, and Agathe Watrin—who were condemned to death by Fouquier-Tinville, because they had presented flowers to the Prussians on their entry into the town, and distributed money and other relief among the emigrants.

A short time afterwards Victor Hugo won the golden lily for another of his compositions, a poem on the subject of the erection of Henry IV.'s statue on the Pont Neuf, a ceremony of which the young writer had himself been a spectator.

In these competitions at Toulouse, Victor's brother Abel, who likewise showed considerable literary talent, gained several honors.

The ode on the statue of Henry IV. was composed in a single night, and under circumstances that make it a touching tribute of filial affection. Madame Hugo was suffering from inflammation of the chest, and her two younger sons were taking their turn to sit up with her at night. On the 5th of February, 1819, it was Victor's turn to remain in the invalid's room. In the course of the evening, his mother, ever keenly interested in his performances, and a firm believer in his future name, and knowing that the following day, according to the rules of the competition, was the latest on which contributions could be received, alluded to his composition, supposing it to have been duly sent off. Victor was obliged to confess that the ode had not been written, and pleaded that he had had too many occupations to be able to attend to it. His mother rebuked him gently; but the youth could see plainly enough that she laid herself down with a feeling of sore disappointment weighing on her heart.

No sooner was she asleep than Victor set to work; he wrote diligently all through the night, and when she awoke at daybreak he had the completed ode to lay before her as a morning greeting. The manuscript that was sent forthwith to Toulouse went after being first bedewed with a mother's tears.

At the next competition at the Académie in Toulouse a fresh poem that Victor Hugo sent in, upon the subject of Moses on the Nile, gained for him the degree of "maître-ès-jeux-floraux," and the director wrote him the following letter:

"SIR,—Since we have received your odes we have spoken much of your talents and of your extraordinary literary promise. Your age of seventeen is a matter of surprise to us all, to some almost a matter of incredulity. You are an enigma of which the Muses keep the key. . . ."

All this time Victor's general studies had been progressing, and were now so far advanced that he was quite capable of entering the École Polytechnique. In his own mind, however, he was convinced that a military life was not in the least his vocation, and both he and his brother begged not to be obliged to present themselves at the examination. Only with extreme reluctance did General Hugo acquiesce in their desire. Soldiers do not often believe in their sons' dreams of literary glory, and doubtless they are frequently right. But, finding his own wishes thwarted by so strong an opposition, he resigned himself to circumstances: he exhibited, however, the annoyance that he felt by withdrawing the moderate allowance he had hitherto made his younger sons, and leaving them to their own resources.

As the result of this, Victor left the pension, having kept all the school-terms, and went to live with his mother, who, since the change in the position of her husband—now reduced to half-pay—had been obliged to leave her apartments in the Cherche-Midi and to find a less expensive place of abode.

She first removed to the Rue des Veilles-Tuileries, and resided on the ground-floor of a house of which Madame Lacotte occupied the first floor. Thence she moved again to the Rue des Vieux-Augustins, into a house now long since pulled down, but formerly part of the Musée des Petits-Augustins. It had originally been a convent; its site at present is occupied by the court-yard of the Palais des Beaux Arts.

Here it was that Madame Hugo was so seriously ill; and, as her bedroom was on the third floor, she attributed the slowness of her recovery to the difficulty of getting open-air exercise, and to obviate this she made another move in the beginning of 1821 to 10 Rue de Mézières. Here there was a garden.

As already remarked, the prevailing work of demolition seems never to have had any regard for the various residences of the youthful poet. Only a portion of the house in the Rue de Mézières is now in existence.

Victor Hugo was now beginning to make himself a name. For two years previously he had been applying himself zealously to work, and, as Rabbe remarks in his biography, 1819 and 1820 were among the busiest and most decisive years in his life.

Then it was with his own will that he entered into the lists with Fortune ; and though in the daily labors of his young life he dreamed of glory, he knew that it could be won only by arduous and incessant toil.

At various short intervals he composed the odes, loyal and religious, that were collected into his first published volume of poetry.

With regard to his principles, it has been said :

"It is known how he acquired his royalist partialities. His religion found its way into his heart through his imagination, and there he saw pre-eminently the highest form of human thought and the foremost line of poetical perspective. The society into which he was thrown, and which received him with

unbounded adulation, kept up unbroken his illusions about his creed; but all along the basis of his political doctrine was personal independence, and, although partially obliterated by Catholic symbols, the positive philosophy of his early training flowed on persistently beneath."

Among other occupations at this period, he was contributing to a periodical called the *Conservateur Littéraire,* to which reference has been already made. The magazine is hardly to be found now, but we have ourselves perused it in the "Bibliothèque Nationale." It consists of three volumes, and was published by Boucher in 1820 and 1821.

Originally it was started by the three young Hugos, Victor being then eighteen. Eugène contributed numerous essays, and Abel supplied the third volume with several articles. The rest of the contributors were Ader, Théodore Pavie, J. Sainte-Marie, Jules de Saint-Félix, Madame Tastu, Alfred de Vigny, Émile Deschamps, Alexandre Soumet, with a few others; but the bulk of the work belonged to the three brothers, Victor's share amounting to at least a third of the whole.

From these articles of his in the *Conservateur,* Victor made a selection in 1834, abbreviating and revising them, and under the title of a "Journal des Idées, des Opinions, et des Lectures d'un Jeune Jacobite," composed the first part of his "Littérature et Philosophie Mêlées;" but, as the author of the "Bibliographie Romantique," Ch. Asélineau, has remarked, it is in the magazine as originally issued that we must seek the polemical, satirical, and Jacobite poet in all the freshness and vivacity of his opinions and genius.

The opening pages of each number were reserved for poetry, and at the commencement of the first part appears a satire signed V. M. Hugo, and entitled "L'Enrôleur Politique." Prefixed to it as a motto is the Scripture verse, "The light shineth in darkness, and the darkness comprehended it not." The poem is a dialogue between an art-student and a recruiting-sergeant. The adept, who regards the study of literature as paramount to everything, exclaims,

"A fool I'd be, your colors would forsake,
My rhymes in peace at my own choice to make !
In lonely den I'd rather be a bear,
Thinking with Pascal, laughing with Voltaire !"

At the end of the piece, with a maturity of expression which is quite surprising, the young author pours forth his wonted echo of his mother's teaching. He makes a pro-

VICTOR HUGO AT HIS MOTHER'S BEDSIDE.

fession of his royalist faith, enunciating a creed which would not permanently command his assent.

In the very first number the *Conservateur* betrays unmistakable indication of its satirical tendency. It announces the sale of a stock of literature, the property of a well-known man of letters, comprising, among other rarities, a collection of documents relating to a variety of departments of human knowledge —the documents being extracts from the best authors copied out on small squares of paper, duly arranged according to their subjects, and carefully spitted on iron files. Then follows the catalogue:

A file of birds;
A file of fish, including the great **sea-serpent**;
A file of roses;
A file of English costumes;
A file of famous dogs, Munito **and the** great Newfoundland lately added;
A file of conjugal fidelity, ever since **Lucretia**;
A file of disinterestedness (this file runs **short**);
A file of deeds of valor;
A file of ancient cookery, etc.

The editor adds that any man of the least intelligence might, by merely copying the documents verbatim, concoct an educational or any other work that was demanded of him; and the notice winds up by saying that the disposer of the property has employed no other means in the composition of his own books.

It will be obvious from the foregoing example that the *Conservateur Littéraire* was not deficient in humor. The facetious notice was preceded by Victor Hugo's first prose article—a curious review of the complete works of André Chenier. It is signed with the initial "E.;" others are signed "H.;" and two humorous letters upon "L'Art Politique"— a poem by Berchoux—bore the fanciful signature "Publicola Petisot." Subsequently the young writer subscribed his name in full, and gives his reasons for doing so in a letter addressed to his fellow-contributors on the subject of the "Biographie Nouvelle des Contemporains," saying that, as he found himself compelled to make some vehement attacks, he felt it right to take the responsibility, and to bear the consequences of his own opinions.

Previously to this, however, twenty-one articles of various kinds had appeared, signed simply with the letter "V." Some of these were in prose and some in verse, and the greater number of them have never been reproduced. The composition of the verses is for the most part classical, sedate, and pure. The prose articles, which are reviews of Casimir Delavigne, Byron, Moore, Ancelot, Gaspard de Pons, Walter Scott, Jacques Delille, Châteaubriand, Madame Desbordes Valmore, and others, are excellent studies, and exhibit the author's deep reading and rich fund of knowledge. Their style is varied, intellectual, and well balanced.

The editor of the *Conservateur* manifestly had all the qualifications for being a first-rate journalist, and his talent for criticism would doubtless have been developed to a remarkable degree if his imagination had not transported his genius into another direction.

From time to time there appeared in the magazine various translations from Lucan and from Virgil, signed M. d'Auverney. Auverney, or Auverné, is a village seven or eight miles from Châteaubriant, in the department of the Loire Inférieure, where General Hugo had a small property that entitled him to the name. Victor took advantage of this, and borrowed it for a *nom de plume*.

Among his other works we must not omit to mention his dramatic reviews. That the future author of "Hernani" should, in 1820, have analyzed "L'Homme Poli," a poetical comedy in five acts by M. Merville, as well as some pieces by Dupin and Carmouche, "Le Cadet Roussel Procida" of the Porte-Saint-Martin, and some vaudevilles by M. Pain and M. Bouilly—or Pain-Bouilly, as they were conjointly called—was a whim, or perhaps rather an irony of fate, that demands a record.

But the most curious, as the most remarkable, of his critiques was that which he wrote upon Lamartine's "Premières Méditations Poétiques," which had just been published anonymously.

"On reading such verses," he says, "who would not exclaim with La Harpe, 'Dost thou not hear a poet's song?' I have read this book more than once, and, in spite of the carelessness, the neologisms, the repetitions, and the obscurity that I notice in various parts, I am tempted to say to the author, 'Courage, young man! you are one of those whom Plato would have overwhelmed with honor and banished from his republic. You must expect to be driven from our land of ignorance and anarchy; but in your exile you will fail to find the palms, the trumpets, and the wreaths of flowers that Plato accorded to the poets.'"

LAMARTINE.

With an enthusiasm that was thoroughly sincere, the reviewer expresses his wonder at the appearance of such a book; and, recognizing the embryo glory of an inspired singer, in spite of his severity as a purist, he commiserates the age, which he fears will only scoff at the productions of the noble and unknown hand.

It was not long before he became acquainted with Lamartine, who has himself recorded their first interview. The account was written when he was advanced in years:

"Youth is the time for forming friendships. I love Hugo because I knew and loved him at an age when the heart is still expanding within the breast. I remember, as though it were but yesterday, the day when the great Duc de Rohan, then a musketeer, though afterwards a cardinal, came to my quarters on the Quai d'Orsay, and said, 'Come with me and behold a phenomenon that promises a great man for France. Châteaubriand has already named him "L'enfant sublime." You will some day congratulate yourself that you have seen the oak within the acorn.'

"Following the duke, I started off, and soon found myself on the ground-floor of an obscure house at the end of a court.

"There a grave, melancholy mother was industriously instructing some boys of various ages—her sons. She showed us into a low room, a little way apart, at the farther end of which, either reading or writing, sat a studious youth, with a fine, massive head, intelligent and thoughtful. This was Victor Hugo, the man whose pen can now charm or terrify the world.

"Already he had written odes and elegies; already was the inspiration of a great poet foreshadowed in his productions—works of which no man with a soul within his breast could fail to feel the power."

Subsequently we shall find that Lamartine became less lavish in his praise, but at that time his admiration of the young author knew no bounds. Our object here is to show that even the first essays of Victor Hugo attracted the attention of all lovers of literature. We shall hereafter see how his reputation continued to increase.

CHAPTER VIII.

The Pamphlets of 1819.—A Cruel Separation.—Publication of the First Odes.—Hard Work.—Mother's Death.—An Affecting Betrothal.—Offer of Marriage.—Duel with a Life-guardsman.—Poverty Bravely Borne.—A Young Poet's Budget.—Publication of the "Odes et Ballades."—Their Success.—The Author's Ideas on Odes.—Corrections of Manuscript.—Lodging in the Rue du Dragon.—Account of Royal Pension.

ONLY a portion of the lyrical pieces dated 1819 have been reprinted. They are not to be found anywhere except in the literary reviews of the period, and are of no interest beyond what they afford to men of letters. Those that were published in pamphlet form have become so rare that none but book-fanciers can procure them. In 1880, Charles Monselet discovered a satire on "Le Télégraphe," an octavo pamphlet of twelve pages, with prose notes at the end, signed V. M. Hugo, and bearing the date 1819. The bookseller refused to let him have it for its weight in gold; but Monselet read it, and pronounced that although the first part was written in an antiquated style, and might have come from the pen of Ancelot, the second part took a higher tone, and presented a colored imagery that shadowed forth the future author of the "Odes et Ballades."

The young poet was now working with increasing energy. His greatest pleasure was to accompany his mother to M. Foucher's house, and there spend long evenings in unspoken admiration of the maiden to whom his whole heart was devoted. It was not long before these admiring glances were noticed by the parents, to whom the danger of encouraging such a passion was apparent, as both the young people were of an age when marriage was out of the question. By mutual consent the two families broke off all intimacy for a time.

Victor Hugo found expression for his grief at the separation in a poem that is full of sad and gentle dignity. It is entitled "Le Premier Soupir."

"Be happy, sweet one! all thy days be peace,
    Enjoy calm slumber on life's flowing stream,
    And waves of gladness lave each hour of thine!
But, oh, how soon doth all my rapture cease!
    My wounded soul dark in despair doth seem,
    Once forced to love, now bidden to resign!"

In spite, however, of this apparent resignation, the obstacles placed in the way of his passion only increased its intensity, and absence, instead of extinguishing his love, served only to increase it. His fevered imagination devised a thousand means by which he might catch a glimpse of one without whom he felt it was impossible to exist. Numberless are the stratagems he contrived, and incredible the ingenuity with which they were executed; the freshness of his romance was itself an exquisite idyl.

An instance of the secret understanding between the lovers has since been discovered. "Han d'Islande," which we shall have to describe at a later page, though it did not appear till 1823, was commenced in 1820. It would hardly have been suspected how, amid the recitals of crime and the conglomeration of terrible adventures, and beneath its scenes of thrilling horror, there lurks, as it were, a love-letter in some yawning and hideous gulf, a message of tenderness for one young girl. The pages of gloom and horror were for jailers, the passages of love were for her.

Victor never despaired. He lived confident in his future happiness; but in the midst of his anticipations he was overwhelmed by a terrible blow.

Madame Hugo took cold; inflammation of the chest again set in, and this time no devotion on the part of her sons could arrest the malady.

The fondly loved mother died on the 27th of June, 1821. Abel, the eldest son, was summoned with all speed, and the three brothers followed the body to the Church of St. Sulpice, and thence to the Cemetery of Mont Parnasse.

It seemed impossible for Victor to realize, as he returned to his desolate home, that he had lost forever the sweetness of maternal love:

"the love that none forgets;
The bread which God divides and multiplies;
A table ever spread where bounteous grace
To each his portion gives, to none denies."

Yet he was to partake of that portion no more. He had lost a mother who to him had been more than a mother, inspiring him with his love for the beautiful and his reverence for the good.

In the evening of the day of the funeral he returned to the cemetery, and there, overcome with grief and choked by sobs, he wandered up and down. He continued his walk till late, recalling his mother's image, and ever and again repeating her name, until he felt himself involuntarily attracted towards the being who alone could soften the bitterness of his sorrow. He wanted tenderness to console him for the tender love that he had lost.

Hurrying off to the Rue du Cherche-Midi, he looked into the window of the house and saw Adèle wearing a wreath of flowers and dancing. She knew nothing of what had happened; it was her birthday, and her father, not to mar her pleasure, had concealed from her the circumstance of Madame Hugo's death.

Victor called on the following day. The young lovers shed tears together over his bereavement, and exchanged afresh their vows of mutual fidelity.

Mademoiselle Foucher had felt the separation of the two families as keenly as her lover; like him, she had sighed in secret; and when, a few weeks later, he came in his mourning attire, more dejected than ever through his life of solitude, and made a formal offer of marriage, the young girl simply said that she already considered herself his *fiancée*. Her strength of purpose was so great and her affection so sincere that her parents knew that any opposition on their part would be of no avail; but, as neither of them had any fortune, it was imperative that the marriage should be deferred until Victor's resources from his profession should enable him to maintain a home. The promise, however, went far to revive his spirits.

A few weeks before this time he had met with an adventure which had somewhat serious consequences, and might have been fatal. As a diversion in his sorrow, he took an excursion to Versailles, where, after taking his luncheon at a *café*, he sat holding a newspaper in his hand, but which he was too absorbed in his own sad thoughts to read. Sitting by his side was a life-guardsman, who, growing impatient in his anxiety to read the news, and observing that his neighbor was not using it, snatched the paper roughly from his hand. The young man,

who looked little more than a boy, turned pale with rage, and forthwith challenged the soldier.

A duel was arranged, the meeting taking place the same day. The parties fought in a room attached to one of the principal barracks in Versailles; and, in order to avoid any commotion, a company of soldiers was exercised in front of the door. Gaspard de Pous, an officer of the Royal Guard, and Alfred de Vigny were Hugo's seconds. In the second round he received a deepish sword-cut in his left arm below the shoulder. When the guardsman was informed that he had wounded "l'enfant sublime," his consternation was great, and he declared:

"If I had known who he was, I would have let him run me through the body."

It took a fortnight for the wound to heal, and the poet applied himself afresh to his labors.

His prospects could not be considered brilliant. As already mentioned, his allowance from his father had been withdrawn, and he was solely dependent on his own exertions. His indomitable spirit, however, and his undaunted confidence in the future, supported him through all his season of poverty, and, with the utmost fortitude, he underwent that fine but trying ordeal from which "the weak emerge infamous, the strong sublime."

The account, written long afterwards, of the early years of Marius in "Les Misérables" may be accepted as by no means an inaccurate description of this period of his life. In his own wonderfully graphic language he there describes how the young man swept out his own landing, how he would buy a pennyworth of cheese at the grocer's, waiting till dusk to creep out to the baker's to get a loaf of bread, with which he would slink home as furtively as if he had stolen it; how, carrying his book under his arm, he would surreptitiously make his way to the butcher's at the corner, and, after being elbowed and jeered at by a lot of servant-girls, till he felt the sweat standing on his forehead, he would take off his hat to the astonished butcher and his shopboy and ask for a mutton cutlet, with which he would go off to cook it for himself, and to make it last for at least three days.

For a whole year he lived on seven hundred francs, which were the proceeds of his pamphlets and the articles in the *Conservateur*. But at length, acting on his brother's advice, he determined to collect his odes and issue them in a single volume. Lamartine's "Méditations" had been published two years previously, and he was sanguine of a similar success for his own venture.

This first volume of the "Odes et Ballades" was printed by Guiraudet in the Rue Saint-Honoré, and published by Pelicier, 245 Place du Palais Royal. In its exterior it had nothing to recommend it to the connoisseur in books, the paper being bad, and the printing vile.

The volume was, in truth, the book of the author's youth.

The first edition contains some pieces that were afterwards suppressed — "Raymond d'Assoli," an elegy; "Les Derniers Bardes," a poem; and an "Idylle," being a dialogue between an old and a young man. The last of these has been introduced into the third volume of the "Annales Romantiques" under the title of "Les Deux Âges."

Not only in Paris, but in the country, the book made a considerable sensation; fresh editions had to be brought out year by year. That issued in 1829, on the page facing "L'Ode à la Colonne," contains a curious portrait of Hugo in a long frock-coat, lounging with his elbows on a sofa cushion; on the right, in a prismatic ray, stands the Vendôme Column with a group of eagles hovering over it; on the ground lie some papers and a terrestrial globe.

It would be too long a task to enumerate all the editions of the work. Its immediate effect was to bring the author into prominence, and, as a consequence of its success, there were some who endeavored to stir up Lamartine's jealousy against a writer who had risen to such popularity. It is impossible to judge whether Lamartine was sincere in his protestations that he entertained no feeling of the kind; but it is at least certain that, notwithstanding their wide difference of style and subsequent divergence of opinion, no one ever succeeded in bringing to open variance the two great men that seemed born to understand and respect each other. Envy is a sentiment that never for a moment found an entrance into Victor Hugo's lofty soul.

There is no need to conceal that the "Odes et Ballades" present many ideas that would find no approval now; but the poet, nevertheless, has declared that he could proudly and conscientiously place them side by side with the democratical books and poems of his matured manhood. This, he says, he should be prepared to do because, in the fierce strife against early prejudices imbibed with a mother's milk, and in the slow, rough ascent from the false to the true, which, to a certain extent, makes up the substance of every man's life, and causes the development of his conscience to be the type of human progress in general, each step so taken represents some material sacrifice to moral advancement, some interest abandoned, some vanity eschewed, some worldly benefit renounced—nay, perhaps some risk of home or even life incurred.

Victor Hugo is all the more justified in being proud of these productions when it is considered that, only twenty years old, and not yet an object of envy, he was so applauded by the best critics of the time, and so patronized by the chief personages of the Restoration, that he could easily have turned his position into a source of profit. The royalist party then in power was in urgent need of rising men, not simply of talent and energy, but of high character.

The poet, however, was faithful to his love of art. His dreams were of a glorious future; and although his prosperity appeared for the time to depend upon compliance with the temptation held out to him, and notwithstanding that the poverty with which he was struggling was the sole obstacle to his marriage, he would not for a moment lend his ear to any of the solicitations with which he was plied. He kept aloof from all intrigue, and, unabashed by his restricted circumstances, he held his head erect and maintained the moral dignity that was his rule of life.

To him poetry was too dear to be made subordinate to other interests. He wished that his whole soul should appear in his odes, his whole imagination in his ballads; and from the first appearance of his work in 1822 he gave indications, not to be misunderstood, of his literary aim.

Although but twenty, he ventured to assert that if, during the last thirty years, the French ode had lost much of its power in depicting the touching and the terrible, the stern and the startling, the mysterious and the marvellous, the defect was not to be attributed in the least to the essence of the ode, but to the form with which the lyric writers had clothed it.

To his mind it seemed that the chilliness and monotony that pervaded the modern

A PROVOCATION.

ode were to be attributed to the superabundance of apostrophes, exclamations, personifications of inanimate objects, and similar forms of vehemence that were thrown into them with the effect of burdening rather than of tiring the imagination. He conceived that by placing the movement of the verses rather in the ideas than in the diction, by having one fundamental subject as the basis of all, and by substituting for the staid old colors of the heathen mythology the newer tints of Christianity, the ode might be invested with something of dramatic interest, and so be constructed to utter language that, though it might be stern, should yet be consoling.

Here, then, was the first declaration of war against the style of poetry designated the classical; it was the prelude of numberless battles; but from that day forward we may recognize the goal towards which the poet advances with a steady tread, resolved to rear a flag of liberty for art. For this, as we shall see, his efforts had to be unwearied.

The manuscript sheets of the "Odes et Ballades" are covered with corrections; the alterations, some of which are noted in the final edition, consist of verses entirely rewritten and lines frequently revised and inverted. In the *ne varietur* edition it has been deemed inexpedient to reproduce certain verses written in the author's youth which he himself when a man subsequently condemned; he found it hard to please himself, but wished to have his due.

After his mother's death, he remained for a short time in a small room in the Rue de Mézières, but afterwards left it for 30 Rue du Dragon (formerly Rue du Sépulcre), where he shared a couple of rooms at the top of the house with one of his cousins, a young law-student.

The front room, which looked out upon the street, served as a parlor, and was furnished with a table and a few chairs, the prizes gained in the Jeux Floraux being arranged over the mantel-piece. This apartment opened into a bedroom containing two little wooden bedsteads, and overlooking a yard.

At that time the young author had only three white shirts in his possession, but his scanty supply of linen did not prevent him from always looking scrupulously neat. Out of his little capital he had bought a bright-blue coat with gilt buttons, which he wore on any occasion when he happened to dine out. Not caring for ordinary amusements, he endeavored to form associations that were worth cultivating, and was invited to *salons* to which admission was not generally easy, and where he was made much of. Literary people felt that they were doing well to give encouragement to the proud young poet, who asked no assistance from others, and was determined to show his father that he was capable of maintaining himself. At the commencement of the century it was the wont of polished society to take an interest in young beginners who appeared to be maintaining the brilliancy of early promise; and Victor in this way formed the valuable friendship of such men as Soumet, Alexandre Guiraud, Pichat, Jules Lefèvre, Émile Deschamps, and Alfred de Vigny, some of whom would visit him in his garret, and listen to him as with his thrilling voice he read his first superb strophes.

The first edition of the "Odes" having brought in a profit of 700 francs, a second edition immediately followed, and, as "it never rains but it pours," Louis XVIII. conceived the idea of allowing the poet a pension of 1000 francs from his privy purse. The king had been flattered by allusions to himself in some verses to which his reader had called his attention; but he had a further reason for his generosity, to which we must presently refer.

The pension came at a timely hour; together with his improved resources, it enabled Victor Hugo to press his offer of marriage. For some months he went to reside with his brother Abel in the Rue du Vieux-Colombier, in a house for which he has since sought in vain, but which, as far as he remembers, was by the side of the quarters of the fire-brigade.

Hitherto the young poet had had but few opportunities of seeing his *fiancée*, their interviews being limited to a weekly visit at her father's house, and some rare meetings which Madame Foucher permitted in the Luxembourg; but at this period he spent a whole summer with the lady and her family at Gentilly, close to Bicêtre. From the house was a view of the verdant valley of the Bièvre, where with happy walks in loving companionship the season passed joyfully away; for the future all looked bright.

And thus there came an end to the sighings of the youth, who, in his letters to Adèle, had lamented the cruelty of fate, and de-

THE ROOM IN THE RUE DU DRAGON.

5

clared that patience was not one of his virtues. But for him love had been an elevating sentiment; it had raised his thoughts above the distractions of earth by associating them with a higher sphere; such love cannot fail to bring its own recompense.

Victor now asked his father's consent. General Hugo had some little time previously to this contracted a second marriage, and had retired to Blois; he had begun to feel a certain amount of confidence in his son's attainments, and did not hesitate to accede to his request.

Lamennais, the eminent priest destined to be a convert to democracy, and, in the name of reason, to reject his Catholic creed, to whom the young poet had been introduced by M. de Rohan, gave him his certificate of confession. By a strange coincidence this priest was then residing in the old house in the Impasse des Feuillantines. Many times in letters afterwards quoted by Madame Victor Hugo, he expressed his esteem for the man who, in his advanced years, was to write "Religions et Religion;" paths almost parallel in the field of philosophy seemed to lie before the two mighty intellects.

It was without any application on his own part that Victor Hugo had been assigned a pension by Louis XVIII. The poet attributed the act of generosity to the publication of the "Odes," but, as already hinted, there was another motive in the background.

In 1822 the Saumur plot took place. Among the conspirators were Berton, Cafe, who opened his veins with a piece of glass, and a young man named Delon, who, when Victor was a child, had often shared his romps in the courtyard of the Rue de Clichy.

Delon's father, formerly an officer serving under General Hugo, had been the informant in General Lahorie's case, causing his arrest, and in consequence of that all intercourse between the families had been broken off; but Victor had never forgotten his old playfellow, and as soon as he heard that he was in danger he resolved to offer him a refuge.

He wrote to Delon's mother, the wife of a royal lieutenant residing at St. Denis, telling her that, although he was himself living in the Rue du Dragon, he had a room at his disposal in the Rue de Mézières. "Let your son conceal himself there; my devotion to the Bourbons is too well known for him to be sought in such a retreat."

This letter, addressed to the mother of a man who had all the police upon his track, was unsuspiciously put by Victor into the post. Evening after evening he took his stand in the street close to the proposed asylum, seeing in every passenger that came beneath the shadow of the wall the friend he thought to recognize; but Delon was far too prudent to venture.

As might have been anticipated, the letter had been conveyed from the post-office to the council-chamber, and there submitted to Louis. The king smiled and said, "That young man has a good heart as well as a great genius; he is an honorable fellow; I shall take care he has the next pension that falls vacant."

Such was the real origin of what was presumed to be simply an act of royal patronage.

The letter was reclosed and forwarded to its address. Had Delon accepted the proposal, there can be no doubt that he would have been arrested, and very probably he would have been executed.

At a later date Victor Hugo heard this account from the postmaster himself, a M. Roger, who aspired to be a dramatic author, publishing several works having no claims to remembrance. It was a joke of the period that "the Académie and the post-office had almost made M. Roger a man of letters."

On hearing the facts, the poet rushed from the postmaster's office with an exclamation of horror that ever his pension should have been awarded as the price of blood.

Delon was far too well acquainted with the ways of the police to listen to any suggestion of the kind; he took good care to make his way abroad—but henceforward Victor Hugo began to doubt the prudence of putting confidence in princes.

Nevertheless, at the time the pension so far contributed to Hugo's happiness that it enabled him to leave his humble lodgings, and to accelerate the marriage which he had been contemplating so eagerly and so long.

CHAPTER IX.

The Poet's Marriage.—Illness and Death of Eugène Hugo.—General Hugo in Paris.—His Influence on Victor.—"Han d'Islande."—Scope of the Work.—Its Reception by the Critics.—Charles Nodier's Approval.—Partisans of the Book.—Drama Founded on it.—Fortune Smiles on the Poet.—The House in the Rue de Vaugirard.—*La Revue Française.*—Victor Hugo's Opinion of Voltaire in 1824.—His Observations on Lamennais, Walter Scott, and Byron.—Achille Devéria and Louis Boulanger.

IN October, 1822, Victor Hugo was married in the chapel of the Church of St. Sulpice, where, eighteen months before, he had attended his mother's funeral. M. Soumet and M. Ancelot were the witnesses, and Alfred de Vigny was likewise present.

The wedding took place from the house of M. Foucher, the bride's father, who still resided in the hotel of the War Office. There it was that hospitality was first provided for the young couple, whose united ages were under two-score, and who started in life without a dowry. The bridegroom, whose entire fortune consisted of 800 francs, had presented his bride with a wedding-dress of French cashmere. The cashmere had been purchased from the proceeds of the "Odes et Ballades!" Could a queen boast of a robe of more costly **fabric?**

The breakfast that followed the religious ceremony was given, by a strange coincidence, **in** the hall where General Lahorie **had** received his sentence of death.

In that giant existence of which we are tracing the story, sorrow rarely seems to have been disassociated with its joy. A terrible event marred the brightness of the occasion. The wedding breakfast was hardly over when Victor's brother Eugène, who for some little time had been exhibiting symptoms of over-excitement of the brain, was seized with a fit of madness.

This young man, who had preceded Victor as a poet—contributing, as has been already said, a number of articles to the *Conservateur Littéraire*—had given tokens **of** considerable **promise.** He has left only some novels and **pieces** of verse, of which a critic has re-**marked** that "they are types of his own melancholy fate; his reviews, too, of new work and **dramas,** while they exhibit intense conscientiousness, always express any **cen**-sure with an anxiety which seems affrighted at the **future.**" He was endowed with an over-vivid imagination, and his natural tendency to melancholy was, in consequence of an unfortunate attachment, aggravated into a morbid madness. Dr. Esquirol was called in, but his skill was of no avail, and in a very short time Eugène succumbed to his malady.

General Hugo had not been present at the marriage, but he came to Paris to take a last farewell of his second son. During his visit his behavior to Victor was most affectionate; and whatever differences of opinion might exist between the soldier of the Empire and the son of the Vendean who in the storms of 1793 had saved nineteen priests, all seemed to be forgotten.

In a letter written two years previously to one of his intimate friends, Victor Hugo has mentioned how one day, when he had been enunciating his royalist principles, his father, who had listened in silence, turned to General L——, who was standing by, and said, "Give him time; as a youth he holds his mother's opinions, as a man he will adopt the father's."

The prediction set the poet thinking. **He** could not fail to observe that young men on their first awakening to political life were in strange perplexity. They found their fathers hailing Napoleon Bonaparte as the hero who conferred on them their epaulets, while their mothers only saw in him the adventurer who robbed them of their sons.

The same letter goes on: "Born under **the** Consulate, we children grew up at our mothers' knees while our fathers were in camp; and often have those mothers, bereaved perhaps of husband or brother by the insatiable craving for conquest of a single man, fixed upon us their loving eyes, all full of tears, and thought how their little ones, now eight or ten years old, would be conscripts in 1820, and either colonels or corpses in 1825.

"The acclamations that greeted **Louis** XVIII. were an outburst of maternal ecstasy.

"Taken altogether, there are few young men of our generation who did not imbibe with their mothers' milk an abhorrence of the two tempestuous periods preceding the Restoration. In 1803 the children's bugbear was Robespierre ; in 1815 their terror was Napoleon."

Victor Hugo concludes his letter by admitting that experience may modify our first impressions of life, but insisting that an honest man is bound to submit all such modifications to the rigid scrutiny of conscience. For himself, indeed, it was his conscience that he always consulted. It was not at once that he renounced the hatred for the conquering despot with which he had been imbued; but little by little he was won over by his father's enthusiasm, so that in course of time he fulfilled the prediction that had been made about himself, and proceeded to celebrate in verse the armies of the *"chef prodigieux,"* and to swell the honors of l'Arc de l'Étoile as the portal of victory.

But this change, though in a measure foreseen, carried with it its own fate. Led away for a time by what seemed great issues, he embraced his father's views ; but his conscience, enlightened day by day, soon dictated quite another bias.

With the indefatigable industry that appertained to him, Victor Hugo set to work immediately after his marriage, and in a few months completed his romance "Han d'Islande."

The first edition appeared anonymously in 1823, and he received 1000 francs from the sale. At that time it was quite unusual for young authors to prefix their names to their works : Lamartine's "Premières Méditations" had been published without the writer's name, and about the same time M. Thiers, then making his début in public life, brought out "L'Histoire de la Révolution Française" under the *nom de plume* of Felix Bodin.

The original work was in four volumes. The issue of these was temporarily interrupted because the editor suspended his payments, and a correspondence was opened with the author. The letters, which are somewhat bitter in tone, are to be found partly in *L'Éclair*, a royalist journal, and partly in the liberal publication *Le Miroir* of May, 1823.

But this incidental difficulty did not prevent public curiosity being keenly interested in the book. The poet's powerful imagination is revealed in the thrilling situations, the magnificent descriptions of scenery, and the careful historical studies that the story con-

tains; while coincident with an aggregation of the most hideous crimes lies a charming picture of chaste and ideal love.

As Victor Hugo has himself remarked, it is the work not merely of a young man, but of a very young man. In reading it one is conscious that the comparative youth who began to write it during the paroxysms of the fever of 1821 had as yet no experience either of men, of things, or of truth, and was only guessing at them all. According to the author's own estimate, "Han d'Islande" is merely a fanciful romance in which a young man's love is the one object felt, and a young girl's love the one subject observed. It is his own statement that, "afraid to trust to any living soul the secret love and grief that he felt within him," he chose his paper to be the confidant of his spirit in the hour that separated him from the object of his passion.

Certain parts of "Han d'Islande" bear a marked resemblance to the style of Sir Walter Scott. The plot turns entirely upon the search prosecuted by young Captain Ordener for papers that will save the life of Chancellor Schumaker, the father of Estel, his promised bride ; the main interest centres in a miners' conspiracy, in which the old man is erroneously supposed to be implicated.

The hero of the romance, the legendary Han d'Islande, is a monster who drinks seawater and blood out of his son's skull, and is the terror of the whole country-side. With him it comes about that the captain finally to dispute the possession of the documents, and it is only by the interposition of a bear that the monster escapes becoming the victim of Ordener's fury.

Received by the critics with equal astonishment and irritation, the work was handled with a severity that almost amounted to insult. On the other hand, there were men of both judgment and talent who did not hesitate to pronounce in its favor.

So far from censuring this early venture, Charles Nodier welcomed it with enthusiasm. He told his friends that the unknown author had put forth a marvellous ideal of nightmare ; and he wrote a long article in the *Quotidienne*, in which he observed that it was characteristic of very few to commence only with faults voluntarily introduced, and which they already knew were open to criticism. Delighted to see any one break a lance with classic literature, he prognosticated an immense success for "Han d'Islande," maintaining that it was the outcome of a strong

HAN D'ISLANDE.

CHARLES NODIER.

intellect and great study, and that it was written in a bright, picturesque, and nervous style, with a delicacy of touch and refinement of expression that formed a striking contrast to its wild and grotesque play of fancy.

Without delay, Victor Hugo hurried off to tender his thanks to the kind-hearted reviewer. Nodier started with surprise at the revelation that the author of the weird and terrible romance was actually the writer of the "Odes et Ballades;" but, on recovering from his amazement, he gave him a hearty greeting, and the interview was the commencement of a lasting friendship between the two.

Another partisan, hardly less energetic, of the production that was the subject of so much attack was Méry, the author of a great many charming standard books, and a fellow-contributor with Barthélemy to the *Némésis.* After a series of singular adventures at Marseilles, this matchless journalist and brilliant orator had just come to Paris. Conjointly with M. Rabbe, who was then writing his history of the popes, he asserted in the *Tablettes Universelles* that "Han d'Islande" was a meritorious work, in every way deserving the study and attention of the public.

After thus recording the praise of such men as Charles Nodier and Méry, we may well feel ourselves more than justified in ignoring the many adverse and insulting strictures of certain critics of little or of no authority.

M. Rabbe himself awarded unbounded praise to "Han d'Islande." We have already quoted some of his opinions on Victor Hugo's early years; he was his devoted friend and his biographer. He died young, the victim of a disease that disfigured him so terribly as to embitter his existence.

In spite, if not in consequence, of the numerous fierce attacks upon the book, there was very soon a demand for a new edition. In a humorous preface to this, the author expresses his satisfaction at the enormous success of his work, some half-dozen people at least having read it from beginning to end. He tenders his acknowledgments to the fair readers, who, he has been informed, have made up their own idea of what the author is like; he describes how flattered he feels by hearing that they have invested him with red hair, frizzly beard, and haggard eyes; he is overwhelmed by the honor they do him in representing that he never cuts his nails; but on bended knee he begs them not to believe that he carries his ferocity so far as to devour little infants alive; in conclusion, he assures them that he will do his best to merit their kind sentiments by striving to attain the high renown of the authors of "Lolotte et Fanfan" and of "Monsieur Botte."

The irony of the defence conveys some idea of the virulence of the attack. The classics declared that the journals in which "Han d'Islande" got a chance commendation were edited by bricklayers, barbers, and tinkers; but the savage critics received an unanswerable rebuke when it transpired that the booksellers Lecointre and Durey had purchased the second edition for 10,000 francs.

Fortune was now smiling on the poet, and the young couple were enjoying what to them seemed an inundation of wealth. About the same time, too, the king doubled the amount of the pension, and the modest household, which had hitherto found its quarters in a small residence in the Rue du Cherche-Midi, now shifted to a more permanent settlement at 90 Rue de Vaugirard. Nodier, without any ceremony, accompanied by his wife and daughter Marie, attended at a house-warming entertainment.

In recognition of his devoted loyalty, as well as of his literary attainments, Nodier about this time was appointed librarian at the Arsenal. The amiable and accomplished writer managed his reputation with considerable tact. He maintained the most friendly relations with all who were in any way famous during the great literary epoch of the Restoration, and throughout his life was always surrounded by illustrious society.

At the time when Victor Hugo, who called him his master, was becoming the leader of the new school, Charles Nodier kept his *salon* open as a common rendezvous alike for classics and romantics, for royalists and liberals. But his preference was specially for the author of "Han d'Islande;" as he was one of the first to pay his homage to the work, so he never ceased to regard the poet with esteem and admiration.

With one further reference we may conclude our notice of "Han d'Islande."

On the 25th of January, 1832, a grand melodrama in three acts and of eight scenes, founded upon the romance, was brought out at the Théâtre de l'Ambigu-Comique. The authors responsible for the adaptation were named Palmir, Octo, and Rameau. The music was by M. Adrien, the scenery by M. Desfontaines, and the divertisement by M. Théodore: this last consisted of a village *fête*, and could not be said to do much credit to M. Théodore's powers of imagination.

The hero, who was usually attired in skins and armed with a hatchet, chiefly attracted attention in the difficult part he had to play by the loud roars that signalized his entrances and exits. The utility of this fanciful melodrama was not altogether apparent; and, in spite of the excellent intentions of the adapters, the original plot was by no means left intact. One peculiarity very much commends the piece to the lovers of spectacle. M. Montigny, who afterwards became the intelligent manager of the Gymnase Dramatique, *doubled* the part of Han d'Islande, which had been created by M. Francisque.

It would have been an oversight on the part of the historian to omit all notice of this dramatic curiosity.

During the year succeeding his marriage, Victor Hugo was a contributor to a magazine called *La Revue Française*, which had been started by Soumet, Guiraud, and Émile Deschamps. The review was but short-lived, but the young writer gave such decided proof of his knowledge and power, his literary judgment and his fine imagination, that every member of the artistic world was anxious to make his acquaintance.

Among those of his artist friends whose attachment to him was then most sincere, and whose belief in his future fame was most confident, should be mentioned Achille Devéria, who drew the beautiful vignettes for the early editions of the "Odes et Ballades," "Bug-Jargal," and "Hernani." By this large-hearted and talented man, the truly French art of illustration, which was in its infancy in 1825, was developed with surprising brilliancy; and it was by the help of his singular skill that the "Bibliothèque" was enabled to set on foot the formation of a collection of engravings on a scientific and practical basis. His pupils were his brother Eugène, who, however, did not fulfil his early promise, and Louis Boulanger, who was, as a painter, the first sincere apostle of the romantic school. In after-years Louis Boulanger painted a striking portrait of Victor Hugo, who, after thus giving him his patronage, dedicated to him some clever verses. Endowed with an imagination of which the fertility seemed inexhaustible, this leading spirit of the 1830 school produced some brilliant pictures of scenes in "Notre Dame de Paris" and "Lucrèce Borgia." Victor Hugo always designated him his painter and his friend.

But, as we have said, in the early days of his career Achille Devéria was the most intimate of all the poet's companions. In 1825 the two families met nearly every day; either Hugo would dine with Devéria, or Devéria with Hugo. It would not appear that these repasts were by any means worthy of Lucullus, but intellect and wit gave flavor to the viands, merriment and laughter supplied the place of the *entremets*, and gave its own effervescence to the meagre wine that filled their glasses. Even to his old-age it was an intimacy to which Victor Hugo could ever allude as one of the most pleasing associations of his life.

About this time Victor Hugo was commissioned to write a notice of Voltaire. This was subsequently reprinted in his "Mélanges de Littérature." Written by a Catholic royalist, the eulogium on the philosopher could not be otherwise than very qualified in its tone, but nevertheless, in spite of all restrictions and prejudices, and after asserting of Voltaire that he had developed and aggravated the latent disorders of the age, Victor Hugo renders homage to the marvellous intellect of which as yet he did not comprehend the full power; he pronounced him to have attraction without grace, fascination without charm, and brilliancy without dignity. In short, it is plain that he had not yet reached the point when he could properly appreciate what Voltaire was.

Fifty-four years later, at Voltaire's centenary, we shall see that he held a very different estimate. Then he beheld the immortal author of the "Essai sur les Mœurs" in a finer light; he glorified him as one "who had waged the war of the just against the unjust, the oppressed against the oppressor; the war of gentleness, the war of kindness," and lauded him as one "who united the tenderness of a woman to the fire of a hero, a being of noble spirit and of expansive heart!"

These differences of opinion should be brought out into bold relief and open contrast. Victor Hugo has ever been ready to recall them, in order that he might frankly compare them as illustrating how the contradictions of his life are superficial rather than radical, and as showing by what secret affinities ideas that are apparently divergent may unite themselves in one central thought that gradually detaches itself from their midst and ultimately absorbs them all.

Although in the critical essay of 1824 Victor Hugo had thus handled Voltaire rather severely, he had nothing but unqualified praise for his illustrious friend the Abbé de Lamennais, who had just published his "Essai sur l'Indifférence en Matière de Religion." In reference to this venerable priest, Victor Hugo said that he seemed to have come casually in contact with glory to mount at once to the topmost heights of literary celebrity, and added: "This dignified and impassioned writer, with a simplicity that is magnificent, with an earnestness that is vehement, and with an intensity that is sublime, appeals to the heart by every tenderness, to the understanding by every artifice, to the soul by every enthusiasm. . . . He has been assailed by a storm of reproaches that every one who makes them should direct to his own individual conscience; he has made all the vices that he would expunge from the human heart cry out like the buyers and sellers expelled from the temple. . . . We have heard it declared that his austere temper would cast a melancholy cloud over human life, and that the gloomy priest wants to pluck up every flower that grows along man's path. It may be so; but the flowers to be plucked up are only those that conceal an abyss."

Only a short time before issuing this glowing eulogium upon Lamennais, Victor Hugo had written a critique upon Sir Walter Scott, in which he gave his opinion that "Quentin Durward" is a book that well portrays how

loyalty, though its representative may be young, obscure, and needy, is certain to attain its end more readily than perfidy, even when assisted by all the resources of wealth, power, and experience.

Again, in June, 1824, he published his ideas of Lord Byron, who had just fallen a victim to his noble ambition, the regeneration of Greece. The poet of France bears magnanimous tribute to the talent of England. He dwells with lofty enthusiasm upon the proud portals of Westminster Abbey, opening, as it were, of their own accord that Byron's tomb might dignify the resting-place of kings, and he bitterly reproaches Paris for having cast contempt upon his coffin.

Byron's school at the beginning of this century was commonly designated the Satanic school. With reference to this expression Victor Hugo has wittily remarked in a note that the literary *mots* of a period may represent not so much the character of the works of the time as the sentiments of those who, often unknown to the authors themselves, have had the leading part in inventing them.

The article upon Byron contains some important paragraphs. Although the author of the "Odes et Ballades" at twenty-two years of age could congratulate himself that he had formed ties of friendship with not a few of the leading spirits of his day, he expresses his great regret that he has never made Lord Byron's acquaintance, and applies to him a touching line of verse which a poet of his school had addressed to the generous shade of André Chénier:

"Farewell, young friend! my friend, though never seen;"

and then he goes on to declare his astonishment that there were minds capable of believing that the literature denominated classic had an existence still; he maintains that the literature of ages passed away, though leaving behind it immortal monuments, has departed with the social life and political ideas of those who were its exponents.

This was the commencement of the war; this was the crossing of the Rubicon! The spear was now poised for the strife; and it becomes our task to recount the battles from which the poet came out triumphant, bearing the palm of victory.

CHAPTER X.

Journey to Blois.—Victor Hugo Made Chevalier of the Legion of Honor.—Coronation of Charles X.—Visit to Lamartine.—Trip Across the Alps.—Return to Paris.—Proclamation of Literary Liberty.—Birth of Romanticism.—Wrath of the Classics.—Literature of the First Empire.—Revival at the Beginning of the Present Century.—Prelude of a Great War.—Caricature of a Classic.—" L'Ode à la Colonne."

"I SHALL hope to see you soon at Blois," were General Hugo's farewell words to Victor on leaving Paris, whither he had come, as we have related, on the melancholy errand of attending Eugène's death-bed. The old soldier of the Empire had now settled in Blois, and was living in complete retirement, occupying his leisure as usefully as he could.

The invitation was accepted, and the journey undertaken in April, 1825. The poet booked three places in the Bordeaux diligence, being accompanied by his wife and by his little daughter Léopoldine, who had been born the previous year, just about the same time that the new volume of the " Odes " had been published. The infant grew up to be a charming girl, and was married, but died by an accident very soon after her wedding-day.

After Victor Hugo had set his foot upon the diligence, he was hailed by a messenger who was running after him at full speed, having been to his house only to find him departed. The messenger delivered to him a packet bearing the royal seal, which turned out to be a patent appointing him a Chevalier of the Legion of Honor.

The circumstances under which the decoration was conferred have been related by Alexandre Dumas. At first Victor Hugo and Lamartine had been included among a batch of others selected for a general promotion; but on the list being presented to Charles X., he struck out both the names. The Count de la Rochefoucauld, who had himself drawn up the list, and who took a great interest in the young poet, ventured to express his surprise at the two most deserving of the names being cancelled. The king replied that they were both far too illustrious to be included with the rest, and that they must be assigned a special promotion by themselves.

During his journey to Blois, Victor composed his ballad of " Les Deux Archers." On his arrival he flung himself into the arms of his father and joyfully exhibited the papers which he had received at the moment of his setting out; the General at once detached from his uniform one of the ribbons that he had won on the field of battle, and fastened it with his own hands on the breast of his son.

The days sped happily away in the veteran's modest dwelling that has been sketched by the poet's own pen.

" Its roof of slate; of stone its white square walls,
On which the green hill's slanting shadow falls;
Though to the roadside somewhat closely placed,
On either hand by smiling orchards graced;
. . . Here doth my father dwell;
Enjoys the ease his sword has won so well."

The visit was not of long duration, but it served to strengthen the ties of family affection; not that anything which the father said could wean the son from his devotion to royalty. Victor firmly believed in the liberal promises made by the successor of Louis XVIII., placing every confidence in the new king's assurances that not only was he anxious to introduce many reforms, but was prepared to abolish the censorship of the press.

While he was at Blois, Victor Hugo received an invitation from Charles X. to be present at his coronation at Rheims. Leaving his wife and child behind, the young poet started off without delay. From Paris to Rheims he travelled in company with Charles Nodier. The incidents of his journey, which occupied four days, have been related by Madame Victor Hugo, and therefore need not be repeated here; suffice it to say that he thought the coronation very fine, but was somewhat shocked to see the king, according to custom, bow down in the cathedral at the archbishop's feet.

At Rheims Victor Hugo met Lamartine. Both poets made a worthy acknowledgment of the royal invitation; the one, who had already outvied Châteaubriand in celebrating the obsequies of Louis XVIII., wrote the author of Charles X.," while the other combiner of the "Chant du Sacre." They ended by becoming thoroughly acquainted, and Lamartine reminded his rival of a promise he had made him to go and see him at St. Point. Victor Hugo accordingly arranged to pay the visit at once. Nodier was of the party, and both the friends were accompanied by their families, Hugo stowing his little daughter's cradle in the post-chaise.

Once at Mâcon it seemed to them an opportunity not to be lost for paying a visit to the Alps, and it was arranged that the expenses of the trip should be defrayed by the proceeds of a book in which they would all three have a hand.

A book written by Lamartine, Victor Hugo, and Charles Nodier was sure of success, and a publisher was soon found, but unfortunately he fell into difficulties before the work could be issued. Victor Hugo, however, had completed his portion, which contained his impressions and experiences from Sallenches to Chamouni. Picturesque and attractive, full of episodes that are striking and dramatic, and abounding in descriptions equally accurate and vivid, the narrative subsequently appeared in the *Revue des Deux Mondes*, and was afterwards re-edited by Madame Victor Hugo.

On his return from this trip to Mont Blanc, the poet recommenced his literary labors in January, 1826. In a preface to a new edition of the "Odes," that were now separated from the "Ballades," he avowed his principles of liberty in the world of literature. The hour for the transformation he declares has arrived, and proceeds to expound his creed.

He cannot comprehend why, in reference to literary productions, he hears so incessantly of what is called the dignity of one style and the propriety of another, of the limits of this and the latitude of that; and, failing to understand these distinctions, he considers them to be without sense, because, as he puts it, nothing can belong to the good and beautiful unless it is good and beautiful throughout; the works of the intellect must be simply good or simply bad.

"This liberty," he goes on to say, "need not result in disorder; liberty need not be anarchy, nor can any originality serve as a pretext for inaccuracy. In a literary production, the bolder the conception the more irreproachable should be the execution."

Such statements, prudent and pacific as they were, would not now be construed as a declaration of war, but at the time when they were first published they extorted yells of wrath from the partisans of the old literature, who still preferred to drag themselves along the dusty paths of routine and imitation.

By its birth Romanticism was to clear the temple of Art of the dealers in insipid prose; and the classics, aware of what was coming upon them, overwhelmed the innovators with obloquy. But, in spite of the howls of the eunuchs that guarded the necropolis of Tradition, the time for the infusion of new blood into French literature had now arrived. Casting aside her chains, Art was to rise all-radiant from her tomb, and, overturning her dismal guardians with one blow of her wing, was, all-triumphant, to rise aloft.

It can hardly be imagined to what a degree of insignificance and decay French national literature had sunk. Under the Empire, the voices of authors had been stifled by the thunder of cannon. To Napoleon I. poets were merely men who made fine arrangements of words, and were useful only so far as they sounded his praises. Not that the great emperor had any actual design that letters should be neglected; on the contrary, in the interval between two campaigns, he occasionally gave his thoughts to their revival. During the periods of his armistices the laurels of Louis Quatorze would rise before him as a vision, and he would have dreams of making a similar name for his own dynasty, and thus adding another ray to his own glory. Having ordered Talma to create some tragedies, he promised him an audience of kings, and was as good as his word; but Talma was not successful in anything but in interpreting the classical *chefs-d'œuvre* which had received applause in the reign of the Grand Monarque.

Bonaparte, who proscribed Châteaubriand and Madame de Staël, had expected to be supplied with dramatists in the same way that he was provided with his conscripts, little thinking that while he was enlisting 300,000 young men every year he was incurring the risk of killing an indefinite number of playwriters.

Among those who eluded slaughter because they were either too old or too weak to be soldiers should be mentioned Alexandre Duval, Baour-Lormian, Mercier, and especially Raynouard, who was the most illustrious of the imperial authors. To these may be added the celebrated Luce de Lancival and the

ROMANTICISM.

great Delrieu, who never forgave the comedians of the Théâtre Français for always choosing free days on which to play his pieces. The conqueror's fame can hardly be said to have been much enhanced by the dramatic authors of his day.

Other branches of literature were represented very much in the same qualified way. The productions of the intellect were gradually becoming more marked by feebleness, insipidity, and insignificance; and it seemed as though the power of thought had departed from the human brain, and that wit, imagination, and enthusiasm had ceased to exist.

In painting too, just as in poetry, there was nothing but what was utterly flat and commonplace. But the young generation at length was aroused, and, waving the flag of Romanticism and shouting the hurrahs of independence, they rushed forward to the assault of the classic citadel.

The word "romanticism" is no longer used in any but an historical sense, and only vaguely expresses some ill-defined doctrines; but it is a *nom de guerre* implying the principles of a party: and the romantics were indeed an army of bold and valorous champions, elevated by the love of their art, and ready to dare every conflict in order to secure the triumph of their instinctive tendencies and aspirations towards the ideal.

And whence sprang this Romanticism? It appears to have had its first starting in Germany, towards the end of the eighteenth century, by the political school of which Ludwig Tieck was one of the principal leaders. From Germany it was imported into France.

French literature has never lost its own distinctive marks of originality, but at various times has submitted to be directed by foreign influence, although at other times it has itself been dominant and communicated its tone to the whole of Europe. In this way German literature during the seventeenth and eighteenth centuries had been very much the mere reflex of the French; but at the beginning of the nineteenth it took an entirely new turn, receiving fresh life and elevation from Klopstock, Herder, Schiller, and Goethe, to whose "Faust" Madame de Staël applies the saying that it treats "de omnibus rebus et quibusdam aliis."

But still, as Philarète Chasles has observed, between France and Germany there has ever flowed the Rhine, and the credit is due to Madame de Staël for having brought across this boundary the German literature which,

received at first with a cordial welcome, still bears its prolific fruits. To that accomplished lady must be assigned the honor of nationalizing among the French the "romanticism" which she herself describes as "the poetry originating in the songs of the troubadours—the offspring of chivalry and Christianity."

If this definition of Madame de Staël's were correct, romanticism would have to be regarded as the intellect of the Romance races in conflict with the intellect of classical antiquity, or simply modern genius in antagonism to the Greeks and Romans; but in reality it is nothing of the kind: as Victor Hugo, Champfleury, and a hundred others have over and over again affirmed, it means nothing else but the development of liberalism in literature.

At the time when Germany was commencing the grand task of emancipation in the world of letters, Byron in England was issuing the poems which gained for him the distinction of "the satanic," and which by their high coloring seemed to reveal to the young sons of France a new sphere for themselves, just awakening as they were to the appreciation of Shakespeare, and beginning to dream of originality.

Simultaneously with Madame de Staël, Châteaubriand was contributing to the revival in France by the publication of "Le Génie du Christianisme," "Atala," "René," a translation of Milton's "Paradise Lost," and "Les Martyrs." Flowing as they seemed from new and refreshing springs of thought, his works had the effect not only of kindling admiration for the Gothic cathedrals to which they referred, but of inspiring a requickened love for Nature in all her phases.

No sooner was the path discovered than a multitude of the young were ready to venture themselves along it.

"When it is remembered," said Asselineau in his "Bibliographie Romantique," "from what point this generation started, and when it is considered what it has replaced, what it has reformed, and what it has revived, there are not praises enough to be found for the venerable flag that it has defended—a flag which, torn and pierced in the strife of battles, ought to be suspended in the vault of a pantheon, as having been the ensign of safety to the commonwealth of letters. The hands that waved it were victorious. To those who carried it is to be attributed the certainty that romance arose and shook off the tameness and frivolity of the last century; that there was the issue from the press of manly productions such as could be read and listened to without a blush; that the drama regained a power to attract and an energy to thrill; that verse re-echoed with a new life; and that prose, resuscitated from the torpid languor of the academic style, began to glow afresh with the vitality of health. To their sincerity, their detestation of tediousness, their sympathy with life and joy and freshness, as well as to their youthful audacity, that was not abashed either by ridicule or insult, belongs the honor of securing to the nineteenth century the triumph of liberty, invaluable in its preciousness, in the world of art."

Having thus exalted their victory, Asselineau proceeds to enumerate the stars of the literary Pleiades. Next after Châteaubriand and Madame de Staël, he recapitulates the names of Victor Hugo, Lamartine, Alexandre Dumas, Charles Nodier, Alfred de Vigny, Sainte-Beuve, Émile and Antony Deschamps, Balzac, Auguste Barbier, Georges Sand, Théophile Gautier, Mérimée, Philarète Chasles, Alfred de Musset, Jules Janin, and Marcelline Valmore. Such was the cluster of which each individual, in his turn, was branded with the epithet "romantic."

We use the term "branded" advisedly, because at that period whoever was disposed to call things by their proper names, or whoever did not choose to make his verses run two and two, "like yoked oxen," was regarded not only simply as tasteless or shameless, but as thoroughly demented.

"Romanticism," wrote the Academician Duvergier de Hauranne, "is not a matter for ridicule; it is a disease as much as somnambulism or epilepsy. A romantic is a man whose brain has gone wrong; he is to be pitied, and should be reasoned with in order to bring him back gradually to his senses, but he must not be laughed at, as he is more properly a subject for medical diagnosis."

This is a specimen of the way in which the young authors were treated who ventured to brave the public sneers in order to deliver that public from poring and yawning over books of the familiar stamp. It was their aim to make literature cease to be wearisome, but it was by no means an easy task to wean the multitudes from a style to which they had been habituated.

At the time when the reform was being worked out, the classics, finding themselves threatened with annihilation, did everything in their power to stir up the wrath of the professed disciples of order, and spared no pains in holding up the reformers to public reprobation. This led Victor Hugo to declare that if the romantics had been thieves, murderers, and monsters of crime, they could not have been exposed to severer objurgations.

It may well be supposed that the poet had no great affection for these Philistines who came down to assault. One day in the neighborhood of Bingen he met a bear that had escaped from a menagerie. The physiognomy of the brute, he said, reminded him of the sleepy, sanctimonious expression ever worn by the old habitués of the theatres as they sat listening to their favorite tragedies.

Some time afterwards, in one of his jocose moods, he scribbled down on the margin of a page in M. Auguste Vacquerie's "Profils et Grimaces" an off-hand caricature which he described as a portrait of a classic.

For whom that portrait was designed must

CARICATURE OF A CLASSIC.
(Drawn by Victor Hugo.)

be left to conjecture. Perhaps the insolent old fop thrusting his thumbs under his vest, while he sneers as he expresses his detestation for "nebulous" poetry, is Destigny the satirical, who described the romantics as being as frantic and ridiculous as

"A maniac herd from Charenton escaped !"

Or perhaps it was Duvergier de Hauranne, or the renowned Viennet, who, in association with Baour-Lormian, was one of the most stubborn of the antagonists who waged war to the knife against the romantic party.

Or if it was not Viennet that Victor Hugo meant to caricature by his rough sketch, it is possible that it was that other "immortal" who called the romantics swine; or it might have been intended for the famous Népomucène Lemercier, who invoked the vengeance of his country upon the works of the new school, and thundered forth his Alexandrine,

"Shall Hugos thus unpunish'd verses make ?"

However erroneous these conjectures may be, it is at least certain that the poet amply avenged himself. But this is long past, and he has done better than that: he has forgiven all his opponents, and no longer recollects their impotent and ridiculous outbreaks of wrath.

Such were some of the preliminary skirmishes in the great epic struggle, which had its heroic as well as its ludicrous side, and which terminated, as we shall presently find, in a decisive victory for Romanticism and its most prominent leader.

But while Victor Hugo was incurring all this literary obloquy he was also alienating himself from the sympathies of the royalists in consequence of an incident that made a great sensation at the time.

In February, 1827, the Austrian ambassador in Paris gave a soirée, to which all the most illustrious French personages were invited. All the marshals who had been raised to the peerage by Napoleon I. attended the reception. On their arrival, however, the ambassador's usher, acting under instructions given beforehand, omitted all their titles and announced them simply by their family name. Thus when the Duc de Dalmatie entered he was introduced as M. le Maréchal Soult; the Duc de Trévise was

announced as Maréchal Mortier; the Duc de Raguse as Maréchal Marmont; and so on with the Duc de Reggio, the Duc de Tarente, and all the other peers of the imperial creation, although in every case they had informed the usher of their proper rank as noblemen.

This was an insult to the whole army, it was the way in which Austria chose to exact her vengeance for Napoleon's victories. The marshals retired in silence, but the circumstance caused a deal of scandal, and Victor Hugo, indignant at the slight put upon his father's former companions in arms, took upon himself to avenge the affront.

He immediately wrote the "Ode à la Colonne Vendôme," which, like many others of his political poems, was printed separately. Glorifying what he called the monument of vengeance, the glistening column of sovereign bronze, he broke out into a strain of indignation which may be approximately rendered—

"Though grovelling Austria strove to tread us down,
  The giant strength of France has trampled on her
      crown :
  The pen of history the blazoned truth shall spread,
  What stands engraven on her vulture's doubled
      head:
      On one, great Charlemagne's all-crushing heel;
      On one, Napoleon's piercing spur of steel !"

The entire ode was full of the praises of the column that recorded the victories that had been achieved, and upon which the stranger should gaze in silence and in wonder. Its wrathful tone, foreshadowing the writer of "Les Châtiments," at once brought him into suspicion and caused him to be accused of deserting the Bourbons, who had come back to France in the train of Austria; and, in truth, for a time he seemed as if he were fulfilling his father's prediction.

So indignant was Victor Hugo at the insult offered to the valiant marshals that, for the moment, he appeared to be altered into another man. Regardless of any animosity that might be stirred up against himself by his own party, he denounced without mercy the intruders into his country, thus causing himself not only to be forsaken, but traduced, by the royalists, and at this critical hour doubling the number of his enemies.

CHAPTER XI.

AMONG the leading critics who reviewed Victor Hugo's works at the latter period of the Restoration was Sainte-Beuve. His articles upon the productions of the new school brought him into notice and obtained for him an admittance into the Cénacle, a name given by the more zealous romantics to a club that they had established, of which the author of the "Odes et Ballades" was the ruling spirit.

In their enthusiasm the members of the Cénacle looked upon themselves as ordained apostles of the new art. Their efforts were originally centred upon a magazine which they started, called *La Muse Française*, and they held frequent meetings, the society including Alfred de Vigny, Jules de Rességuier, Émile and Antony Deschamps, Ulrich Guttinger, and about twenty others. The members called one another by their Christian names. In the winter they met at each other's houses to read verses, and in the summer they turned out in a body for walks in the country, occasionally mounting the towers of Notre Dame to admire the sunset and to watch the parting glow of daylight vanish in the waters of the Seine.

After the fall of Châteaubriand, the Cénacle was virtually broken up. Some of the members, however, persevered in holding their meetings until the time when the romantics claimed an undisputed victory, and Victor Hugo devoted himself to theatrical labors. Although it had but a transitory existence, the society was like a beautiful morning dawn; its atmosphere was all-radiant with the ardent generosity of youth.

In his "Portraits Contemporains" Sainte-Beuve has referred to the charming visions and the fruitful labor of that happy time; and in his "Joseph Delorme" he has dedicated some laudatory verses to the young associates of the club, the general tone of which may be conjectured from the concluding lines, which run something in the following strain:

"Both good and great they were, from jealous passion free;
Nor suffered that the honey of their verse should be Barbed with an angry sting;
Though high as zenith-sun their fame, and all ablaze,
It ne'er was known to burn with scorching rays
The tin1est flower of spring."

Previously to his rushing into the agitation of the romantic fray, Sainte-Beuve, a critic at the beginning as well as at the end of his career, had written a very qualified review of the "Odes et Ballades." While he allowed that the author's imagination was of a first-class order, uniformly deep and true, he expressed his regret at the frequency with which he had introduced exaggerated similes, prosaic incidents, and over-minute analysis into the most brilliant periods of his verse.

Victor Hugo, always ready to acknowledge that whatever he wrote was open to criticism, felt no annoyance at the review, but, on the contrary, soon found himself on very friendly terms with the young reviewer, though the friendship was of short duration.

The details of the commencement of this amicable intimacy are related in a letter written by Sainte-Beuve towards the end of his life, and which has not been generally circulated. He writes:

"I knew Victor Hugo before the publication of 'Les Orientales.' In 1826 and 1827 I was critic to the *Globe*, then under the editorship of M. Dubois. Without knowing anything whatever of the author of the 'Odes et Ballades' beyond his name, I was instructed to write a review of his publication. This I did in two successive articles. Victor Hugo called to thank me. It turned out that, without knowing it, we had been almost next-door neighbors, he living at 90 and I at 94 in the Rue de Vaugirard. I was not at home when he left his card, but I returned his call on the following day, and we soon became acquainted. I confided to his ears some verses which I had composed, but which I had hitherto kept a secret, feeling that the *Globe* was rather an organ for criticism than for the publication of original poetry. We were all very formal then; and I was formal too; for all the world I would not have chosen to be introduced to an author whose works I should have to review. At that time I was every inch a critic; subsequently there came the period when the faculty was suspended and forgotten."

This last avowal of Sainte-Beuve's is worth observing. He did indeed enter enthusiastically into the romantic movement, and, having embraced the cause, exhibited himself as a most ardent disciple, outrunning his master and exaggerating his style. But at a later date he changed his mind: he burned the idol he had worshipped, and, by way of excuse for having joined Victor Hugo's party, protested with an intolerable vanity that he had only made a pretence of belonging to its ranks.

The occasion will subsequently occur on which we shall be called upon to pass a severe judgment not so much on Sainte-Beuve's apostasy from the cause of Romanticism which he had espoused, as upon the odious ingratitude of the man who, in 1827, after making Victor Hugo's acquaintance, sought his friendship and advice, and read to him both " Joseph Delorme" and the " Consolations."

About this date it was that Victor Hugo first began to turn his serious attention to the stage. Reform in poetry might be said to be all but achieved, but reform in the drama had yet to be accomplished.

M. Taylor was then royal commissioner at the Comédie Française. He had formerly been aide-de-camp to General d'Orsay, and had retired with the rank of major. From that time until the end of his long and noble career he devoted himself with all the ardor of his energetic nature to the cause of art. Familiarized with the freedom of English literature, his mind was too independent to submit to routine, and, possessing large ideas, he maintained strict impartiality in literary pursuits, and to him is due the honor of having procured the admission of the romantics to the stage. He inquired of Victor Hugo why he had not given his attention to play-writing. The poet's answer was ready: " I have already commenced a drama upon Cromwell."

The only performer who was capable at

that date of representing Cromwell was Talma. M. Taylor lost no time in inviting him to meet Hugo at dinner, and the poet and the actor had a long conversation together.

Talma was now approaching the limit of his fine career, but was full of bitter complaints of his profession. Though he could not withhold a certain measure of admiration for the style of tragedy in which he had made his reputation, he had always longed for more reality to be combined with the wonted dignity and decorum of the parts he had to play. He had conceptions of kings who should be human as well as regal; he yearned to express emotions that were natural rather than strained; he wanted new subjects, but when he asked for Shakespeare they gave him Ducis, and left him no medium for gratifying his realism beyond what he could invent in his costumes!

He proceeded to expatiate on his position: "No one knows what I should have been if only I had come across the author for whom I have been looking. Without his rôle an actor is nothing. I shall go to my grave without acting as my soul would prompt me to act. M. Hugo, you are young, you are enterprising; surely you could devise a character adapted to my faculty. Taylor tells me you are writing a 'Cromwell.' Cromwell is a part that I have ever longed to play. Tell me what your piece is like. I am sure beforehand that it is out of the old routine."

" I should imagine," replied Victor Hugo, " that the part that you are longing to play is precisely what I am longing to write."

And the poet proceeded to propound to the tragedian the ideas that he afterwards expanded in the preface to the play.

He said that he intended to claim for an author the right to submit to no other rule than that of his own imagination, and to survey everything from his own point of view.

"There are three epochs in poetry," he asserted, "each corresponding to an era in society : these are the ode, the epic, and the drama. Primitive ages are the lyric, ancient times the heroic, and modern times the dramatic. The ode sings of eternity, the epic records history, the drama depicts life. The characteristic of the first is *naïveté*, of the second simplicity, of the last truth. The rhapsodists mark the transition from the lyric to the epic, as the romancists make the change from the epic to the dramatic. Historians begin to exist in the second epoch, critics and essayists come to light with the third. The characters of the ode are colossal—Adam, Cain, Noah; those of the epic are gigantic—Achilles, Atreus, Orestes; those of the drama are human—Hamlet, Othello, Macbeth. The ode contemplates the ideal; the epic the sublime; the drama the real. And, to sum up the whole, this poetical triad emanates from three fountain-heads—the Bible, Homer, and Shakespeare.

"Society, in fact, begins by singing of what it has dreamed, then proceeds to recount what it has done, and finally begins to paint what it has felt.

"The poetry of our own time, therefore, is the drama, of which reality is the essential characteristic, and this reality is the resultant of two types, the sublime and grotesque, which are there combined as they are in creation and in common life. Poetry, to be true, should consist in the harmony of contrasts, and everything that exists in nature should exist in art."

With much elegance and perspicuity Victor Hugo enlarged upon these points. Talma was delighted, nor did his ecstasy diminish when he listened to the various quotations from the unfinished play which were read to him. He promised to undertake the chief character; but he died a few months before the drama was completed.

Thus left without the interpreter on whom he had reckoned, Victor Hugo extended the piece to seven thousand verses, making it of a length which precluded its representation on the stage, but giving him scope to work out a full and elaborate study of one of the grandest characters in history.

Alphonse Esquiros has remarked upon this point that we seem to be made to penetrate into Cromwell's inmost soul; we spy out every idea that crosses the brain of the protector of the English commonwealth—that strange genius, that curious mixture of magnanimity and meanness, of love of despotism and love of liberty, of faith and hypocrisy; we can hear him pray, or laugh, or dictate a death-warrant; we can probe his bleeding heart-wounds, and in this great stroke of a master-hand we may see before us—

"Cromwell an Attila by Machiavelli made!"

It is thus that the power of dramatic genius reanimates the form of the departed hero; it initiates the multitude into the secrets of a heart that had great aspirations; it explores a human soul so as to lay bare its passions in such a way as to render them a prolific and attractive source of edification.

An analysis of the work has been made by Victor Hugo himself, who has represented its design in the following terms:

"There is one special period in Cromwell's life at which all the variety of the phases of his wonderful character might almost be said to exhibit themselves at once. That period is not, as might be at first imagined, the trial of Charles I., full of terrible interest though that crisis was; but it is the period when his ambition made him eager to realize the benefits of the king's death, when having attained what any other man would have reckoned the summit of fortune, being not only master of England, but by his army, his navy, and his diplomacy master of Europe too, he was urged onwards to fulfil the visions of his youth, and to make himself a king. Never has history veiled a loftier lesson under a loftier drama. In the earliest stage he causes himself to be solicited to come forward; the scene commences with addresses by corporations, by cities, by counties; these are followed by a bill in Parliament, Cromwell all the while, though the author of the plot, appearing dissatisfied with what is being done. We see him hold out his hand for the sceptre and then withdraw it; we see him, as it were, wriggling sideways towards the steps of the throne from which he has just displaced the representative of the established dynasty. But at length he comes abruptly to a decision; Westminster is decked with flags at his command; the platform is erected; the crown ordered from the goldsmith; the day of coronation is fixed. But then comes a strange denouement! On that very day, and on that very platform in Westminster Hall from which he had resolved that, in the presence of the people, the soldiers, and the Commons, he would descend a king, he wakes all of a sudden, as it were out of a sleep. All at once he has become alive to the true meaning of a crown: he asks what the formality implies; he asks whether he has been dreaming; and, finally, after agitating the question for three hours, comes to the determination not to assume the regal dignity.

"Whence the hesitation? Why this change? No contemporary document solves the mystery; but so much the better for the poet, whose liberty is more complete, and who is left to give his drama the latitude which history does not refuse. The scene is unique, it is the great turning-point of Cromwell's life, it is the moment when his chimera escapes him, when his present demolishes his future, and, to use an expressive phrase, his destiny turns out 'a flash in the pan.'

"Cromwell's entire soul is at work in the great comedy that is played out between England and himself. Such is the man and such the period that this drama aspires to depict."

The piece was published at the end of 1827. The preface, however, attracted more attention and excited more discussion than the poem; it started a species of poetry that was altogether new in its form, so that its production may be reckoned as one of the greatest literary events of the time.

Not that the poem itself was at all wanting in boldness and originality; it contains many beauties, and the verses offer very fine examples of the sense of one line being involved and completed in the next; but the preface was nothing less than a startling manifesto, in which the rules of the rising modern style of dramatic art are exhibited in a way which one of the classic critics describes as "pitiless."

In thus making a statement of his principles, Victor Hugo offers himself as a champion of his cause, and, by arguments as solid as they are brilliant, overturns the framework of the system which would detain every line of thought in one uniform mould.

The point upon which he takes his stand as a reformer is this: the drama is a mirror in which all nature is reflected, a glass from which *must* be thrown back upon the vision everything which has had its existence in history, in life, or in man.

Art, as it were with a magic wand, turns over the pages of centuries and of nature, consults chronicles, and studies to reproduce the *reality* of facts, especially the reality of manners and of character. Nothing should be neglected or forgotten.

From beginning to end the programme is traced with the vigor that was already characteristic of the powerful intellect of the young master-mind, and it is instructive to remark that it comprises all the theories that have since been claimed as inventions by those who profess to be leaders of the realistic school. Victor Hugo desired that notice should be taken not only of the beautiful, but also of the ordinary and the trivial, every figure being restored to its salient trait of individuality. As we have said, the naturalists made discovery of nothing; they simply repeated that which since 1830 has been ac-

cepted as a recognized rule, an author's right, and so without any adequate reason they have occupied the attention of the world with a dispute as futile in its issue as it was uproarious in the mode in which it was carried on.

Long before the time of these wrangling contenders, the true leader of the romantic school was writing that the proper mission of the drama and of the dramatist was to represent *nature;* Cromwell should be allowed to retain his grotesqueness, Henry IV. should still utter his oaths; the touches of weakness in the hero, and the glimpses of humanity in the tyrant, should be portrayed with fidelity; tears should be mingled with smiles; the hideous placed side by side with the graceful; the spiritual brought into contact with the brutal, and this solely because truth demands it.

Nor was this all. In his famous preface, Victor Hugo goes on to say that a language can never be at a standstill, a rule to which the French is no exception. He writes:

"The language of Montaigne is no longer the language of Rabelais, as that of Pascal is not the language of Montaigne, nor that of Montesquieu, again, the language of Pascal. Individually, as being original, each is to be admired; every epoch, as having its own ideas, necessarily has its own words to represent them. . . . Our literary Joshuas may call upon language to stay its course, but language will now no more than the sun be arrested on its way. When languages stop, they die. A writer, then, may safely invent his own style; he has the right to do so, but only on one condition—he must write well, for Racine contains Vaugelas."

He claims the same liberty for verse as he does for prose. To Corneille, to Racine, to Molière, and to all the master-minds of the past whose names were brought up against him, he paid the most respectful homage; they were all great poets, being, as Théodore de Banville has rightly designated them, giants of superhuman strength; but it was by genius, and not by art, that they produced their immortal *chefs-d'œuvre,* for "so far as it was known to them, the art of versification was so utterly bad that, after having hampered and perplexed them all the days of their life, it was never of any service whatever to their successors; while, thanks to Victor Hugo and his disciples, the instrument that we have now at our disposal is so excellent that the most illiterate, when once he has learned its use,

OLIVER CROMWELL.

becomes capable of composing verses that should be fairly good."*

Finally, the preface to " Cromwell" repudiates two out of the three unities consecrated by the classics: it rejects the unity of place, as being absurd and in contrariety to what is probable; and it discards the unity of time, as being ludicrous because it limits an action to a period of twenty-four hours. One unity alone is recognized—the unity of action—excluding the other two simply because neither the eye nor the mind can properly take in more than one idea at a time. The same theory was held by Goethe, who acknowledged only the unity of comprehensiveness, "das Fassliche."

In an article devoted to the manifesto in the *Revue de Paris*, Charles Nodier writes:

"Since liberty is recognized as an almost universal benefit, it would be extraordinary if liberty were to be withheld from the imagination, that very one of our faculties which it affects the most."

It can hardly be imagined now what bitterness and polemical spite were aroused by these assertions, which looked like attempts to overturn a fabric that had been deemed eternal. A volume might be filled with the mere catalogue of the pamphlets and *feuilletons* by which the revolutionist was assailed. Never did malice and vituperation find a more open field.

" These fanciful whims," patronizingly wrote the *Gazette de France*, "have no stable basis; they have indeed a ludicrous side which might be amusing if only they had any talent to back them: but to fight with giant's strength is indispensable; and when an attempt is made to dethrone writers that entire generations have agreed to admire, the attack ought to be made with weapons which, if not equal, ought at least to be sufficiently good, and to be wielded with intelligence and not in impotence. What harm can be feared from any who write *like the author of the preface that we are reviewing?*" This concluding sentence suffices to exhibit the rage and rancor of the classics.

Victor Hugo had to stand against a perfect storm of such banter and sarcasm; but vehement as was the assault, he was quite capable of making a vigorous defence.

In the *Globe*, a journal of moderate views, and the tone of which was then regarded as the "juste milieu," M. de Rémusat wrote a

very judicious article, in which he repeated Voltaire's opinion that the dispute between the ancient and the modern is a question still pending. Other newspapers, more courageous still, openly expressed their enthusiasm, and the preface to " Cromwell" became a sort of watchword for the young men of the day.

Theophile Gautier, who had not yet allied himself to the romantic party, was furious when he read the vindictive abuse in the small classical journals. To his eye and to that of his associates the preface appeared to stand with an authority as supreme as the Decalogue, and its enactments to admit of no reply.

These few instances may serve to give an idea of the sensation produced by the work. It was published by Ambroise Dupont, and had this dedication.

" To my father: as the book to him is dedicated, so to him is the author devoted."

General Hugo had left Blois, the town of picturesque old mansions that Victor had delighted to sketch, and, having been restored by the existing government to his proper rank and honors, was now residing in Paris. He had married again, as already said, and, after coming to Paris to be present at the marriage of his son Abel with Mlle. Julie de Monferrier, he had made up his mind to remain for some time and enjoy the society of his children and grandchildren.

Besides his daughter, Léopoldine, Victor Hugo had now a son, Charles; and a third child, Victor François, was born shortly afterwards. The general took apartments quite near the young children, so that he might see them every day.

But his enjoyment was very brief. On the 28th of January, 1828, Victor, after dining with his father, was called up in the middle of the night only to find that the general had succumbed to a fit of apoplexy. Madame Foucher had died only a few months before: so that sorrow seemed, as ever, to be an attendant upon all the poet's seasons of rejoicing.

The general, as we have said, besides being a distinguished soldier, was a military author of no inconsiderable repute. In addition to his historical journal of the blockade of Thionville, he left a treatise on the means of supplying the place of negro slaves by free laborers. He likewise wrote two volumes of memoirs that are still used as books of reference, and which, according to Michaud, are

---

* Banville, " Traité de Poésie Française."

put together with much clearness and precision, and contain many minute details connected with La Vendée, Naples, and more particularly Spain. To these must be added a romance called "L'Aventure Tyrolienne,"

With reference to this work on fortification, it is said that a foreign government, having been apprised of its importance and merits, offered the general a considerable sum for the copyright, but he indignantly rejected

AN OLD HOUSE IN BLOIS.
(*From a drawing by Victor Hugo.*)

which he published under the *nom de plume* of Sigisbert; and, finally, he composed an elaborate treatise upon fortified places, the compilation of which occupied a great deal of his time.

the proposal. The manuscript, by the desire of the French government, was handed over to their keeping, but by some mismanagement of the administration it remained buried in some forgotten portfolio, the general being too magnanimous ever to make any complaint of the neglect.

The death of his father was a great grief to the poet: he mourned for him sincerely, and sought for solace by renewed application to work.

Before resuming the story of Victor Hugo's conflicts, we should not omit to mention that a piece which he had written in conjunction with Soumet was loudly hissed at the Odéon. It was founded on Sir Walter Scott's "Kenilworth," and was named "Amy Robsart." Of this drama, the first three acts had been written by Victor Hugo when he was only nineteen. Upon his showing them to Soumet, he found that they did not meet with his approval, and he gave Soumet permission to alter them and finish them in his own way, bestowing no more pains upon the piece himself until the success of Shakespeare, as performed in Paris, put it into the mind of his brother-in-law, M. Paul Foucher, that a play combining comedy and tragedy might prove acceptable to the public.

It was these representations of Shakespeare that had induced Victor Hugo to put forth many of the statements in his preface to "Cromwell;" and in the strength of his convictions he handed over his "Amy Robsart" to his brother-in-law, Paul Foucher, as an experiment. Foucher produced the piece in his own name; but when it proved so complete a failure, Victor Hugo at once came forward and avowed his own share in the production, taking the responsibility of the non-success.

"Amy Robsart" was, however, never published among the poet's works. Victor Hugo gave the manuscript to Alexandre Dumas, who had it for a long time in his possession.

CHAPTER XII.

MAINTAINING, as he was always prepared to do most thoroughly, that an author should remedy the production of a work that proved a failure by the production of another **work** and a better, Victor Hugo applied himself **to** the composition of "Marion Delorme."

This drama was preceded in its **issue by** two other important works — "Les **Orien**tales" and "Le Dernier Jour **d'un Condam**né." Of these **we shall have to speak later** on, **but meanwhile must diverge a little from the chronological order of the poet's produc**tions, **that we may dwell upon his experi**ences as a dramatist.

Thanks to the liberal influence of M. Taylor, a bold experiment had been made at the Théâtre **Français** in the beginning of **1829,** and "Henry **III.,"the fine "**romantic" drama by Alexandre **Dumas,** had been produced with considerable success. It was at its first performance that its distinguished author first made the acquaintance of Alfred **de Vigny and** Victor Hugo. Victor, **encouraged by** the success of the play, **turned to its fortu**nate writer and said,

"**Now it** is my turn!"

Immediately, from among the various historical figures with which his mind and imagination were stored, he chose the character of Marion Delorme, and henceforth lived a while with her image ever in **his** fancy, and creating the characters with which to surround her.

This **mode of** operation is peculiar to great artists; **they** do not take up their **pen** or pencil until **the** persons that they are about to call into being have assumed a definite shape. As Minerva emerged armed **from** the head of Jupiter, **so** do the heroic offspring of the poets, **with** all their passions, **virtues,** and vices fully developed, leap forth **direct from the author's** brain.

No important work of Victor Hugo's has **ever been** written without much prelimina**ry thought. The** manuscripts **of** his finest verses and most striking scenes exhibit hardly a sign of erasure or correction. Obedient **to** the creative faculty of the master, the **hand** moves easily and speedily across the paper.

On the 1st of June, 1829, rather more than four months after the first appearance of "Henry III.," he considered himself ready to commence writing "Marion Delorme." He set to work assiduously, and by the 19th he had finished the first three acts; on the 20th he began the fourth, at which he worked unremittingly for twenty-four hours without taking either food or sleep. On the 24th the play was complete, except that it received a few finishing-touches until the 27th.

Having composed his "Cromwell" in such a style that it was impossible for it to be represented on the stage, he was very anxious now to construct a drama suitable for performance. The report of what he had done was soon circulated; and he agreed, though not altogether without hesitation, **to** give a reading of his drama at Devéria's house.

Every star in the literary Pleiad turned to be present; accordingly the assemblage on the occasion was very large, including Taylor, De Vigny, Émile Deschamps, Sainte-Beuve, Soumet, Boulanger, Beauchesne, Alexandre Dumas, Balzac, Eugène Delacroix, Alfred de Musset, Madame Tastu, Villemain, Mérimée, Frédéric Soulié, and several others.

The piece, to which he originally gave the name "Un Duel sous Richelieu," was much applauded, and Victor Hugo was more gratified than if he had had an audience of kings.

Dumas, ever free from envy, manifested the greatest enthusiasm. He afterwards wrote:

"I listened with admiration the most intense, but yet an admiration that was tinged with sadness, for I felt that I could never attain to such a powerful style. . . . I was sitting near Taylor; at the conclusion **of the** reading he turned and asked me my opinion, and I told him that I should be much mistaken if it did not prove one of Victor's finest compositions. It exhibited all the qualities of a matured mind, and none of the faults of youth. . . . I congratulated Hugo very heartily, telling him that I, deficient in style as I was, had been quite overwhelmed by the magnificence of his; and if I could have attained to his style by the sacrifice of ten years of my life, I would willingly have made the surrender."

ALEXANDRE DUMAS.

There was, however, one point in the plot that was no small grievance to the amiable Dumas; he could not feel satisfied that Didier met his death without forgiving Marion. Mérimée and Sainte-Beuve joined with him in requesting that the restored courtesan might receive pardon, and Hugo acceded to their request.

One is almost tempted to call it an unfortunate alteration, the original idea being so much the more powerful as well as the more logical. The love that is deep and sincere may pardon the offending objects upon which it has been lavished, but it cannot reinstate them; the only pretext that Didier has for the kind of forgiveness that he bestows is that he is on the point of death. He knows well enough that it would be impossible for him to live again with her who, in two lines, afterwards suppressed for fear of shocking the public modesty, says that she is ready—

" . . . . free to leave my naked breast
On which whoe'er first comes an hour may rest."

He knows it would be impossible for one bearing the honored name of Didier to love a woman so degraded and so debased ; and he knows, moreover, that the courtesan is false to herself when she exclaims,

" For me to be again impure, that could not be !
Nay, though thy very life depended upon me.
No, Didier, no ! thy quick'ning breath once more
Doth all my first and fresh virginity restore."

It might be true that, in the agitating hour when she was about to be parted from a being that she passionately loved, she would persuade herself that she felt like this; but it is, after all, a mere delusion, and the empty vision of desperation.

The poet was quite justified in complaining that these four lines, as well as the other two, had to be sacrificed to the susceptibility of the least respectable portion of the public, who ought to have been impressed by their artistic purity, and to have been capable of listening to chaste words with chaste ears; he was bound to write what he felt Marion, in the madness of her passion, would have thought; he had no alternative but to make his language an echo of his conceptions. Genius may claim its own rights.

According to M. Auguste Vacquerie, Marion has come across an honorable man who is seeking a paragon of a woman, and she generously undertakes to find him what he wants. So far, so good. But as the attempt proves a failure, Didier would have been a grander character if he had remained inflexible. It is only the scaffold before him that can account for his clemency; and if he could escape that, what could possibly happen next?

Penitence can never restore the fallen to a condition of equality with the unfallen; it cannot bring back forfeited innocence. No insult should be offered to fallen women; but they must not be placed on the same level with those who have never lost their honor, nor should their eyes be dazzled by the hope of any possible recompense for their shame.

Had Marion, in spite of her heroism and her repentance, been adequately chastised for her lapse from virtue, probably much of the sentimentality would have been avoided, which, although now exploded, at the time caused a great depravity of taste, and invested the "Dames aux Camellias" and the "Mimis" of Bohemian life with an interest that they did not deserve.

The sensation produced by the reading of

DIDIER IN "MARION DELORME."

"Marion Delorme" soon spread through Paris. The members of the Cénacle expressed an almost unqualified admiration of it wherever they went. One evening, as Émile Deschamps was passing the Théâtre Français, he saw that "Britannicus" was announced; he shrugged his shoulders and said, "Can they not perform something better than this?"

After the reading of his drama, theatrical managers flocked to the young poet's house. The first to arrive was M. Harel, manager of the Odéon. Catching sight of the manuscript as he entered, he took up a pen and wrote across its front page, "Accepted at the Théâtre de l'Odéon, July 14, 1829." Victor Hugo meanwhile came in and informed him that the piece had been already pledged to M. Taylor for the Comédie Française, and that the character of Marion was to be undertaken by Mlle. Mars. Harel left the house, but not without insisting upon his own claim to the work.

Two days later, M. Crosnier, the general superintendent of the Porte-Saint-Martin, called upon him as the representative of the proprietor, M. Jouslin de Lassalle. Introduced to him in the *salon*, and never suspecting that the beardless young man was the author of whom so much had been said for years, he asked him whether he could speak to his father. Victor replied that his father had died about a year ago, but at the same time he had no doubt that the visit was intended for himself.

M. Crosnier stammered out his apologies, and proceeded to explain that he had come to bespeak "Marion Delorme" for the Porte-Saint-Martin. Victor Hugo smiled, and handed him the manuscript, to show that Harel had already been before him, and that even Harel had come too late.

"Oh, that's all nonsense!" rejoined Crosnier; "you can never tell beforehand where any piece will be performed. Permit me, if you please, to write my claim below Harel's, and perhaps, after all, it may turn out that the third comer is the luckiest of all."

The signature was made, and subsequent events proved the truth of his prognostications. Two years later Crosnier brought out "Marion Delorme" upon his stage.

Nothing could be more enthusiastic than the reception of "Marion" by the company of the Comédie Française; and in the course of the summer the rehearsals were commenced. Mlle. Mars undertook the rôle of the heroine, Firmin that of Didier, and Joanny became responsible for Nangis and Menjaud. Hardly, however, had the arrangements been made and the scenery completed when a rumor arose that the censorship was about to interfere and oppose the representation.

Ever cringing to the power which maintained them in their useless office, the censors alleged as a reason for their veto that, in the fourth act of the play, Louis XIII. was represented as a ridiculously weak prince, as cruel as he was superstitious, and that they considered such a character might provoke public malevolence and lead to a disparagement of his Majesty Charles X.

M. Taylor, who was long accustomed to the absurd proceedings of the censors, had already guessed what would occur, but the poet had properly refused to alter an historical delineation that was not only accurately true, but on which he had bestowed such especial care.

Knowing how it had happened more than once, that by taking vigorous action managers and authors had contrived to elude the talons of the censorship, and recalling the circumstance that Dumas' "Henri III." had finally been sanctioned after having been first prohibited, Victor Hugo determined to go and see M. de Martignac. This minister, whose "liberal" tendencies were hurrying on his downfall, was considered a friend of letters and an independent statesman; he had been associated with Scribe and Casimir Delavigne, but did not see his way to entertain any views at all in advance of theirs.

He gave the author of "Marion Delorme" a very frigid reception, and maintained the fiat of prohibition. The matter, he insisted, concerned an ancestor of the king, and none but the king was entitled to give a judgment in the case.

Pressed by M. Taylor to urge the request, Victor Hugo asked for a royal audience. According to the indispensable rule, he dressed himself in a court-suit, put on a sword, and thus prepared to appear in the presence of Charles.

After a long wait in the anteroom at St. Cloud, he was conducted into the audience-chamber, and entered into explanations with the king, telling him, as he had told every one else, that it was from a purely artistic point of view he had endeavored to depict Louis XIII., and that his representation could not in any **way concern that** monarch's descendants.

Charles **X. was at** this time mainly consulting his **own** liberty by sternly repressing liberty, and was about displacing Martignac and confiding the fate of the throne to Polignac of mournful memory, and did not conceal his sentiments from the young poet.

Victor Hugo, in some well-known verses that were published subsequently, **has himself** described the interview and criticised the motives, alike literary and political, **that** led to his application being refused without power of appeal:

" And, curious, seek you now to know the thing
Debated thus between the poet and decrepit king?
Their conversation on a contrite Magdalen falls
Whose chastened love her former purity recalls;
Shall Marion still her degradation feel
Because a censor's serpent-tongue hath bit **her** heel?"

The king hesitated, **and,** without alluding to the moral aspect of the drama, turned his observations to its political bearing, and expressed his intention not to allow his dead ancestors to be disturbed in their tomb, confessing his fear **that**

"Forth from the drama's scenes,
As from a sepulchre, the lurid spark might break,
And all the fire of revolution's storm awake."

He went on to avow his conviction **that** there was far too much **liberty** everywhere and in everything, and protested that

" **For** fifteen years the dangerous flood **has held its** way;
Now must the dike be reared, the dangerous flood to stay!"

The poet, as **a** prophetic monitor, warned him how

" The swelling wave of time resistless ever rolls,
Nor bridge, nor dike, nor dam its onward rush controls;
He, He alone, who can the raging ocean bind
Can check the mighty progress of a people's mind."

But the poet warned him in vain; and **just as** vainly did he remind the monarch **how, under** Louis XIV., Racine was happy, **and Molière** was free; yet all to no purpose. **Charles X.** had arrived at that time of **life when he** could listen neither to counsel **nor to** warning. Still, he **made an** effort to be gracious; he made an apology for what he was doing, **even** while he persisted in prohibiting the piece from being performed during his reign.

Anxious, however, to conciliate the author and to make some sort of compensation, the king proposed to **raise** his pension from 2000 to 6000 francs. The poet, with **prompt** decision, declined the offer.

This refusal on the part of Victor Hugo of course immediately aroused the wrath of the ministerial journals, all **of** them being exceedingly indignant that a man of letters should have the conceit and audacity to spurn a present offered by **a** sovereign's hand. The opposition papers, on the other hand, highly applauded the poet's determination, and some of the disciples of Romanticism paid him the compliment of celebrating his magnanimity in verse.

Many of Victor Hugo's friends employed their talent in singing of his future glory; and although this nineteenth century has suffered their names and their works to be forgotten, there are not a few of their productions which really deserve to be read and remembered. Such are the names of Ernest Fouinet, Dovalle, Regnier Destourbet, Jean Polonius, Ulric Guttinger, Drouineau, Théodore Carlier, Jules de Saint-Félix, and Arvers, whose magnificent sonnet survives the general oblivion. Besides these, some mention ought to be made of Fontaney, who, on the 19th of August, 1829, addressed a sonnet to Victor Hugo on the subject of the rejected pension, which long enjoyed much popularity, as being one of the most perfect examples of the poetical renaissance. It was found on the margin of the famous Ronsard Album, dedicated by Sainte-Beuve to the author of the "Odes et Ballades."

No tribute of admiration, however, from brother poets, and no congratulations from the literary world in general, availed to prevent "Marion Delorme" from being a prohibited piece. M. Taylor, who had rested all his prospects upon it for the winter season, was quite in despair. "We have nothing else in our portfolio," he sighed, reckoning as comparatively nothing some eight or ten pieces by Viennet, a "Pertinax" by Arnault, and some stray productions of Delrieu and Le Mercier.

"Never mind," said **Victor** Hugo, "we must see what can be done. This is only August; you were not yet about to commence rehearsing. Come to me again on the 1st of October."

M. Taylor did not forget the appointment. He made his call on the precise day that had been fixed, and the poet put into his hands the manuscript of "Hernani." The writing of this had been begun on the 17th of September, and the drama was completely finished on the 25th.

Like the "Marion," it was received with acclamations by the company of the Théâtre Français; but it had likewise the fate to fall foul of the censorship.

The report of the censors has been discovered; it is signed by Baron Trouvé, the inspector of theatres, and by Brifaut, Chéron, Laya, and Sauvo. Such a monument of stupidity is a rarity; it concludes as follows

"Our analysis has extended to a considerable length; but it gives, after all, a very imperfect idea of the whimsical conception and defective execution of 'Hernani.' To us it appears to be a tissue of extravagancies, generally trivial and often coarse, to which the author has failed to give anything of an elevated character. It abounds in improprieties; it makes the king express himself like a bandit, and the bandit treat the king like a brigand; it represents the daughter of a Spanish grandee as a mere licentious creature, deficient alike in dignity and modesty. But while we animadvert upon these flagrant faults, we are of opinion that not only is there no harm in sanctioning the representation of the piece, but that it would be unadvisable to curtail it by a single word. It will be for the benefit of the public to see to what extremes the human mind will go when freed from all restraint."

To this report of the committee Baron Trouvé added a note, specifying certain corrections that were to be made:

"1. The name of Jesus to be removed from every passage in which it occurs.

"2. The words 'You are a coward and a madman,' as addressed to the king, to be replaced by a less bitter expression.

"3. The verse—

"'Think'st thou that kings to me have aught of sacredness?'

to be altered.

"4. The verses beginning 'a vile king' to be suppressed. The sentence had better end with the preceding verse, 'A king thou art, Don Carlos,' as the allusions that follow appear dangerous.

"5. The two lines which bear so harshly upon courtiers to be revised; the court being described as a poultry-yard—

"'Wherein the easy king, solicited for food, Squanders his grains of grandeur on the brood.'

"6. The tirade against kings to be removed, commencing—

"'Poor fools! at empire aiming with proud eye and head erect,'

and terminating with—

"'Their rule the dictate of the necromancer's art.'

The whole passage is merely a paraphrase of Frederic's saying, that 'God is on the side of great armies,' and ought to be cut out, if only on account of the couplet about 'right' and 'the scaffold.' The idea is tolerable enough, but is sufficiently worked out in the preceding lines."

The entire document is a literary curiosity, and as such we introduce the above extract. The censors, of whom it was said that they only escaped contempt by ridicule, had their own way, and the poet was obliged to remodel all the condemned passages of his play.

M. Vitet, afterwards an Academician, and one of the most enthusiastic admirers of Victor Hugo's acted drama, had read "Hernani" to the minister in the censors' office. When he finished, the secretary pronounced the piece "excessively stupid;" but the censors did not venture to prohibit its performance, and the rehearsals proceeded accordingly. The part of Hernani was given to M. Firmin, that of Don Carlos to Michelot, while the important rôle of Doña Sol was assigned to Mlle. Mars.

Carried on during the terrible winter of 1829–30, these rehearsals did not proceed quite so smoothly as they should. The sympathy of the actors at the Théâtre Français did not altogether lie with the romantics, and Mlle. Mars could only half conceal her own dislike of the new school. Fifty years of life, moreover, had not improved her temper, and Dumas, Victor's faithful admirer, has recorded several instances of the disagreements that arose. One of these may be mentioned.

Pausing in the middle of a rehearsal, Mlle. Mars suddenly said to the performer who was acting with her,

"Pardon me, I have a word to say to the author."

She advanced to the footlights, and, shading her eyes, looked round about in every direction, as if trying to discover him, although she was perfectly aware that he was sitting in the orchestra close to her.

"Is M. Hugo here?" she inquired.

"Here, mademoiselle, at your service," replied Hugo.

"Ah, yes; thank you, I want to speak to you about this line—

DOÑA SOL IN "HERNANI."

"'And thou, my lion, how proud and generous thou
    art!'
that I am made to say."

"Quite right," rejoined Hugo; "Hernani
addresses you, and says,

"'Alas! I love thee with a love for tears too deep;
    Together let us die. E'en though the world were
        mine,
    Its choicest, richest store of blessing should be thine.
    Unhappy I!'

And you say to him,

"'And thou, my lion, how proud and generous thou
    art!'"

"And you really like that?" inquired the
actress.

"Like *what?*" demanded the author.

"The term 'my lion.'"

"Yes, I wrote it because I liked it best."

"And you wish me to retain it?"

"Certainly; unless you can suggest something better."

"I am not the author; it is not my place,
but yours, to find something better," insisted
Mlle. Mars.

"Well, then, we will, if you please, leave
the words as they stand," retorted Hugo.

"But I feel it so odd to have to call M. Firmin *my lion.*"

"That is only because you want to remain
Mlle. Mars instead of becoming Doña Sol.
Once get yourself absorbed so as to feel yourself the Castilian lady, the noble daughter of
the sixteenth century, and the pupil of Gomez
de Sylva, and you will have no thought of
M. Firmin; you will see before you none
other than Hernani, the robber chief, making
the monarch tremble in his capital. Be such
a woman, and to such a man you will open
your soul, and say *my lion.*"

"Well, then," assented the actress, in her
harsh, dry voice, "if you decide so, I will say
no more. My business is to deliver what the
manuscript directs; it makes no difference to
me. Come, Firmin, we will proceed:

"'And thou, my lion, how proud and generous thou
    art!'"

The rehearsal was then resumed; but the
very next day the same contention arose
again, and Mlle. Mars insisted upon substituting "mon seigneur" for "mon lion." Annoyed at the interruption, Victor Hugo determined at once both to put an end to the
grumbling, and to be himself treated with
proper respect; accordingly, he requested
Mlle. Mars to throw up her part. Accustomed
though she had been to have all the writers
of the world bowing down to her talent, Mlle.
Mars soon discovered that she had now to
deal with a character of another kind. She
forthwith became polite, and promised the
author that she would perform her rôle as no
one else could.

When the hour of trial came, she amply
vindicated her word.

CHAPTER XIII.

First Performance of "Hernani."—A Petition from the Classics.—Intrigues of the Philistines.—Appearance of "Young France,"—Théophile Gautier's Red Waistcoat.—A *Quene* at the Theatre Door.—Seven Hours' Wait.—Scene in the House.—Homage to Beauty.—The Battle.—A Blunder.—Down with Sycophants.—Mlle. Mars's Costume.—A Child's Question.—The Triumph of Romanticism.—Parodies of "Hernani."—The Press in 1830.—After the Victory.

THE first performance of " Hernani " was fixed for February 25, 1830, a day that will ever be memorable in theatrical annals as being the occasion of a battle that, in its own field, may be compared in importance with Marengo or Austerlitz, although many of the details are not generally known.

After the prohibition of "Marion Delorme," and the commotion that had been made during the rehearsals of " Hernani," public curiosity was excited to the highest pitch. The classics did their utmost to prevent the performance of the piece. Their animosity is not hard to understand, as the innovators were set upon displacing them from a stage which they had hitherto regarded as their own peculiar property. Accordingly seven Academicians, a worn-out remnant of the imperial literati who had been long accustomed to supply dramas for the Théâtre Français, addressed a petition to the king requiring that the house should be closed against all productions of the new school, and be reserved exclusively for writers who really apprehended the true and the beautiful. The petition specially demanded that the rehearsals of " Hernani" should be stopped.

Charles X. gave these benighted individuals an appropriate answer.

" In literary matters," he said, " my place, gentlemen, is only, like yours, among the audience."

The complainants, however, were not inclined to allow that they were beaten; they brought every kind of official influence to bear so effectually that, during the early part of Louis Philippe's reign, they contrived to keep an interdict upon all Victor Hugo's dramatic works; but now, meanwhile, in 1830, " Hernani " was about to be performed, and they had to insure its being received with hoots and hisses.

A watch, as strict as possible, was always kept during the rehearsals at the door of the theatre; but, in spite of this, one of the classic confraternity had succeeded in concealing himself somewhere within the house. In this way a certain knowledge of the piece was obtained beforehand, and a number of ridiculous verses were hawked about to bring the play into contempt and make it fall flat. In addition to this, a parody on the forthcoming drama was performed at the Vaudeville several days before the piece was brought out at the Théâtre Français.

Joining with the cabal, the censorship, in the strangest fashion, published an abusive notice of the manuscript, which had been submitted to them by order.

These various manœuvres are described in a curious article in the *Journal des Débats* of February 24, 1830, from which it is evident to how limited an extent the word of some of the censors was to be trusted.

One of them, who had studied "Marion Delorme" from his own point of view, said to the poet shortly afterwards, " For my part, I consider that a censor who should knowingly divulge the contents of a work that it had been his duty to inspect would be acting in a way as odious and unworthy as a priest who should reveal the secrets of the confessional."

But, notwithstanding this vehement declaration, there was a breach of confidence somewhere: some verses of the play were published, many of them so altered that they were quite grotesque. The poet knew pretty well that the treachery had not come from the theatre, and, suspecting the real source of the attack, made his complaint to the aforesaid incorruptible censor, receiving in reply a letter which, with his usual magnanimity, he abstained from publishing, but which contained the following passage:

" What, sir, is your grievance? Have your spies informed you that I have revealed the secret of your drama? Have you been told that I have been repeating your verses and turning them into ridicule? And suppose it is so, what harm have I done? Are your works sacred? And as to the lines that have been quoted, there can hardly be more than three at the utmost."

The excuse that is thus pleaded reminds us very much of the thief in "Jodelle," who, when he was caught in the act of stealing, gave himself credit for only taking three louis-d'or when he had the whole pile before him from which he could help himself. The scrupulous censor had evidently lost all sense of shame.

All Paris, as might be expected, was intent upon witnessing the first performance, and the competition for the smallest boxes was very keen. M. Thiers, Benjamin Constant, and many more who were interested in literature, applied to the author to secure them places.

Just on the eve of the important day, Victor Hugo, to the consternation of the actors and actresses, came to the resolution that he should refuse admission to all *claqueurs*. Besides that his pride made him entertain a dislike to paid applause, there was another reason that weighed with him—he felt that he could have no confidence in men who had always been in the service of the classics; and it was one of not the least curious signs of those heroic times that the "knights of the chandelier," in their passionate attachment to tragedy of the old school, might begin to hiss instead of to applaud.

Fired with an unprecedented zeal, a bevy of the literary scions of the day came forward and offered themselves as a substitute for the professional *claqueurs*, who were evidently unreliable. Gérard de Nerval undertook to recruit and organize the voluntary troop ready for the evening that threatened to be so stormy. This refined and elegant writer had a brave and generous nature, and well deserved the confidential friendship to which Victor Hugo admitted him. His first step was to select a certain number of "captains" on whom he knew he might rely, and commission them to enlist a company of recruits. To the summons thus issued Petrus Borel, Balzac, Berlioz, Auguste Maquet, Préault, Jehan du Seigneur, Joseph Bouchardy, and a number of others quickly responded, all of them ready to rally to the trumpet-call of "Hernani," and, as they said, "resolved to take their stand upon the rugged mount of Romanticism, and valiantly to defend its passes against the assaults of the classics.". De Nerval distributed to them their tickets, which consisted of squares of red paper signed at the corner with the word *hierro*, the Spanish for "iron."

Among those on whom the lot of captain fell none was prouder than Théophile Gautier, who had long been burning with a zealous eagerness to fight against the hydra of "perruquinism." Wild and boundless was the enthusiasm with which the light-hearted young poet demanded of his followers, on their honor, that they would give no quarter to the Philistines! Unparalleled was the devotion with which he regarded the author, to whom he was ready to say, as Dante of old said to Virgil, "Thou art the guide and master of my thought!" And touching are the pages, exuberant in their passion and rich in their flow, which he has dedicated to the immortal day of "Hernani!" And fervent was the frenzy with which he pressed to his bosom the crimson ticket with its motto, bidding him to be strong and trusty as Castilian steel! He was but nineteen years of age; but having made up his mind to be a champion and a warrior in the cause, he concluded that it would be out of character for him to appear in the ordinary costume of a citizen, and felt that it behooved him to adopt some special uniform. For some time he had visions of fanciful doublets and feudal armor, but at last decided upon wearing a red waistcoat. He declared that he had a special predilection for red, not only as a noble color that had been dishonored by political strife, but as the type of blood and life and heat; a hue that blends with equal perfectness with marble or with gold, and which he deplored as having vanished so entirely from modern life and modern art. He discerned, as he thought, a fitting occasion whereon red might be brought from oblivion, and reinstated in an honor that it should henceforth never lose. He would constitute himself "the lion of the red," and would flash its brilliancy upon "the grays," as he designated the classics, who had no sympathy with the light of poetry. The bullocks, though terrified at the color, should have to face the red of Hugo's verse!

Having thus made up his mind about the dress he would wear, he sent for Gaulois, his tailor. Gaulois made a good many objections; it seemed to him a proceeding out of all reason for a waistcoat not only to be red, but that it should be made to button behind. One by one the tailor's objections were overruled: Gautier first gave him a pattern which he had himself cut out of a piece of gray cloth, and although he was looked upon as little short of raving mad when he selected some scarlet satin for the material, he held to his order so firmly that resistance was useless, and the waistcoat was made.

The rest of Théophile Gautier's costume, as described in "L'Histoire de Romanti-

tered ribbon did duty both for collar and cravat. It is the red waistcoat, however, that will be remembered for ages yet to come!

In his "Légende du Gilet Rouge" Gautier himself writes:

"Any one who has the least acquaintance

THÉOPHILE GAUTIER IN 1860.

cisme," consisted of a pair of pale-green trousers with a stripe of black velvet down the seams, a black coat with broad velvet facings, and a voluminous gray overcoat turned up with green satin. A piece of wa-

with French character will own that to present one's self with hair as long as Albert Dürer's, and a waistcoat as red as an Andalusian bull-fighter's, in a place of amusement where all Paris is assembled, requires a sort of courage very different from that which inspires a man to storm a redoubt that is bristling with cannon. Never has there been a war but there has always been the heroic band, the forlorn - hope, volunteering to accomplish the daring deed; but hitherto there has been found only a solitary Frenchman venturing to flaunt upon his breast a piece of stuff of so rare, so dazzling, so aggressive a hue!

"And now we must wear it bravely, no good for us to try to tear it off; it must cling to us like the coat of Nessus. It is the hallucination of the *bourgeoisie* that they never can see us without it; we may put on garments of olive, of chestnut, of ochre, of London soot, of pickle color, or any other of the neutral tints that a sober civilization may approve, but nevertheless we shall never be recognized as otherwise than wearing the red waistcoat.

"Precisely so also with the hair. Cut it as short as we will, we shall always be presumed to be wearing it long; so that even were we to present ourselves to the orchestra with our polls as polished as ivory or as smooth and shiny as ostrich-eggs, the whole artillery of opera-glasses would assuredly reveal that a perfect cascade of Merovingian locks was falling around our shoulders."

Many other of the "Hernani" partisans appeared in costume scarcely less eccentric. The young men had asked to be allowed admission into the theatre before the general public, so that they might preoccupy the obscure places or any corners in which some "hissers" might be likely to make an ambush. This request was conceded on condition that they should all be at the door by three o'clock, but so anxious were they not to be thwarted in their plan that they actually assembled at noon.

The passengers along the street stopped and stared at them with amazement; such a fantastic assemblage baffled their comprehension. Some of them wore soft felt hats; some appeared in coats of velvet or satin, frogged, braided, or trimmed with fur; others, enveloped in Spanish cloaks, stood with their arms akimbo; and many more wore velvet caps of the most extraordinary shapes. It looked as though a costumier's store had been ransacked, and "young France" had run off with the spoil to deck themselves out as Rubens, Velasquez, or some of the old heroes of the Revolution.

It was not, howeve. the motley costumes that so much offended "the good taste" of the *bourgeoisie*, as the way in which the hair was allowed to fall round the neck and the prodigious growth of beards. At that date beards were considered so improper that in no station of life would a young man have ventured to be married wearing either beard or whiskers or mustache. The two Devérias, in 1825, were the first to raise the standard of revolt in this respect, and they were only allowed the privilege because their friend Victor Hugo had encouraged it. Their example was ultimately followed by a host of others.

Altogether the long hair was decidedly the feature that most of all provoked the wrath of the citizens. The flowing locks might be carefully trimmed, and the mustaches might be elegantly curled, but nevertheless they created a great deal of scandal. The classic journals, great and small, announced that the corps of the romanticists was made up of rough, fierce, and dirty vagabonds; "brigands of thought," as Philothée O'Neddy designated them—such alone were capable of espousing the cause of "Hernani."

But, "brigands" though they were called, they were nevertheless poets, reviewers, journalists, architects, painters, and sculptors; for the most part, they belonged to good families, and were well educated, and sincere in their love of art and liberty. At the same time, it must be allowed that it was a misfortune that they should elect to manifest their craving for reform and their detestation of the prevailing flatness of style by adopting such an eccentricity of dress and personal appearance.

It was a whim which involved them in considerable discomfort, at times exposing them to violent assaults; and as they now stood in their places in the *queue* in the Rue de Valois, they were pelted with cabbage-stalks and every variety of filth. Balzac himself was struck on the face.

They knew well enough that any retaliation on their part would only provoke a row, bringing about the interference of the police; accordingly, they only smiled and allowed the mob to bespatter them at will.

At two o'clock the doors of the theatre were opened, and the troop rushed in, making it their first business to explore the most obscure places in the house, in case any of their adversaries should be in hiding. Some chose the pit, some the upper gallery, those most devoted to the cause always selecting the most inferior positions.

There were more than six hours to wait

"YOUNG FRANCE" OUTSIDE THE THÉÂTRE FRANÇAIS.

before the curtain would rise. They had, at any rate, got the start of the classics, but the next question was how they should conduct themselves during the long interval.

It cannot be said that they behaved particularly well. The far-seeing ones, the notaries of the future, had provided themselves with refreshments: they had brought in their hard-boiled eggs and their sausages, smelling sufficiently strong of garlic, and they had not forgotten their bottles of wine. Accordingly, they ate and drank and chattered, and then they proceeded to sing their studio songs; but the hours, nevertheless, passed somewhat tediously away.

Among other things they discussed the various titles that had been proposed for the forthcoming piece. Victor Hugo himself had first intended calling it "Trois pour Une," truly a romantic title, and one which, in the opinion of some of them—although the minority—was a fine challenge to the old tragic party. A good many, however, preferred calling it "L'Honneur Castillan," as in a certain degree indicating the leading idea of the play. Still, the predominant feeling was in favor of naming it simply "Hernani," the title which had been retained, although Mame's first edition, published in 1830, was entitled "Hernani, ou l'Honneur Castillan."

Some of the young enthusiasts related how Victor Hugo, in coming from Spain to France as a little child, had passed through the town of Ernani, and maintained that its sonorous name had fastened itself upon the poet's memory; others of them recited some of the verses of the drama which their intimacy with the author had enabled them to learn by heart; and thus, by means of sandwiches, songs, and recitations, the time waned and the momentous hour drew nigh.

The chandelier was lighted, and the business of the evening commenced long before the rising of the curtain, as whenever a box-door was opened the eyes of "young France" were turned in that direction, and as often as any graceful girl was admitted to her seat there was a general outburst of applause.

The young connoisseurs were far more attracted by personal beauty than they were captivated either by sparkling jewels or costly toilets. When Mlle. Delphine Gay, who afterwards became Madame de Girardin, made her appearance, her chiselled features, her fair hair, and the finished elegance of her attire evoked for her a triple round of cheers; and yet she wore nothing but the plainest white muslin dress, fastened with a blue sash, her entire costume, as she told the Duc de Montmorency the next day, having cost only eight-and-twenty francs. But the color of the sash, the perfect fit of the robe, and her own sweet countenance formed a *tout-ensemble* so charming that it could not fail to arouse enthusiasm.

In due time the classics also began to arrive, and the heads of the Academicians began to "pave the orchestra." Then commenced the fray. At first, low murmurs and angry growls were heard amid the throng. The two armies, or, as they have been significantly called, "the two civilizations," found themselves face to face; with war in their hearts and with head erect, they glared upon each other ready to discharge their volleys of vituperation. Gautier's red waistcoat was of course a conspicuous object, and became the theme of perpetual banter; but the young romantic only smiled contemptuously, and, disdaining all ridicule, stood with his fists closed, ready to resent any direct provocation that should be given. Endowed with prodigious strength, he seemed only waiting his opportunity to show himself a Samson among the Philistines.

The storm still gathered, the tumult increased, and the cross-fire of invectives became more continuous, until there is little doubt that blows would ultimately have followed, had not the three sharp raps, the well-known signal for the lifting of the curtain, temporarily at least calmed the excitement.

But the play did not proceed far without interruption. The scene of the first act is a bedchamber, in which a crimson curtain covers the window and a secret door is seen, at which Hernani is accustomed to knock. The old duenna, Josepha Duarte, having drawn the curtain and listened at the door for the arrival of Hernani to visit her mistress, proceeds to say,

"Serait-ce déjà lui? C'est bien à l'escalier Dérobé. . . ."

Immediately the commotion burst out afresh, and loud protestations were heard on every side.

The classics had never known such wanton audacity; to put "dérobé" in such a place, at the beginning of another line! Preposterous!

"But that," exclaimed a red-haired artist, "is just the beauty of it; the position of the word precisely answers to the mystery of the secret staircase!"

The loud cries of "Silence!" "Hush!" "Turn him out!" had the effect of making the offender hold his tongue; but the tumult could not be long suppressed.

We may again quote Théophile Gautier, who, though an active partisan, may yet be accepted as a competent witness of what transpired with regard to this struggle. He subsequently writes:

"Now that men's minds have become accustomed to regard as classical the very novelties that at first were treated as pure barbarisms, it is difficult to describe the effect produced upon an audience by verses so singular and strong, and yet of a style so strange, containing a ring of both Corneille and Shakespeare. Before the excitement can be comprehended, it is necessary to realize the extent to which the mere honor for words was carried in France, alike in poetry and in prose; and, after all, it will be next to impossible to conceive the horror which was originally experienced, though now, like other prejudices, it may have passed away.

"Let any one nowadays attend a performance of 'Hernani,' following the play with an old copy in his hand, upon the margin of which there are marks indicating the passages which at first were the signal for uproar and contention, and he will find that these are the very passages at which the applause rises like the flapping of the wings of gigantic birds; the very points which once were the occasion of battles fought and refought, of ambuscades of reviling epithets, of bloodhounds let loose to fasten on the throats of the foe, are now hailed with universal favor. The present generation can never duly comprehend the efforts that were made to liberate them from the long-established bonds of foolery.

"How could any one imagine that such a line as

"'Est-il minuit—minuit bientôt,'

aroused a storm so violent that it raged for days together?"

Throughout the performance, everything that night served as a pretext for an uproar; and when, at the end of the first act, Hernani uttered his cry of anger:

"De ta suite—j'en suis."

the whole tribe of baldheads was lashed into incredible fury.

It must not be concealed, however, that the defence was as furious and occasionally quite as senseless as the attack. For instance, when Ruy Gomez is about to marry his kinswoman, Doña Sol, he confides her to the care of King Carlos, whereupon Hernani exclaims to Gomez, "Vieillard stupide [you old stupid], he is in love with her!" A veritable classic, M. Perseval de Grandmaison, who was rather deaf, imagined that the words were "Vieil as de piques" (old ace of spades). Full of indignation, he cried out,

"This is too much! Shame!"

"What did you say?" inquired Lassailly, who was sitting in the adjoining stall and had not observed the words to which he alluded.

"I say it is a great shame to call a worthy character like Ruy Gomez an old ace of spades."

"Shame, sir? not at all!" retorted Lassailly; "he has a perfect right to do so; cards were invented—yes, M. l'Académicien, I should have thought you would have known that cards were invented in the days of Charles VI. Bravo, Hugo! Bravo, old ace of spades!"

This anecdote is related in the "Mémoires de Dumas."

Whenever the groans of the Philistines became too unbearable, the enthusiasts of the pit would drown them by shouting, "To the guillotine with the sycophants!"

But, however fierce was the outcry, no doubt could remain that the old strongholds were captured, and Romanticism had proved triumphant; Romanticism, which, according to Baudelaire, is but the modern expression for the beautiful, had asserted its power, and at the conclusion of the performance the name of the author was proclaimed as that of a victorious general, and the shouts of acclamation overwhelmed the storm of hisses.

The next day Châteaubriand wrote to Victor Hugo, expressing his admiration of his genius, and hailed him as one rising to the world just at the time that his own star was setting.

Before the rising of the drop for the fifth act, M. Mame, the publisher, had asked Victor Hugo to give him an interview for a few minutes in the street outside, and, as the result of a short conversation, he offered him six thousand francs for the manuscript of the play. The bargain was forthwith concluded, and the money immediately paid

down in a tobacconist's shop close at hand.
The payment came very opportunely. Victor Hugo, who has himself related the fact,
had not at the time more than fifty francs
in the world. He re-entered the theatre in
high spirits.

All the actors and actresses had gone
through their parts bravely, and the poet
made due acknowledgments to each of
them. With regard to Mlle. Mars, he owned that none but those who saw her could
have any idea of the effect that she had produced as Doña Sol, so skilfully had she developed the part, her talent carrying her from
the graceful to the sublime, and back from
the sublime to the pathetic.

Nevertheless, the popular actress had had
her own way; she had never been able to
reconcile herself to call M. Firmin "mon
lion," and had persisted in substituting what
appeared to her the more appropriate title
of "mon seigneur;" neither would she allow any interference with her toilette, for, although she made her appearance in white,
she would not be induced to wear anything
on her head but one of the fanciful little
hats that were all the rage in Paris at the
time. Nothing, of course, could be more in-
congruous for a Spanish girl at the beginning of the sixteenth century, but her resolution was fixed. The costume, which is
worthy of being included in a collection of
caricatures, may be found in one of the departments of the Bibliothèque Nationale.

In spite of all minor defects, the piece retained its place in the play-bill with the most
brilliant pecuniary results, standing its ground
notwithstanding the ridicule with which it
continued to be greeted.

Listening to the play as it was repeated
night after night, Victor Hugo found by
marking his manuscript that there was not a
line, nor a half-line, that did not in its turn
come in for the fate of being hooted. One
evening his little sister-in-law, hardly more
than a child, was taken to the theatre, and,
on her return, asked her sister whether the
hisses that went on all through the intervals
between the acts were of the same account
as those which were kept up during the performance. The question could not give much
consolation to Madame Victor Hugo, who
waited anxiously every night to hear how the
play had gone off.

The wrath of the public was fanned by the
press, which had never been more unjust in
its criticisms. With the exception of the

Journal des Débats and one or two reviews,
there was not a single newspaper found to
defend the work. Unfortunately, we have
not the means of reproducing the insults that
were heaped upon the poet at this period,
and it is beyond conception with what disgust the innovations of the romantics were
received. Women were up in arms about
the immorality of the piece, considering it
horrible and monstrous for any one to allow
the imagination to be sullied by such shameful scenes. It was done under the name of
the national dignity, and with an ostentation
of respect for the purity of their tongue and
admiration of the beautiful; but the most eminent critics did not scruple to denounce the
romantics as slovens, rascals, drunkards, and
madmen, and to declare that "Hernani" was
utterly foul and abominable.

Foremost among the assailants was Armand Carrel, who, in his earliest contributions to the *National*, delivered himself of
some terrible onslaughts.

After reading his first article on "Hernani,"
Victor Hugo wrote him an explanatory letter, in which he reminded him of various
peculiarities characteristic of the *soi-disant*
classics of 1830.

Carrel immediately replied,

"It is quite true that I take my stand by
the classics, but the classics that I am proud
of acknowledging have all long been dead."

And having said this, the brilliant polemist
went on to declare his conviction that no opposition was too vehement to be brought to
bear on a production that was calculated to
inspire minds naturally refined and well-bal-
anced with a deplorable spirit of emulation.
Blinded with rage, he had not the penetra-
tion to foresee that the author of "Hernani"
would ultimately come to rank among the
greatest of "classics," who, by restoring the
lyric to the drama, would link it afresh to the
ancients—to Æschylus, Sophocles, and Eurip-
ides as well as to the modern Corneille and
Shakespeare.

The literary war rose to such importance
that it occupied public attention almost as
much as the appointment of Polignac as
minister. It created a vast sensation even in
the provinces, and a young man was killed in
a duel of which a quarrel about "Hernani"
was the cause.

Victor Hugo received numberless anonymous letters, not only full of insult, but some
of them containing threats against his life;
and so seriously did his friends regard the con-

dition of things that they never failed every night when he left the theatre to accompany him to his own house.

The parodies on the play were too numerous to be recounted. The most notorious were those entitled "Harnali, ou la Contrainte par Cor," by A. de Lauzanne: "N. I. Ni, ou le Danger des Castilles," a wild rigmarole by Carmouche and Dupeuty; and one styled "Fanfan le Troubadour à la Représentation d'Hernani." Countless also were the pamphlets published about the "rococos" armed for war against the vandal partisans of the Goth.

These feuds have long since passed away. Time, to whom Æschylus dedicated his tragedies, has once again vindicated the assertion that genius will always in the long-run attract men's souls. As Paul de Saint-Victor has remarked, it will be to Victor Hugo's honor that he has gained in grandeur by the storm; his glory has been reared by insult as much as by applause.

"The flag of liberty in art was first planted by 'Hernani' on the breach of an assaulted citadel. What the Cid was for the ancient stage, such was 'Hernani' to the new, at once a revolution and a renaissance. The mission of 'Hernani,' when it appeared in 1830, was to overturn the false classic tragedy that Corneille had reared in marble, and Campestron to De Jouy had imitated in plaster. Hernani sounded his horn as Joshua blew his trumpet, and the three unities tottered to their fall. A long array of living personages, genuine flesh and blood, natural, with human passions, fanciful and lyrical, strange it might be, and picturesque in their attire, came trooping in from every epoch of history, to take the places where hitherto abstract kings had been accustomed to recount their abstract dreams. . . . The main design of this literary revolution was to annihilate the trashy repetitions of the old drama, and to stamp out the commonplace conventionalities of comedy where true eloquence was only aped by a laborious rhetoric. The romantics have been likened to barbarians, and they may do worse than accept the comparison. Wherever the horse of Attila set his hoof, the grass would grow no more; so where Victor Hugo's drama has made good its footing, the miserable thistles and the artificial flowers of the false classic style have never again been seen. The renaissance was magnificent, and requickened every form of language and of thought."

In consequence of Mlle. Mars having to leave, the performance of "Hernani" was discontinued, and the play was not again acted until eight years afterwards.

CHAPTER XIV.

The Revolution of July, 1830.—Performance of "Marion Delorme."—Reasons for Delay.—Reception by the Public.—Parodies.—Jules Janin's Indignation.—"Le Roi s'Amuse."—First Performance.—A Severe Critic.—Immediate Prohibition.—Causes of Prohibition.—Louis Philippe's Ministry.—Trial before the Board of Trade.—Disgraceful Hostility of the Newspapers.—The Poet's Reply.—"Lucrèce Borgia."—Its Actors.—Immense Success.—A Duel Avoided.

"To fight for **liberty**" **was** the romantic motto that had now **become the** watchword of the people. Roused to indignation by the edicts promulgated **by Charles** X., and by the policy of his minister, Polignac, Paris at last **revolted, and at** the end of July, 1830, requested the king to retire into exile, and there **to meditate upon** the mischief **of** despotism.

The political revolution was effected simultaneously with the literary, but unfortunately the Republican party was not strong **enough** to establish itself, and the **crown merely** changed hands by passing from the elder to the younger branch of the Bourbons. **After** lurking behind the throne, Louis **Philippe** now succeeded in mounting the **steps, and made** an attempt to naturalize that **bastard form** of government which **in France** will **ever be an** impossibility—a constitutional monarchy.

Victor Hugo's relations with Louis Philippe will be introduced hereafter, but, adhering to our programme, we will continue to recount the incidents connected **with his** dramatic labors.

The expulsion **of** Charles X. removed the impediment **to the** production **of** " Marion Delorme,**" which, it** will be remembered, was prohibited by the censorship and by the royal veto in 1829. **But,** now that liberty was restored to **the stage, the** Comédie Française bethought **themselves of the** piece, and the poet received a **number of** applications urging him to allow it to be produced. It was conjectured, not without some show of reason, **that** during this time of political reaction **the fourth act,** which had been such a **bugbear to Charles** X., would prove **a brilliant success.**

But, as the author has explained **in one of** his prefaces to the printed **editions of the play, it was just** this likelihood **of reactionary** success that induced him to detain the work a little longer in his portfolio. He felt that he was in a somewhat peculiar **position.** He

had indeed for some years been in the foremost ranks of the opposition, and since reaching man's estate he had been on the side of all that encouraged liberty and improvement; moreover, he had entered into certain **contracts about this "** Marion Delorme;" but at the same time he could not forget how, when he **had** first been launched into the literary **world at the** age of sixteen, all his sympathies **and** opinions had been royalist and Vendean. **He might be convinced now** that his sentiments then had **been mere delusions, but he could not fail** to remember that he had once written **"a coronation ode,"** though he could plead **that it was composed when the** people's **king had announced amid universal** acclamations that **there should be "no more censorship** ! no more halberds!**"** And now he **did** not want to have the past thrown up against him. **He felt** in his heart **that** he had acted conscientiously and disinterestedly; he had only **done his** duty, acting according to his lights; **but** he was satisfied that now his voice ought to **be uplifted rather on the part** of those who applauded **the people** than of those who cursed the king, and accordingly he refused to sanction the performance, not caring for a success that was the result either of political allusions or of scandal.

When, however, another year had elapsed, and Charles X. and his censorship had fallen into oblivion, there could be no further reason for postponing the representation of an historical drama simply because Louis XIII. was one of the characters.

Certain, therefore, that his work would no longer **be supposed to** convey any insinuation **against the** Bourbons, Victor Hugo allowed **the** rehearsals **to commence;** but, in spite of **the solicitations of Mlle.** Mars, and of the **manager of the Théâtre** Français, he selected **the theatre of the** Porte-Saint-Martin, thus fulfilling **the prediction of M.** Crosnier, who had now become **the** proprietor of the house.

The unavowed hostility that still lurked in

the Rue Richelieu against all works of the romantic school decided Victor Hugo upon making this change. He considered it advisable to have a manager who would take all responsibility, and he promised M. Crosnier to provide him with two pieces a year, upon the condition that he would have it announced in the play-bills that M. Hugo's works would not be submitted to the censorship.

The first performance of "Marion Delorme" took place on August 11, 1831, succeeding upon a run of Alexandre Dumas' "Antony." Madame Dorval took the part of Marion, and M. Bocage that of Didier. The excitement of the audience was quite as great as it had been at the first performance of "Hernani;" but, in spite of all the tumult, the piece was obviously a success.

From the production of "Marion Delorme," however, the receipts were less than they had been in the case of the previous play, but the enemies of the poet were not yet completely disarmed, although perhaps it is not entirely to be attributed to their spleen that there was at the time a pecuniary failure of a piece which is now always received with unbounded applause, and which throughout its five acts never fails to arouse the spectator alternately to laughter and terror, and to charm him by the flow of its magnificent verse.

With the exception of the principal rôles, all the parts, although they really require thoroughly good acting, were taken by players of no note and devoid of talent. The public taste, too, was not yet educated to the new style, and Victor Hugo had still many struggles to make before he could attain his object of reforming the stage. Moreover, political affairs were particularly grave, and all men's more serious interests were absorbed in matters that seemed of larger importance than poetry and the drama. The *Journal Officiel* of the 12th of August does not even mention the performance of the "Marion," while all the other journals mention the piece only to condemn it, with the exception of the *Journal des Débats*, and even that is somewhat severe.

It was in a Normandy diligence that Alexandre Dumas, who was coming from Trouville, expecting to be in time to witness the production of the play, was informed by a writer on the staff of the *Débats* that he had come too late. But, in order to console him, the contributor to a paper that was always a supporter of Victor Hugo's interests added,

"However, you have not lost much. The audience received it coldly, very coldly. As poetry it is weaker than 'Hernani;' and as for the plot, why, that is prigged from De Vigny's romance!"

And the critic rubbed his hands with a self-satisfied air, and doubtless, had the conversation been continued, was quite ready to go on to avow that Victor Hugo had really no talent whatever.

The *Moniteur*, in criticising the piece on the 15th, after observing that talent should never overstep the rules of good taste, goes on to say that "this maxim could not be too often inculcated upon M. Victor Hugo, who seems no more inclined to recognize it now than he did in the merry days of 'Hernani.' A few beardless novices, eager perhaps to keep him down to their own level, may flatter him into the belief that his productions are all *chefs-d'œuvre*, but never yet has he conceived anything more meagre and commonplace, and at the same time more full of eccentricities, than 'Marion Delorme.'" In reply to this, the *Revue des Deux Mondes* insisted that M. Hugo had never so truly shown himself a poet, nor attained to so high a range of vision nor so wide a field of judgment as now.

As well as being attacked by the press, the play was travestied by parodies at the minor theatres. At the Variétés there was "Une Nuit de Marion Delorme," by Théric and Girau ; and at the Vaudeville, the 'Gothon du Passage Delorme," by Dupeuty and Duvert. Nor can it be imagined what coarse, stupid jokes these burlesques contained ; they were as bits of mud thrown at the poet's mantle, yet so foul was their nature that at length Jules Janin uttered an indignant protest against their odious nonsense. The poet himself did not deign to notice insults emanating from so low a source; he felt himself strong enough to despise his traducers, confident that he should gain renown in spite of his violation of antiquated rules, and that he should rise to be admired in defiance of the public and the press. Calm and undisturbed he continued his work, and his fame emerged all the greater from the wranglings and disputes.

"Marion Delorme" was succeeded by "Le Roi s'Amuse," which Victor Hugo began on the 1st of June, 1832, and finished during one of the periods of disturbance that were so frequent in Louis Philippe's reign. Immediately afterwards he wrote "Lucrèce Borgia."

M. Taylor, having heard of the completion of the two dramas, the first of which was in verse and the second in prose, put in his claim for "Le Roi s'Amuse." The author acceded to his request, and the piece was at once rehearsed, M. Ligier appearing as Triboulet, M. Joanny as St. Vallier, M. Perrier as François I., and Mlle. Anaïs as Blanche.

The rehearsals went on quietly enough through the summer, and by November everything was ready for the performance, when M. d'Argout, the minister for the time being, sent for the manuscript. As the censorship was presumed to be abolished, the author refused to comply with the demand, but went to call upon M. d'Argout, who he found had been informed by some one that "Le Roi s'Amuse" contained certain allusions that were derogatory to Louis Philippe. Victor Hugo emphatically denied the application, and asserted that in depicting François I. in his true historical colors he had no more thought of Louis Philippe than he had thought of Charles X. in depicting Louis XIII.

The minister yielded to his representations, and the first performance took place on November 22, 1832.

Just as usual the young men were at their posts, with Théophile Gautier and Célestin Nanteuil at their head; but "young France" was now beginning to interest itself in politics, and as the *élite* of beauty and fashion entered the boxes they were not greeted as before by rounds of applause, but by the strains of the "Marseillaise" and "La Carmagnole." The effect produced upon the *habitués* of the Théâtre Français may be more easily imagined than described. To crown all, just before the curtain rose it was reported that a pistol had been fired at the king; voices rose high and loud, and the house became the scene of a regular tumult. Nevertheless, when the play commenced, the faithful "rowdies" who had been the heroes in the "Hernani" fight vigorously endeavored to hold their own against the supporters of the old tragic style.

"Le Roi s'Amuse" was more vehemently hissed than either "Hernani" or "Marion Delorme," and the press was absolutely merciless in its criticisms. To such an extent were men's minds blinded by their literary fury that the very journals that were most liberal in their politics, and most opposed to Louis Philippe's government, sided against the poet, who at the same time lost several

of the friends on whom he had thought he might most confidently rely.

The very day after the performance the most astounding accusations were circulated, and some criticisms were published that might be described as comical in their severity.

One critic, writing anonymously, complained that he had hitherto failed in inducing M. Hugo to listen to truth; and asserted that his productions revealed absolute weakness and sterility in their conception, and betrayed a vicious system that, instead of leading to originality, only dragged him into the trivial and absurd.

The writer continued:

"M. Hugo in his former dramas, though verging on the grotesque, has hitherto preserved some faint idea of the good and beautiful, some semblance of sentiment, of morality and propriety. In 'Le Roi s'Amuse' he has overstepped all bounds: history, reason, morality, artistic dignity, and refinement are all trampled underfoot. Such is his progress. . . . He traduces historical personages, such as François I. and Clément Marot, the poet; . . . the conversation of the courtiers is far from edifying; . . . the whole piece is monstrous; history is set at nought, and the most noble characters are slandered and vilified. . . . The play is entirely void of interest, and the horrible, the mean, and the immoral are all jumbled together into a kind of chaos.

"The performance was scandalized by a madcap set of the author's partisans, who, in return for every hiss, shouted out 'Down with the idiots! Turn out the fools!' This carefully organized band had been introduced into the house before the proper hour, and made it their business to applaud most whatever the public received with most disgust. In spite, however, of the strenuous efforts of these extraordinary *claqueurs*, the hissing was so overpowering that M. Hugo's name was drowned in the tumult. Notwithstanding the utter failure of the piece, a second performance is all the same announced for Thursday next."

Such was the treatment accorded to what is now acknowledged to be one of the most admirable works of the modern stage, and one of the finest tragic poems that have ever been conceived. And it is with ill-disguised delight that the critic appends to his venomous article a postscript:

"We learn this evening that the prime-minister has issued an order to stop the performance of the piece."

Incredible as it may seem, the intelligence was perfectly true. The constitutional monarchy was acting in precisely the same way as the monarchy that ruled "by right divine."

Academicians and deputies had betaken themselves with all speed to the minister, and informed him that "Le Roi s'Amuse" was not a simple outrage on good taste and public morality, it was absolutely indecent; and, moreover, contained disrespectful allusions to Louis Philippe, and all this just at the very time when assassins were making a target of his sacred head.

The minister straightway summoned a council, and the council decided that such a scandal could not be tolerated. Hence it came to pass that just as Victor Hugo was going to breakfast he received the following note from M. Jouslin de la Salle, who had formerly been manager of the Porte-Saint-Martin, and was now manager of the Théâtre Français:

"Nov. 28.

"It is now half-past ten, and I have just received orders to suspend the performances of 'Le Roi s'Amuse.' M. Taylor has made the communication to me on behalf of the prime-minister."

It was Victor Hugo's first impression that there must be some mistake. Not being able to credit a proceeding that seemed at once so senseless and so overbearing, he ran to the theatre, but only to find the information confirmed, and to be told that "the minister had given the order in virtue of his divine ministerial right. There was no other reason to be alleged."

The Comédie Française, whose proposal to submit his drama to the censorship Victor Hugo had indignantly rejected, were quite bewildered, and made some efforts to get the decision reversed; but all their attempts were utterly vain, as not only was the order of suspension confirmed, but a formal prohibition was issued. The objectionable words "Le Roi s'Amuse" were to be erased from the play-bills under the penalty of withdrawal of the license from the theatre.

Thus deprived of his rights, and thwarted in his professional occupation, the poet was not going to humiliate himself by hanging about the doors of ministerial antechambers. He considered that to ask a favor of a power was to recognize its authority, and consequently he resolved to make a wider appeal.

Two tribunals were open to him: he would appeal to public opinion, and he would appeal to a court of justice.

In a manifesto which he addressed to the public he writes:

"It appears that those who appoint themselves our censors profess to be scandalized by 'Le Roi s'Amuse;' the piece has shocked the modesty of the gendarmes; the Léotaud brigade has voted it obscene; the chamber of morals has put its hands before its eyes, and M. Vidocq has been made to blush. In short, the watchword that has been lisped for some days around us has now been given to the police—*the piece is immoral!* Come, my good sirs, and let us look into the matter.

"Do you really believe there is any immorality in the play? Listen and see! Triboulet is deformed, he is sickly, and he is court fool; this triple misfortune causes his weakness. Triboulet hates the king because he is a king, he hates the aristocracy because they are the aristocracy, and he hates men in general because they have not all got a hump upon their back. He depraves, corrupts, and brutalizes the king; he spurs him on to ignorance, tyranny, and vice; he sets him loose in the bosoms of reputable families, pointing him out the wife to corrupt, the sister to seduce, and the daughter to dishonor. One day, in the middle of some festival, just as he is urging the king to elope with the wife of M. de Cossé, M. de Saint-Vallier makes his way up to the monarch, and reproaches him with having dishonored Diane de Poitiers, his daughter. Triboulet commences insulting the parent whom the king has thus injured, and the father then raises his hand and utters a fearful curse. This is the turning-point of the piece.

"Triboulet, upon whom the curse has thus fallen, is not, after all, a man utterly without heart. He has a daughter, Blanche, whom he has nurtured in a solitary house in a deserted place far away from the eyes of the world. He is bringing her up in purity and faith and innocence. His great fear is lest she should fall into the wickedness, the misery of which he knows so well.

"Now it falls out that the curse of old De Saint-Vallier overtakes Triboulet through this one object of his love. The very king who has been encouraged in vileness by Triboulet seduces Triboulet's child. The fool is smitten by an avenging fate in exactly the same way as the man who cursed him had been smitten before him.

"Then Triboulet lays a snare for the king, who has carried off his daughter, but into this the daughter falls and becomes a victim. Thus Triboulet has had two pupils — the monarch whom he has led into vice, and his child whom he has educated in virtue—and the former becomes the destroyer of the latter. The result happens in this way. In his design to carry off Madame de Cossé for the king, he carries off his own child; and then, in attempting to avenge himself upon the royal seducer, he assassinates that child with his own hand. Vengeance is not stayed half-way—the curse of the father of Diane is accomplished upon the father of Blanche.

"Whether this idea is dramatic, it is not for me to decide. All that I contend for is that it is not immoral."

In a long preface, published on the last day of this month, after giving a dignified and wholesome caution to the ill-advised power, the poet goes on to say that the matter must not be regarded as a petty literary *coup d'état,* but must be considered as touching the general property and liberty. In accordance with this, he announces his intention to have the cause pleaded judicially, and to institute a suit before the Board of Trade: first, to compel the Théâtre Français to perform "Le Roi s'Amuse;" and, secondly, to compel the government to sanction the performance.

The trial commenced on the 19th of December, 1832.

All the journals, and especially the *Débats,* record that large crowds assembled to hear the case. As early as nine o'clock in the morning hundreds of people stood waiting *en queue* in the galleries of the Palais de la Bourse, where the Board of Trade then held its sittings.

The court was divided into four parts: the enclosure of the tribunal, which was generally filled with a select audience, chiefly composed of fashionably dressed ladies, assembled long before the hour of hearing; the bar, reserved for solicitors, barristers, and political celebrities; the third part was a space into which some privileged spectators were admitted as into the pit of a theatre; while at the rear was the compartment allotted to the general public.

At noon the doors were opened, and a few minutes sufficed to fill every corner to overflowing. Even the hall of the Pas-Perdus, a spacious vestibule separated from the court by glass doors, was crowded with an eager multitude. As Victor Hugo entered with his counsel he was loudly cheered, the spectators mounting their seats to get a better view; and it was amid great excitement that the officials, under the presidency of M. Aubé, took their seats.

The double action was then commenced. The first was Victor Hugo's claim upon the Théâtre Français; the second was the demand for compensation by the Comédie Française from M. d'Argout, the Minister of Trade and Public Works, as having jurisdiction over the theatres.

M. Chaix d'Est-Ange opened the pleadings as counsel for the minister of the crown. He commenced by proposing that the court should declare itself incompetent to give judgment in these proceedings, as it was not provided with powers of administration.

Victor Hugo's counsel, M. Odilon Barrot, rose and opposed this motion in a brilliant speech. He described his client's mission as one of talent and of genius, and claimed not only for him in particular, but for authors in general, the right of liberty of thought in the production of dramatic compositions. He called forth protests and shouts of ironical laughter from the audience by making the advocate of the Comédie Française read the document in which the Comte d'Argout had prohibited the performance of "Le Roi s'Amuse," because "many passages therein were an outrage upon public morals;" and he reminded the court that the functions of the censorship had been abolished by charter in 1830, and how M. de Montalivet, the Minister of the Interior, had endorsed the scheme for the management of theatres with the sentence "The censorship is dead." He wound up by claiming damages from the Comédie Française for the non-fulfilment of their covenant.

The reply of the counsel for the Comédie Française produced such a tumult that the President had to order one section of the court to be cleared and the adjoining vestibule to be closed.

Victor Hugo then came forward, and in an effective speech, which he had prepared beforehand, he argued that his suit had no other origin than the illegal order of the minister, an order which, as he had no right to make it, the stage had no call to follow. After asserting that the government was gradually withdrawing from the French people rights and privileges which forty years of

TRIBOULET IN "LE ROI S'AMUSE."

revolution had secured to them, he concluded by saying :

"To-day a censor deprives me **of my liberty as a poet;** to-morrow **a gendarme will** deprive **me of** my liberty as a citizen. To-day I am banished from the theatre; to-morrow I shall be banished from the country. To-day I am gagged; to-morrow **I shall** be transported. To-day there is a **state** of siege in the commonwealth of letters; to-morrow there will be a state of **siege** in the city. No longer do we hear of privilege, of security, of the charter, or of the public rights. Nothing of the sort. But the government must listen **to advice.** It must stay its downward course; **otherwise we** shall soon have once **more the despotism of** 1807, barring its glory !"

These fine and prophetic words were greeted **with** fresh bursts of applause.

M. Chaix d'Est-Ange replied, and the court rose.

As Victor Hugo passed through the waiting **crowds** on his way home, he was loudly **cheered.**

A fortnight afterwards **judgment was given in** favor of the minister.

The poet was not **in the least** discouraged by the sentence, which was only what he had anticipated. Genius is patient; **it is conscious that it** can afford to wait, and nothing can divert it from its course.

M. **Paul** Foucher, in his interesting book "Entre Cour et Jardin," has described how, on the night of the first performance of "Le Roi s'Amuse," when the whole **theatre** was in an uproar, **so** that Hugo's name was drowned in the sea of roaring voices, the author's face exhibited no sign of despondency at the failure any more than it had shown **passion or excitement** during the struggle. **His Olympian brow had** withstood the tempest **with the firmness of a** rock, and after the **curtain fell he went** to offer his thanks and encouragements **to the** actors and actresses, saying,

"You are a little discomposed to-night; but you will find it different the day after to-morrow !"

In spite of the hissing, he **was sanguine** about his play; nevertheless, **it was not** destined to be repeated.

"Hernani" had been performed fifty-three times, "**Marion Delorme**" sixty-one; "Le Roi s'Amuse" appeared once, and **has** never **been put upon** the stage again. **Since his last return to Paris the** poet has at various **times been solicited to** authorize its repro-

duction; but, although he has offered no opposition, the performance has never taken place. The part of Triboulet is undoubtedly very difficult, and it is feared might overtask the powers of the actor; but, on the other hand, it has been reported, though perhaps in mere gossip, that the rôle has been coveted by several performers of equal ability, and that their mutual rivalry has created an impediment **to the representation of** the piece upon the stage. **It is to** be trusted, however, that **the** obstacle, whatever it is, will not prove to be insurmountable, and that there will be a chance before long of witnessing a *chef-d'œuvre* that succumbed originally to an attack at **once so** violent and so ridiculous.

The ministerial organs **in France in 1832** were by **no** means satisfied **with the final** prohibition of the play. **Irritated beyond** measure by Victor Hugo's proud and defiant attitude, the official journals began to load him with reproaches because he continued to receive the original pension of two thousand francs which had been granted to him as well **as to Lamartine.**

We have already seen how the poet, as a matter of conscience, had declined accepting the increase of pension offered by Charles X. as compensation for the interdiction of "Marion Delorme." Hitherto, however, he had experienced **no scruples as** to the propriety of his receiving **pecuniary assistance** from the nation, and it **was only in** consequence of many virulent **attacks** in certain newspapers that he sent a **letter, marked** by moderation and reserve, but still full of dignity, in which he tendered his resignation of the pension. M. d'Argout remonstrated with him, but he adhered to his resolution, and refused to re-**ceive the** money any longer, although at that **time his** resources were far from considerable.

His line of action, magnanimous as it was, did not have much effect in mitigating the severity of his reviewers. Nevertheless, although they continued to depreciate his power as a dramatic author, they began to do some justice to him as a poet; and one of his most inveterate enemies, Gustave Planche, was fain to acknowledge that in manipulation of language "Victor Hugo is unrivalled, because he wields the French idiom at his will; he forges it as solid as iron, he tempers it like steel, he engraves it as silver, he moulds it like bronze, he chisels it as marble; the blades of Toledo are not keener, nor the mosaics of Florence more delicate, than the verses which his skilful workmanship has produced."

And Planché, hard and spiteful as he often is, has said even more: he has owned that when he witnessed Triboulet's grief in the play he was overcome with admiration and moved to tears; and what stronger testimony than such a confession could be rendered in praise of a dramatist whose leading aim it was to excite the emotions of his audience?

The violence of the outcry against Victor Hugo's last work had no permanent effect in discouraging the theatrical managers, and before the end of 1832 M. Harel sought the author's permission to perform his drama, hitherto unpublished, of "Le Souper à Ferrure," the title originally given to "Lucrèce Borgia."

M. Harel's company at that time included Frédéric Lemaître and Mlle. Georges. This lady, though no longer young, having been born in 1786, still retained an extraordinary beauty. Not only had she a figure which might have enraptured Phidias, but her marvellous form was animated by intelligence, passion, and genius; a true soul underlay her chiselled grace. Frédérick Lemaître, too, was in the zenith of his talent.

The proposal was accepted, and, Delafosse taking the part of Don Alphonse d'Este, and Mlle. Juliette that of the Princess Negroni, the rehearsals commenced forthwith.

Every rehearsal was made with closed doors, and the author declined admitting even his brother Abel to the dress rehearsal on the night preceding the first public performance. The slightest indiscretion was known to be enough to feed the fury of Hugo's traducers, and he wished to avoid any of the scenes of his drama being hawked about the city and made the subject of ridicule. He could not, however, find it in his heart to resist the entreaties of Sainte-Beuve, who always professed himself the most sincere and devoted of friends. Having obtained permission to witness the rehearsal, he came, listened most attentively, congratulated the author most warmly on his production, and then went out and circulated it everywhere that "Lucrèce Borgia" was an utter piece of absurdity.

The incident was but a type of this man's character. It was solely due to his treachery and infamous gossip that on the morning of the day on which the piece was to be performed in the evening, several newspapers

announced that the
the plot, and that th
in the highest degr
gies terrible and ind

In spite of every
formance was a com
was the name of the
clamation, but he w
dience to appear be
to this, notwithstand
he refused to con
awaited his departu
ped the cab in which
pelled him to retur
by hundreds of adm
went.

Faithful to his co
tor Hugo had returi
of his life; indeed,
labor before he ha
petty political adve
most to distract; wi
drama had been p
with another, thus c
ernment that its he
and that art and libe
up in a night, thou
trample them dowr
be his resolve to co
gle simultaneously
would maintain hi
giving up his priva
hands, he said; one
one another.

In forming his ov
that he had last fir
ured to predict th
s'Amuse" would p
political era, and "I
cipal literary era, of
two works, though
sign, were in reality
idea.

Both represent de
cal and hideous; bu
he is, has a soul, ar
purest sentiment t
paternal love—a po
degraded nature int
imates to the sublin

"Lucrèce Borgia
no less complete ar
hers is a moral def
lieved by the pure
tains to woman, ma

These are his wor

"Embody a moth

and the monster will not fail to excite interest, and may be sympathy. . . . Physical deformity, sanctified by paternal love, this is what you have in ' Le Roi s'Amuse;' moral deformity, purified by maternal love, this is what you find in ' Lucrèce Borgia.' "

Convinced that social problems are by no pict the misery to which humanity is heir, it is fitting that the veil of some serious and consoling thought should be thrown over the naked truth, which in itself would be too painful to contemplate.

Nowadays no one fails to discern the philosophy of Victor Hugo's dramatic

MLLE. GEORGES AS LUCRÈCE BORGIA.

means independent of literary matters, Victor Hugo has consistently maintained that an audience ought never to be allowed to leave a theatrical spectacle without carrying away some instinct of morality both deep and stern; but, at the same time, whenever it becomes necessary to lay open the wounds and to de-works, but the triumph of "Lucrèce Borgia" was unquestionably a memorable epoch in his career. He was then thirty years of age.

But the enthusiasm of the general public had not by any means the effect of bringing the classics to consider themselves defeated. Armand Carrel remained inflexibly among the ranks of the irreconcilables, and criticised the play somewhat captiously, although he could not help acknowledging that it was skilfully put together, and that it was in general conformity with historical tradition, inasmuch as "Lucrèce Borgia" was the true Lucrèce of the legend, having the mingled is one in verse which should hardly be passed over in silence, if only on account of its mercilessness. It was by Destigny, whose name we have already had occasion to mention. The vindictive poet, in his angry indignation, commences by designating Victor Hugo as

"A Homer waiting on a harlot's will;"

MLLE. JULIETTE AS PRINCESS NEGRONI.

blood of the courtesan and of the pope flowing in her veins.

Parodies, of course, did not fail to be forthcoming, but none of them were worthy of special notice.

Among the satires, however, that were published after the performance of the drama there and, not satisfied with this shameful appellation, proceeds to say,

" Behold the produce of your mediæval stage!
  Lust and adultery it connsels to our age.
  In mercy's name, no more these ancient crimes exhume,
  But leave the Borgias in their own polluted tomb!
  *   *   *   *   *   *   *

8

Of this be sure, ye playwrights infamous and vile,
'Tis you that all our women and our youth defile."

The author had the satisfaction of bestowing his unqualified approval upon all the interpreters of his work. He congratulated Frédéric Lemaître, whose easy yet dignified grace, terrible yet tender, manly yet childlike, modest yet severe, had fully realized the Gennaro of his own conception. He tendered his acknowledgments to Mlle. Georges, who, in vengeance, in chastisement, and in insult, was ever the great tragedienne; and he complimented Mlle. Juliette, who, though she merely represented an apparition, threw such vivid animation into the beautiful countenance of the young Princess Negroni, and gave such force to the few words she had to utter, that she revealed a talent that was conspicuous in spirit, passion, and truth.

It was long since the Théâtre de la Porte-Saint-Martin had realized profits so large, and the manager lost no time in claiming another piece from the author. His demand, however, was made in such a way as not only to excite the anger of Victor Hugo, but the quarrel became so violent that a duel was determined upon.

Happily, while the seconds were arranging the details of meeting, the parties came to terms. M. Harel acknowledged himself in the wrong, but still held to his claim for a new drama. Victor Hugo acquiesced in the demand, and at the end of August the irascible manager was informed that "Marie Tudor" had been completed, and that it was quite at his service.

Before concluding this notice of "Lucrèce Borgia," or rather of its first performance (for the reproduction of Victor Hugo's dramas will have to be recorded subsequently), it should be mentioned that an opera called "Lucrezia Borgia" was performed in Milan, at the Teatro della Scala, in 1834. It was afterwards introduced at the Théâtre Italien, in Paris, when Victor Hugo was obliged to assert his claim to the copyright.

A similar difficulty afterwards arose about "Ernani," but the matter was settled amicably.

CHAPTER XV.

ORIGINALLY entitled "Marie d'Angleterre," the play of "Marie Tudor" was performed at the Porte-Saint-Martin on the 6th of November, 1833.

This important piece cannot be analyzed here, but it must suffice to say that its interest as an historical drama concentrates itself "upon the terrible reality of the formidable trio so often found in history, and here so fully depicted—a queen, a favorite, and an executioner."

The play, which covers a period of three days, is in prose. It is touching, full of bold and novel incident, and presents a striking picture of the civil discords in England at the time.

M. Harel, the manager, threw repeated obstacles in the way of its production; but in spite of the hisses that never failed to be the accompaniment of Victor Hugo's "first nights," the piece turned out a complete success.

Mlle. Georges played Marie with all her wonted fire and talent. In his *Notices Romantiques*, Théophile Gautier eulogizes her acting in this way: "It is with ever dazzled bewilderment that we recall the smile with which she opened the second act, as she lay half reclining on a pile of cushions, dressed in orange-colored velvet slashed with silver brocade, her royal hand lightly touching the brown curls of Fabiano Fabiani, who knelt at her side. Her pearl-white profile stood out from a rich and sombre background; she seemed to glitter, and, as it were, to be bathed in light; her beauty flashed with brilliant gleams, and presented the perfect personification of power inebriated by love. Before she uttered a word, thunders of applause were heard from the pit to the roof of the house."

But this applause was not long maintained. The piece had not proceeded much further when Mlle. Georges was vehemently hissed, as was also Mlle. Juliette, who took the part of Jane.

Yet in spite of this adverse reception, and in defiance, moreover, of the ridicule of Gustave Planche and his brother critics, the piece continued to draw, the proceeds being very satisfactory, and the representations numerous.

Nearly eighteen months now elapsed before Victor Hugo had another drama ready for the stage; but on the 28th of April, 1835, "Angelo," also in prose, was produced at the Théâtre Français. In this drama the author has said that it was his design to depict two sad but contrasted characters—the woman in society, and the woman out of society. The one he has endeavored to deliver from despotism, the other he has striven to defend from contempt; he has shown the temptations resisted by the virtue of the one, and the tears shed over her guilt by the other; he has cast blame where blame is due—upon man in his strength, and upon society in its absurdity. In contrariety to the two women, he has delineated two men, the husband and the lover, one a sovereign and one an outlaw, and by various subordinate methods has given a sort of summary of the relations, regular and irregular, in which a man can stand with a woman, on the one hand, and with society in general, on the other.

In all the dramatic works of this great writer, which are invariably as full of instruction as they are thrilling in interest, it is ever by the method of social antithesis that he proceeds to his point. Every scene of this masterpiece is overflowing with passion, and is written in a vivid and sparkling style. It was a triumph alike for author and actor. Incidents succeed one another with rapidity, and are as startling in their ingenuity as they are natural in their power and touching in their pathos.

Besides moving its audience alternately to shouts of applause and tears of sympathy, "Angelo" was the cause of a bitter rivalry between Mlle. Mars and Madame Dorval.

Madame Dorval, who had so much delighted the poet by her magnificent interpretation of "Marion Delorme," happened to be disengaged at the time, and Victor Hugo succeeded in obtaining her services for the Comédie Française, to undertake the part of Catarina in the forthcoming piece. Like Frédéric Lemaitre, Madame Dorval could personify romantic genius, and to a certain extent realized the ideal of the writers of the Renaissance. Her feeling, her fire, and enthusiasm would always bring down the house. Her cry of distress had all the poignancy of truth; her sobs were heart-rending, her intonation so natural, and her tears so perfect in their counterfeited sincerity, that the stage seemed to be utterly forgotten, and it appeared incredible that her agony was only simulated. Her talent was essentially modern; she actually lived in the ideas, the passions, the loves, the errors, of her time; as a dramatist, rather than a tragedienne, she followed the fortunes of the literary reformers, and thus found herself in the right place.

It may easily be imagined that Mlle. Mars, never remarkable for either amiability or good temper, took considerable umbrage at this introduction of so formidable a rival; the "tragedienne" of long-established renown conducted herself with intolerable haughtiness towards the rising "dramatist," and to such an extent did her insolence increase during the period of the rehearsals that Victor Hugo was compelled to interfere. Mlle. Mars only gave in when seriously threatened with the withdrawal of her rôle; but whenever she found herself in the presence of an audience all her rancor was totally-forgotten, and, notwithstanding the absurd headgear which she persisted in wearing, she always succeeded in meriting the ovation which, as well as her rival, she was sure to obtain. Rachel, in later days, gained one of her grand triumphs in the part now undertaken by Mlle. Mars.

Shortly after the success of "Angelo," Victor Hugo, at the request of several of his friends, made up from his romance "Notre Dame de Paris" the libretto of an opera called "La Esmeralda," of which the music, composed by Mlle. Bertin, the daughter of the editor of the *Journal des Débats*, was hissed on its performance at the Royal Academy on the 14th of November, 1836.

The libretto, which was full of poetry, life, and passion, ended with the word "fatality."

Madame Victor Hugo has pointed out that, curiously enough, the first crushing failure was not the only fatality attending a work of which M. Nourrit and Mlle. Falcon were the executants, a lady of recognized talent the composer, Victor Hugo the librettist, and "Notre Dame de Paris" the subject. The fatality seemed to pursue the very actors: Mlle. Falcon lost her voice; M. Nourrit shortly afterwards committed suicide in Italy About the same time, too, a vessel called the "Esmeralda," on her passage from England to Ireland, foundered with all her crew; and a valuable mare with the same ill-starred name, belonging to the Duc d'Orléans, ran foul of a horse in a steeple-chase and sustained a fracture of the skull.

As nearly as possible two years had elapsed when, on the 8th of November, 1838, Victor Hugo brought out "Ruy Blas" at the Renaissance, a theatre that had been built by royal permission for the special benefit of the romantic school. The drama, which was in verse and in five acts, had been written during the previous July and the early part of August; its moral contemplates the yearning of the population for higher things; its human subject is the passion of a man for a woman; its dramatic point the love of a lackey for a queen.

This play (to which, with others that were afterwards produced with better success, we shall have to refer again) was at first the subject of as much contention as any that preceded it. Notwithstanding that Frédéric Lemaitre devoted his best powers to the part of Ruy Blas, the valet and minister beloved of the queen, the piece was performed scarcely more than fifty times, being persistently hissed on every occasion.

M. Auguste Vacquerie travelled between 200 and 300 miles in order to be present at the first performance. He had known Victor Hugo for some time, and, like Paul Meurice and Paul Foucher, he remained among the number of his intimate and most devoted friends; but, at that time, the devotion and admiration of men of letters seemed utterly unable to prevail against the corrupt taste of the multitude. Years had yet to elapse before the poet's immortal works were appreciated according to their merits, and assigned the glory they can never lose. The struggle was long and fierce, but the decisive victory that he ultimately achieved has long consoled him for the injustice that he

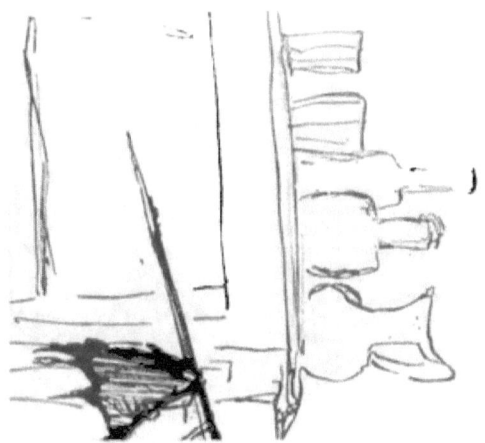

suffered at the hands of the contemporaries of his youth.

Not until 1843 did any fresh work appear on the stage from Victor Hugo's pen; but on the 8th of March in that year "Les Burgraves" was produced at the Comédie Française, being the last of his dramas that he allowed to be performed. The splendid trilogy, in respect of which the poet might fitly be compared to Æschylus, was destined to be unappreciated throughout. Æschylus, the first of Greek tragedians, after he had long stirred the emotions of the Athenians, was finally deserted by them; they preferred Sophocles to him; and, full of dejection, he went into exile, saying, "I dedicate my works to Time." And Time at last did him ample justice, though he did not live to enjoy his triumph.

Like Æschylus, Victor Hugo had now to find out that the people of Paris had discovered a Sophocles for themselves in the person of Ponsard, who proved to be a poet of very mediocre talents. His "Lucrèce" was being played at this date, and a certain clique were lauding its success, in order to insure the failure of "Les Burgraves."

After the performance of "Lucrèce," Jules Janin had introduced Ponsard to Lamartine, who received the new-comer very kindly. De Lacretelle thus writes upon the subject:

"It was quite an event. Hugo, Lamartine, Vigny, and Sainte-Beuve had long been recognized as the leaders of the romantic party, to which we youngsters were all attached. Our instincts had drawn us on towards the beautiful, and we had become the slaves of Shakespeare, whose power was revealed to us in the brilliancies of 'Hernani,' 'Marion Delorme,' 'Le Roi s'Amuse,' and 'Ruy Blas.' Now the classic party, having discovered some beauties in 'Lucrèce,' were making an effort to avenge their dethronement by exaggerating these beauties, and, as a consequence, by trying to elevate Ponsard in opposition to Hugo; to keep up a constitutional monarch, instead of acknowledging a Charlemagne. Our own love of liberty was expressed in our romantic creed. We were indignant with Lamartine for patronizing Ponsard, and we were sorely tempted to bring against him the overt charge of deserting our cause. Happy times! in which the only civil war that raged was between the party which observed the three unities, and that which set them at defiance. But such were Lamartine's estimable qualities as a

man, and his genius as a poet, that we soon got over our annoyance, and gradually forgave him for regarding Ponsard with favor." [*]

This confession on the part of one of Lamartine's most devoted admirers gives a very good idea of the state of public feeling at the time of the representation of "Les Burgraves." The classics lifted up their heads again at the appearance of Ponsard, and it is impossible to withhold an expression of regret that Lamartine's name should be associated with their efforts at revival.

Considerably disturbed at the resuscitated vitality of their classic rivals, Auguste Vacquerie and Paul Meurice set themselves to work to reorganize the youthful alliance of 1830, going for that purpose to Célestin Nanteuil, and asking him for "three hundred Spartans ready to conquer or die in defending their Thermopylæ against the hordes of the barbarians."

Nanteuil, who had been a bold champion in all the battles that had been fought, shook his long hair and sighed. Turning to Vacquerie, he said,

"Go, tell your master that there are no young men now; to enroll three hundred would be utterly impossible!"

He was right; the rising generation had ceased to be enamoured of poetry; they had begun to think about getting rich, rapidly becoming "*embourgeoisés.*"

Although the talent of the author may be said to have reached its apogee in this work, which may be declared to be Titanic in its power, yet the representation of "Les Burgraves" was not allowed to proceed without perpetual excitement; jeers and hisses never ceased to mingle with the applause. The piece was only performed thirty times.

Very sharp were the criticisms both in the *Revue des Deux Mondes* and the *Gazette de France*, neither of which could forgive M. Hugo for putting forward independent views in politics. Only two journals spoke favorably of the work—the *Messager*, in which M. Édouard Thierry maintained that the poet was being driven from the stage, just as men of mark were ostracized by the Athenians when they were weary of them; and the *Presse*, in which Théophile Gautier wrote to this effect:

"What marvellous ability it has demanded thus to revive an epoch that had faded in the

---

[*] Henri de Lacretelle's "Lamartine et ses Amis."

obscurity of the past! What a gigantic effort, nerved with the vigor of an architect of the Middle Ages, it has taken to build up the impregnable fortress, with its walls traversed by gloomy galleries, its vaults thrilling in their mystery, its ancient family portraits, and its suits of armor that murmur still so strangely, as if they continued to be haunted by the forms that wore them! What wondrous power of imagination was necessary to blend the legendary phantoms with living persons, and to supply appropriate discourse to imperial lips! In our day there is no one except M. Hugo who is capable of giving the epic tone to three great acts, or of maintaining their lyric swing. . . . Every moment seems to produce a magnificent verse that resounds like the stroke of an eagle's wing, and exalts us to the supremest height of lyric poetry. The play is diversified in tone, and displays a singular flexibility of rhythm, making its transitions from the tender to the terrible, from the smile to the tear, with a happy facility that no other author has attained."

This judgment has now become the universal judgment of posterity, but at that time the storm of contention was so violent that Victor Hugo felt it useless to contend against it, and resolved that he would bring out no more dramas on the stage. He has kept steadfastly to his resolution, and none of his then unpublished works have since been performed; and when it is submitted to him that there is no fear left of any hisses being heard now, and that he ought not to deprive the world of any of the productions of his genius, his answer is invariably the same. He says,

"My decision is final. Under no pretext shall any more of my plays appear on the stage during my life."

The pieces of which we speak are locked away with some other manuscripts in an iron chest, and only a few favored friends have had the privilege of hearing them read by the master in his own rare and perfect manner. They are called "Torquemada," "La Grand'mère," "L'Épée," and "Peut-être Frère de Garoche;" and there is likewise a pantomime, "La Forêt Mouillée," in which trees and flowers are made to talk.

Having indicated the philosophical range of Victor Hugo's dramatic writings, it yet remains for us to point out how they brought about, to a certain extent, the revival of the representation of love upon the stage.

Charles Nodier, in epitomizing the literary history of the classic period previous to 1830,

has remarked that love had come to play a most unimportant part, and that since Malherbe, "whose appearance might very well have been dispensed with," the classical school had exhibited a positive antipathy to that sentiment; and in his own discriminating way this able critic goes on to observe that except in a few scenes by Molière, a small number of effusions by La Fontaine, some outbursts of Phèdre and of Ariadne, and some tears of Andromache, some fine passages in the "Cid," and a magnificent hemistich by Sertorius, the classics had made it clear that they understood no more of love than of liberty.

And in his own brilliant style Nodier expresses his indignation that a literature based upon the poetry of love should no longer be understood by its natural interpreters; and he inquires, with considerable warmth, how it had happened that metaphysics, affected rather than subtle, had been introduced by people of culture into the affairs of the heart, and why sentiment had grown as pedantic as the philosophy of the Encyclopædists, and whence had come the voluptuousness as foul and brutal as the *spinthrées* of the Parc-aux-Cerfs. Convinced in his own mind that love had no longer any part in the literary productions of the present century, just as it had no part in the marriages of the middle classes, he went on to affirm that it had taken refuge among "the people" — that asylum for all elevated human thought that society rejects, because it is among the people that all the elements of civilization are preserved, developed, and reanimated, even as it is in the earth that the germs are concealed which renew the blossoms of the spring.

With Romanticism, and with Victor Hugo as its representative, love found its regeneration. Its heroes were taken from the people, and inspired with the passions of the people; they were the "Hernani," the "Marion Delorme," and the "Ruy Blas" of the stage. These are characters that live and weep and suffer with a common humanity; as such they have become types—that is to say, they are the embodiment of a truth, the expression of an idea, and at the same time the sign of a creation.

Now creation, or invention, is the stamp of genius. The commonplace artist simply copies; the true artist gives animation to an individual being by making it the representative of an entire group. The classics were reproducing the types of antiquity, copying their models with unvarying precision; there was to them only the one ideal of beauty in literature as in painting; and, consecrated as that was by the admiration of ages, they did not venture to acknowledge any other. Why should they desist, they asked, from admiring what the world had never ceased to admire before?

Thus the road to success was to be subservient to the established taste, and to run along the common groove. To deviate from the accustomed path was only to court insult and derision.

But the romantics had the audacity to brave that derision. They saw that the time was come for producing something new, even at the risk of rendering themselves liable to indecorous violation of custom; they were persuaded that the national genius should no longer be denied the exercise of that faculty of invention in which it was so especially strong, declaring that liberty should not be to them a mere empty sound, however much it had been disputed hitherto — sometimes in the name of Aristotle and the Greeks, sometimes in the name of the Sorbonne, the University, or the Academy, and sometimes in the name of Liberty herself. It is for Victor Hugo that Charles Nodier goes on to claim the honor of being, after Rabelais and Molière, one of the most original geniuses that French literature ever saw; but his talent was of the very kind that explains the aversion with which he was regarded by the incapables who, by their intrigues, contrived to hold their own, and to prevent his productions from being performed on the stage.

Political chicanery had much to do with the literary persecution; and in reference to this Victor Hugo remarks how strange it was that the prejudices, feuds, and plots that he had to encounter should have such solidity that they could be piled up into a barricade that should effectually close the door of a theatre.

It was a barricade, however, upon the demolition of which Victor Hugo was determined. It remained undisturbed through the earlier years of Louis Philippe's reign; but in 1837 the poet commenced another suit before the Board of Trade to compel the Comédie Française to complete their engagements with him by performing his plays, and to compensate him for the long delay in producing them.

M. Paillard de Villeneuve was Victor Hugo's counsel, and acquitted himself well. He pointed out the injustice of a theatre supported by the State becoming the monopoly of a clique; he detailed all the particulars of the covenant which had been made between the Comédie Française and the plaintiff; he denounced the party-spirit that had threatened to withdraw the State grant if the "innovators" were allowed to have their way; and he concluded by asserting that no pieces had ever realized greater profits, and that even now, while they were prohibited in France, they were drawing large and appreciative audiences in London, in Vienna, in Madrid, in Valladolid, in Moscow—in short, everywhere except in Paris.

Following his counsel, Victor Hugo rose and made a few extempore remarks, to show how the manager of the Théâtre Français had applied for his pieces, but now had allowed it to be seen that he had two faces, or rather two masks—one of which he wore to deceive authors, and the other to delude justice.

Judgment was given in his favor. The Board sentenced the Comédie Française to pay 6000 francs as damages, and bound the company over to perform "Hernani," "Marion Delorme," and "Angelo" without further delay.

Against this judgment an appeal was lodged before the Royal Court in December; and when the matter came on for trial, Victor Hugo pleaded in person, and represented that a small clique, in ambush behind the Minister of the Interior, was putting forth its energies to keep the stage closed against a new and rising school of literature, simply for no other reason except that the new school entertained ideas that were not in accordance with their own.

Amid a general expression of approval, the court upheld the previous judgment, dismissing the appeal. In this way justice at last asserted her right in opposition to the ministerial clique.

"Hernani" was the first of the disputed pieces to be reproduced. It was universally applauded; and, in order to account for the favor with which it was received, a classic critic issued a review to the effect that Victor Hugo, the author, had altered nearly every line!

CHAPTER XVI.

'Les Orientales."—A Portrait of Victor Hugo.—Respect Inspired by the Past.—Changes of Residence.—
The House in the Rue Jean-Goujon.—An Attempt at Murder.—The *Revue des Deux Mondes.*—M. Buloz.—
M. Xavier Marmier.—Domestic Life.—'' Les Feuilles d'Automne.''—Manuscripts.—'' Les Chants du
Crépuscule.''—'' Les Voix Intérieures.—'' Les Rayons et les Ombres.''

Thus did Victor Hugo achieve the triumph of liberty for literature; hereafter he would become the champion of liberty in politics. All that he did and all that he spoke had but one single aim—the emancipation of the human race.

With the object of combining into a continuous narrative the account of what Victor Hugo calls his "attempt at drama," we have collected his various plays into a group by themselves, but for this purpose have been led to depart somewhat from the chronological order of his publications. It will consequently be necessary now to go back a few years to take his lyrical compositions into review.

"Les Orientales" first appeared in 1829. These poems, with their bright and sparkling color, mark what we may call the poet's second lyric style; they are a series of Eastern visions, full of imagery as bright as it is pure. The cadence of their rhyme is full of harmony, and beneath the skill of the artist's hand the Oriental landscapes spring forth to life; while simultaneously the poet extols the most generous sentiments, the love of independence and the spirit of patriotism.

After describing Navarino and the lightning, he passes with a charming facility from the proud demand of the Greek child for ammunition to the idyllic reveries of "Sara la Baigneuse;" and, as a reviewer has pointed out, "never had the material aspect of things been so vividly depicted, and never had French versification exhibited such picturesqueness, grace, and melody."

The author of "Les Orientales" has been reproved for drawing an East that is entirely imaginary, having nothing real or historical in its character. Asked what was the good of the book, he replied that he really did not know; he had only to say that the idea had entered his head one summer evening as he was watching the sunset at Vanves, according to his wont, and that he was not aware that there was any forbidden fruit in the garden of poetry.

Criticism, however, did not prevent the volume from reaching a seventh edition in the course of a few weeks: it was the first work in which the author gave free scope to his imagination, while retaining his own peculiar style. One reviewer has observed that the poetry might fairly be likened to the Gothic architecture of the fifteenth century, being ornate, fanciful, and florid; and that its diversity, embracing every form of conception from the love-ballad to the war-song, vindicates the claim for the author that he had never been surpassed in flexibility and fertility of thought.

The appearance of the book redoubled the admiration felt for Victor Hugo by his disciples; and in the following year Théophile Gautier, the most enthusiastic of them all, begged for an introduction to the "grand chef." His account of the interview, which he has written in his own fashion, is worth recording, as giving a characteristic portrait of the poet at this period. He writes, in his "Notices Romantiques:"

"After all our battles in his behalf, we felt that such an introduction was little short of our right, and it could readily be accomplished, as either Gérard de Nerval or Petrus Borel would take us to the house. But, to say the truth, we were overpowered with shyness at the thought of our wish being actually fulfilled, so that it was a sort of relief to find, from time to time, that something had occurred to prevent our keeping the appointment with Gérard or Petrus. The very delay enabled us to breathe more freely.

"Twice did we mount his staircase, our feet dragging as if they were shod with lead; in our excitement, the sweat stood upon our brow; we laid our hand upon the knocker and our terror became too much for us; we turned, and, taking four stairs at a time, made a hurried retreat, our friends meanwhile standing and laughing at our alarm.

"But the third attempt proved more successful. Having gained a few moments' grace for our legs to recover from their tottering, we took a seat on the stairs, when suddenly the door was open, and lo! himself the

en sceptre for our encouragement. But he was too much accustomed to see small poets in a state of swoon to exhibit any astonishment. He courteously raised us from our seat, and, observing that he would give up the walk on which he was about to start, he led the way into his study.

SARA LA BAIGNEUSE ("LES ORIENTALES").

centre of a flood of light, like Phœbus Apollo in his glory, there stood Victor Hugo!

"Like Esther before Ahasuerus, we were ready to faint; it was almost a matter of surprise that the monarch did not, like the satrap to the beautiful Jewess, extend his gold-

"Heine has related how, when he was going to have an interview with Goethe, he prepared an elaborate speech beforehand, but when he found himself in the great man's presence he could think of nothing better to say than that the plum-trees on the road between Jena and Weimar bore plums that were very nice when one was thirsty; whereupon the Jupiter Mansuetus of German poetry smiled gently, perhaps more flattered by his visitor's bewilderment than he would have been by the most finished harangue and by the most glowing eulogium. Just so was it with us! Our eloquence was mute: the long apostrophe of praise which we had spent whole evenings in composing all came to nought!

ment, rose above his calm and earnest countenance: the beauty of that forehead was well-nigh superhuman; the deepest of thoughts might be written within, but it was capable of bearing the coronet of gold or the chaplet of laurel with all the dignity of a divinity or a Cæsar. This splendid brow was set in a frame of rich chestnut hair that was allowed to grow to considerable length behind. His face was closely shaven, its peculiar paleness being relieved by the lustre of a pair of hazel

VICTOR HUGO AT THE AGE OF TWENTY-EIGHT.

"Gods, kings, fair women and poets can be stared at with more impunity than ordinary mortals. Victor Hugo was manifestly not in the least disconcerted by the intense admiration with which we fixed our gaze upon him.

"He was then twenty-eight years of age, and nothing about him was more striking than his forehead, that, like a marble monu-

eyes, keen as an eagle's. The curved lips betokened a firm determination, and, when half opened in a smile, displayed a set of teeth of charming whiteness. His attire was neat and faultless, consisting of black frock-coat, gray trousers, and a small lay-down collar. Nothing in his appearance could ever have led any one to suspect that this perfect gentleman was the leader of the rough-bearded, dishevelled set that was the terror of the smooth-faced *bourgeoisie.*

"Such was Victor Hugo. His image as we saw it in that first interview has never faded from our memory. It is a portrait that we cherish tenderly; its smiles, beaming with talent, continue with us, ever diffusing a clear and phosphorescent glory!"

Enthusiastic as this outburst is, it bears its own special testimony to the respect that Victor Hugo had gained at an age when poets are ordinarily only just emerging into fame. Already he had inspired men scarcely younger than himself with a veneration that did not arise solely from the works that he had published, but was to be attributed in a measure to the dignity of his private life and the worth of his moral character. Although a member of the Cénacle, and living in close intimacy with his literary contemporaries, he never lost his courteous reserve and gentle gravity; he was kind yet serious, cheerful yet not familiar, many of his most fervent supporters never knew him intimately, and only a few of his associates ever ventured to say to him "thee" or "thou." He has been insulted and slandered, but never treated with contempt; and we shall subsequently have occasion to notice the personal influence he exercised upon all who were brought into contact with him.

Since 1828, when he had left the Rue de Vaugirard to take up his abode at 11 Rue Notre Dame des Champs, all the men of letters who visited him had come to regard him as their master. Among those who called upon him most frequently was Louis Boulanger; another constant visitor was Sainte-Beuve, who owned that Victor Hugo had taught him a method in the art of poetry, instructing him both in style and versification. He never hesitated to declare that the great leader of Romanticism had captivated him from the first day he saw him.

Every evening in Victor Hugo's house was at this period devoted to readings, to which both his daughter Leópoldine and his little son Charles, a chubby boy nicknamed Charlot, were invited to listen, while Victor, the baby, slumbered in his cradle; the family party being frequently increased by Alfred de Musset, Émile Deschamps, Gustave Planche, Mérimée, Béranger, and Paul Foucher, who, himself a noble-hearted and imaginative writer, never ceased to regard his distinguished brother-in-law with loving admiration.

The house in the Rue Notre Dame des Champs, in which so many fine verses were composed, is now destroyed; it had a garden on one side and a court-yard on the other: the landlady occupied the ground-floor, the poet had the floor above. The court-yard was approached by an avenue of trees shut in by a wall. The residence suited Madame Victor Hugo well enough, but her stay in it was brought to rather a sudden end; for, after the performance of "Hernani," the apartments of the author were besieged by such an influx of visitors, especially late at night, that the landlady declared she could not have her rest disturbed in that way, and accordingly gave her tenants notice to quit. They moved to the Rue Jean-Goujon, a street then being formed in the Quartier François I. At that time the house they occupied was the only one finished; it was afterwards distinguished as No. 9; all around it were gardens and the Champs Élysées, then in a very desolate condition, but affording sufficient solitude to enable Victor Hugo, according to his habit, to compose as he walked. The unfinished thoroughfare was remarkable for a great bowling-alley, enclosed by a hoarding, which was a favorite Sunday resort for the *bourgeois.*

The change of residence did not bring any immediate comfort. Just at that period the Revolution of 1830 broke out, fighting went on in the Champs Élysées, and bullets perpetually whistled round the solitary house in the Rue Jean-Goujon, so that it was considered desirable to send the most valuable part of the property away to the Rue du Cherche-Midi. It was not long, however, before peace was restored.

It was Victor Hugo's habit to go out after dark and wander about for hours composing either some verses, a scene of a play, or a chapter of a romance, which he would commit to paper on his return, and, notwithstanding the various dangers that threatened him, he persisted in always going alone. The fury that "Hernani" excited was quite alarming. One dramatic author, whose name, in spite of his marvellous memory, Victor Hugo has quite forgotten, sent him a challenge; and the poet received many letters that were not only insulting, but menacing. Madame Victor Hugo has mentioned one of them which ran to this effect: "If you do not withdraw your vile play, you shall soon be sent beyond the taste of bread."

Victor Hugo only smiled at all this; but

one night, after returning from a stroll in which he had composed a page of the "Feuilles d'Automne," he lighted his lamp, and was writing at about two o'clock in the morning, when he heard a loud report, and immediately felt the window-pane at his side shivered to atoms. In vain he looked down into the street; not a soul was visible; but on examining the room he discovered that a bullet had passed only a few inches above his head, making a hole right through a picture of Boulanger's that was hanging on the opposite wall. He put out his lamp and went to bed; but he made no report of what had happened, and took no measures to ascertain who was the would-be assassin.

In the house in the Rue Jean-Goujon, the ground-floor was occupied by the owner; the floor above had been taken by Victor Hugo; over him were two more stories, in one of which resided Général Vicomte de Cavaignac, the uncle of Godefroy and Eugène Cavaignac, and whose son was afterwards made a French peer; the uppermost floor of all being the lodging of Baron de Mortemart de Boisse, of whom Émile Deschamps, who ever loved his joke, used to say that he was neither "*baron* nor *mort,* nor *de Boisse,* but simply *emart.*"

This Mortemart de Boisse, who was brother-in-law to the Vicomte de Cavaignac, was then editor of the *Revue des Deux Mondes,* a periodical now of world-wide celebrity, though for some years after it was started (in 1829) by Ségur-Duperron and Mauroy it was a publication of comparatively no importance, and devoted principally to geography. The editor informed Victor Hugo that the proprietors were anxious to dispose of it, and asked him whether he knew of any one who was likely to be a purchaser. It happened that quite recently M. Buloz had had a small legacy, and he had confided to Victor Hugo his desire to start a journal. To him the poet communicated what De Cavaignac had mentioned; the matter was soon negotiated, and thus M. Buloz became the proprietor of the review. He at once requested Victor Hugo to be a contributor; to this application Victor Hugo replied that he could not write for him regularly, but consented to his publishing the account he had written of his journey to the Alps in company with Nodier and Lamartine.

As the success of the review became established, M. Buloz became more urgent in his solicitations.

"My subscribers," he said, "are full of inquiries about you, and when I tell them Hugo is the greatest poet of the age, they naturally say, 'Then give us Hugo.'"

But the poet's answer never deviated; he invariably maintained that he was not disposed to write in magazines, till Buloz, irritated with disappointment, rejoined,

"Be it so; but mark you, henceforward *my* journal is not *your* journal."

And forthwith the *Revue des Deux Mondes* changed its tone of admiration into the most furious attacks upon all Victor Hugo's productions. M. Buloz never forgave him.

Another picture of the poet in his home has been sketched by M. Xavier Marmier, a young man devoted to art, and subsequently a distinguished writer in the *Revue,* and an Academician. One evening, in the winter of 1831, he presented himself in the Rue Jean-Goujon; he had no letter of introduction, but, convinced that any sincere lover of literature would be sure of a welcome, he called to submit a book of poems to the poet, and to request his criticism and advice, which he knew would be equally wise and candid. Ushered into a large room, furnished with simple and yet elegant taste, he was struck by the womanly beauty of Madame Victor Hugo, who had one of her children upon her knee; and when he saw the poet sitting reading close by at the fireside, he was vividly impressed with the resemblance of the entire scene to one of Van Dyck's finest pictures; and, although it is now fifty years ago, he retains all the clearness of his first impression.

It is in a new aspect that we have now to see the poet.

Family affection had ever been a deep feeling of his heart, but the "Feuilles d'Automne," which next appeared, revealed to what extent paternal love had now asserted its hold upon him. He sings no longer of the woman of his early love, but he dwells upon the praises of the mother, and henceforward seems to have an infinity of tenderness to lavish upon his children, who, while they charmed him by their sprightly grace, yet brought him much anxiety and care.

Justly are the "Feuilles d'Automne" still esteemed the most touching of all his lyrics. In them he dwells upon all his inmost joys, and, as M. Alfred Nettement writes,

"His lay is of what he has seen, of what he has felt, of what he has loved. He sings of his wife, the ornament of his home; of his children, fascinating in their fair-haired beauty; of landscapes ever widening in their horizon; of trees under which he has enjoyed a grateful shade."

Here, in what perhaps may claim to be the most finished of all his works, he records his sickly infancy, and his love for his affectionate mother and his honored father. Not only has the power of his style developed itself marvellously, but his ideas have widened so as to embrace a new and beautiful life. Whatever sadness and disappointment might arise, all seemed to be cheered, if not dispelled, by the unfailing pleasures of family union. He takes a retrospect of the past; he wonders how the happy hours have sped away so rapidly, and exclaims:

" Years of my fleeting youth! did I e'er do you wrong,
    That you so swiftly on your transit haste along
        And leave me to complain?
    What have I done? No more your smiling joys ye
    bring,
    No more ye carry me enraptured on your wing;
        My heart must sigh with pain!"

And then he asks himself where suffering humanity may find relief; and, shrinking from the destiny before him, utters a murmur of resignation somewhat in this strain:

" Forget, forget the past! and let th' unresting air
    That wafted once our youth, our waning lives now
    bear
        On to the mystic shore.
    Nought of ourselves is constant; perishable all;
    The very shadows that we cast upon the wall,
        Seen henceforth never more!"

But this philosophy, sombre as it is, is, after all, no cry of desperation. Though the poet, himself a type of humanity, may groan and travail, his tears are all stayed by the thought of the smiles of those he loves.

Sainte-Beuve, who subsequently became a freethinker, reproached the author because in his book he had forgotten God, and Planche reviewed it with his wonted spitefulness; it was, moreover, published just at the crisis of a revolution, but neither political agitation, severe criticism, nor theological reproof availed to diminish its circulation. It was soon in the hands of every one. The verse captivated alike by its rhythm and its genius, and was felt to have the highest of all charms—that it appealed to all, and could be understood by all.

Happy in what he had accomplished, Victor Hugo did not rest from his labors; but though he was giving new life to the stage by his dramas, and creating romances stirring in their novel interest, he continued to work

as a poet, and in 1835 produced "Les Chants du Crépuscule."

Such was the title that the poet elected to prefix to his new volume, as indicating the general gloom of twilight and uncertainty that seemed to be settling upon society and the world in general. It was almost as if a note of interrogation were appended to every thought as it arose in the mind. As compared with what had gone before, the book exhibits the same ideas; the poet is identically the same poet, but his brow is furrowed by deeper lines, and maturity is more stamped upon his years; he laments that he cannot comprehend the semi-darkness that is gathering around; his hope seems damped by hesitation; his love-songs die away in sighs of misgiving; and when he sees the people enveloped in doubt, he begins to be conscious of faltering too. But from all his temper of despondency he quickly rallies, and returns to a bright assurance of a grand development of the human race.

Meanwhile, over this uncertainty, political and social, he breathes out his poetic soul; midway between what is positive and negative, he will not despair, but ventures to hope. He discerns the sound of the waves of human life as they roll along, sometimes placid and sometimes angry, just as the sea-breeze will carry across the summit of the cliff the murmur of the rippling water or the boisterousness of the raging breaker.

The Revolution of 1830 was a popular movement; he divines not what it would produce; he has a presentiment that what it established would be void of advantage, and yet he knows not wherewith to replace it:

" And yet, what matter? we may sleep or wake,
    The world around its destined course will take,
    But if for weal or woe man knoweth not;
    The age approaches its unerring lot!

" And hark! from yon horizon's farthest bound
    There breaketh forth a vague and mystic sound;
    Upon that distant margin fix thine eyes,
    The shade shall deepen, or the star shall rise!

" And anxious thus the doubtful east to scan,
    The poet hears the mingled plaints of man;
    He hears the saddened sigh of weary life,
    He marks the uproar of a nation's strife.

" And yet, amid the sadness of his song,
    A gentle echo doth its note prolong—
    Echo of noblest dreamings of the soul,
    That should each waiting, harassed heart console!"

Intermingled with such verses as these are songs of pity and of indignation. The poet consigns to the pillory the man who betrayed

"LES FEUILLES D'AUTOMNE."

the Duchesse de Berri, and he enters his protest against insults being heaped upon fallen woman; he meditates as he works, desiring that his poetry should be the instructor of his own soul, according to what he wrote some years later.

After a diligent prosecution of his philosophical and social studies, Victor Hugo, in 1837, published a new volume entitled "Les Voix Intérieures." He dedicated it to his father, as one whose name was not originally inscribed upon the Arc de l'Étoile, although the government ultimately rectified the omission.

The poet in this production regards life under its threefold aspect—at home, abroad, and at work; he maintains that it is the mission of the poet not to suffer the past to become an illusion to blind him in the present, but to survey all things calmly, to be ever stanch yet kind, to be impartial and equally free from petty wrath and petty vanity; in everything to be sincere and disinterested. Such was his ideal, and in accordance with it Victor Hugo spared no effort to improve the minds and morals of men in general, and by his poetry, as well as by his romances and his plays, he desired to constitute himself the champion of amelioration.

With that scornful severity to which he ever yielded, Planche consigned the volume to oblivion; but, in defiance of all condemnation, its power and animation were too plain to be overlooked. It contains magnificent outbursts on the fate of empires side by side with tender appeals to the tiny child whom he addresses as

"The little bandit with the rosy lips."

His references to children are very touching. After reproving his own children for having burned some of his verses, he immediately feels compunction, "recalls," as he says, "the startled birds," asks their pardon for scolding them, and tells them that in their absence his life grows weary:

"Come back, my children! hope before you lies:
For you too soon 'tis folly to be wise:
Not yet has trouble mingled with your fate;
You know not yet the cares that men await.
Yes, come, my children, come and bring the smile
That shall the weary poet cheer awhile!"

As to this entire work, Victor Hugo has himself defined it as exhibiting

"How, stone on stone, two sacred columns rise,
Where creed on creed extinct and fallen lies;
Columns that time is impotent to move—
Respect for age, for children holy love!"

In 1840 Victor Hugo submitted his next work, "Les Rayons et les Ombres," to the public, having already read it at the house of M. de Lacretelle, where Lamartine, Émile Deschamps, Jules Le Fèvre, and many other literary men were accustomed to resort. In this he claims the right of expressing his good-will for all who labor, his aversion to all who oppress; his love for all who serve the good cause, and his pity for all that suffer in its behalf; he declares himself free to bow down to every misery and to pay homage to all self-sacrifice.

The theme of Victor Hugo's poetry, just as it was the aim of his life, was *liberty of thought*. This will be developed more completely in a subsequent chapter which we shall devote to his political opinions, but at present we are occupied solely with the lyrical compositions of his earlier years.

In this the last of the series there are not many pieces that are purely political, although various allusions are continually made to the generally discouraging aspect of affairs at the time in which they were published; and it was in consequence, perhaps, of the lack of anything to arouse enthusiasm in the condition of the national life that the poet felt himself thrown back upon the joys of home and the beauties of nature. Thus he dwells upon the memories of childhood—the old home where the birds sang and his mother smiled, the old scenes now tenanted by other occupants, careless of all interests but their own. These are touched with a delicacy and a power that must be owned to be very attractive.

Never does Victor Hugo fail either to denounce the selfish or to sympathize with the suffering. As in "Les Voix Intérieures" he lashes the heartless Dives who lives only for his gold, dead to every sentiment of generosity—so in "Les Rayons et les Ombres" he gazes upon the poor girl, the daughter of the people, singing in contentment and simplicity over her work, and bids her to be industrious and pure, and listen to no counsel but that of virtue.

Though he admired Voltaire, he had nothing but the most earnest protests to deliver against that sceptical Voltairianism that was becoming the watchword of the middle classes; for, notwithstanding that the romantics had declared war against the ancient literary régime, they were by no means of the mind to accept the guidance of this new philosopher.

Go, my soul, refined and pure,
  In the peaceful concert sing!
Go, thou sacred flower, and bloom
  By the desert's lonely spring!
Dreamer, seek thy rest discreet
In the grotto's calm retreat;
  Hear, in shade, the voice of love;
Find, in glooms, the light of day—
Light that gleams with tender ray,
  Voice that whispers from above.

(Les Rayons et les Ombres.)

Onwards from the period of the Revolution of July, Victor stood forward as a socialist fighting for the amelioration of the people's sufferings; and the more he pondered, the more his sympathies enlarged. He struggled more perfectly to recognize his own mission, and he studied human codes that he might be better equipped to mitigate human hardships.

In his view, deep instruction was to be drawn alike from royal crimes and popular vices; and he held that a writer was bound to employ history so as to inspire his readers with veneration for the old, respect for women, duty to parents, tenderness to the suffering, and especially with sentiments of honor, hope, and love. And what he thus portrayed is what he has demonstrated himself to be. Various as are his productions, there is the one essential element that pervades them all; like the growth from the earth, there may be many species, but they are kept in vigor by the rising of the one sap. He believes in the unity of his own work, and, though he does not put himself forward as a civilizing artist, he has made civilization his leading principle and his loftiest aim.

Long before his exile, Victor Hugo affirmed that a poet ought to have in him the worship of conscience, the worship of thought, and the worship of nature; he should be like Juvenal, who felt that day and night were perpetual witnesses within him; he should be like Dante, who defined the lost to be those who could no longer think; he should be like St. Augustine, who, heedless of any accusation of pantheism, declared the sky to be an "intelligent" creation. Under such inspiration he has attempted to write the poem of humanity. He loves brightness and sunshine. The Bible has been his book; Virgil and Dante have been his masters; he has labored to reconcile truth and poetry, knowing that knowledge must precede thought, and that thought must precede imagination; while knowledge, thought, and imagination combined are the secret of power.

To the detractors who have risen up to traduce him, his works are the fittest reply, and Victor Hugo need never regret the attacks of his enemies, inasmuch as they have only served to accelerate his greatness. To-day he is read by all who read, and admired by all who have capacity to admire. He has gathered in the produce of the harvest of which he sowed the seed; from the first he had a confidence in the future which has now been vindicated perfectly.

A comprehensive glance at the earlier career of Victor Hugo thus far depicted cannot fail to leave before our gaze the portrait of a man pure in life, earnest in purpose, honorable and independent in action, and ever actuated by the ardent and indwelling principle of the love of liberty.

CHAPTER XVII.

"Litterature et Philosophie Mêlées."—Jacobite in 1819, Revolutionist in 1830.—The Poet's Judgment on his
Early Works.—Study of Conscience.—Thoughts upon Art.—History of the French Language.—Candida-
ture for the Académie.—Failure Thrice.—Malice of Casimir Delavigne.—Wrath of Alexandre Duval.—
Châteaubriand and Viennet.—Formal Reception.—A Satirical Quatrain.—Speeches of the New Member.

MEANWHILE, during this fine and prolific period, Victor Hugo was producing other works. Not only did he publish "Notre Dame de Paris," to which we shall have to devote a special notice hereafter, but in 1834 he committed to the press a review of the part he had been taking in literary and political matters. By putting together a number of notes of his own proceedings "during fifteen years of progress," he exhibited how a loyal mind in the time of revolution may become its own critic.

This collection of miscellaneous pieces and criticisms was published in two volumes, and was entitled "Littérature et Philosophie Mêlées." The first volume commences with the journal of a Jacobite in 1819, and declares the creed of the author of "Han d'Islande." Thence he takes the multitude, as it were, into his confidence, and reckons up every step of the ladder by which he has mounted until he comes to hold the opinions of a revolutionist in 1834; his object being to demonstrate how his line of thought has been gradually drawn out and his range of vision perpetually widened, but still how his conscience has consistently led him on in the path of progress.

In thus tracing the development of his views, he believes he is portraying the condition of mind of a large proportion of his generation, and the summary he gives becomes not simply the picture of a youthful royalist, but an instructive historical document.

The outline of what was working in his brain in 1819 was necessarily half effaced by the lapse of time, but the judgment which he passes upon his own early productions is not devoid of interest; he says:

"There were historical sketches and miscellaneous essays, there were criticism and poetry; but the criticism was weak, the poetry weaker still. The verses were some of them light and frivolous, some of them trag-ically grand; the declamations against regicides were as furious as they were honest; the men of 1793 were lampooned with epigrams of 1754, a species of satire now obsolete, but very fashionable at the date at which they were published. Next came visions of regeneration for the stage, and vows of loyalty to the State; every variety of style is represented; every branch of classical knowledge is made subordinate to literary reform; finally, there are schemes of government and studies of tragedies all conceived in college or at school."

Smartly, however, as Victor Hugo thus animadverts upon his first literary efforts, he asserts that amid the general chaos there was the fermentation of one element which would ultimately assimilate all to itself; there was an undercurrent of a spirit of liberty, which, in course of time, would modify and pervade his every thought of literature, of art, and of society.

He describes the work "as a sort of herbarium in which is preserved a labelled specimen of each of his various blossomings;" and, regarded in this light, the "Littérature et Philosophie Mêlées" offers an attractive study to any one who wishes to get a comprehensive view of the development of one of the master-minds of his age.

In the preface Victor Hugo enunciates his opinion about art; he denies having ever seriously applied the terms "classic" and "romantic" to any one, and expresses his satisfaction at the termination of the literary wars of the early period of the Restoration, making the remark that "it is a good sign of progress in a discussion when party names come to be disregarded." He asserts that style is an absolute property, and that in poetry an idea is inseparable from its style of expression. "Take away Homer's style," he says, "and you have only Bitaubé." He next proceeds to give a résumé of the history of the French language, noting its progress and anticipating that it will preserve its dignity in the hands of writers of style; and he concludes with some admirable advice to such as intend devoting themselves to letters, and bids them cherish a lofty aim and make it their ambition to appeal straight to men's hearts.

The entire composition reveals the secret of Victor Hugo's thought. His intellect is enlarging; his horizon is becoming more extensive; he feels that he can no longer be content with his lyre; he burns to throw himself into public action, and to bring his energies into contact with the great social struggles of his day. For this purpose he must make his way to the tribune.

Under Louis Philippe there were but two tribunes, the Chamber of Deputies and the Chamber of Peers. For Victor Hugo to be elected a deputy was out of the question; he was not a householder and he had no private fortune. The peerage was only open to him on condition of his becoming a member of one of the corporations from which the king nominated the peers. Of these the Académie was the chief, and accordingly for the Académie the poet resolved to become a candidate, and a vacancy occurred in 1836.

Dumas has remarked that it was a strange whim on the part of the author of the "Odes," "Marion Delorme," and "Notre Dame de Paris" to wish to become a colleague with such men as M. Droz, M. Briffaut, and M. Viennet; but, though he did not see that the title would add anything to the poet's renown, he began vigorously to canvass for votes to gratify his fancy. He called upon Casimir Delavigne, imagining that the author of the "Messéniennes" would only be too glad to support so illustrious a candidate; he found himself utterly mistaken, and in his own charming way relates how vehemently Delavigne protested that he would vote for Dumas with all his heart, but for Hugo never. Casimir Delavigne hated Victor Hugo most cordially. The reason of this antipathy, Dumas observes, he could never discover; but when he himself remarks that Delavigne, with his feeble constitution, had only produced one work, and that a very consumptive one, he really assigns the true explanation. The poet of the imperial era was sickly and asthmatic, and he detested Victor Hugo simply for his robustness and his power.

Meanwhile the Academicians had a very limited choice of candidates, and were much perplexed how to act. At length, in mere despair, they elected Dupaty, a name burdened with so light a literary reputation that its weight has long ceased to be felt.

In his defeat, Victor Hugo consoled himself by saying,

"I always thought the way to the Académie was across the Pont des Arts; I find that it is across the Pont Neuf."

In 1839 another seat fell vacant, and Victor Hugo renewed his canvass, going, according to custom, from the house of one Academician to another, but being received everywhere with the same frigid politeness. For were not the majority his sworn foes? were they not writers of the very school who were scandalized at his popularity? Nevertheless, he always jocosely said he never regretted the expense of his cabriolet fares; it was well worth the money to see these literary pontiffs arrayed in their dressing-gowns, and it was a source of infinite amusement to hear them snarl out their contemptuous judgment on his various works. Even now he can recall the stately pose of Briffaut and of Lacuée de Cessac, and remembers how, when he called upon the celebrated Baour-Lormian, the concierge was absent, but that while wandering about the passage he came upon a pair of shoes so monstrous that he knew at which door to knock. Nobody but Baour-Lormian could be the wearer of such shoes as those!

Nor does he forget how Alexandre Duval received him with ill-disguised hostility.

"What had you done to offend him?" we asked the poet, recently.

"I had written 'Hernani,'" he replied, with a smile.

It was Duval who, in a dying condition, insisted upon being conveyed to the Académie to record his vote against Hugo. When Royer-Collard saw the poor creature almost at his last gasp, he inquired,

"Who is the infamous candidate that drags this expiring mortal from his bed? Tell me, and I will vote against him."

But when he heard it was Hugo, he changed his tone, and voted in his favor.

The successful candidate in 1839 was M. Molé.

Another vacancy occurred in 1840, and for the third time Victor Hugo was unsuccessful, the choice of the Academicians on this occasion falling on M. Flourens.

At last, in the following year, 1841, he secured his election, the majority who voted for him being Lamartine, Châteaubriand, Royer - Collard, Villemain, Charles Nodier, Philippe de Ségur, Lacretelle, Salvandy, **Molé**, Pongerville, Soumet, Mignet, Cousin, Lebrun, Dupin the elder, Thiers, and Viennet. In the minority were Casimir Delavigne, Scribe, Dupaty, Roger, Jouy, Jay, Briffaut, Campenon, Feletz, Étienne, Tissot, Lacuée **de** Cessac, Flourens, and Baour. Guizot arrived too late to record his vote; Châteaubriand, a rare attendant at the Académie, took care to be in time, considering it was an event for which he might well put himself a little out of the way, and being anxious for the fourth time to render his tribute to a writer whose great future he had predicted.

A name remarkable among those who **voted** for Victor Hugo was that of M. Viennet. At the time when Victor Hugo was made a chevalier of the Legion of Honor, he wrote a letter, never very widely circulated, to the effect that he should like to claim "the cross of a chevalier for every one who had the courage to read right through any work of a romantic, and the cross of an officer for every one who had **the wit** to understand it." Poor Viennet! **he was** converted **afterwards**, and must be forgiven.

One candidate refused to stand against Hugo. This was Balzac, who subsequently presented himself in 1849, but was defeated by M. **de** Noailles, a writer whose literary talent was by no means conspicuous. Discouraged by his failure, Balzac wrote to M. Laurant Jan, begging him to convey his thanks to the *two* Academicians who had honored him with their support, and adding,

"The Académie has preferred M. de Noailles to myself. As an author I am his inferior; but in courtesy and magnanimity I **am** his superior, for I formerly retired in favor of Hugo."

Notwithstanding that many of the elections have been the issue of literary feuds, or of what is called "political necessity," the Académie as a whole contains many names that are really illustrious, and accordingly merits a high respect. But public spleen, which entertains respect for nothing, has vented itself in various epigrams on the institution, by no **means** reckoning that adoption into its society is a *sine quâ non* of genius. Victor Hugo's **congratulations on** his admission **were by** no **means universal, and** on the **very day of** his **election he received** a quatrain sent to him **under** cover by an unknown hand, and entitled "The Emperor and the Poet:"

"Ambitions both, **both with perfidious rivals matched,**
They now **the highest prizes of their hope have**
snatched:
Napoleon at the Invalides his quarters takes,
While Hugo to the Institute his entry makes!"

The poet took his **seat** on June 3, 1841, in the room of Népomucène Lemercier.

His inauguration speech opened with a brilliant picture of the rule of Napoleon. He referred to the emperor's power **as being that** before which the whole universe, **with the** exception of six contemplative poets, **was** bowing down in homage. "Those **poets,**" he said, "were Ducis, Delille, Madame **de** Staël, Benjamin Constant, Châteaubriand, **and** Lemercier. But what did their resistance mean? Europe was dazzled, and lay **as it** were vanquished and absorbed in the glory of France. What did these six resentful spirits represent? Why, they represented for Europe the only thing in which Europe failed: they represented independence: and they represented for France the only thing in which France was wanting; they represented liberty."

According to custom, he proceeded to eulogize his predecessor: he spoke of the nobleness of his life, and told how he was on terms of brotherly intimacy with Bonaparte the consul; but how, when the consul became an emperor, he was no longer his friend.

He concluded his oration by declaring how it was the mission of every author to diffuse civilization, and avowed that, for his own part, it had ever been his aim to devote his abilities to the development of good - fellowship, feeling it his duty to be unawed by a mob, but to respect the people; and although he could not always sympathize with every form of liberty which was advocated, yet he was ever ready to hold out the hand **of** encouragement to all who were languishing through want of air and space, and whose prospects of the future seemed full of gloom and despair. To ameliorate the condition of the masses, he would have every generous and thinking mind lay **itself** out to devise fresh schemes of improvement; and libraries, studios, schools, should be multiplied, as all tending **to the advancement** of the human race, and **to the propagation** of the love of law and liberty.

His harangue **was warmly** applauded by the Académie, and received **a** much more enthusiastic welcome than **the** somewhat feeble reply of M. Salvandy, who was by no means anxious to foster any new or bold litcnary theories. It was likewise highly praised by all the independent journals, which hastened to express satisfaction at the delivery of so strong an appeal for the liberty of the press.

Two years afterwards, when, according to rotation, Victor Hugo was president. Casimir Delavigne died, and accordingly it fell to his lot, by virtue of his office, to deliver a funeral oration over one who, for some inexplicable reason, had always shown himself his enemy. But to bear malice was not in his nature. In a few words he bore witness to the fine talents of Delavigne, in whom he recognized a calm and lofty soul, a kind and gentle heart, and an intellect guided by conscience; and he wound up his peroration by exclaiming, "And now let all the petty jealousies that follow high renown, let all disputes of the conflicting schools, let all the turmoil of party-feeling and literary rivalry, be forgotten! let them pass into the silence into which the departed poet has gone to take his long repose!"

On the 16th of January, 1845, Victor Hugo had to reply to the speech of M. Saint-Marc Girardin, who had been elected in the room of M. Campenon; and on the following 27th of February he had to respond to the opening address of M. Sainte-Beuve.

To pass any eulogium upon Sainte-Beuve was for him a difficult and almost a cruel task. Sainte-Beuve had once been his friend and admirer, but had long changed into an unrelenting enemy and unscrupulous critic. As far back as 1835 he had written to M. Louis Noel, who, like himself, had been one of Victor Hugo's admirers, to the following effect: "You have been, I feel, under some delusion about Hugo. . . . He was not what his friends imagined. . . . I was once fascinated with him; I have now learned to understand his true character. His pride is intense, . . . his egotism is unbounded, and he recognizes no existence beyond his own: . this is his chief fault; his other failings may be mere weaknesses to be treated with indulgence." Nor had Sainte-Beuve contented himself with these treacherous insinuations. he had gone so far as to publish in one of his books, which he named "Poison," the most slanderous calumnies against one who had welcomed him to his own fireside as a brother.

For all this, Victor Hugo had turned him off. The critic vowed that he would have his revenge, and he took it in his own fash-

ion: and on the 1st of March, 1840, he had the audacity to publish an article in the *Revue des Deux Mondes* which he entitled "Dix Ans après en Littérature," and which is a perfect specimen of literary treachery. It must have been a very difficult article to write, as the author had to contradict and renounce all his previous statements and opinions. The few extracts that follow will show that he set about the business rather awkwardly. He commences thus:

"We who have preached more crusades than one, and those not always of the most orthodox character; we who, it may be feared, have been too keen in our love of adventure, not stopping short of the rape of Helen and of an imprudent assault, now find it proper and opportune—nay, imperative—to effect a kind of second marriage and new union of reason between talents that are matured."

He goes on to explain:

"The union between classics and romanticists is a noble idea. The basis of the alliance is this: the romanticists have not fulfilled their pledges, and consequently the only alternative left to French literature is to betroth them to the classics."

He proceeds to deliver a pompous eulogium upon Châteaubriand, whom he exalts as "the pre-eminent and most lasting writer of his time; a grandsire who had seen the birth and death of many sons and grandsons," and bestows unstinted praise upon Guizot, Cousin, Villemain, Thierry, Thiers, and Jouffroy. He speaks in flattering terms of Lamennais and of Lamartine; but when he comes to allude to Victor Hugo, Sainte-Beuve has nothing but ill-concealed censure and stern rigidity. He allows, indeed, that within the last ten years he had given sufficient proof of his lyrical genius in "Les Feuilles d'Automne," and of his power as a prose-writer in "Notre Dame de Paris," and immediately goes on to say:

"Yet all these signs of magnificent promise do we forget as soon as we think of his numerous stubborn relapses, or consider the way in which he holds to theories which public opinion has already condemned. Sentiments of humanizing art, which might easily enough be praised, are utterly ignored, and M. Hugo clings with a steadfast persistence to his own peculiar style." In the reactionary movement which appeals for a moderate coalition, M. Hugo holds himself entirely aloof. He is no longer the leader of a school of thought; he is no longer an author of whom

Sainte-Beuve could write, as he had written ten years before, that "all his works are characterized by progress in art, in genius, and in intensity of emotion." He is now only "a man who shines as it were from afar; whose sole influence is upon minds that are capable of development."

Such is the extent to which an ordinarily enlightened intellect may fall when blinded by malice! Such is the depth of meanness to which a writer with an ill-balanced mind will condescend!

And now Sainte-Beuve had been elected to the Académie, and it would be the duty of Victor Hugo to respond to his inauguration speech. The occasion naturally excited the public curiosity. Tickets of admission were eagerly sought for, but no party-feeling of the audience was destined to be gratified. Not a single word of personal allusion found its way into Victor Hugo's speech, unless the following sentence, which is of doubtful interpretation, may be considered in this light: "You, as a poet, must know that those who suffer retire within themselves under a sense of uneasiness, which in fallen souls is shame and in pure souls is modesty."

It will be necessary to add only one more characteristic of Victor Hugo as an Academician.

During the first ten years in which he held his seat, from 1841 to 1851, he was a most conscientious member, attending all the debates. In common with his associates, he had to peruse the books sent in for competition and to award the prizes, but on such occasions he would never consent to make a written report, always limiting his judgment to a verbal opinion. Sometimes he found himself alone in a minority, but it nearly always turned out that his adjudication was correct.

One day, when some one was speaking of the historical dictionary which the Académie was preparing, he made the observation that, at the rate at which it was progressing, it would take about 3000 years to finish. M. Renan, afterwards his colleague, subsequently said to him,

"At first I thought your reckoning much exaggerated, but I have since verified it and found that it is perfectly accurate."

The form of our narrative has led us to leave Victor Hugo's great romance temporarily on one side, but we may now turn our attention to "Notre Dame de Paris."

CHAPTER XVIII.

"Notre Dame de Paris." — A Shawl and a Bottle of Ink. — Author's Aim in the Work. — Archæology and Philosophy. — Criticism. — Opinions of Sainte-Beuve and Jules Janin. — Victor Hugo's Erudition. — His Vocabulary. — Complaints of the *Savans.* — A Well-informed Cicerone. — Plays Adapted from "Notre Dame de Paris."—Contemplated Romances.—"Le Rhin."—A Conscientious Tourist.—Mediæval Architecture.

It was in 1831, ten years before he entered the Académie, and at the period when he was aiming at the regeneration of the stage by renovating the style of the drama, and while he was giving fresh vitality to the art of poetry, that Victor Hugo brought out "Notre Dame de Paris," a romance published in two volumes, and a work which of itself would suffice to immortalize its author's name.

He had made a contract some time previously with M. Gosselin, the publisher, to supply him with the work; but when he got into arrears with it and gave fresh annoyance to M. Gosselin, who had already been vexed at not having been the publisher of "Hernani," he was threatened with legal proceedings to compel him to fulfil his undertaking.

The original agreement had been that the manuscript should be ready by the end of 1829; but in July, 1830, not a line of it had been written. A fresh arrangement was made, including a covenant that the book should be completed by the following December. The author, however, had scarcely commenced his task when the Revolution broke out, and as the house in the Rue Jean-Goujon was in a dangerous situation, he considered it desirable to shift his manuscripts to the Rue du Cherche-Midi, and had the misfortune to find that, in the general hurry, a book of notes, the result of two months' labor, had been mislaid.

The missing chapters, which were called "Impopularité," "Abbas Beati Martini," and "Ceci tuera cela," did not appear in "Notre Dame de Paris" until the eighth edition, in 1832, after the author had recovered them. They did not, he said, affect the plot, but he inserted them in order to give a more complete view of his æsthetical and philosophical ideas.

Desiring that the manuscript should be finished under every advantage, M. Gosselin conceded a further delay, stipulating that the work should be in his hands by February, 1831, thus leaving Victor Hugo five months to accomplish it.

"The witness of his life" has informed us what steps he now took: he purchased a great gray woollen wrapper, that covered him from head to foot; he locked up all his clothes, lest he should be tempted to go out; and, carrying off his ink-bottle to his study, applied himself to his labor just as if he had been in prison. He never left the table except for food and sleep, and the sole recreation that he allowed himself was an hour's chat after dinner with M. Pierre Leroux, or any other friend who might drop in, and to whom he would occasionally read over the day's work.

Shortly before the manuscript was finished, M. Gosselin wrote to inquire in what terms the book ought to be described in the preliminary advertisements. Victor Hugo replied, "It is a description of Paris in the fifteenth century, and of the fifteenth century as far as regards Paris. Louis XI. figures in one chapter, and is associated with the denouement of the whole. The book does not pretend to be historical; nevertheless, with a certain amount of knowledge, and with a certain amount of conscientiousness, it gives glimpses of the morality, the creed, the laws, the arts, and the civilization of the period. And yet this is not the most important feature of the work; if it has any special merit, that merit lies in its being the creation of imagination, fancy, and caprice."

Universally known as this powerful work has become, it cannot be expected that we should attempt any elaborate analysis of its plot; we should only wish to throw what light we can upon the intention of the author, who, in opening up some of the aspects of the Middle Ages, has brought this particular period so vividly before us.

As an archæologist he has revived for us the monuments of ancient Paris; he has ransacked the annals of the cathedral of which the foundations and earliest portions date back to the twelfth century, and which, as the result of the mutilations of some ages and the enlargements of others, has become one of the purest of *chefs-d'œuvre* of religious architecture; that architecture which, from the first epoch of history down to the invention of printing, might be reckoned as "the great book of humanity, appealing as a force and an intelligence to the various stages of its development."

Victor Hugo has always had an intense veneration for the national architecture; he has ever tried to defend the ancient monuments from modern vandalism, and thus, to his mind, the imposing cathedral of Paris has become the symbol of art and ideas long passed away, so that he has delighted to make it, as it were, the heroine of his romance.

And to this artistic enthusiasm he has joined the erudition of the historian; he has studied and brought to light the superstitions of the Parisians of the Middle Ages; and he has thrown life into the physiognomies, alike strange and interesting, of scholars, vagrants, alchemists, poets, merchants, and magistrates, carrying us through by-ways to the Palais de Justice, conducting us from the cloister to the Place de Grève, and taking us from the Porch of Notre Dame to the Cour des Miracles, where dirt predominates, and a swarming populace of bandits keep up a tongue elsewhere unknown or rather forgotten.

Having deciphered the word ἀνάγκη upon the wall of a cell under the towers of Notre Dame, Victor Hugo took it as an epigraph of the cathedral; and, recognizing the stern fatality that urges on the career of every mortal in the turmoil of life who is not controlled by the civilized laws of duty, he represented it as the secret of the celibate priest being surrendered to love, the Bohemian being subjected to the priest, and the mother being impelled to lead her daughter to the gallows. Thus it was that, obedient to the inexorable sway of fatality, Gringoire became the type of the literary misery of the period; the same power being owned by Jean Frollo, the scholar; by Trouillefou, king of the vagrants; by Quasimodo, the ideal of deformity; and by Esmeralda, the ideal of grace — this Esmeralda being a young girl with slim figure and rich brunette complexion, arrayed in bodice of gold and variegated

skirt, dancing in the porch upon a fragment of old Persian carpet, curving her arms and striking her tambourine, and flashing lightning glances from her large black eyes.

The basis of the romance is art as exemplified in architecture, but the architecture of the cathedral becomes a magnificent framework for a drama full of excitement.

"In the style," writes Sainte-Beuve at a period when his judgment was as yet unbiassed, "there is a magical facility and freedom in saying all that should be said; there is a striking keenness of observation; especially there is a profound knowledge of the populace, and a deep insight into man in his vanity, his emptiness, and his glory, whether he be mendicant, vagabond, *savant*, or sensualist. Moreover, there is an unexampled comprehension of form—an unrivalled expression of grace, material beauty, and greatness; and altogether a worthy production of an abiding and gigantic monument. Alike in the pretty prattlings of the nymph-like child, in the cravings of the she-wolf mother, and in the surging passion, almost reaching to delirium, that rages in a man's brain, there is the moulding and wielding of everything just at the author's will."

Alfred de Musset acknowledged that the work was colossal, but professed himself unable to take in its scope.

Other critics were more pronounced; one of them, a contributor to a leading journal in Paris, giving his judgment that "'Notre Dame de Paris' is merely an insipid copy of Voltaire's 'Mérope.' The discovery of a daughter by a mother constitutes the whole plot; of invention there is absolutely nothing!"

On the other hand, Jules Janin's judgment was more than favorable. He wrote, with enthusiasm:

"'Notre Dame de Paris' is powerful and thrilling reading that leaves a terrible impression on the mind, like a distressing nightmare. Of all the works of the author, it is pre-eminently that in which his fire of genius, his inflexible calmness, and his indomitable will are most conspicuous. What accumulation of misfortunes is piled up in these mournful pages! What a gathering together there is of ruinous passion and bewildering incident! All the foulness and all the faith of the Middle Ages are kneaded together with a trowel of gold and of iron. At the sound of the poet's voice, all that was in ruins has risen to its fullest height.

reanimated by his breath. What movements are stirred up in those narrow streets, those crowded quarters, those ancient churches! What fiery, warring passions are excited in the minds of those merchants, that soldiery, those cut - throats! Each one, priest and woman alike, is arrayed in the proper garb; unless, indeed, the passion is naked, as of a beast in the wilderness!

"Victor Hugo has followed his vocation as poet and architect, as writer of history and romance; his pen has been guided alike by ancient chronicle and by his own personal genius; he has made the bells of the great city all to clang out their notes; and he has made every heart of the population, except that of Louis XI., to beat with life! Such is the book; it is a brilliant page of our history which cannot fail to be a crowning glory in the career of its author."

To add anything to such a testimony as this would be superfluous, as it would be to speak any more in praise of a work which has been lauded by Eugène Sue and by Béranger; it is worthy of the minister of which its title bears the name; it has been read only to be read again. None now would venture to disparage the romance as a work of genius; it is only about the use of a few technical terms and the employment of some obsolete expressions that there is any longer any dispute.

Undoubtedly Victor Hugo's vocabulary is very extensive, and he does not hesitate to employ terms that are by no means generally understood by the masses. He has bestowed almost unlimited time upon lexicons, and has not contented himself with the ordinary medium of communicating his thoughts; not but what his usual style is sufficiently clear, and when it suits him he can be terse and concise; it is only when he deems it necessary to make his words a picture of what he would describe that he resorts to language which was peculiar to the age in which his characters lived and acted. Erudition, he held, was not unbecoming in an author; and thus, in "Notre Dame de Paris," he reckoned it advantageous to have so far studied the glossaries of the Middle Ages as to utilize the phraseology, to revive with truth and accuracy the manners and the features of the time.

The result of this has been that certain commentators have alleged that his vocabulary has been based upon a counterfeit science, and that it would inflict unnecessary torture

upon the Saumaises of the future, who would be driven to desperation to discover the meaning of such terms as *la casaque à mahoîtres, les voulgiers, les craacquiniers, le gallimard taché d'encre, le hasteur,* and such like.

But in reply it may be urged that genuine students, worthy of the name, have not been required to make any deep researches to establish the ignorance of such critics. A very little investigation might have served to inform them that in the time of Louis XI. the *casaque à mahoîtres* was a robe with puffed sleeves; while in the chronicle of Jacques Duclere (1467) it is recorded that the highborn ladies of the court of Philip le Bon wore great *mahoîtres* on their shoulders in order to make themselves look more dressy and to show off the slope of their necks. And just so in the other cases: *voulgiers* were foot-soldiers armed with the *voulge* or *vouge,* a single-edged blade fixed to a pole; *craacquiniers* were cross-bowmen; a *gallimard taché d'encre* was simply an inkstand; a *hasteur,* a keeper of a cook-shop; the whole of which might have been ascertained by merely consulting Ducange's "Glossarium Mediæ et Infimæ Latinitatis."

A correspondent of the curious magazine called the *Intermédiaire* has remarked that the author, in order to give his romance the true archaic coloring, has gone to the fountain-head for his knowledge, and that consequently every incident and every expression may be justified by reference to Monteil's "Histoire des Français," De Sauval's "Histoire des Antiquités de Paris," and Roquefort's "Glossaire Roman."

Not content with accusing Victor Hugo of pedantry, some of the reviewers began to charge him with ignorance of grammar, the dispute turning very much upon the gender of the word *amulette,* and serving in a way to recall the remark made, we believe, by Alfred Delvau, to the effect that critics have no right "to amuse themselves like so many monkeys by picking the vermin from the lion's skin."

Notwithstanding the anxiety felt by its publisher, "Notre Dame de Paris" had an immediate success. Within a year it reached an eighth edition, and the original vignettes by Tony Johannot were replaced by some engravings by Célestin Nanteuil.* The num-

* For these engravings, four in number, Nanteuil received the sum of sixty francs—a statement that may serve to measure the liberality of publishers in Paris fifty years ago.

LA ESMERALDA.

ber of subsequent editions can scarcely be estimated.

The sensation caused by the work was not long in attracting crowds to the old basilica of Philippe Auguste, where the cicerone made a good harvest. One day while Victor Hugo was conducting a party of ladies over "his cathedral," the cicerone came as usual to render his services. On reaching the belfry-entrance above the gallery, he opened the door of a cell, and proceeded to tell his story:

"Here is the cell where the illustrious M. Hugo wrote his popular work. He never left the spot till he had finished writing. There you see his table, his chair, his bed. He took hardly any food, and that of the plainest kind."

The poet gravely thanked the intelligent verger for these historical details, and, with a gracious smile, bowed, and slipped a gratuity into his expectant hand.

Hardly had the book issued from the press before an attempt was made by a dramatist named Dubois, of the Théâtre de Versailles, to convert it into a play. This consisted of seven scenes, in three acts, Quasimodo being made the principal character. The theatrical registries make no mention of the work, to which we here refer chiefly as a literary curiosity. It was published both in Paris and Versailles, and sold by booksellers who dealt in novelties; but it was performed only a few times at the Théâtre du Temple.

Altogether of a different character was the drama in five acts compiled by Paul Foucher, Victor Hugo's brother-in-law, and brought out in 1850. This proved a great success. It was afterwards revised and modified by M. Paul Meurice, who made it adhere still more closely to the original work. In this improved form it had a long run at the Porte-Saint-Martin in 1879.

At the solicitation of M. Gosselin and other publishers, Victor Hugo consented to write some more romances, and they were advertised as being in preparation. One of these was to be called "La Quiquengrogne." It was intended to give an idea of feudal mediævalism corresponding to the picture of ecclesiastical mediævalism that had been drawn in "Notre Dame de Paris." It was to be followed by another, of which the title was "Le Fils de la Bossue." Neither of these books, however, was published; and, although they were conceived some fifty years ago, they have never yet appeared. The

romance that was next in order to "Notre Dame de Paris" was "Les Misérables."

Having now reviewed all Victor Hugo's romances as far as 1840, we may mention "Le Dernier Jour d'un Condamné" and "Claude Gueux," and leave them awhile, to be the subject of a later chapter.

Enough has been said to demonstrate how the poet had now made his mark in every form of literature so as to rank at the head of the writers of his time; and it will be seen not only how constant were the difficulties with which he had to contend, but how versatile was the power and how singular the courage that characterized all his productions.

About this time he wrote "Le Rhin," a work that exhibits another side of his genius. This consists of a series of letters, supposed to be written to a friend, giving a humorous account of an archæological tour. The style is racy, but affords the author every opportunity of illustrating his wide erudition. Under the character of a good-natured *savant*, he carries his readers from Aix-la-Chapelle to Cologne, thence to Mayence and Frankfort, visiting the numerous monuments on his way, relating the various legends connected with town, village, or castle, digressing into philosophy and politics, and introducing a number of graphic stories full of interest and amusement.

He sketches as he goes, and his drawings manifest his unbounded admiration of the scenery of the river and the old "burgs" upon its banks. As a tourist he is singularly intrepid, clinging to branches and tufts of grass, and clambering all alone to obtain views from the summit of the ruins. He describes with much minuteness the architecture that he admires, and rarely fails to vent his wrath upon white façades with green shutters. At the same time, he sees beauties where others would espy defects, and owns that he has a perfect mania for investigating old tumble-down buildings and for deciphering obliterated inscriptions, declaring that he no more gets weary of repetitions in art than a lover grows tired of painting the portrait of his mistress. At times he is indignant at the discovery of some incongruity, as spiral volutes intermingled with ogives; but at times, too, he is enchanted by arabesques that were worthy of Raphael.

His descriptions and his illustrations are equally admirable: the painter and the poet go hand-in-hand.

For the commonplace he seems to have

NOTRE DAME DE PARIS.

no eye. His affection is lavished upon the mediæval ages which he had so laboriously brought back to life; and, as he looks upon the venerable ruins, nothing stirs up his wrath more vehemently than to see what attempts have been made to embellish them in later times, and it is a very pang to his heart to find any dilapidated tower of Germany not left to the beauty of natural decay, but utilized by some hideous transformation designed as an improvement by some modern architect.

CASTLE ON THE RHINE.

(Drawn by Victor Hugo.)

CHAPTER XIX.

WHILE the rehearsals of " Le Roi s'Amuse " were going on in October, 1832, **Victor** Hugo removed from the Rue Jean-Goujon to the Place Royale.

The **house in which he took up his** residence was **No. 6, the same which it was** said had been the home of **Marion** Delorme. His reason for settling in this locality was that he **might be near Charles Nodier, who was then at the Arsenal; and it happened also about the same time that Théophile Gautier came to live at the opposite corner of the square. The poet's suite of apartments was on the second floor, and was approached by a wide and handsome staircase. A door opened into the dining - room, which was adorned with** some fine tapestry, representing scenes in the "**Romance of the Rose;**" at the farther end were two doors, one leading to the *salon*, the other to a passage **in which were** the bed-chambers; beyond **which was the** study, a room full of quaint **pieces of furniture,** and overlooking an inner **court-yard.**

The ceiling in the study was decorated with a painting by Auguste de Châtillon, called " Le Moine Rouge "—**almost** as strange a production as Louis Boulanger's " **Ronde** du Sabbat," **its subject** being a priest robed **in red** lying **full length** and reading a Bible, which is supported **by a nude** female figure. Châtillon, **although he could not** be **said to be** famous in **1823,** was acquiring a reputation which he **never was able to** maintain. He squandered away his talents, and **ultimately** died in extreme poverty, without **leaving behind** him any valuable monument **of his powers.** In 1836 he painted a picture **representing the first communion of Victor Hugo's eldest son in the church of Fourqueux, which was never exhibited, but was retained by Madame Victor Hugo in her own chamber. It is now in Guernsey. He likewise painted a portrait of Victor Hugo himself, upon which Méry, in his "Melodies Poétiques," has composed a fine ode, into which he intro-**

duced many of the leading points in the poet's life.

As **for the** *salon*, it might **almost be** described as a picture-gallery, so numerous **were the** artists, including Achille Devéria, **Célestin** Nanteuil, David d'Angers, and **others,** who sought the honor of being allowed **to** contribute to the decoration of the apartment. At one end was a high mantel-piece after **the** taste of the poet, covered with **drapery, and** holding some fine China vases; on the **left was a sort of dais, which demands especial notice, inasmuch as it has given rise to some absurd stories.**

It has been alleged that Victor Hugo, in his vanity, used to sit on a throne upon this dais beneath a canopy, and extend his hand to be kissed by his admirers, who **would mount the steps upon** their knees. As **matter of fact, there were no steps** and no throne; there was simply **some** drapery arranged in an artistic way, having a banner, that had been brought from the palace of the Dey of Algiers, as a background, under which stood a common sofa, which was ordinarily used as a seat, although occasionally it did duty as a bed. About the year 1840 Victor Hugo's bust was placed close beside it.

Some arm-chairs of the time **of Louis XV.,** made of gilt wood and covered with **tapestry, completed the furniture of the reception-room.**

Opposite the dais were three large windows reaching to the ground, and opening on to a balcony that ran the whole length of the *salon*, and overlooked the square. Here it was that the poet's **friends** would sip their coffee and chat with him until quite late, especially **on Sundays, when the gatherings** would be **most numerous. The** stone **balcony** no longer **exists; it fell down** shortly after the poet left the place.

Never was *salon* **more** hospitable. It was the resort for all who had a name in literature or art, and who came not attracted more by the glory of the master than by his kindness and affability. Among many others Pierre Dupont, the future author of "Les Bœufs," there found a welcome, enjoying a fireside where he might try his pinions, and, with seeing his friends at home, rarely going anywhere, even to visit Charles Nodier, who lived close by.

The influx of new visitors that now found their way to the Place Royale made

VICTOR HUGO'S HOUSE IN THE PLACE ROYALE.

according to Baudelaire's expression, allow the flowers of his brain to begin to expand.

For some time Victor Hugo had been in the habit of attending the receptions of Madame Ancelot, who called him "the great rebel;" but he now began to content himself some little commotion among the earlier friends of the poet, and various petty jealousies were the result. Among the older admirers of Victor Hugo who had been drawn to him by his genius were Auguste Le Prevost, the Norman antiquary, and his fellow-

10

countryman Ulric Guttinger, the poet. One day, however, Guttinger felt himself so neglected in comparison with the new-comers who were receiving such a large share of attention that he left the house in disgust, and, vowing that he would never cross the threshold again, started back to Normandy. In vain his friend Le Prevost remonstrated with him; he wrote him a letter urging him to accept Hugo's invitations as an honor; but no representations could make Guttinger overlook his grievance.

One of the most noteworthy among the new-comers, both on account of his talents and his unwavering attachment to Victor Hugo, was Auguste Vacquerie. He had come to Paris with the especial object of making the poet's acquaintance, and he has described the aspirations of his youth in a volume of exquisite poetry, which he sent forth to the world under the title of "Mes Premières Années de Paris." Born at Villequier, in La Seine Inférieure, in 1820, he commenced his education at the Lycée in Rouen; his school career being so successful as to justify him in desiring to go to the metropolis in order to devote himself to art.* His father, a ship-owner at Havre, readily acquiesced in his wish.

It was quite common at that time for the Parisian colleges to employ agents to make the round of the provincial schools, and to pick up the clever lads who would be likely to carry off the prizes in open competitions, such success on the part of their students being always attended with pecuniary advantages to the institutions themselves. One of these travelling agents offered an exhibition to Auguste Vacquerie if he would come up to the Pension Favart. His father declined the exhibition, but Auguste, nevertheless, proceeded to the pension in preference to any other, mainly because it was only a few steps from Victor Hugo's residence in the Place Royale.

The principal at the Pension Favart considered it would be best for his young Rouen student to go in for a double *second*, and Auguste consented to the proposal. Un-

fortunately, at the examination, the professor was a whimsical old man who had a special aversion to Normandy and all its people, and who, consequently, gave him only an ordinary second-class certificate.

Naturally disappointed, Auguste went to the principal and claimed his right to enter his name for the examination in rhetoric. This could not be refused him, but so irritated was the principal at the result of the former examination that he lost no opportunity of chastising the young student. One pretext for punishment was of perpetual recurrence. Although the educational department was well attended to, the domestic arrangements were miserably neglected, and the food was often so bad that Auguste refused to touch it, and made his meal from a dry crust of bread. One day when the soup was more disgusting than usual, and he was about to receive his wonted chastisement for daintiness, a messenger came in bringing the honor list from the Collége Charlemagne. A mere glance was enough to show the principal that the name at the head of the roll was that of Auguste Vacquerie. In a moment his wrath subsided, and, tasting the soup, he allowed that it was "execrable," and threatened to dismiss the cook. Thenceforward not only were the meals better served, but the successful pupil was treated with proper consideration.

At this examination it was that Auguste Vacquerie and Paul Meurice first met, the result being a sincere and lasting friendship between them. Paul Meurice, the son of a goldsmith, had great talents and a large heart; he was brother, on the mother's side, of Froment Meurice, the well-known artist. The bond of union between Auguste and Paul was confirmed in the discovery that they both "lived in the same poet;" equally to them both the name of Victor Hugo was the name of a master, of whom, in ardent enthusiasm, they were mutually ready to own themselves the loyal though humble disciples.

Never losing sight of the inducement which had originally brought him to Paris, Auguste Vacquerie ventured after a while to compose an epistle in verse, stating his ambition to be introduced to the great poet, and had it conveyed to the Place Royale. Victor Hugo, always kind to the young and obscure, replied that he should be most happy to receive a visit.

To describe the pride and ecstasy with which the young student received the invita-

---

* He has expressed his longing in a poem dedicated to Paul Meurice:

"The world had brought the wondrous echo near,
  I longed the very voice itself to hear:
But though for Paris ardently I sighed,
  Paris to me meant Hugo, nought beside;
Paris itself the shrine of Hugo's fame,
  The towers of Notre Dame proclaimed his name!"

THE SALON IN THE PLACE ROYALE.

tion would be impossible. Like Théophile Gautier, he trembled with agitation, but lost no time in availing himself of the kind permission. Victor Hugo quite appreciated the young man's devotion, and accurately discerned his talent. He invited him to dine with him nearly every week, and in a short time insisted upon his friend Paul Meurice tention to him; she constantly sent him nutritious delicacies, and when he was convalescent he felt himself bound to the poet's family by a still closer affection. In acknowledgment of the kind care that had been bestowed upon his son, M. Vacquerie begged to be allowed to place his château at Villequier at Madame Victor Hugo's dis-

CHARLES VACQUERIE.

accompanying him. The intimacy gradually grew closer; the two friends were constantly in the poet's *salon*, especially on Sundays, when nothing would delight them more than to take his sons for a walk.

Just before the close of his college career Auguste Vacquerie fell seriously ill, and Madame Victor Hugo was unwearied in her at- posal for the summer vacation. She gratefully accepted the offer, and in due time started off with her four children, all highly delighted at the prospect of visiting Normandy.

During this holiday visit Auguste's brother Charles became acquainted with Léopoldine Hugo. Falling in love almost at first sight, they were soon formally engaged, and their marriage took place in the following spring in 1843, the wedding breakfast being given at the Place Royale.

Victor Hugo expressed his good wishes for his daughter's happiness in some verses that were afterwards included in the collection published as " Les Contemplations:"

"Thy lover love, and in his constant love abide !
 That lover wooes thee, wins thee, claims thee for his
   bride.
      Fain would we keep thee lingering here awhile ;
 But now a double duty claims thy equal care.
 Leave us thy fond regrets, one tear of anguish spare,
   Then greet thy new abode with beaming smile."

Five months later this union had a fatal termination under most distressing circumstances.

The Vacquerie family property at Villequier is on the banks of the Seine, which is tidal as far as Rouen ; but the periodical rising of the water was a matter of no uneasiness to the family, who were accustomed to make excursions almost daily from Villequier to Caudebec. One of these excursions was arranged for the 4th of September, when M. Charles Vacquerie, with his wife, his uncle, and cousin, started to make a trial trip in a large new boat. They all set out in high spirits upon what was quite an ordinary outing ; but a sudden squall came on, and the boat capsized. Léopoldine had always been taught that, in the event of being upset, the safest thing to do was to cling to the boat, and accordingly she now instinctively grasped its side with convulsive alarm. Her husband was a good swimmer, and, anxious to carry her off, did his utmost to make her relax her hold. But all his efforts were unavailing ; in her agony she seemed to have embedded her finger-nails in the wood ; his very attempt to break her fingers proved ineffectual. He was but a few yards from the shore, but finding it impossible to save her, he determined not to survive her, and taking her into his embrace, sank with her in the stream. The two bodies were recovered a few hours afterwards.

They were buried in the little cemetery at Villequier. Close beside them lies Léopoldine's mother, Madame Victor Hugo, whose remains, at her own dying request, were brought hither from Brussels in 1870, under the care of her two devoted friends, Auguste Vacquerie and Paul Meurice.

Madame Victor Hugo felt her daughter's loss most acutely ; her tears fell bitterly in the home of which she was the ornament and the pride. The Adèle Foucher who had been the substance of his early dreams had now long been the presiding genius of the poet's household. Something of the dark Spanish beauty and attractive form of his wife may always be detected lurking beneath the conception of La Esmeralda, Doña Sol, Sara la Baigneuse, Thisbé, and all the other brunettes who animate Victor Hugo's poetical seraglio. Raphael perpetually reproduced the head of La Fornarina in his pictures, but Victor Hugo may be said to have set the first example among Frenchmen of a poet devoting his lyre so constantly to his wife.

A contemporary, in a work entitled " Les Jolies Femmes de Paris et de la Province," has remarked this specialty by observing how unweariedly he seeks to immortalize the companion of his joys and sorrows, illustrating his notice by the following verses, which are but a specimen of others that are similar, and which in the original make the reader hardly know whether to admire most the poet who composed or the woman who inspired them:

"To thee my duteous lyre shall sing ;
 To thee its constant homage bring !

"None but pure and lofty deed
 Can from thy pure soul proceed ;
 Soul by passion ne'er oppressed,
 Nor by anger e'er distressed !

"Give her thy blessing, whosoe'er thou art ;
 She sheds a radiance on each loving heart !
 To me a solace 'midst life's anxious fears,
 Retreat hereafter in decaying years ;
 A tutelary saint, whate'er betides,
 That o'er the Lares of my home presides !"

As Victor Hugo's fame increased, the calm serenity of his early years of married life was necessarily somewhat disturbed by the troubles and anxieties that glory brings, but in the Place Royale Madame Victor Hugo relates that they lived in much happiness with the children who were their pride and their delight. Their friend, M. Louis Boulanger, painted a portrait of the charming lady, which was exhibited at the Salon, and which received much notice, being thus described :

"A full, well-developed bust, white arms of perfect form ; a pair of plump, delicate hands that a queen might envy ; the hips high, and setting off a figure that was faultless in its contour and flexibility."

Such was the companion whom Victor

THE ACCIDENT AT VILLEQUIER.

Hugo ever cherished with the utmost tenderness. She performed her duties as a hostess with infinite grace, and her *salon* was filled with celebrities like Lamartine, who would write verses in her album, and with accomplished women like Madame de Girardin.

late it might be, Victor Hugo made it a rule to go out for a stroll by himself; and, armed with nothing but a cane, would cross the Champs Elysées and wander as far as the Arc de Triomphe. This was his favorite hour for work, and he has himself informed

AN ATTACK.

Visitors flocked daily to the hospitable dwelling, attracted both by the fascinations of the hostess and by the refinement and joyousness of the poet.

After his guests had departed, however

us that some of his finest thoughts have come to him more readily in the midnight hours of the silent streets, and in the shadow of the trees that line the pathways, than in the solitude of his study.

He continued this practice for a long time without any interruption. Once, however, an accident befell him when he stumbled over a pile of chairs that had been left in the avenue, and over which he had to clamber; and once he met with an adventure of a more startling character. As he was sauntering along near the Rue des Tournelles, he was attacked and knocked down by some pickpockets who were waiting at the corner of the street, and he would certainly have been robbed if some passers-by had not disturbed the ruffians, and made them take to their heels. The poet immediately regained his feet, and, running after the thieves, cane in hand, called out "Help! help!" but in so low a tone that it was plain he did not want the rascals to be caught.

The attack had not the least effect in making him discontinue his wanderings in the dark. He rarely referred to the incident; and, although he has since had to contend with bandits of another sort, he has never ceased to regard Paris as the securest of all the cities of the world, so long as those who concoct *coups d'état* are not lurking in ambush.

CHAPTER XX.

Victor Hugo's Politics during the Reign of Louis Philippe. — His Convictions in 1830. — Revolutionary Sentiments. — Literary Liberty followed by Political Liberty.—Connection with the Press.—Relations with the King.—Portrait of Louis Philippe.—Raised to the Peerage.—First Speeches in the Chamber.—Preludes to the Revolution of 1848.

It was the avowal of an honest and illustrious writer, "I have never passed a day without correcting some fault," and it was almost an echo of this which Victor Hugo spoke when he represented himself as a son of this century, and, alluding to his own modified sentiments, said,

" At its own folly startled, year by year,
Some error from my wakened soul gets clear !"

He is ever ready to own that he has made political mistakes, but is quite prepared for his whole life to be thrown open to the inspection of his contemporaries. His early education had the effect with him, as with many others at the beginning of the century, of introducing an apparent inconsistency into his principles. He was illogical, yet upright; a legitimist and yet a Voltairian, a Bonapartist and yet a liberal. He was a socialist groping blindly about among the things of royalty; but, amid all the discrepancies caused by the struggle in his mind between the doctrines he had been taught by his mother and the priests, and the doctrines of freedom which he subsequently grew to appreciate, he is satisfied that he never wrote a line but what was designed to promote the love of that true liberty which in philosophy is reason, in art is aspiration, and in politics is right.

The briefest outline of the internal changes of his conscience would suffice to attest the sincerity of his assertions.

By 1830 it had become impossible for him to put any confidence in the promises of the Bourbons, and he was quite prepared to swear allegiance to Louis Philippe. Nevertheless, he did not lose his respect for the past, nor could he bear that the name of Bourbon should be treated with scorn when the gray locks of the old king had ceased to be circled by a crown; but as his veneration could not blind his eyes to the faults that seemed inseparable from the dynasty, he regarded the change of government as a true and necessary step in advance.

Hitherto he had been "the man of letters," working revolution in the world of literature by his brilliant efforts; the time seemed to him now come when he was called upon to throw himself into political strife, and he joined the Revolution of July rather because it appeared to satisfy his liberal instincts than because it roused him to any enthusiasm.

His honesty was evident; for, however divergent may have been the apparent lines of principle he followed, it is incontestable that he ever kept one law, one aim, in view. Louis Blanc is correct in asserting that the unity of his life has been his one constant advance towards "the good," and his one determined ascent towards "the right;" and M. Spuller is equally correct when, in his recent eulogium, he pronounces that the three French poetical geniuses of the nineteenth century—Châteaubriand, Lamartine, and Hugo—all born outside the pale of the Revolution, proved the very men to come forward to serve and glorify the democracy; and he implies that Victor Hugo is the greatest of them all, as having defended the social truths that will be the law of future society.

Hitherto, however, Victor Hugo had never believed that the formation of a republic was practicable. At that time he could write in his "Journal de ses Idées et de ses Opinions Révolutionnaires" such sentiments as these:

" What we want is a republican government under the name of a monarchy."

" To-day is for kings, to-morrow for the people."

" Some people think that a republic means a warfare waged by those who have neither brains, money, nor virtue, against those who have all or any of the three."

" Of that republic not yet matured, but which all Europe is destined to see a century hence, my own idea is that of society governed by society itself: a national guard for its defence; a jury for its judge; a commune for its administration: an electoral college for its government."

"In such a republic the four appurtenances of a monarchy—the army, the magistracy, the cabinet, and the peerage — will be excrescences that will speedily wither and die away."

"The electoral law will be complete when its Article I. shall be — Every Frenchman is an elector; and its Article II. — Every Frenchman is eligible."

"Revolution is the embryo of civilization."

Such pronounced sentiments were altogether in advance of public opinion. At that time the citizen-king, in the eyes of the majority of the people, represented the best of republics; the republicans, themselves without power or organization, regarding the newly established monarchy as a dawn in which nothing was wanting, "not even the cock."

With age and experience Victor Hugo's old royalist and Catholic prepossessions crumbled away piecemeal; and, according to his own showing, if any fragment of them survived in his mind, it was only like a ruin at which he might gaze with veneration, but at which he could never again pour forth his devotion. He deems it a poor compliment to a man to say that he has not modified his political opinions for forty years. It is to his view equivalent to asserting that he has had no experience and gained no fresh power of thought; like praising water for being stagnant, or a tree for being dead; it is like preferring an oyster to an eagle. All opinion is liable to variation, and nothing should be absolute in politics except their morality. Movement belongs to vitality, and the political creed of a man may change without dishonor to himself, so long as his conscience remains uncorrupt and his convictions are not subordinate to his interests.

The formation of Victor Hugo's character is all the more laudable because he had made every step of his progress only by a resolute struggle with himself, never ceasing to persevere in comprehending what is right, and never flinching from the greatest sacrifices in order to attain to what is true.

There are those who have said of Victor Hugo, "He is the greatest of poets, but nothing in politics;" but they speak either maliciously, lacking his integrity, or else ignorantly, lacking his foresight. There are those likewise who reproach him for his fickleness; such, however, for the most part, have been the creatures of Louis Philippe,

who afterwards kissed the hand of the emperor, accepting offices and honors from "the man of December," while the object of their revilings, in vindication of his honesty, has stood alone and made his protest against violated law and outraged justice.

And now, after 1830, he became the reflex of the popular mind. Like the people, he seemed to hesitate, sharing their shifting emotions during the troublous reign of Louis Philippe. Checked in her aspirations, France seemed hardly to realize whether she was under a monarchy or a republic, and honest minds were led away to confound liberalism with Bonapartism, and to regard progress with a kind of suspicion; but Victor Hugo saw farther than the people. Brought face to face with the general agitation and with the rebellious spirits that were harassing the heart of society, he felt it his duty to fling himself into the conflict:

"Nought, nought but shame
To thinkers who their members maim,
And who themselves will mutilate
Sighing to leave the city gate!"

He asked himself what a government born of a population in revolt was likely to effect; and in 1832, after one of the insurrections so common at the time, when Paris was put into a state of siege, in which bloodshed appeared imminent, and the *National* published a protest to which signatures might be appended, he requested that his own name might be added to the list.

In writing to one of his friends, he said,

" I trust that they will not venture to sprinkle the walls of Grenelle with young brains, which, though hasty, were yet generous. If the guardians of public order should resolve upon a political execution, and if four brave men would rise up to rescue the victims, I would join them as a fifth. . . . Some day we shall have a republic, and it will be a good one. But we must not gather in May the fruit which will only be ripe in August. We must learn to be patient, and the republic proclaimed by France will be the crown of our hoary heads."

Thus already, notwithstanding the conflicting sentiments that were agitating his mind, the Victor Hugo of Guernsey and Jersey can be discerned, and already "the tribune is appearing from beneath the dreamer." No sooner did he make the open avowal that he deemed it unworthy of himself to take no interest in public questions than the newspapers sought his co-operation; and Émile de

Girardin, on starting *La Presse*, a journal destined to exercise a considerable influence upon public opinion, was extremely anxious to have Victor Hugo for its sponsor. The poet accordingly drew up the prospectus, introducing a passage to this effect:

" Let us endeavor to rally men of the highest gifts and the highest spirit round the idea of progress, so as to form a superior party qualified to represent the civilization of those who hardly fathom their own desires."

It was an elevating design, the formation of such a party being ever the dream of upright men, weary of revolutions and reaction.

The prefaces to the various volumes of Victor Hugo's poetry during the early days of constitutional monarchy exhibit to how large an extent politics all along had been occupying his thoughts. In 1831, when "Les Feuilles d'Automne" appeared, he considered revolutions as changes fraught with glorious issues for time and for humanity. In the preface to "Marion Delorme" he states that the shock produced by the Revolution of July was an effort for freedom that was a necessity for art ; while in the preface to " Les Rayons et les Ombres " he expresses his desire that no ill-feeling towards the king may intrude itself into his affection for the people; and in the introduction to the " Contemplations " he describes himself as a spirit proceeding from light to light, after having passed through visions of tumult, trouble, and strife.

Step by step the change is effected ; study and meditation bring it about that he beholds a republic diffusing its glory over the future, and to an old friend who was wont to deplore his altered views he gives his own account of his conversion :

" Must I still wear the chain of ignorance, forsooth,
Because a narrow teaching trained my early youth ?
Because La Vendée once obscured La France, must I
' Get thee behind me ' to the dawning spirit cry ?
Must I go on forever Breton's fame to raise,
Choman, not Marceau, Stofflet and not Danton
    praise ?
Because of old the royalist song I joyed to chant,
Must I, unwise, to freedom's progress cry Avaunt ?
Nay, nay ; no longer cloistered in a narrow cell,
To wider, nobler scope my soul's true instincts
    swell."

The modification of his political creed was so natural and so honest that it need not be any further illustrated. Like many of his contemporaries, he groped his way slowly but surely towards the light, and he may justly feel proud of the course that he has taken.

It was not long before he came to be on almost intimate terms with Louis Philippe. The king, who at first had only admired him as a writer, grew to be much interested in him personally. Victor Hugo's opinion of the king is given at length in a striking chapter of " Les Misérables," in which he has borne favorable testimony to the ruler of whose throne he did not approve, but of whose kindness he was the recipient. He has been discriminating and just in his judgment, without manifesting either contempt or partiality, dealing fairly with him as a sovereign, and leniently with him as a man.

Others have been much more severe, expressing their regret, with some show of reason, that Louis Philippe did not make an effort to organize the democracy, and contending that he neither understood nor cared for the laboring classes.

According to Daniel Stern (Madame d'Agoult), who wrote one of the best histories of the Revolution of 1848, it was his aim to keep a high-minded nation down to the level of an upstart *bourgeoisie*, which, in its narrow-minded egotism, furnished him with the type, and almost, it might be said, with the material, for his government.

So far, however, was he from entertaining any real regard for the *bourgeoisie* which he was endeavoring to conciliate, that he did his utmost to enslave and debase it. To grow rich became the corrupt ambition of the middle-class, and it was precisely in consequence of this that in the hour of his misfortunes there was no manifestation of devoted courage or generous disinterestedness on his behalf. When the democracy awoke to power, those whom he thought he had made subservient to himself abandoned him with utter indifference.

In literature, as in everything else, Louis Philippe was a sceptic, and for art had no shadow of genuine care. Upon this point the opposition journals left him no peace, and it was by way of making some gracious advances towards the poets that, upon the marriage of the Duc d'Orléans, Victor Hugo was invited to attend the festivities at Versailles. The invitation was at first declined; but the bridegroom, at the instigation, it is said, of his young bride, again sent him so pressing a message that he was induced to reconsider his determination. He went to Versailles, and was introduced to the duchess, who received the author of "Notre Dame de Paris" with the graceful compliment,

"The first building, monsieur, that I visited on coming to Paris was *your* church."

This introduction, which took place in June, 1837, was the prelude to numerous interviews between the king and Victor Hugo.

After having thoroughly determined to devote himself to politics, he began to entertain the idea of getting returned for the Chamber of Deputies, notwithstanding the difficulties that lay in the way of his eligibility. In this project he was promised every possible assistance by Paul Meurice's brother Froment. This talented artist was the restorer of an art that had fallen into decay; and many of his caskets, vases, ewers, and swords are masterpieces of their kind. His occupation as a goldsmith and jeweller gave him a very considerable influence in the city, which he was quite prepared to place at the disposal of the new candidate; but the elections were postponed, and the design was abandoned.

His admission to the Academy afterwards gave him the requisite qualification for being nominated to the peerage, though he had the prospect in his early days of deriving a title in two separate ways, as two of his mother's cousins—M. de Chasseboeuf (Volney) and M. Cornet—had been peers of France. There is no doubt that M. de Chasseboeuf would have gladly left his title to his young kinsman if he had not considered his political views too advanced. M. Cornet, moreover, had actually decided upon making him his heir; but his mother, Madame Hugo, had protested against his consenting to add the name of Cornet to his own, declaring that "Hugo-Cornet" was too ridiculous to be tolerated.

Thus practically precluded from acquiring a title by inheritance, the poet found another avenue to the Chamber. Discovering, although somewhat tardily, that the brilliant intellect of Victor Hugo might be made serviceable to him, Louis Philippe invited him to come and see him, and the visits gradually became more and more frequent. On one of these occasions the king, always remarkable for conversational power, found his visitor's society so agreeable that he forgot all about the hour; and the servants in the Tuileries, imagining that their master had retired to rest as usual, put out all the lights and went to bed. When at last the guest rose to take his leave, Louis Philippe, discovering what had happened, took up one of the large candelabra from the table of the room where he

was sitting, and escorted the poet down the staircase, staying to talk with him a considerable time longer in the hall.

Victor Hugo had always a great facility of speech. His phraseology is easy, fluent, and intelligent. His marvellous memory, his power of imagination, and vivacity combine to make his conversation unusually attractive; and he has the rare faculty of being able to introduce into what he says the striking antithesis which is so characteristic a feature in his writings. There are not a few authors who only have control over their thoughts while they are sitting at their writing-desk; with him it was always the case that he could bring his ideas at once to bear, and could clothe them with the attraction of personal kindness. This accounts for his success with Louis Philippe, who, though perpetually reproached with setting no value on poets until they became politicians, certainly professed a high regard for him.

More and more the *salon* in the Place Royale became transformed into a political rendezvous, and on the 13th of April, 1845, Victor Hugo was made a French peer. The choice was hailed with much satisfaction by the general public, and only a few republicans, who were by no means content with the liberalism of the Chamber, manifested any discontent. One anonymous satirist launched forth at him a series of little verses, of which the wit was supposed to reside in their being published to represent the tail of a congreve rocket:

> "Grand, petit
> Tout finit,
> Loi supreme!
> Hugo même
> La subit,
> Vivace
> Il passe
> Pair!"

Victor Hugo, however, now republican in heart, and who had done so much to break down the old literary *régime*, had but little affection for the peerage, which he regarded as the remnant of an antiquated political system. Nevertheless, it was the only channel that seemed open to him by which he could associate himself with political transactions, and by accepting the dignity he no more compromised his conscience than did the democrats who swore allegiance to the Empire, because it was their only means of defending the rights of the democracy.

Some idea may be formed of the venerable age of the French peers at that time when

VICTOR HUGO AND LOUIS PHILIPPE.

it is recorded that the new statesman took his place by the side of the Vicomte de Pontécoulant, who had voted for the death of Louis XVI. In front of him sat Soult, who had been a maréchal since 1802; while the president was Duc Pasquier, who, as a young councillor, had passed sentence on Beaumarchais, who died in 1799.

At first the newly created peer professed himself an independent conservative; and, while he did all the justice he could to the monarch who from the throne promulgated words of universal peace, he refused to be subservient to the policy of his ministers.

He mounted the tribune for the first time on the 18th of February, 1846, when, after his two rivals, Lamartine and Châteaubriand, had been making some powerful speeches, he made a vigorous defence of artists and their copyright. On the 10th of the following month he delivered his first political harangue, on the subject of Poland.

M. Guizot had avowed his conviction that France could do nothing towards re-establishing the Polish nationality. Victor Hugo unhesitatingly denounced so selfish a policy; he maintained that it was not a material but a moral intervention that was required, and that such intervention ought to be made in the name of European civilization, of which the French were the missionaries and the Poles the champions; he reminded his audience how Sobieski had been to Poland what Leonidas had been to Greece, and he claimed the gratitude and moral support of France for a people who had done their part in the noble defence of freedom.

He might as well have spoken to the winds. To assert in the French Chamber of Peers that the oppression of a people is an offence against law or justice was a sort of heresy. His speech was very coldly received.

His next effort was to consolidate some measures for the protection of the coast, and he entered into many technical details, and gave much practical advice.

In June, 1847, he supported the petition of Prince Jérome Napoleon Bonaparte, requesting that his family might be permitted to return to France. In his speech he exhorted the Chamber to be magnanimous, and to evidence its strength by its generosity; he pronounced it to be repugnant to his feelings that any countryman of his should be an exile or an outlaw, and he asserted that it was impossible for any pretender to be otherwise than harmless in the midst of a nation

where there was freedom of work and freedom of thought; in mercifulness they would establish their power.

On the evening of the same day on which this appeal had been urged, Louis Philippe, after reading the speech, informed Maréchal Soult, the president of his council, that he had come to the conclusion to allow the Bonapartes to return to the country.

Early in 1848 Victor Hugo made an oration in favor of Italian unity. The Pope, Pius IX., was at that time regarded as a revolutionist in many quarters, in consequence of certain prospects of liberty which he was holding out, although he afterwards falsified them all by his Syllabus; and, in spite of vehement opposition, Victor Hugo took up the matter, and pleaded for the unification of the Italian government.

However much all these parliamentary struggles occupied his energies, they did not prevent him either from continuing his poetical labors, or from exercising a powerful influence upon literature generally. Nor did he neglect his friends; for about this time he obtained the dramatic editorship of *L'Époque* for Auguste Vacquerie, whose talents he justly appreciated.

Simultaneously with Lamartine he notified his adhesion to Louis Blanc, who was then about to start the *Revue du Progrès*, and he wrote to him to say that the next great work to be effected was the peaceful, gradual, and logical formation of a social order, in which the principles newly evolved by the Revolution should be combined with the ancient and eternal principles of all true civilization, the basis of the order being that social questions should be substituted for political.

Already he had warned the ruling powers that they must bestow a more active attention upon the masses of the people, who were so courageous, intelligent, and patriotic; already he had set forward the consequences of the government of July; he saw how conscience was becoming debased, corruption was on the increase, and that the highest offices were being beset with the basest of passions. All this filled him with profound regret.

If Louis Philippe's government had only been true to its promises, upholding liberty and devoting itself to the solution of social difficulties, there can hardly be a doubt that the great poet, overflowing with benevolence, would have remained a social philosopher, content to be watchful, and suggesting counsels of philanthropy; but when the errors of that government drove the people into insurrection, and the tempest arose that swept away the throne, Victor Hugo was impelled into more decided action. At first, mindful of his oath of allegiance, he proposed that the Duchess of Orleans should be declared regent; but subsequently, carried along with the current of the time, he gave his assent to the Republic, which he has defined as being a "social majesty," and which, as our ancestors have beheld it great and terrible in the past, he hoped that posterity would behold grand and beneficent in the future.

CHAPTER XXI.

As Victor Hugo has himself acknowledged, he had some hesitation, in 1848, in deciding what line he should follow. For the time, he says, liberty *lui masqua la République;* it closed his eyes for the present to the form of government which he was ultimately to support so ardently.

In the month of March some electors wrote to him, proposing that he should become a candidate for the National Assembly. He replied that he was at the service of his country; his antecedents were well known; he had written thirty-two books and eight dramas; his speeches could all be read in *Le Moniteur*, and consequently the world was capable of judging whether he was suited for a political career.

In accordance with the new electoral law, which was the basis of universal suffrage, and the most democratic that had hitherto been carried anywhere, the elections were fixed by the Provisional Government for the 23d of April.

The first name drawn from the urn was that of Lamartine, with 259,800 votes; it was followed by the names of Dupont (de l'Eure), Arago, Garnier-Pagès, Armand Marast, Marie, and Crémieux. Victor Hugo was not elected; he was forty-eighth in the Paris list, with 59,446 votes; Barbès and Lacordaire, who also were not elected, having a few more votes; General Changarnier, Raspail, and Pierre Leroux having polled a few less.

Within six weeks, in consequence either of the retirement of some candidates or of the double election of others, Paris had to elect eleven new representatives; and in response to the solicitation of 60,000 electors, Victor Hugo again came forward.

He expounded his views in a telling speech, delivered shortly before the election at a meeting of the five associations of art and industry; he was much applauded, and on the day of election received 86,965 votes, his name as a successful candidate appearing, by a strange coincidence, between those of Pierre Leroux and Louis Napoleon Bonaparte. Caussidière, General Changarnier, Thiers, and Proudhon were elected at the same time.

Not immediately on his election did he decide what part to take in the Assembly. With his personal freedom from ambition and prejudice, on being first called to take a part in the administration of public affairs, he did not draw any definite line of action, but contented himself by voting independently, according to his conscience, now with the Right and now with the Left, without identifying himself with any section.

His first speech was made on the 20th of June, when he took part in the debate upon the national factories. These had now been in operation for four months, and had brought about none but deplorable results. Admitting the necessity which might seem to justify their establishment, he insisted that practically they had had a most disastrous influence upon business, and pointed out the serious danger which they threatened, not alone to the finances but to the population of Paris. As a socialist he addressed himself to socialists, and invoked them to labor in behalf of the perishing, but to labor without causing alarm to the world at large; he implored them to bestow upon the disendowed classes, as they were called, all the benefits of civilization, to provide them with education, with the means of cheap living; and, in short, to put them in the way of accumulating wealth instead of multiplying misery. In conclusion, he recommended patience alike towards the people themselves and towards those who were desirous of ameliorating their condition.

It was a speech that betokened a rupture with the reactionary party. The noble sentiments that he uttered found an echo, and thenceforward Victor Hugo's pleading of the cause of the degraded and oppressed earned him the gratitude and gained him the love of those whose welfare he desired.

Yet, as a representative, he allied himself with the guardians of the public peace. He was anxious, above all things, to prevent bloodshed. He went from barricade to barricade, entreating the insurgents, and bidding them, in the name of the National Assembly, to lay down their arms; at the risk of his life he forced his way where the uproar was loudest —into the Rue St. Louis and the Rue Vieille du Temple. But effort was in vain. Nothing could avert the tragedy of the three days of June.

Was this terrible insurrection necessary? Was it right? Such are the questions that Victor Hugo asked in the beginning of the book which he entitled "Depuis l'Exil." And in giving his own reply he says that he is tempted to say both Yes and No; "Yes," if the end to be accomplished by the Republic is taken into consideration: "No," if only the means employed be regarded—means which involved the fatal mistake of slaying what it ought to save.

He goes on to say:

"The insurrection of June took a mistaken course; but, alas! the very thing that especially made it terrible was that it demanded respect. It was the outcome of a people's despair. The first duty of the Republic was to suppress the revolt; the next was to pardon it. The National Assembly met the former obligation, but failed in the latter, and for the omission will be held responsible by History."

We shall have occasion to remark hereafter how precisely similar to these were the sentiments which Victor Hugo expressed about the Communist insurrection in 1870. In 1848 he was not slow in putting his theories into practice, by saving the lives of several of the insurgents.

When he returned to his apartments in the Place Royale, he discovered that the rooms had all been ransacked by the rebels, in the hope of finding arms, but that no further theft or mischief had been committed, and he found the house now occupied by a troop of the National Guard, who accused the concierge of opening a back door to the insurgents, and, having made him kneel down against a wall, were about to shoot him forthwith. Victor Hugo, with equal promptitude and earnestness, represented to the soldiers how such retaliation would be of no service, and only sully their own reputation; and the man's life was accordingly spared.

Others whom he was the means of rescuing from summary punishment were a literary man whose name we have forgotten, an architect named Roland, Georges Biscarrat, the nephew of his old tutor at the Pension Cordier, the Comte de Fouchécourt, a legitimist who had taken an active part in the insurrection, and four more; all of whom, at the imminent risk of his personal safety, he conveyed past the sentinels under the pretext that they were his own servants.

And he was not content with saving those who thus casually came in his way. At an early meeting of the Assembly he proposed that an entire amnesty should be proclaimed. Immediately a man rose and embraced him. That man was Victor Schœlcher, of whom Lamartine has said, "He has never thought of himself for an hour. Justice is in his every breath, sacrifice in his every movement, uprightness in his every word; all his thoughts lead upwards to what we call heaven; and yet he is a materialist, owning not the existence of God. How can such a man evolve such virtue from himself?" He was one of the most energetic advocates for the emancipation of the negroes, and became one of the poet's most faithful friends. It was a delight not soon to be forgotten to hear them discuss their sentiments. Spiritualism was the one subject on which they did not agree, but in spite of this diversity in creed they were one in heart; in goodness they are the same.

During Cavaignac's administration Victor Hugo did not entirely separate himself from the Moderates; he repudiated the project of taking proceedings against Louis Blanc and Caussidière; he refused to declare that Cavaignac deserved the gratitude of his country; and he opposed the formation of the constitution that was proposed on the ground that he approved of two Chambers, and held a single Chamber to be dangerous, if not disastrous. This opinion has been combated by many arguments, but it can hardly be questioned that the existence of a second Chamber at the time would probably have interposed an insuperable obstacle to the *coup d'état.*

Victor Hugo went on to claim liberty for the press, which had been temporarily suspended during the state of siege. He also pleaded for the abolition of capital punishment; and, in common with a number of his colleagues who were not discerning enough to anticipate the future, he opposed Grévy's amendment, which, by suppressing the presidency of the Republic, would have rendered

11

the establishment of the Empire impossible.

It was in his anxiety to use every means for the advancement of liberty that on the 1st of April, 1848, he started *L'Événement*, a journal whose design was declared by its motto, "Intense hatred to anarchy, tender love for the people." At first it was proposed to call this paper *La Pensée*. It is a curious monument of French journalism. The prospectus, drawn up by the poet himself, thus describes its intention:

"This journal will be a daily attack of fever to the nation in travail with civilization. France, from her pangs, will soon bring forth a constitution, and then more tranquil days will dawn. Constitutions require storms for their birth, peace and quietness for their life. The human heart is even as the soil; it requires first the plough and afterwards the sun.

"Our present purpose is to secure work and to develop art; work to supply men's bodies with sustenance, art to supply their souls with nourishment. We want to banish from the brightness of our sphere the last fatal shadows of ignorance, which makes the night-time of the heart."

The contributors to the paper were Auguste Vacquerie, Paul Meurice, Théophile Gautier, the poet's two sons, Auguste Vitu, with several others.

What has been said about the paper having been issued for Victor Hugo's private emolument or personal advantage is entirely false. Admired and respected—nay, loved—by the people, he had no thought beyond the people's benefit. There can be no doubt that he was actuated by the desire to eradicate the prejudice which he deemed to be absurd, that because a man was a poet he was therefore incompetent to deal with human affairs. The journal, in its enthusiasm, described the editor as "arm and head, steel and torch, strength and gentleness, conqueror and legislator, king and prophet, lyre and sword;" above all, it defended the cause of the Revolution. Nevertheless, its early success was changed into ultimate failure.

On the 29th of January, in the following year, amid murmurs of strong dissatisfaction from the Left, a motion was brought forward that it would be for the public advantage if the Constituent Assembly were dissolved and a Legislative Assembly elected in its place. The motion was carried, and a dissolution ensued.

Under the auspices of the pronounced revolutionary party, Victor Hugo came forward as a candidate in May, and was elected, his name standing tenth on the list of the twenty-eight deputies for Paris.

In the new Assembly, his attitude was no longer one of hesitation. He had now reckoned up the requirements of the times, and as the truth revealed itself his perplexities vanished. At once and forever he severed himself from his former friends and became the most powerful organ of the republican party.

Both by word of mouth and by his pen, he has distinctly avowed that the year 1849 is a great era in his life, as then he first grasped the problems that had to be solved, and the reforms that had to be made. He beheld the majority casting aside its mask of hypocrisy, and he understood it all. "An inanimate body was lying on the ground; he was told that that lifeless thing was the Republic; he drew near and gazed, and lo! it was Liberty; he bent over it and raised it to his bosom. Before him might be ruin, insult, banishment, and scorn; but he took it unto him as a wife! . . . From that moment there existed within his very soul the union between Liberty and the Republic. . . . Such is the history of what has been called his apostasy." [*]

As the champion of democracy he now began to mount the tribune more frequently. On the questions of education, electoral reform, transportation, the protection of the press, and the reorganization of the Constitution, he was ever anxious to give his opinion; and his speeches, full of fire and marked by a captivating eloquence, moved the Assembly, on the one hand, to admiration, and, on the other, to wrath. For the next three years there was a succession of oratorical contests as brilliant as they were impassioned.

In one of the speeches which may be reckoned among his masterpieces, Victor Hugo made the statement that he held misery to be a thing that it was quite possible to annihilate. A storm of dissent immediately broke out from the Right. M. Poujoulat shouted that it was "a downright fallacy," while M. Benoît d'Azy, supported by the majority, maintained that such a proposition was simply ridiculous.

At this period it was that the melancholy episode in Italian history occurred wherein Rome was entered by the French, and the

---

[*] " Le Droit et la Loi."

Pope was restored to the protection of the tricolor. For a considerable time Victor Hugo had looked upon Pius IX. as a man of liberal sentiments; but now he declared that the papacy was holding itself isolated from the general march of intellect, and failed to comprehend aright the demands of the people and the age. His denunciation of the abuses which followed in the train of ecclesiastical domination called forth against him the invectives of M. Montalembert, who reproached him with his treachery, not only quoting some of his earlier verses, but jeering him unmercifully for having to submit to such a chastisement as the applause of republicans.

The poet's reply was simple enough:

" Call it chastisement if you will; I regard it as an honor. Other applause like that of the tormentors of Hungary, or the oppressors of Poland, I count not. Let those accept it who choose. There was a time—I regret to have to remind M. Montalembert of it—there was a time when he employed his noble talents better. He defended Poland as now I defend Italy. I was with him then; he is against me now. The explanation is not far to seek. He has gone over to the side of the oppressors; I have remained on the side of the oppressed."

The speech had the effect of quieting M. Montalembert; but his supporters, men who afterwards swore fidelity to the Empire, kept up their raillery, calling Victor Hugo a sun-worshipper, and taunting him with his conversion. Once, when he referred to the threatened dictatorship, and ventured to speak of the United States of Europe, M. Molé rose up and left the Assembly in indignation, imagining that he would be followed by the majority; but, discovering that the deputies kept their seats, he had to return to his place again somewhat discomfited and abashed. No amount of uproar, hisses, or laughter ever discomposed Victor Hugo. He calmly reclined with half-closed eyes against the side of the tribune, and was always prepared, as soon as the noise had subsided, gravely to take up the thread of his discourse, and to vindicate the opinions for which he counted no sacrifice too great, in defence of the people and their rights.

On the 21st of August, 1849, the Peace Congress was held in Paris. Victor Hugo was elected president, and Mr. Cobden vice-president.

In his opening address the poet offered greetings to those who had come from the most distant parts of the world, inspired by one grand and holy thought. He spoke to them as men who had met together to work, not for the benefit of a single nation, but for the welfare of all nations. He addressed them as a throng of representatives coming on a mission of mercy, and bringing the best sentiments of the most illustrious peoples.

" You have come," he said, " to turn over, if it may be, the last and most august page of the Gospel, the page that ordains peace among the children of the one Creator; and here in this city, which has rejoiced to proclaim fraternity to its own citizens, you have assembled to proclaim fraternity to all men. Welcome, welcome to you all!"

The orator then proceeded to demonstrate his view that peace — universal peace — was not only an object that was attainable, but was a result that was inevitable; maintaining that as its final accomplishment might be retarded, so also it might be accelerated.

This prediction of the future concord of nations was couched in terms equally elevated and pathetic, and his speech was repeatedly interrupted by loud bursts of applause.

For three days the congress discussed the great question with dignity and propriety, but it was the final session on the 24th that was most crowded and enthusiastic.

In his closing speech, Victor Hugo exclaimed, " From this day forward, gentlemen, we have a common fatherland; we are henceforth all compatriots. . . . What, for the last three days, has been the vision before your gaze? It has been that of England grasping the hand of France, and America grasping the hand of Europe. I know not what sight could be finer. . . . And now go back to your homes, and announce that you have come from your fellow-countrymen of France."

While, that morning, M. l'Abbé Duquerry, the *curé* of the Madeleine, had been speaking on the subject of charity, a member of the congress had interrupted him, to remind him that the 24th of August was St. Bartholomew's Day. The venerable priest had simply turned his head away, as if he rejected the association. Victor Hugo, however, took occasion to refer to the coincidence.

" Yes," he said, " on this very day, two hundred and seventy-seven years ago, this city of Paris was aroused in terror amid the darkness of the night. The bell, known as the silver bell, chimed from the Palais de Justice, and a bloody deed, unprecedented in the annals of crime, was perpetrated; and now, on that self-same date, in that self-same city, God has brought together into one general concourse the representatives of that old antagonism, and has bidden them transform their sentiments into sentiments of love. The sad significance of this mournful anniversary is removed; each drop of blood is replaced by a ray of light. Well-nigh beneath the shadow of that tower whence tolled the fatal vespers of St. Bartholomew, not only Englishmen and Frenchmen, Germans and Italians, Europeans and Americans, but actually Papists and Huguenots have been content to meet, happy—nay, proud—to unite themselves together in an embrace alike honorable and indissoluble."

As he pronounced these words, M. l'Abbé Duquerry and M. Coquerel, the Protestant pastor, threw themselves into each other's arms in front of the president's chair. Enthusiastic applause broke from the platform and from the audience in the public seats; English and Americans rose to their feet, waving their hats and handkerchiefs, and, at the prompting of Mr. Cobden, gave three times three cheers for the orator.

In January, 1850, M. de Falloux, who had been appointed Minister of Public Instruction, brought in a new educational bill, which seemed to many to give the monopoly of teaching into the hands of the clergy. In the debate that ensued M. Barthélemy Saint-Hilaire declared himself a most decided adversary to the proposed law, and was followed by Victor Hugo, who criticised it with extreme severity. He affirmed that, with his consent, the education of youth should never be intrusted to the clerical party, who were ever seeking to put restrictions on the human mind; the Church and State must each hold its separate course. "Your law," he said to M. de Falloux, "is a law with a mask. It says one thing, it does another. It may bear the aspect of liberty, but it means thraldom. It is practically confiscation under the name of a deed of gift. But it is all one with your usual policy. Every time that you forge a new chain you cry, 'See, here is freedom!'"

A few months later Victor Hugo felt himself called upon to raise his voice against the law of transportation, under which political criminals were not only to be sent to Noukahiva, but were liable to be shut up in citadels. A convict, Tronçon-Ducoudray, aptly designated its aim as "a dry guillotine." The

poet, on this occasion, delivered a speech of great oratorical power; he appealed strenuously for mercy to the vanquished, and warned the conquerors not to assign penalties which sooner or later might return upon their own heads. He asserted that there were far better occupations than creating political galleys, and that while the problems of civilization were waiting to be solved there was no time to be lost in devising schemes of mischief to one another.

The very day after the delivery of his speech a subscription was set on foot to distribute it over the country. M. de Girardin proposed that a medal should be struck, bearing an effigy of the orator, and having for its motto the extract from the harangue, "When men introduce injustice into their laws, God supplies the justice, and, through the law, smites the authors of it." The government could not interfere to prevent the issue of the medal, but it put a veto upon the inscription.

And now the hour was approaching when M. Thiers was to make the announcement that "the Empire is made!"—the hour in which was enacted one of the most odious and bloody crimes ever registered in history.

For some time Victor Hugo had foreboded the danger that was threatening the Republic. During the days that followed upon the Revolution of 1848, he had, by means of *L'Événement*, kept up an attack upon General Cavaignac, whose dictatorship he distrusted, and he had supported Prince Louis Napoleon Bonaparte, even so far as to give him his vote. It was a heavy penalty that he had to pay for this error, but it was shared by many others besides himself.

At first the conduct of the prince gave no cause for uneasiness; he was universally regarded as the offspring of the Revolution, and no one thought of him as a Napoleon; in the common reckoning he was a democrat. During his imprisonment and exile he had published "L'Extinction du Paupérisme," "L'Analyse de la Question des Sucres," and "Les Idées Napoléoniennes," all of them books that seemed inspired by a yearning for progress, by democratic sentiments, and by social sympathies.

Calling himself a humanitarian, he avowed himself a citizen rather than a Bonaparte. In "Les Rêveries Politiques," he professed himself a sincere republican. After the Revolution of February he succeeded in securing his election to the Constitutional Assembly;

AN EPISODE OF THE COUP D'ÉTAT (LES CHÂTIMENTS).

and, having hailed the Republic, he declared from the tribune that his life should be devoted to consolidation, and that he had no thought other than for liberty.

Louis Blanc, as well as Degeorges, Peaucher, and other pronounced republicans, who had visited him in his confinement at Ham, had been quite charmed by his doctrines; he was then studying the extinction of pauperism. Though no one regarded him as gifted with a strong intellect, he was credited with a genuine honesty of purpose that had been established by his misfortunes and enlarged by the failure of his plans. He was considered as a victim of Louis Philippe's, and the articles that he published in the *Revue du Pas de Calais* were applauded by the republican press. The poorer classes were utterly misled by his promises, his name of Napoleon having the effect of shedding a certain halo of glory around his person. He had been cordially received in 1848 by the representatives of the people, who never thought of regarding him as dangerous. Those who mistrusted his convictions called him an idiot.

On his return from exile he went to see Victor Hugo, and said to him :

"What would it be for me to be Napoleon over again? Why, it would not simply be an ambition, it would be a crime. Why should you suppose me a fool? I am not a great man, and when the Republic is made I shall never follow the steps of Napoleon. As for me, I am honest; and I shall follow in the way of Washington."

And what he said was heard by Saint-Priest, the Academician, who, while he listened, believed in the speaker's sincerity. Those who abide in integrity are slow in suspecting treachery

When Louis Napoleon was elected President of the Republic, he laid his hand upon his heart and swore fidelity to the Constitu-

tion. Again and again he subsequently declared that he was bound by his oath.

It was not long, however, before intrigues began to be discovered, and men of far-seeing power began to be anxious.

Proudhon wrote that the people had taken a fancy to a prince; and "Citizen Bonaparte, who but yesterday was a mere speck in the fiery heavens, has become an ominous cloud, bearing storm and tempest in its bosom."

Victor Hugo's eyes were then opened, and he saw how miserably he had been duped. When the promoters of the Empire were scheming to mutilate the law of universal suffrage, he mounted the tribune and made a speech in its defence, the peroration of which, in the way of oratory, has rarely been surpassed. To the people he said, "When once you shall have the right of voting, you will be the sovereign power, and you will no longer make or foster disturbance." As often as any effort was made to stifle liberty he rose as a champion, and, grave and pale amid the ever-increasing tumult, and disdaining the abuse and contempt with which he was assailed, he vindicated the freedom of the press, and eulogized the benefits of the Revolution.

The *coup d'état*, therefore, did not take him by surprise. Already he had foreseen it; and when the hour of the struggle came, he did his duty, and did it well. He exerted himself to organize some resistance. When the bullets of the hired soldiers were killing women and children in the streets, and police-agents were breaking open with crowbars the desks of those who were loyal to the Republic, he held firmly to his principles. This fatal struggle has been recorded by the poet in his marvellous trilogy, "Napoléon le Petit," "Les Châtiments," and "L'Histoire d'un Crime," which were the first works of his exile, when "indignation added a brazen string to his lyre."

CHAPTER XXII.

Acts Leading to Banishment. — A Price Set upon the Poet's Head.—Drive Through Paris.—A Woman's Devotion.—Sons and Friends in Prison.—Arrival in Brussels.—"L'Histoire d'un Crime."—"Les Hommes de l'Exil."—Proposition to the Literary Society of France.—La Grande Place in Brussels.—"Napoléon le Petit."—Alarm of the Belgian Government.—The Exile's Expulsion.

And now the penalty of exile awaited the patriot. Victor Hugo had asked the Assembly whether, having had a Napoleon the Great, they were now to have a Napoleon the Little; he had inquired of the Royalists how it was that they entered into such strange fellowship with the Empire, pointing out significantly how the Imperialists, who had murdered the Duc d'Enghien, and the Legitimists, who had shot Murat, were now grasping each other's blood-stained hands. From the tribune he had proclaimed that the Republic is invincible, and that in France it would prove itself indestructible as being identical on the one hand with the age, on the other with the people. In lofty language, alike prophetic of the future and condemnatory of the present, he had poured out his indignation in the ears of the nation. The result of all this was that Bonaparte wrote his name at the head of the list of the proscribed.

All the details of his struggle have been related by himself in his well-known work, "L'Histoire d'un Crime," so that it is unnecessary to dwell upon them here.

Though a representative of the people, he was turned out of the Palais Bourbon with the other members of the Left; he took an active part in the efforts made by the Committee of Resistance; he drew up the placards that announced the deposition of the perjured prince, but at last, when the people were terrified and Paris had become the prey of the myrmidons in power, Victor Hugo had no alternative but to fly.

A price was set upon his head; a reward of 25,000 francs was offered to any one who would either kill him or arrest him; but as he knew that the sacrifice of his life could be of no benefit to any one, he did his best to escape the assassin's hand, and, leaving his home and his family, he started off through Paris in a *fiacre*.

Madame Drouet, a brave and noble wom-

an, did her utmost to secure the poet a safe asylum. She applied at many doors; and, undiscouraged by the denials she received, she persevered in her attendance, and devised many schemes for his escape with undaunted determination.

The drive was sufficiently terrible. It was past ruined barricades and pointed cannon; it was amid drunken patrols thirsting for blood, and police agents in pursuit of honest men. From time to time they were brought to a standstill; Victor Hugo had to crouch in a corner of the carriage, while Madame Drouet would mount the stairs to the apartments of her friends, and appeal to them to return her past favors by sheltering the poet. But every appeal was in vain; every door was closed, friendship was terror-stricken, and gratitude a thing of the past.

At last, after weary hours spent in anxiety and fatigue, the fugitives, almost sinking in despair, found a retreat under the roof of a relation of Victor Hugo's, who was the manager of a Legitimist journal. With generous sympathy, he took the risk of receiving the proscribed man into his house, and, after keeping him concealed for five days, procured a passport, by means of which the outlaw, having adopted a complete disguise, was enabled to depart on the 12th of December from the Northern Railway station.

He arrived in Brussels the following morning at daybreak, and immediately wrote to inform his family and benefactors of his safety.

His sons had been unable to come to his assistance; they were co-editors of *L'Événement*, and the whole of the staff, six in number, had been thrown into prison. Charles Hugo had already been confined four months in the Conciergerie because he had written an article on capital punishment, in reference to the terrible execution of Montcharmont; his brother François (who had dropped the name of Victor in order that his writings might not bear the same signature as his father's) was undergoing a similar penalty on account of his having taken part with the outlaws; Paul Meurice, who, besides being one of the joint editors, was the manager of the paper, was their fellow-prisoner for nine months; and Auguste Vacquerie exposed himself to a similar punishment, for when the paper was suspended for a month he endeavored to start it afresh under a new title, *L'Avènement du Peuple*; and, after being charged under five indictments, one of which rendered him liable to death, he escaped with a sentence of six months' imprisonment.

At this same period the walls of the Conciergerie detained Proudhon, the representative of *Le Peuple*, Louis Jourdain of *Le Siècle*, Nefftzer of *La Presse*, and some scores of other journalists. Bonaparte had found that the readiest way of suppressing the papers was to lock up the editors.

In their prison-cells the sons and friends of Victor Hugo could hear the roar of cannon and the rattle of musketry; and from time to time they saw groups of wounded and dying brought in to swell their numbers, lest they should recover sufficient strength to rouse themselves to fresh efforts in defence of liberty.

For a while Victor Hugo's privilege as deputy protected him from arrest; but when Bonaparte began to feel the inconvenience of the restriction, he did not hesitate to seize his victims at night-time in their beds, so that when Victor Hugo effected his escape Paul Meurice quite believed that he had been shot, though, out of consideration for the sons, he kept his presentiments to himself.

Arrived in Brussels, Victor Hugo took up his quarters in the Grande Place, and soon sent for his wife and prepared to recommence his work.

He felt that a new duty now devolved upon him. Hitherto he had sung of humanity, of women and of children; he had been the consoler of the afflicted and of those in despair; now he would be an avenger. Accordingly, he tasked himself to compile a history; his lashes should reach to the faces of Napoleon and his acolytes at the Tuileries; he became at once the Tacitus and the Juvenal of his time, only his accents were mightier than theirs because his indignation was greater and his wrath more just. He resolved to give in his own words the record of the crime that had been committed, and in all their terrible reality he has depicted the scenes which

he witnessed, and told of all the atrocious phases of the outrage.

Each morning brought many knocks at the door of the little room he occupied, as other outlaws, who had escaped like himself, came to bring him fresh information or new documents to aid him in the history he was composing.

Cournet came to tell him how he had strangled in a fly the police spy who had arrested him and was carrying him off to be shot; and Camille Berru, who had been one of the editors of *L'Événement*, came to relate his experiences. Then there was Noël Parfait, who, although he was under no compulsion to quit Paris, yet felt it his duty to seek poverty in exile; leaving his wife and his son Paul, himself a writer of talent, behind him, he came to Brussels, utterly without resources, and was only too glad to betake himself to Victor Hugo; he undertook the office of secretary and amanuensis to his friend Dumas, and, as Charles Hugo has incidentally mentioned in the charming pages of " Les Hommes de l'Exil," he found the engagement anything but light.

Dumas had been residing in Brussels for some time, not on account of any political necessity, but because he found himself best able there to apply himself to his work. He had never cared much for politics; but when he found that Victor Hugo was driven into banishment, he made up his mind never to see Louis Napoleon again, although he had previously been on intimate terms with him. He kept his word, never going either to Compiègne or the Tuileries any more.

It was during this period that he was writing his "Mémoires," and it was almost by the immediate dictation of Victor Hugo, whom he saw well-nigh every day, that he depicted the leading incidents of the poet's childhood and youth.

Victor Schœlcher, who made his escape in the disguise of a priest, was another friend who came to console the exile. He expressed his contrition for having mistrusted him through so many years, and for having failed to perceive his true love for the democracy. The testimony of this venerable man was but one of many marks of esteem that Victor Hugo received. Thus cheered and supported by sympathy and affection, he persevered in writing "L'Histoire d'un Crime," completing his work in the five months between December, 1851, and May, 1852. But the book was never published until 1877, when it appeared probable that reaction would bring about a second *coup d'état.*

After this production was finished, and Victor Hugo commenced " Napoléon le Petit," his visitors became more numerous than ever. His door seemed never closed; and all who knocked obtained admittance. Intent upon his writing, the author would hardly look up to see who had arrived, and would motion his guest to take a seat, not entering into conversation until he had finished the chapter on which he was engaged.

Among the most frequent of his visitors was General Lamoricière, who, arm in arm with Charras, Bedeau, or Hetzel, refugees like himself, might constantly be seen perambulating the streets and inveighing vehemently against the state of things in Paris. Morning after morning he would make his appearance in Victor Hugo's study, light his pipe, and fling himself on a sofa, twirling his mustache until the writer should please good-naturedly to read him a few pages of " Napoléon le Petit." This would generally act as a sort of narcotic upon him, and he would be calmer for a few hours, like a man who has applied a sedative to an aching tooth. The hero of many battle-fields has been described by Charles Hugo as having been captivated by the monarchy and tempted by the republic. He subsequently placed his sword at the disposal of the Pope, in whom, however, he had not much faith; and in 1852, under the influence of his illustrious fellow-exiles, he avowed himself a stanch supporter of the republican cause.

Émile de Girardin was another who had taken refuge in Brussels, at the Hôtel de Belle Vue. Thus temporarily removed from the agitating world of politics in which alone he seemed able to exist, he occupied himself in studying a number of questions in which he took no little interest; he investigated the relations between children and the State, and wrote one of his most interesting works upon the subject of women and marriage. But he could not remain long away from Paris, which he loved so well; when guns were silent, pens were weapons, and he was unable to resist the desire of taking up afresh the paper warfare. He returned to France just at the time when some obscure author, a tondy of the *coup d'état,* was proposing to the Literary Society of Paris that it should erase from its roll the name of the writer of " Notre Dame" and " Les Feuilles d'Automne," as well as that of Villemain, one of

the founders of the society; and he had the mortification of seeing that the proposal was received with approbation, so abject was the fear that filled the general mind.

Brussels did not offer quarters that could altogether be considered hospitable, and out of the seven thousand proscribed Frenchmen who found refuge in Belgium, only two hundred and forty-seven stayed there for any length of time. In this number were included generals, officers of lower rank, freeholders, magistrates, notaries, barristers, merchants, bankers, artists, and mechanics, the names of them all being specified in Charles Hugo's touching account. The myrmidons of the *coup d'état* might call them "drinkers of blood," but they were in truth a pleiad of upright men, the *élite* of the brave and illustrious. Among them, either in the capital or other towns of Belgium, were David the sculptor, Ledru-Rollin, Michel de Bourges, Bancel, Louis Blanc, Eugène Sue, Charras, Barbès, and Pauline Rolland. All the talent and genius, the virtue and honor, the integrity and intellect, the vital energy, and whatever constituted the glory of the nation, seemed to be expelled from France by the Empire, and driven among foreigners to eat the bitter bread of poverty and exile.

Victor Hugo, the most illustrious of all, was also the most courageous; he encountered adversity with a placid brow; and, with a mingling of scorn and good-nature, with indignation that did not disturb his gentleness, he fought with indomitable perseverance for vengeance and for life.

As soon as his sons were set at liberty, they hastened to his side; and in January, 1852, they found him in the third place of residence he had had in Brussels, at No. 27 in the Grande Place. There, beneath a tobacconist's signboard, just opposite the glory of Belgium, the magnificent Hôtel de Ville, the poet occupied a fairly spacious apartment on the first floor of a house that he has rendered historical. The principal furniture of the room was a sofa that served for a bed, a table that had to be used both for writing and for meals, and an old mirror over the mantelpiece.

The view of the Hôtel de Ville from his window was a perpetual satisfaction to him, as he had ever been an enthusiastic admirer of stately architecture; and he made up his mind to continue in his modest quarters so long as Napoleon III. should be at the Tuileries. Fate, however, ruled otherwise.

On his first coming to Brussels he was, as a Knight of the Order of Leopold, entitled to the respect of the Belgians, and was very cordially received by the government. The people liked him; the burgomaster paid him almost daily visits; his partners in exile had constant recourse to his ready aid, and he was the means of saving more than one of them from starvation.

But under an over-strong government a people has not the free disposal of its sympathies. The triumph of the Empire overawed the statesmen of Belgium.

From an inkstand long preserved as a relic by the prince the poet wrote a work which made the heart of Bonaparte tremble. "Napoléon le Petit" had so wide a circulation, and produced so great an impression, that the Belgian government took alarm. Afraid of Napoleon III., it came to the resolution that Victor Hugo must be expelled. In order to justify this violation of the right of asylum in a free country, the Chamber had to pass a new law, which still bears the name of Faider, its author, a shrewd magistrate who had obtained rapid promotion in Paris in 1852. Fortified by this act, the authorities informed Victor Hugo that he must seek a refuge elsewhere. Immediately he went to Antwerp, whence he embarked for England, having been accompanied to the port by a number of his proscribed countrymen, and by not a few Belgians who were not responsible for the decision of their rulers.

At parting, Victor Hugo spoke a few words to his friends, several of whom were destined to die in exile. Addressing Madier-Montjau, Charras, Deschanel, Dussoubs, Perdiguier, and the Belgians, he said that although he had been attainted with treason, hunted away first from Paris, and now from Brussels, he should ever remember with gratitude the land that had received him.

Cheers and sobs followed him to the vessel on which he embarked for a land where the law would be respected.

LA LOI

CHAPTER XXIII.

Jersey.—Reception of the Exiles.—Victor Hugo's Resources.—Sale of Furniture.—Apartments in the Rue de La Tour d'Auvergne.—Vacquerie's Sketches.—Formalities of Society.—The Privileges of a French Peer.—An Imperial Spy.

VICTOR HUGO merely passed through England, and on the 5th of August, 1852, landed in Jersey, where he was received by a party of French outlaws, who were awaiting him upon the pier at St. Hélier. In a few feeling words he thanked them for their kind welcome, and exhorted them to maintain entire concord among themselves, insisting that there ought to be unity between those who shared the same sorrows and the same hopes.

tle colony was not destined to remain long undisturbed; but at the time of the poet's arrival there was no immediate ground for suspicion of danger, either to its moral or material liberty.

Victor Hugo took a small detached house on the sea-shore, on a part known as Marine Terrace. It was only one story high, and had a balcony, a terrace, and a garden. The rent of this modest residence was 1500 francs

A JERSEY LANDSCAPE.

The number of exiles that had betaken themselves to Jersey after the *coup d'état* was not very large; but the island, with its independent constitution and local government, seemed a spot well adapted to protect the rights of banished men whose object it was to live by their own industry. The lit-

a year. The poet's resources did not allow him to occupy a more commodious dwelling, his entire income now amounting to only 7000 francs, out of which he had nine persons to keep.

No more money was to be expected from France. "Hernani," "Ruy Blas," and "Marion Delorme" had been strictly forbidden by the future author of "The Life of Cæsar," who at one time thought of being a candidate for the Académie. Neither were there any more author's profits to be received. His very poems, though not actually prohibited, were cried down and insulted; any one who had a copy of "Les Contemplations" or "Les Feuilles d'Automne" in his house ran the risk of coming under the suspicion of the ruling powers. The partisans of the Empire had burned or hidden "Notre Dame de

handcuffed. So successful was this policy that for the time it was an utter impossibility for the exile on a foreign shore to derive any emolument from his literary labors. "L'Histoire d'un Crime," as we have already stated, had not yet been published; "Napoléon le Petit" had been secretly printed in Brussels, and a considerable number of copies had been sold clandestinely, but all the profits went to the booksellers. Honorable as the Belgians as a nation are, it is known only too well that some of

THE EXILE.

Paris" and "Les Odes et Ballades," and the superintendents of police were waging war against the books as being dangerous. It was almost as much as a man's place was worth to mention the name of Victor Hugo at all, while to eulogize it was to incur the hazard of being marched off straight to prison. Silence on such subjects was the order of the day, as enjoined by the ministry of the Empire; and Napoleon found his consolation in beholding genius bound and

these booksellers were not over-conscientious, and took care to look after themselves in the matter of this book, and subsequently of "Les Châtiments," without providing that any of the bank-notes should find their way to the purse of the exiled author.

But Victor Hugo accepted poverty as complacently as he had ever accepted wealth.

He had a mission to fulfil and work to accomplish, and consequently there was no hardship which he was not prepared to endure with fortitude and cheerfulness.

Meanwhile he had a certain position to maintain, and the sum realized by the sale of his effects in Paris was an acceptable addition to his resources.

He had left the Place Royale in 1848, and after a short stay at No. 5 Rue de l'Isly, adjoining the St. Lazare Railway station, he had taken up his residence at No. 37 Rue de La Tour d'Auvergne, in apartments from which there was an extensive view of the city. This was his abode at the time when the *coup d'état* took place, and here it was that he had brought his collection of artistic treasures that had now to be submitted to auction.

Théophile Gautier was at the pains to an-*coup d'état* money was scarce in every quarter. A few of Victor Hugo's friends—among whom, as usual, was Paul Meurice—came to rescue what they could from the hands of the brokers, but the bidding was slow, so that the resources of the exile were not benefited as they ought to have been by the sacrifice of his goods.

Thus it came about that Victor Hugo took up his residence at Marine Terrace in Jersey, with means scarcely adequate to maintain his family in comfort. But his spirit was by no means broken, and his wife did not lack the courage to brave adversity. Bruised he was, but not shattered; and he nerved himself to reconstruct the edifice of his life which had been struck down by this sudden and unexpected blow. Undaunted by disaster, he

VICTOR HUGO'S BEDROOM AT MARINE TERRACE.
(*From a Sketch by Charles Hugo.*)

nounce the sale in a short article in *La Presse*, indulging the hope that a subscription might be raised to secure the property for its owner. But his appeal, bold as it was, found no response; for who could be expected in 1852 to allow his name openly to be associated with such a project?

The apartments in the Rue de La Tour d'Auvergne had been furnished according to the poet's own taste, and were crammed with artistic curiosities. Besides the numerous trinkets that he had picked up in the old parts of Paris, there were shelves full of old china, ornaments of carved ivory, and some choice specimens of Venetian glass. These articles, although of great value to their owner, sold for next to nothing. After the braced himself up to the work which was not yet finished.

Not only did his brethren in exile give him an enthusiastic welcome to Jersey, but the residents themselves were desirous of showing him all respect; and in one of their newspapers they announced his arrival in the island, speaking of him in their own curious dialect as "*un de nos muses les plus distingués.*"

Gratified at his reception, he proceeded to furnish his house with the simplicity that his narrow means necessitated. It contained a considerable number of rooms, which have, for the most part, been reproduced by Auguste Vacquerie, who voluntarily shared the banishment of one whom he considered his master, and by whom he was treated as a son. Auguste employed his leisure in photographing the places and the people about him, and sent a book, which he called "Profils et Grimaces," to Madame Paul Meurice, which we have had the pleasure of inspecting. A few examples of these, and a specimen of Charles Hugo's drawing, are introduced into the adjacent pages.

The bedroom of the poet contained little besides the bedstead and a table, but it overlooked the sea, and the sea was ever a source of delight and inspiration to him.

The habits of the little household were regular and industrious. Victor Hugo's usu-

THE GREENHOUSE AT MARINE TERRACE.

al custom was to rise at daybreak, and work steadily on until midday. After luncheon most of the party took a walk, Madame Victor Hugo retiring to rest in a sheltered conservatory that was almost the sole ornament of the place. On returning from their walk, during which they would frequently bathe, the gentlemen amused themselves with fencing or billiards, and then went back to their own rooms to resume their work. Except that they were expatriated, they were not lacking in all the resources for a happy existence.

It was not the custom of the people of Jersey to quit their houses on Sundays; and the exiles, in order to find recreation after the brain-work of the week, used to play billiards, taking care, however, always to draw down their blinds, and to strike the balls as noiselessly as they could, so as to avoid shocking the susceptibilities of the residents.

The grand secret, however, as Victor Hugo has himself recorded in his jocose way, of his being treated with so much respect by the islanders was not in the least because he was Victor Hugo the poet, but because he was a peer of France. By virtue of this rank, as Gustave Rivet says in his "Victor Hugo chez lui," he enjoyed certain privileges, one of which was that he was exempt from the obligation of sweeping his doorstep and cleaning away the grass from the front of his house. On the other hand, he was bound to supply the suzerain of the duchy of Normandy with two fowls every year, the price of which tribute the tax-gatherer never failed to demand. The residents always addressed the "*muse distingué*" as "My Lord," and even the governor of the island regarded him as being of a rank superior to himself.

Into company the Hugo family entered very little; not only had they very limited time at their disposal for visiting, but they did not quite understand the stiffness of English society. When occasionally they went through the ordeal of a formal call, Madame Victor Hugo used to say to her son Charles, who was somewhat particular in his dress, "You go first; you are the dandy of the party," and Charles would gravely take the precedence, followed by his parents and his brother.

But although Victor Hugo did not associate much with the residents, he found more than enough society for his scanty leisure in the visits of the various refugees, Schœlcher, Pierre Leroux, General Meszaros, General Percsel, General Leftò, Sandor Téléki, Mézaise, Théophile Guérin, Barbier, Bonnet-Duverdier, Kesler, Émile Allix, and Xavier Derrieu. His own immediate circle included Vacquerie, Paul Meurice, Ribeyrolles, and others who were bound to him by every tie of affection.

He never complained. Disdainful of all calumny and insult, he resigned himself to his fate. Work was the law of his life; he watched the sun and the sea, and, "while he contemplated the unceasing surging of the waves, he meditated on the perpetual struggles of imposture with the truth."

As a place of residence, Jersey was in itself delightful; it has been called an idyl of the sea. Marine Terrace was close to the shore, and at the extreme end of the town. Although now included in a suburb, in 1852 the house stood quite alone. Its little garden sloped down to the beach, whence Victor Hugo often turned his eyes to France. Whatever charms the land of exile may boast, they never can compensate for the loss of one's native shores. *Non ubi bene, non ibi patria.* There is ever the unseen bond that attaches us to the country where we were born.

Notwithstanding the beauty of the scenery, the salubrity of the climate, and the luxuriance of the flowers, the poet was ever dreaming of the land which he knew not whether he should see again.

"Exile, see those roses
  Wet with morning dew!
  Each petal to thy view,
A pearly tear discloses.

"Roses homeward ever
  Bid my memory glance;
  But May without my France
Can May be reckon'd never!"

VICTOR HUGO AMONG THE JERSEY ROCKS.

Sometimes in the evening, as he was conversing with his friends upon by-gone times, his eyes would fill with tears, and he would seem tempted to yield to despair. Nor was it always friends that were about him; traitors did not fail to make their way into the society of the proscribed. The French government had their spies in the island, and the apprehension that they were revealing their secrets to their enemies was not the

least of the trials that the exiles had to endure.   They were aware that they were
under a secret surveillance, and that they
were in perpetual danger of being entangled
in a snare.   Whatever letters they either
wrote or received were all opened on the
frontier.

They lived, indeed, upon a free soil, but
that soil was under the rule of England, and
England acknowledged the Emperor of the
French as an ally.   Protected though they
were by the institutions of Jersey, the refugees
were only too well aware that treachery was
lurking among some of the Frenchmen who
were only pretending to be outlaws like
themselves.   The duplicity of one imperial
spy, named Damascène Hubert, was found
out through the jealousy of a woman, and it
was ascertained that he was in the habit of
sending information to the police in Paris.
Those whom he had been betraying formed
a resolution to have his life; but when their
design was communicated to Victor Hugo,
he rose in the middle of the night and succeeded in diverting them from their purpose, and in inducing them to have the spy
committed to prison.   It transpired that he
was in debt to many of his countrymen, and
this formed a pretext for placing him in
confinement.

After he was liberated he managed to sub-
sist for a time by the contributions of some
friends; but when these failed he left Jersey.

It was not to be long before the poet also
took his departure.

CHAPTER XXIV.

"Les Châtiments."—Editions of 1853.—Their Introduction into France.—Attitude of the Exiles in Jersey. —Victor Hugo's Funeral Orations.—Action of the English Government.—Sir Robert Peel.—Ribeyrolles' Reply.—*L'Homme.*—Felix Pyat's Letter.—Meeting at St. Hélier.—Threats.—Denunciation of the Exiles. —Victor Hugo's Protest.—The London Press.—The Second Expulsion.

"LES CHÂTIMENTS" was published during the period of the author's residence in Jersey.

Never had poet been more inspired with patriotic indignation. In verse that burned, he chastised the tyrants who, for twenty years, confiscated France to their own selfishness. In odes, in ballads, in epics, in satires, he smites the authors and the accomplices of the *coup d'état*, the cowards that bend their knees to the dominant power, the priests that chant their Te Deums in honor of a Cæsar whom they despise.

Sometimes he is full of pity for the victims of the dastardly aggression, pouring out his sympathy for those whom the conviction-ships were conveying to the deadly climates of Cayenne and Lambessa, to receive for political offences the fate of the worst of felons; sometimes he sounds forth their virtues in brilliant strophes; and sometimes he rises into grandeur as he scourges the great men of the Second Empire, while at others he uses the lash of satire, and depicts them all as circus-grooms and mountebanks. Page after page seems to bind his victim to an eternal pillory.

He describes the Cemetery of Montmartre; and, addressing the martyrs who had perished by foul play, he inquires what was the tenor of their dying thoughts, and proceeds to cry:

"Ye dead, ye dead whom nought from cruel death
    could save,
What now detains you half outside the silent grave?
Here, when the dark sepulchral cypress mournful
    sighs,
Why start ye forth on heaven to fix your eager eyes?
'Twould almost seem ye hear the judgment clarion
    ring,
That doth Napoleon to the dread tribunal bring;
And while before the bar the perjur'd despot stands,
Ye rise to witness to the blood that stains his hands."

The collection is divided into seven books, the separate titles of which, with cutting irony, represent the various phases of the *coup d'état.* They are: "Society is Saved,"

"Order is Re-established," "The Dynasty is Restored," "Religion is Glorified," "Authority is Consecrated," "Stability is Assured," "The Deliverers will Deliver Themselves." The poet has no mercy for the guilty, and heaps upon them his heaviest malediction, and then proceeds, in a vision of the constant advance of humanity, to pour forth his aspirations for a happier future. Full of indignation, he pleads the cause of a great people which, though blinded for a time, would ultimately reassert its power. And it has been remarked that while such a voice was making itself heard, nothing could be considered as irrevocably lost; it reanimated the people's courage, and kept their consciences alive.

The first edition, which was published in Brussels in 1853, by Henri Samuel, appeared in a mutilated form, the Belgian government having refused to allow the circulation of a certain number of the pieces. The author protested against what he held to be an infringement of liberty, and declared that it would be an astonishment to the future that any country that was the asylum of the proscribed could proceed to such an arbitrary measure.

Quite inexplicable is the awe with which the emperor managed to inspire his neighbors. It resulted inevitably that in their desire to please him they violated their own constitutions.

The second edition, revised and corrected by Victor Hugo himself, was published at St. Hélier in the same year, and contains the portions that were excluded from the Brussels edition. It was sold both in Geneva and in New York, and received a highly favorable notice in the *Illustrated London News.* In spite of all exertions on the part of the police, it achieved an almost universal circulation; indeed, the more it was hunted down, the more thoroughly it penetrated France. It had as many disguises as an outlaw. Sometimes it was enclosed in a sardine-box, or rolled up in a hank of wool; sometimes it crossed the frontier entire, sometimes in fragments; concealed occasionally in plaster busts or clocks, laid in the folds of ladies' dresses, or even sewed in between the double soles of men's boots.

But, however keen was the search, and even though the fishermen's heaps of *vraick* were overhauled, innumerable copies found their way into Paris, to the no slight discomfiture of Napoleon the Little. Into workshops, into cafés, into the Quartier Latin, and into the Faubourg St. Antoine, behind shop-counters, and into *salons*, "Les Châtiments" made its way, and only rarely did a copy find itself in the hands of the police.

Perfect in its expression, this *chef-d'œuvre* has justice and progress for its theme, and by its combination of beauty and truth reaches the very ideal of art. To such as objected that history would very likely not bear out his judgment of the Second Empire, Victor Hugo replied that the wrath of a prophet who does not roar against lions, but who inveighs against tyrants, can never miscarry. It is panegyric that misses its mark. Horace and Virgil were deceived about Augustus, and Pliny was deceived about Trajan; but Isaiah and Ezekiel made no mistake about the monarchs of Egypt, nor Dante about the popes, nor Tacitus about Tiberius, nor Juvenal about Nero.

Neither was Victor Hugo deceived in his judgment of Napoleon. The gentle poet of childhood and womanhood, the lover who had drawn his inspirations from nature in her sweetest moods, was now transformed into a merciless avenger, and his new temper found an echo in every heart that owned any sense of justice or of pride.

Although a great many copies of "Les Châtiments" were sold in Jersey as well as in Brussels, the author derived no more profit than he did from the works he had written in Belgium. The printing had cost him 2500 francs, and he did not even pay his expenses; moreover, he lost a lawsuit in which he engaged at the instigation of Victor Schœlcher, who was incensed at the infringement of copyright.

But, if the book brought pecuniary profit to the booksellers only, it accomplished a higher purpose in kindling men's consciences to energy and right.

Nothing could be a surer proof of the terror that the work inspired than the precau-

tions which were taken to suppress it; and Napoleon felt so uneasy at the proximity of Victor Hugo that he endeavored to have him hunted out of Jersey, and before long succeeded in attaining his end.

From their island refuge the exiles continued to issue their protests, and on all republican anniversaries they made speeches which were regularly reported in the foreign journals. Until 1855 their proceedings attracted no particular notice in England, and they lived peaceably in the enjoyment of their privileges.

Whenever a French exile died, his countrymen would assemble at the Cemetery of St. Jean, and Victor Hugo most frequently would be the orator to commemorate the virtues of the departed. Thus he delivered the funeral harangue over Jean Bousquet, an active soldier of the democracy, who died at the age of thirty-four, broken-hearted at his estrangement from his country. In the course of his speech he declared that whenever the expatriated republicans should return to France they would ask no vengeance, and that no drop of blood should be shed in retaliation of their wrongs. For himself, he required no recompense but the deliverance of the oppressed and the enfranchisement of humanity.

Three months later, in the same cemetery, he made an oration at the obsequies of Louise Julien, a brave woman of the people, who was hunted, imprisoned, and as good as slain by Napoleon, for no other reason than her fidelity to her principles. From her tomb, he said, rose the heart-rending cry of humanity that made the crowned criminal turn pale upon his throne; and while he lauded the self-sacrifice of those who associated themselves with the people's sufferings, he demanded the benefits of a free education for the masses, schools and workshops, and all the apparatus of civilization.

Again, when Félix Bony, another victim to banishment, died (in 1854), Victor Hugo stood beside the grave, and maintained that the funeral processions of the exiles were a credential of the advance of liberty; and he took occasion to refer to the condition to which Europe had been brought by the war in the East, describing the tortures endured by soldiers simply through lack of foresight and care.

Noble and brave as these protests were, they had no effect in rousing the feelings of the British government—generally so active

"LES CHÂTIMENTS."

in defence of freedom. But, before long, an incident that could hardly be foreseen resulted in the withdrawal of the exiles' right of asylum in Jersey.

After the colony of refugees had been resident in the island for nearly three years and a half, Félix Pyat, having chosen London for his retreat, wrote a paper upon the subject of Queen Victoria's visit to France, which he read at a public meeting without incurring any objection or remonstrance. But the paper used strong language about the Emperor; and the English government, having concluded that Napoleon would be a useful ally, determined to allow no insult to be offered to his name.

Already, in 1854, Sir Robert Peel, forgetful of the indignation that had been expressed in England at the *coup d'état*, had said, in reference to the oration delivered at Bony's funeral:

"One individual there is who has a kind of personal quarrel against the distinguished personage that the French nation has chosen as its sovereign. That individual has told the people of Jersey that our alliance with the Emperor of the French is a degradation to our country. In what way is this a matter of concern to M. Victor Hugo? If our people are to hear this kind of nonsense from those who betake themselves for refuge to our borders, I shall deem it my duty to ask the Home Secretary to put an end to it as soon as possible."

It was an open threat, and it called forth a sharp response. The French newspaper in Jersey was *L'Homme.* It was under the charge of various exiled journalists—Jules Cabaigne, Philippe Favre, Esquiros, Étienne Arago, and others—the ostensible editor being Ribeyrolles, a man of vigorous intellect, who took a leading part in the political controversies of the time.* In answer to Sir Robert, he inserted an article in his paper asking whether England intended to allow herself to be led astray by fear, to associate herself with crime, and to hunt down the oppressed. If it were so, and they were driven from their retreat, the cry that would go up from the ship that bore them to their second exile would be the cry that "England is England no longer."

Victor Hugo likewise made his sentiments known:

"I warn M. Bonaparte that I am aware

of the secret springs he has set in motion, and I am aware of what has been said about me in the British Parliament. M. Bonaparte has driven me from France because I have acted on my rights as a citizen, and as a representative of the people; he has driven me from Belgium because I have written 'Napoleon the Little,' and he will probably drive me from England because of the protests that I have made and shall continue to make. Be it so. That concerns England more than it concerns me. America is open to me, and America is sufficiently after my heart. But I warn him that whether it be from France, from Belgium, from England, or from America, my voice shall never cease to declare that sooner or later he will have to expiate the crime of the 2d of December. What is said is true: there is a *personal quarrel* between him and me; there is the old quarrel of the judge upon the bench and the prisoner at the bar."

No immediate action was taken upon the publication of this protest, but the people of England, as well as the people of Jersey, were beginning to think of the advantages which might accrue from an alliance with the Emperor, and accordingly turned against the exiles, their irritation being inflamed by the reproduction in *L'Homme* of the paper by Félix Pyat which has been mentioned.

The paper was in the form of a letter to Queen Victoria. After congratulating her Majesty on her safe return from the fêtes in honor of the Crimean war, the author made some cutting remarks; he reproached her for visiting an upstart tyrant and taking his hand as an ally, and by her coalition with him sacrificing her rank and her pride, and the dignity of her race and sex. In conclusion, he made a joke about her having put Canrobert *au bain.*

This harmless little pun was like a spark to powder. All Jersey was in arms. Their queen had been accused of impropriety; it had been insinuated that she had put a man into a bath!

In a scare the police called an indignation meeting. Colored posters covered the walls, of which one may be given as an example:

"INHABITANTS OF JERSEY,
natives or foreigners,
all who respect the sex to whom you owe your being,
and of which
Queen Victoria
is the brightest ornament,
come and attend a meeting
at the Queen's Assembly Rooms, to-morrow evening.

---

* M. Ribeyrolles died some years afterwards in exile in Brazil.

THE CHIEF-CONSTABLE OF **ST. HÉLIER**
in the chair.
Attend and show your indignation at the infamous
libel published on Wednesday last, and
now sold in your streets.
The exiles whom you **have received with hospitality**
have treated your Queen with **insult.**
MEN OF JERSEY,
your fathers distinguished themselves **by their**
loyalty.
Attend and show that you have not
degenerated."

This **was** by no means the most furious of
the placards; others were intended to stir up
the people of St. Hélier to much more vehement wrath. The agitation, however,
was successful; and on the evening of Saturday, October 13, the room was crowded with
an angry multitude that must have numbered little short of two thousand.

In a violent speech, the chief-constable
maintained that all the exiles ought to be
held alike responsible for the offence; and
an officer, Captain Childers, amid much applause, brought forward a motion that the
outlaws should be forthwith informed that
Jersey was no longer a place of safety for
any of them. The motion was carried by
acclamation, and the audience, in the highest
state of excitement, shouted, "Down with
them!" "Down with them!" "Lynch-law
them!" "Hang them!" "Down with the
Reds!"

To no purpose did a few voices try to
make themselves heard in defence; the mob
was furious, and rushed from the room to
the printing-offices.

Charles Hugo, in his "Les Hommes de
l'Exil," has given a detailed account of that
night of commotion. Had it not been for a
heavy fall of rain and for the energy of a
policeman, who would not allow private
property to be attacked, there would have
been great risk of bloodshed. The workmen
at the printing-offices had barred themselves
in, prepared to make a vigorous defence, and
happily no blows were struck.

Cheers were called for at the meeting for
Queen Victoria, for the Emperor of the
French, and for the Empress Eugénie; and
groans were given for *L'Homme*, a resolution
being carried that a newspaper which defied
authority, backed up assassins, and aspersed
the sovereign should be at once suppressed
as a disgrace to the island and an outrage
upon hospitality and upon all Christian sentiment.

During these proceedings the exiles remained in their homes, somewhat uneasy,
and **Victor Hugo** was warned to be on his
guard. But he had no thought of taking any
unusual measures for his protection; he had
been accustomed to walk unarmed upon the
beach by night as well as by day, and did
not see that any special precaution was needed now. His life, he said, was of little value
to him, but he confessed he should be grieved
if his manuscripts were destroyed.

On hearing this, Préveraud, one of the
exiles who had been condemned to death on
the 2d of December, disguised himself as a
workman, bought a truck, and conveyed
away a strong iron-bound chest to his own
lodgings. The chest contained the result of
thirty years' labors—"Les Contemplations,"
"La Légende des Siècles," and the first portion of "Les Misérables."

The precaution was not altogether unnecessary, as "the Jersey vespers," as Charles
Hugo expresses it, were being preached not
only in the island, but in London, and it was
well to be provided for every emergency.

Victor Hugo's friends were more anxious
for him than he was for himself, and Théophile Guérin, Hennet de Kesler, and
Charles Ribeyrolles came to render his sons
and Auguste Vacquerie any help they could
in protecting his house. Asplet, a military
man, who had incurred the reproof of the
government, likewise came and warned Madame Victor Hugo of the danger; but she
refused to quit her post, which, she said, was
at her husband's side when he was liable to
the assaults of fanatics.

The attention that was attracted in England was considerable. The *Times* of October 17 contained the following paragraph:

"We have already said enough about the
revolutionists for the public ear; but we
recommend M. Félix Pyat's letter to Lord
Palmerston's careful perusal. We have reason to believe that the prime-minister has
already threatened these seditious persons
with transportation."

It did not end with threats. On the day
after the meeting the chief-constable called
upon the three persons who were responsible
for *L'Homme*—namely, Ribeyrolles, the editor; Pianciani, the manager; and Thomas, the
salesman of the paper—and informed them
that the governor could no longer permit
their residence on the island. Following the
example which Louis Napoleon had set with
the French papers, they did not suppress
L'Homme itself, but suppressed the parties
that published it. A week was granted

them for their departure, but, without availing themselves of the respite, they left the island within twenty-four hours.

The exiles were far too intimately involved in one another's proceedings not to feel themselves all equally aggrieved by this violation of English law. They resolved to issue a

violence done to our persons merely causes us a smile."

"But we would not be misunderstood. This is what we exiles from France say to you, the British government: 'Your ally, the puissant Napoleon III., stands legally accused of high-treason. For four years he

MADAME VICTOR HUGO.

protest, and Victor Hugo was deputed to draw it up. The general tenor of this document may be understood by a few extracts:

"The *coup d'état*," wrote the author, "has penetrated into English liberty. England has reached this point, that she now banishes exiles."

"Apart from the outrage upon right, the

has been under a warrant signed by Hardouin, the President of the High Court of Justice, by Delaparne, Pataille, Moreau, and Cauchy; and countersigned by Renouard, Attorney-general. He has broken his oath, he has violated the law, he has imprisoned the representatives of the people, he has expelled the judges.'"

LÆTITIA RERUM.

Qui chante là ? Le rossignol.
  Les chrysalides sont parties.
Le ver de terre a pris son vol
  Et jeté le froc aux orties.

Enfants, dans vos yeux éclatants,
  Je crois voir l'Empyrée éclore.
Vous riez comme le printemps,
  Et vous pleurez comme l'aurore.

LÆTITIA RERUM.

"Treason, perjury, spoliation, and murder are crimes that are punishable under every code in the world: in England by the scaffold; in France, where capital punishment is abolished, by the galleys. The Court of Assizes bides its time to arraign Bonaparte."

"This has been our undeviating opinion; for a long time the bulk of the English press held with us; our opinion remains what it was."

"Expel us if you will."

The protest was signed by Victor Hugo and by thirty-six others. The signature of Victor Schœlcher was sent from London, with the reminder that for eighteen months the press in England had been all but unanimous in calling Louis Napoleon an assassin. Louis Blanc, too, signified his concurrence, and expressed his indignation at the action of the English against those whom they were bound to consider as their guests.

When this document was circulated in London, the wrath of the citizens seemed only to be aggravated; they appeared to be almost jealous of the people of Jersey for having taken the initiative, and were now most energetic in demanding the instant punishment of the offenders. The *Times* announced that a French government vessel was waiting in the harbor of Jersey, ready, no doubt, to embark the refugees; other newspapers printed the protest without making any comment, the *Illustrated London News* going to the length of saying that the "clique of French ruffians" were "miscreants" and "malefactors of the most heinous kind," and that "the fate of Pianori, whom they pretend to look upon as a martyr,

would be no inappropriate one for themselves."

The English government, to say the truth, seemed somewhat embarrassed, and no action was taken for a week; there was, in fact, nothing definite to be alleged against the exiles. The protest made no reference to Pyat's letter to the Queen, it simply remonstrated against their own expulsion. But there is circumstantial evidence that the French government was having its own will, as in the *Moniteur Officiel* of Friday, October 26, the news of the expulsion of Victor Hugo was announced in Paris, while the exiles themselves received no notice of the decision until Saturday, the 27th.

On that day the constable of St. Clément appeared at Victor Hugo's door with the order of the government that he should quit the island by the 2d of November. The exile produced the protest, and, reading it over to the officer, insisted that not only was it true, but that it contained nothing that exceeded the bounds of local privilege. He added:

"I am ready to go. But go you back and report yourself to your superior officer, the lieutenant-governor; he will make his report to the English government, and the English government in turn will report to M. Bonaparte. I need hardly tell you that I do not await the expiration of the respite that is given me. I hasten to quit a land where honor has no place, and which burns my feet."

The other exiles received similar notices, and prepared to leave their asylum in what they had hoped to find a free country. Many of them were entirely without resources; but such is the law of banishment.

CHAPTER XXV.

Departure from Jersey.—Satisfaction of the Bonapartist Journals.—"Les Contemplations."—Criticisms.—
   Opinion of the *Revue des Deux Mondes.*—Reception of the Work in France.—"La Légende des Siècles."
   —Outline of its Aim.—Correspondence with Charles Baudelaire.

BEFORE quitting Jersey, the exiles paid a farewell visit to the graves of their fellow-countrymen who were buried in the little independent cemetery of St. Jean, the resting-place of such as did not belong to either of the twenty-seven places of worship in the island, and then embarked, some for London, some for Germany, and some for Guernsey.

It was to the last of these that the steamer conveyed Victor Hugo and his family on the 31st of October. He left Jersey with considerable regret. In spite of the difficulties which had beset him, he had become much attached to the spot which he afterwards described in "Les Travailleurs de la Mer" as a bouquet as large as London, and where all is perfume, light, and laughter. In verse, too, he has spoken of it as

"Sleeping amid th' eternal thunder of the waves,
    Itself a tiny gem whose shores the ocean laves :
    But though so tiny, still a bold and rocky land:
    With Brittany below and Normandy at hand,
    To us a very France, with France's flowery smile,
    And yet for us with France's tears bedewed awhile."

But though the exile was the victim of the machinations of the Empire, and some portion of the English and the Jersey press contributed to the vengeance that was exacted, Victor Hugo himself has been careful to maintain that the great English nation at large (which he calls "majesty in uprightness") had no share in the blame. He rejoiced in his asylum in the island, which was but a fragment of Gaul detached in the eighth century, and found there not a few warm admirers.

Nevertheless, his expulsion gave rise to a certain amount of misunderstanding; there were those who deemed him responsible for the severity exhibited towards his compatriots; but these were only such as failed to comprehend the true greatness of the protest which he had published. In reality, the sympathies of the islanders are not French at all; and in 1870, during the war, they congratulated themselves on being exempt from the obligation of furnishing military contingents and supplies. At the time of which we are writing, a number of the residents who were true Englishmen at heart accompanied the departing exiles down to the port, raised in their behalf the complimentary shout "Vive la République?" and expressed the hope that they might see them back again to reside among them.

On the part of those who were driven to migrate there was no shadow of rancor or ill-feeling; they had no hatred for anything but wrong; they were indeed the playthings of fortune, and the Bonapartist journals in Paris exulted over their discomfiture.

Meanwhile the poet was not confining his efforts to the task of political vengeance; during his residence in Jersey he wrote both "Les Contemplations" and the first part of "La Légende des Siècles."

"Les Contemplations" was published by Michel Lévy and Pagnerre in Paris, in May, 1856. It is in two volumes, and contains a history of twenty-five years of the author's life—the essence, he says, of all that has filtered through his experiences and sufferings, and deposited itself in the depths of his heart. His very soul speaks from its pages. In describing himself he knows that he is describing others, because there are joys and sorrows, tumults and trials, that are common to all humanity, and he recounts all his recollections and impressions, the realities and phantoms of his life, alike grave and gay.

The first volume bears the title of "Autrefois," the second that of "Aujourd'hui;" the various parts being respectively headed "Aurore," "L'Ame en Fleurs," "Pauca mea," "En Marche," "Au Bord de l'Infini."

Looking back upon the road that he has travelled, he reviews the history of his existence page by page. He has reminiscences of his two young daughters,

"One like a swan, one graceful as a dove."

He goes through the story of his creed, and

makes answer to his accusers; he relates episodes of his early love and of the days in the garden of the Feuillantines; he dedicates his reveries to his friends Auguste Vacquerie, Alexandre Dumas, and Paul Meurice, and that upon his drama "Paris" to Froment Meurice; he deplores the daughter he had lost, addressing her in words of tenderness, and dwelling on the devotion of her husband.

"Their souls conversed beneath the rushing wave;
  'What doest thou?' she cried, 'thou canst not save?'
    'With thee I die,' he ever constant cried:
  And thus in locked embrace their hands they keep,
  Sinking together in the current deep:
  Ah! still we hear the moanings of the tide!

" Yes, thou wast good, and to thy pledges true,
  Her husband thou, her ardent lover too,
    Deserving all the love of thy sweet bride!
  Upon the sculptured tablet o'er thee laid,
  Th' Eternal Godhead ever casts his shade:
    Then sleep, my son, e'er at my daughter's side."

Besides the problems of life that are discussed, "from the complaint of a blade of grass to a father's sob," there is a large portion of "Les Contemplations" devoted to literary and political polemics as well as to philosophy. The poetry of the inner soul is simple, true, and touching; it penetrates to the heart, and while it instructs it never fails to soothe and comfort.

Only courageous critics ventured to praise the book. In the *Revue des Deux Mondes* Gustave Planche again came forward, his spleen by no means diminished by the lapse of time; he allowed that the sentimental verses might be all well enough, but pronounced the philosophical only fitted to provoke the smile of contempt; and he professed himself quite unable to regard Victor Hugo's attempts at reasoning in a serious light at all. In his opinion, whenever the poet left his personal experiences and ventured to touch upon the origin of things, upon the destiny of man, his duties or his rights, and the chastisements that were due to his delinquencies, he became childish, and uttered what probably would be amusing if only it were expressed in plainer language, so as to get rid of its obscurity. The critic added that, although he had no right to be surprised at poetical caprice, he thought it astonishing that there should be such an utter absence of all knowledge of eternal truths. Planche was blinded by his antipathy to the author, for nothing could be more generous or more elevated than the philosophy that pervades the whole of the volumes, which in spite of unscrupulous attack made their way to con-

siderable appreciation. No fault was now found, in any quarter, with the poet's style, and his genius was admitted to be asserting itself more and more completely.

"Les Contemplations" went through numerous editions. Borne down though she was by the weight of despotism, France revived at the perusal of the verses of her ardent poet; envy might try to put its finger on them all, but it was only a debased and a prejudiced mind that was not constrained to find much to applaud; and that did not listen with admiration to the voice of power that sent forth its cry from the place of exile.

Among those who were remarkable for the expression of their gratification at the appearance of the book was Jules Janin, who throughout the continuance of the Empire lost no opportunity of displaying his respect for the banished author. Victor Hugo sent him a handsome copy of the book, containing a drawing in sepia, done by his own hand, accompanied by an autograph letter four pages long. The volume was sold at Jules Janin's sale for 1000 francs. Three years later the brilliant critic received from the author one of the earliest copies of "La Légende des Siècles," with a dedication and a colored frontispiece, that was sold for 635 francs.

We may here add a few words respecting "La Légende des Siècles," of which the first part (in two volumes) completes Victor Hugo's lyrical works in the early years of his exile. It was published by Michel Lévy in Paris, in 1859, and was issued bearing the inscription—

"The winds, my book, shall thee convey
  Back to my native shores!
  The tree uprooted from the soil
  A faded leaf restores."

And yet the leaf was not faded in the least; the tree had never been in greater vigor, and never had thrown out more splendid branches. Again was the acknowledgment forced from the general judgment that the pages now issued were comparable to any that had ever seen the light before.

In this gigantic work the poet, with his incessant yearning towards great conceptions, has formed the design of writing an entire history of the human race by selecting striking and typical epochs so as to indicate, in tracing out the ages in their order, the various changes in the physiognomy of nations, downward from the era of Eve, the mother of men, to the dawn of Revolu-

' des Siècles' seems wonderful.
nghout is stamped with your
p intellect.   The more
written, the more I
re of the same
eps to the
be one
ich

THE JERSEY ROCKS.

VICTOP

He thus describes his own aim: ...y in a kind of cyclic "To display hum successively and simultaneously in its aspects, historical, fabulous, philosophical, religious, and scientific, all of which unite in one vast ascending movement towards the light; to represent as it were in a mirror the one great figure, single and multiplied, gloomy and cheerful, fatal and sacred, Man: this is the idea, this perhaps the ambition, that has been the origin of 'La Légende des Siècles.'

programme, Victor Hugo has depicted some salient point in each of the great epochs—Biblical antiquity, the age of chivalry, mediæval life, and the modern era.

Biblical antiquity is represented by three great poems—"Le Sacre de la Femme," recounting the marvels of creation and the pure joys of Paradise; "La Conscience," in which the punishment of sin is depicted in gloomy coloring worthy of Dante; and "La Première Rencontre du Christ avec le Tombeau," an episode which, if not actually derived from the Gospel, is inspired by the sacred page.

JEANNIE ("LA LÉGENDE DES SIÈCLES.")
(From a Drawing by Victor Hugo.)

"The development of the human race from age to age; man rising from darkness to the ideal; a transfiguration of Paradise from a terrestrial hell; the gradual unfolding of liberty; right for this life, responsibility as regards the next; a hymn of a thousand strophes with sincere faith in its inmost depths and a lofty prayer on its topmost heights; the drama of creation irradiated by the countenance of the Creator: this is the outline of what the poem aspires to be."

In accordance with this comprehensive

Passing on to the legends of the North, side by side with Cain he places Canute, the parricide, who wanders eternally through the darkness of night wrapped in a mantle of snow, upon which there falls incessantly a trickling drop of blood.

The conceptions are independent of all epic framework, and, taken altogether, "La Légende des Siècles" may be ranked with the very finest and most complete of all Victor Hugo's poems. Whether he calls forth Androcles's lion, or speaks of the cedar which at Omer's order covers Jean with its shade, he takes his flight through time and space, ever gifted with supernatural power of thought; and even when he pauses to sympathize with *les pauvres gens*, to weep with Jeannie, the poor fisherman's wife, he pours forth his thoughts in such exquisite pathos that his master skill is felt to be unrivalled.

It may easily be imagined how great a sensation the appearance of the volume produced in France. All the poets of the country wrote to the author to express their admiration of his work; and as it was then as ever Victor Hugo's habit not to allow a letter of any sort to be unanswered, he was brought afresh into correspondence with all the literary men of the day.

'La Légende des Siècles' seems wonderful. Your letter throughout is stamped with your sincere heart and deep intellect. The more you read what I have written, the more I believe you will find that we are of the same mind, advancing with the same steps to the same end. Let us rally beneath the one ideal; let us make for the one goal to which mankind directs the double and eternal effort; let us be true to art and progress!"

The correspondence did not end here. Baudelaire wrote again, promising to send his

THE CEDAR ("LA LÉGENDE DES SIÈCLES.")

Among others, he exchanged notes with Charles Baudelaire, the author of "Les Fleurs du Mal." Baudelaire had told him how much he admired his production; and in reply Victor Hugo wrote:

"Thanks, poet. To me what you say of

translation of Edgar Poe, and begging Victor Hugo not to read any other copy beforehand, as there were certain corrections to be made.

Victor Hugo replied:

"Rest assured I will wait. I understand all you feel; I have had no less than eleven revisions of 'La Légende des Siècles,' all for the sake of a few commas."

These confidences are interesting, inasmuch as they testify to the care bestowed by great artists upon their works, which in their estimation are never perfect.

CHAPTER XXVI.

Guernsey.—Hauteville House.—The Oak Gallery.—Garibaldi's Chamber.—The Study.—Family Pursuits.—
Pets.—"Les Misérables."—Lamartine and his "Cours de Littérature."—Letter from Victor Hugo.—
Dinners to Poor Children.—Banquet in Brussels.—M. Grenier's Criticism.

BETWEEN the people of Jersey and the people of Guernsey there has long been a sort of antipathy; it would almost seem as if the expulsion of the exiles from the one island gave them a claim upon the generosity of the other, and they received a warm welcome upon their arrival at Peterport.

Opportunely Victor Hugo found that there was a large and convenient residence to let, which he lost no time in securing. It was known as Hauteville House. For nine years it had been standing empty. Report said that a woman had been killed there, and that her ghost haunted the place every night; the consequence was that no one ventured to occupy it. But the ghost story had no terrors for the poet, and he not only took possession of the house, but proceeded to improve it by enlarging the rooms, decorating them according to his fancy, and leaving his mark, according to his wont, upon all its surroundings.

The re-arrangement, which was quite an occupation for leisure hours, was not completed at once, but occupied not less than three years; and Victor Hugo referred to the interest which he took in his new abode in a letter which he wrote to Jules Janin, and which has hitherto been unpublished:

"You may fancy me as doing little less than building a house. I have no longer a country, but I want a home.

"England has hardly been a better guardian of my fireside than France. My poor fireside! France broke it up, Belgium broke it up, Jersey broke it up; and now I am beginning with all the patience of an ant to build it up anew. If ever I am driven away again, I shall turn to England, and see whether that worthy prude Albion can help me to find myself at home.

"The curious thing about all my movements is that it is literature that is enabling me to defray all the expenses of my political experiences.

"I have taken a house in Guernsey. It has three stories, a flat roof, a fine flight of steps, a court-yard, a crypt, and a lookout; but it is all being paid for by the proceeds of 'Les Contemplations.'

"'Les Contemplations' it is that gives me my roof over my head; and when you have time to spare to take from yourself and to devote to us, you must come and see us. You have liked the poetry; you should come and see the home that the poetry has purchased."

As its name implies, Hauteville House is situated in the upper part of the town, on the top of a cliff, in a small, narrow, winding street, which, it must be allowed, is somewhat ugly. The front is bare, and painted black, which gives it a melancholy aspect externally; but no sooner has a visitor crossed its threshold than he is conscious of a thrill of emotion. He enters the asylum of a banished poet.

In the outer hall stands an elegant column of carved oak, its panels representing scenes from "Notre Dame de Paris." The staircase ascends from an inner hall, at the farther end of which a door opens into the dining-room.

The walls of the dining-room are adorned with four relievos in white porcelain, representing huge vases of flowers; besides which there are valuable plaques, enamels, and china ornaments. Around the walls are high-backed oak chairs, on which are old paintings in the Flemish style, warlike episodes, with titles furnished to them by the poet himself. The table in the centre is large and square, also of carved oak; while at the extreme end of the room, between two windows overlooking the garden, there is a huge arm-chair attached to the wall by a chain, and called the *Sella Defunctorum*, because it was the seat in which the ancestors of the house had presided at the family meals.

On the left is a large earthenware stove, above which is placed a statuette of the Vir-

THE OAK GALLERY IN HAUTEVILLE HOUSE.

gin and the Child. Victor Hugo metamorphosed the image so as to make it a representation of Liberty, engraving an inscription, which he placed upon the pedestal, indicating that he saw in the holy Child a type of the growing people:

> "Small though the people be, it great shall prove,
>   And from thine arms, prolific mother, rise ;
> Onwards, O Liberty ! thy footsteps move ;
>   Display thy mighty infant to our eyes!"

The same sentiment was repeated in a Latin hexameter engraved upon the side:

> "Libertas populum, populus dum sustinet orbem."

The garden seen from the windows, though not large, is very charming, being full of exotics from the South.

On the ground-floor the other rooms are a smoking-room and two parlors. On the first landing is the room that was occupied by Auguste Vacquerie. The first floor contains the sleeping-apartments of the family and the two *salons*—one known as the red drawing-room, the other as the blue.

In the blue room is a table the history of which has often been told. Before the poet's exile some charitable individuals who were organizing a bazaar came and asked him to allow his inkstand to be put up to auction. Not content with so modest a gift, Victor Hugo wrote to Lamartine, Georges Sand, and Dumas the elder, inviting them to join him in his present, and to make a similar contribution. They all complied with his request, and he had the four inkstands set in the corners of an elegant oak table. When the day of sale arrived, he was himself the purchaser of the article of furniture, for which he paid a liberal price, and which is now preserved among other curiosities at Hauteville House.

The second floor is entirely occupied by the famous Oak Gallery, constituting a museum that is in every way remarkable. Along one side are five large windows overlooking the sea; in the middle is an enormous oak candelabrum with many branches, surmounted by a wooden statue carved by Victor Hugo's own hands. Behind this is an open balustrade likewise carved in oak, and a large couch, originally intended as a bed for Garibaldi, to whom the poet, at the time of the Mentana affair, had sent an offer of hospitality.

The verses in which the invitation was conveyed are well known :

> "Yes, come ! O brother of the bruisèd spirit, come !
> Though exiles we, for thee we gladly find a home.

> Consent to come, and hospitality partake
> With us, of whom no tyrant's power slaves could make.
> For Italy, for France, together let us see
> The promise of the glorious day of liberty !
> Together in the evening wait the dawning light
> When nations shall confess the majesty of right !"

Circumstances prevented the great patriot from accepting this earnest invitation, and the two national emancipators have never met; but that portion of the Oak Gallery has never ceased to be known as Garibaldi's Chamber.

On the third story is the study, a kind of belvedere, with its sides and roof composed of glass. In this study, which overlooked the little town of St. Sampson and its picturesque promontory, the poet did his work, his books lying around him at his feet, and his sheets of manuscript scattered about the sofa, or on the top of the earthenware stove. Without express permission no one was allowed to enter this retreat.

Adjoining the study are several apartments containing books and papers, a bedroom in which the poet not unfrequently reclined, and the modest apartment reserved for Madame Chenay, Victor Hugo's half-sister, who since 1870 has resided in the house alone.

Throughout the house the light is very subdued, reminding one of such residences as Sir Walter Scott is given to describe. Everything about the place bears the impress of its occupier, reflecting in a way his work and genius. Although he did not build it, it may still be reckoned as his own creation ; it is adorned entirely after his own fancy, and enlivened by his own reminiscences and designs. He would appear to have taken upon himself the functions of architect, painter, upholsterer, sculptor, collector, and decorator, and so to have converted the house into a witness of himself, that renders Guernsey henceforth historical.

The mode of life at Hauteville House is generally known. Every member of the household had work to do. The daughter, Adèle, composed music : the elder son wrote dramas and romances; his brother translated Shakespeare, rendering alike the spirit and the letter of the original, and making, as his father said, deep researches into his genius; Madame Victor Hugo collected notes of her husband's life, and commenced the book which her death prevented her from bringing to completion; while Auguste Vacquerie made a daily store of literary studies—learned, descriptive, or humorous — from

VICTOR HUGO'S STUDY AT HAUTEVILLE HOUSE.
13

which he afterwards compiled his popular works "Les Miettes de l'Histoire," and "Profils et Grimaces."

In writing in 1856 to Ernest Lefèvre, Vacqueric says:

"I have a library that is quite unique. Do you know what I have read this year? In poems I have read, 'Dieu,' 'La Fin de Satan,' and 'Les Petites Épopées;' in drama I have got through 'Homo,' 'Le Théâtre en Liberté,' and 'Les Drames de l'Invisible;' in lyrics, 'Les Contemplations,' and 'Chansons des Rues et des Bois;' and in philosophy the 'Essai d'Explication,' a book that twenty-five years of thought have not yet completed. For my library I have Victor Hugo's manuscripts, and I rove at my will among *chefs-d'œuvre* that no eye has hitherto seen. I have 'Ruy Blas' all to myself. It is an indescribable feeling to be all alone in these unpublished realms of thought, among untouched strophes, amid the purity of such creations and the virginity of their dawn. It is like Adam's ecstasy over his first day in Paradise."

Victor Hugo has given his own account of these prolific years of work. In speaking of his sons, he says that they simply did their duty. They served and glorified their country, spending their lives in her service, though they were far away. They honored their mother, they mourned for the sister they had lost, they cherished the sister that was left to them; they assisted their father to bear his banishment, and acted as brothers to their companions in adversity. They proved themselves worthy of the poet, knowing how to struggle and how to endure.

Hauteville House was a general refuge, and no application for admittance was refused. One of the rooms by the side of Victor Hugo's study was placed at the disposal of any Frenchman of letters who wanted to write a book as the occupation of his exile, and Gérard de Nerval, Ourliac, Balzac, and not a few others, at different times occupied the apartment, Victor Hugo providing board as well as lodging, and felicitously calling the retreat "the raft of Medusa."

Not only was the house full of visitors, it abounded with pets, all happy and well cared for. "It gratifies me," said Vacqueric, "that this abode of genius is the abode of animals; the creatures love those that love them, and always pick out the best among us." In his "Profils et Grimaces" he has devoted several pages to these four-footed inmates, giving the history of Ponto, the handsome spaniel, good-tempered and faithless; of Chougna, the watch-dog, brutal in aspect, yet gentle in temper; of Lux, Charles Hugo's favorite; and of Mouche, the great black-and-white cat, equally defiant and morose.

From Belgium Madame Victor Hugo had brought a magnificent greyhound, which was stuffed after its death, and still stands in the house. The inscription on its collar was by the poet himself:

"Whoever shall find me, please to take me whence I came;
I'm Madame Hugo's dog, and Sénat is my name."

The name was doubtless given as a souvenir of the senate of the Second Empire. Altogether, the house seemed to suggest Madame de Staël's words, "The more I know men, the more I love dogs;" not that the love of dogs in the place in the least interfered with the kindness and consideration uniformly shown to human beings.

Such was the home where the author of "La Légende des Siècles" resided, and where, according to the rule that he laid down for himself, he worked almost literally from morning to night.

Here, too, was finished "Les Misérables," that marvellous production which goes far to justify the name that has been bestowed upon it, of "the work of the century." It had been commenced in the Place Royale, and was to have been published by Gosselin and Renduel about 1848, one portion of it being then entitled, "Le Manuscrit de l'Évêque." But political events interrupted the composition, so that its issue was deferred until now. Meanwhile its original design had been much enlarged. Carried away by his imagination, the author continued to expand the work, never wearying of introducing new episodes, inserting new incidents, and even adding new chapters.

In August, 1861, a year before the appearance of the book, Victor Hugo wrote from Schiedam, in Holland, to Paul Foucher, in reply to a request that he had made to be allowed to dramatize the romance:

"My son Charles has already taken notes for this purpose, but it is not impossible that there may be material enough in 'Les Misérables' to form the subject of more than one drama. The work will appear in three parts, each having its own title, and each, in fact, being a separate story, although the whole book revolves around one central, single

JEAN VALJEAN ("LES MISÉRABLES").

figure; it is a sort of planetary system, making the circuit about one giant mind that is the personification of all existing social evil."

When the book really appeared in 1862, it came out in five parts, called respectively "Fantine," "Cosette," "Marius," "L'Idylle Rue Plumet et l'Épopée Rue Saint-Denis," and "Jean Valjean." Moreover, instead of consisting of two octavo volumes, as had been previously announced, it extended to no less than ten. It was published simultaneously in Paris, Brussels, Leipsic, London, Milan, Madrid, Rotterdam, Warsaw, Pesth, and Rio Janeiro.

Seven thousand copies were issued in the original Paris edition, which was published by Pagnerre, every one of which was sold within two days. The printer, Claye, had fortunately taken the precaution to keep a number in reserve, so that a fresh supply was ready in a fortnight afterwards, and thus the aggregate of the first Paris edition amounted to 15,000 copies. The Brussels edition reached 12,000, the Leipsic being 3000. Copies of foreign translations were issued to the number of 23,950, without including those that were pirated. Two illustrated editions were likewise produced, and subsequently a splendid *édition de luxe* was published by Hughes; so that, on the whole, the circulation may be estimated at hundreds of thousands, and the book may be reckoned as one of the most wonderful successes of the kind that have ever been known.

The secret of the success was not hard to find. The powerful voice of Victor Hugo, raised as it had ever been in behalf of the disendowed classes, was bound to be heard by all the world; and here were his whole soul and his ardent love for the people all thrown into a work in a way which made it the culminating point of his social evolution.

Full of pity for such as have been crushed by fate, he becomes the champion of the unfortunate, while he is full of sympathy for those who rise from their degradation. He extends his hand to all who are oppressed in any way by social law, and even pleads for pardon for those whose crimes are the result of hereditary vice or evil example.

All the philosophy of the work is summed up in a few lines in the preface:

"As long as the action of laws and customs is the cause of the existence of a social damnation that artificially creates a hell in the full light of civilization; as long as there is found no solution of the three problems of the age—the degradation of men by the proletarian, the decay of women by hunger, and the atrophy of children by night; as long as social asphyxia is possible in certain regions; or, in other terms, and from a wider point of view, as long as misery and ignorance prevail, so long will it be true that books of this kind have a service to render."

It is not requisite for us here to analyze a work which has been admired by all who have read it. From Jean Valjean to Gavroche, every character that plays a part in "Les Misérables" is universally known. There is scarcely any one who has not been touched by the grace of the descriptions, by the clearness of the portraits, and by the vigor of the incidents. The grandeur of its *tout ensemble*, the artistic richness of its style, the boldness of its composition, explain how it is that not only in France, but throughout the educated world, the book has found such a multitude of readers.

"Something exists," said the poet to us one day, "I know not what, in common with me and the people, that makes us understand each other."

And so it is. The heart of the populace strikes home to his heart, and for that simple reason "Les Misérables" has found its way into every land. During one of his journeys in Eastern Russia, M. Alfred Rambaud came across a Russian translation in a bookseller's shop at Kazan, a town that is half Tartar; and General Lee's niece has related how, during the War of Secession, the American soldiers carried English translations in their knapsacks, and used to read them in the intervals of battle by the light of their camp-fires. This was known as the Volunteer's Edition; and the men would amuse themselves by calling each other Marius, Myriel, Valjean, or some other name that figures in the book. An immense number of copies, moreover, are scattered about the republics of South America; and even Japanese versions are in existence.

Immediately on its appearance, the critics began to deal with it in long and thoughtful articles. Barbey d'Aurevilly, Voirsuon, Courtat, and many more, published elaborate notices sufficient to fill a volume. But the only criticism that we will stop to consider is that given in the pages devoted to "Les Misérables" by Lamartine in his "Cours de Littérature." The familiar conversations on the subject are called "Considérations sur un Chef-d'œuvre, ou le Danger du Génie."

GAVROCHE ("LES MISÉRABLES").

The author of "Les Méditations" begins by owning that he had been much pressed to publish his views on this impassioned and radical criticism on society. But before doing so he wrote to Victor Hugo, telling him that while reading the book he had been alternately charmed by its picturesqueness and shocked by its principles, declaring that its radicalism and denunciation of society were repugnant to him, simply because society, though imperfect as being human, was sacred as being a necessity. He proceeded to say that if he wrote upon "Les Misérables" he should respect the genius and talent of the author, but that no admiration of his skill could prevent him from cordially opposing his theory; and representing that from this opposition to the theory he must involuntarily be brought into collision both with the author and his work. Accordingly he would await a reply before writing a single line of the admiration and of the censure that were simultaneously boiling within him.

Victor Hugo replied two or three times, invariably giving Lamartine full permission to do precisely as he pleased. Among other things, he said to him:

"If radicalism is the ideal, I am a radical. From every point of view I want and demand what is best. The proverb says 'Let well alone;' but that is very much the same as saying that the best and the evil are one. . . .

"Yes, a society that admits misery, a humanity that admits war, seem to me an inferior society and a debased humanity. It is a higher society and a more elevated humanity at which I am aiming—a society without kings, a humanity without barriers.

"I want to universalize property, not to abolish it. I would suppress parasitism. I want to see every man a proprietor, and no man a master. This is my idea of true social economy. The goal may be far distant, but is that a reason for not striving to advance towards it?

"Yes, as much as a man can long for anything, I long to destroy human fatality. I condemn slavery, I chase away misery, I instruct ignorance, I illumine darkness, I discard malice. Hence it is that I have written 'Les Misérables!'

"To my own mind it is a book that has fraternity for its pedestal, and progress for its crown.

"Then, take the book and weigh it well. Literary communications between men of letters are simply ridiculous; but political and social debate between equals—that is to say, philosophers—may be as useful as it is weighty.

"You for your part, it is plain enough, to a great extent desire the same things as I; only perhaps you would take a less precipitous path. For myself, with so much suffering before my gaze, I would strictly avoid all violence and retaliation, but otherwise I would take the very shortest path that is possible."

Lamartine still hesitated, and Victor Hugo shortly afterwards sent him another characteristic letter:

"DEAR LAMARTINE,—So long ago as 1820 my first lisping as a youthful poet was a cry of admiration for your brilliant sun, which was just rising on the world. What I wrote still fills a page in my works, and I still love that page well; it was written, with many others, for your glorification.

"The hour has now come when you have to speak about me. I am proud to know it. For forty years we have loved each other, and we are not dead yet. You will, I am sure, spoil neither the past nor the future. Do what you please with my book. From your hands nothing will proceed but light.

"Your old friend,
"VICTOR HUGO."

Thereupon Lamartine came to his decision, and announced his intention of demonstrating what he believed to be social truth for all men, and even for all intellects. We may take it upon ourselves to say that he was unequal to the task.

In an interminable dialogue between himself and a convict named Baptistin, he tries to prove that "Les Misérables" is a misnomer for the book, which ought rather to have been called "Les Scélérats," "Les Paresseux," "L'Épopée de la Canaille," or even "L'Homme contre la Société." He complains that it can only inspire a single passion—the desire of overturning society as it is, only to re-establish it on a type that is advocated by an erratic man of genius; and he is thus led on into a severe disquisition upon Plato, Jean Jacques Rousseau, Saint-Simon, Proudhon, and finally upon Victor Hugo, whom he represents as suffering from vertigo, and laboring under a sickly sentimentality, like a St. John upon Patmos, weeping tears of indignation, and fancying that he is writing *for* the people, when all the time he is writing *against* them.

He repudiates the idea of sharing in any degree the envy or paltry jealousy of his profession, declaring that Victor Hugo is "a sovereign artist," who, though he sometimes strains his pencil, yet repeatedly makes it deliver thoughts that are immortal; and, besides this, he acknowledges that Victor Hugo was right when he said, "I have an advantage over Lamartine in understanding him, while he could not understand my dramatic genius." He owns, for instance, that he never could comprehend either "Hernani" or "Ruy Blas." Nevertheless, he claims to understand society, and indulges in his own vision of what it ought to be.

Between Victor Hugo and Lamartine there was this great difference—the one had advanced, while the other had been going back. Lamartine reproaches his friend for not having kept faithful to his creed of 1848, the time when he had Hugo's two sons working under him in his office for Foreign Affairs; he laments that the author of "Les Châtiments" should have gone so far as to write revengeful poetry, of which nothing was to be admired but the power; he deplores the production of the diatribes that stigmatize individuals, avowing that if they were written with one hand they ought to be erased with the other; because in politics, although there may be fighting, there should never be insult.

In the end, Lamartine comes to the conclusion that "Les Misérables" is an unjust and exaggerated onslaught upon society, leading men on to abhor the social order which is their salvation, and to rave for a social disorder which would prove their destruction. He takes much precaution in softening all asperity of expression; but, in spite of his care, he passes a stern condemnation upon all Victor Hugo's dramatic works, especially on those of the period of his exile. He confesses, what is not in any way to his honor, that he has arrived at a time of life when he feels that he must yield to the pressure of circumstances, and regard society as it exists to be the accomplishment of centuries. To his mind Victor Hugo is a Utopian, and Utopians are more to be dreaded than knaves, because no one distrusts them, and every one is pleased with their flatteries; and hence he pronounces "Les Misérables" to be a dangerous book, inasmuch as it makes those who are happy fear too much, and those who are unhappy hope too much.

No doubt it is painful to read all this criticism; it exhibits only too plainly the enfeeblement of a great intellect. Lamartine was entering upon the old-age which was not to augment his glory, and apparently he had ceased to believe in human progress. Victor Hugo was full of tenderness for those who mourn and for those who suffer. He could not see why humanity should be condemned to perpetual woe; his wish was not only to ameliorate its lot, but to second the efforts of all who cherished the same aim.

It did not content Victor Hugo while he was in Guernsey to plead the cause of the miserable in his books; from the year 1861 he labored to put his theory into practice by entertaining a number of poor children, who were brought every week to his house by their mothers. At first eight, then fifteen, then twenty, and afterwards forty came to sit at his table, where they were waited on by himself and his household, and regaled with slices of roast beef and glasses of wine, and told "to laugh and be merry." It seemed to Victor Hugo that his idea was worthy of imitation; considering it not "almsgiving," but "fraternity," and holding that this blending of poor families with his own was as advantageous to him as it was to them; it was all in accordance with the spirit of pure democracy, and the result should be that, while we learn to serve them, they should be brought to love us. At Christmas-time especially there were great festivities, and a general distribution of toys, cakes, and clothing.

The poet did not lose the gratification of seeing that this charming institution stirred up many others to imitate his example; as the issue of the initiative that he had taken, thousands of dinners were given away to the needy throughout England and America. Hauteville House was the original starting-point of the movement which has produced such capacious charitable halls in London.

In opening one of his Christmas feasts, Victor Hugo made a speech, and said:

"An act of emancipation it is to succor children. In health and education there is a real liberation; by fortifying a poor suffering body, and by developing an uncultured intellect, we accomplish a great thing ; we remove disease from the body; we take away ignorance from the mind. My idea of providing a substantial dinner for the destitute has been well received almost everywhere; as an institution of fraternity it is accepted with a cordial welcome—accepted by Christians as being in conformity with the Gospel, and by democrats as being agreeable to the principles of the Revolution. Let us bring the brotherhood of the present to bear upon the future: let us lay out what we can; it will all be restored to our children. The child is the field of the coming generation; what grows in it will be the harvest of the next age; he is the germ of the society that is to be. Let us cultivate his mind; let us instil the principles of justice and of joy. By elevating the child we elevate the people of the future."

The English press did not fail to acknowledge what their country owed to the benevolence that prompted the ideas of the French political exiles. The *Times* published a statement declaring that the health of the children in the Westminster Ragged Schools had appreciably improved from the time they were provided with a substantial meal given them once a week. To our mind the association is clear, and so it has been by design that we have introduced this notice of dinners to the poor in direct connection with our review of "Les Misérables," the one work appearing to be the complement of the other.

When the book was given to the world, the publishers in Brussels—Lacroix and Verboeckhoven—sent the author an invitation to a banquet, which he did not hesitate long in accepting. The announcement was known throughout Europe, and excited some attention among the imperial police in Paris. From all quarters—from France, England, Italy, and Spain—Victor Hugo's friends and admirers came flocking to meet him. Mr. Lowe represented the English press, and M. Ferrari the Italian; while associated with them were Louis Blanc, Eugène Pelletan, Nefftzer, De Banville, Champfleury, and a long catalogue of others. The banquet was held in M. Lacroix's house, and was attended by eighty distinguished guests. All the Belgian newspapers were represented, and the principal magistrates were also present. Victor Hugo presided, having the Burgomaster of Brussels on his right hand, and the President of the Chamber of Representatives on his left.

The entertainment passed off without any *contretemps*, and must be admitted to have been an important event, literary as well as political, as being a reunion of the talent and intellect of the civilized world at once protesting against the Empire and manifesting its sympathy with the exile.

Many speeches were delivered. In the name of the international book-trade, MM. Lacroix and Verboeckhoven tendered their thanks to the author of "Les Misérables;" M. Nefftzer spoke for *Le Temps*, M. Berardi for *L'Indépendance Belge*, and M. Pelletan for *Le Siècle*. Louis Blanc pronounced a few touching words; then Champfleury addressed the distinguished guest in the name of the prose-writers; and finally Théodore de Banville on behalf of the poets.

Tears fell from the eyes of the exile as he listened to these speeches, rivalling each other in their tone of admiration and affection. In returning thanks, he said:

"Eleven years ago, my friends, you saw me departing from among you comparatively young. You see me now grown old. But, though my hair has changed, my heart remains the same. I thank you for coming here to-day, and beg you to accept my best and warmest acknowledgments. In the midst of you I seem once more to be breathing my native air; every Frenchman seems to bring me a fragment of France; and while thus I find myself in contact with your spirits, a beautiful glamour appears to encircle my soul, and to charm me like the smile of my mother-country."

Prolonged applause greeted his speech, and, after a few words from the burgomaster, to which Victor Hugo again replied, the memorable gathering broke up.

Meanwhile the critics were going on with their work, and M. Grenier, a man of considerable literary power, and the editor of the *Constitutionnel*, took up the argument of Lamartine, and wrote:

"According to M. Hugo, society as it exists is the origin and author of all the crimes that appal us and all the miseries that afflict us; it is a league of the strong, bound together in a merciless compact by their own selfish interests against the weak, who are imposed upon in their helplessness; it is a universal system of untruth, iniquity, and oppression, which covers the most crying abuses and the worst disorder with the specious varnish which it designates law and justice. Crime has no refuge but crime; shame has nothing to expect but shame; misery has no flight beyond misery. . . . Such is the basis of the teaching of 'Les Misérables.' The doctrine is a misappreciation of human nature; it confines itself to the study of certain deplorable facts that every one regrets, and that it is no one's business to alter."

THE DINNER TO POOR CHILDREN.

But need we reply that to alter them is precisely what ought to be done? All honor is due to those who, holding that society is responsible for the ills of humanity, lay themselves out to rectify its laws. It may be true that any progress that can be made must be slow, but there is no room to deny that such progress may exist.

While, however, M. Grenier took this disparaging view of the philosophy which characterized "Les Misérables," he gave his testimony to the literary charms of the book. He confessed that it sparkled with many beauties; he gave an unqualified admiration to the purity of its eloquence, declaring that the delineation of Fantine was most touching, and the description of Waterloo the work of a true poet.

Before long complete justice was done to the book, which earned for itself in some quarters the title of "The Gospel of the People."

FANTINE.

CHAPTER XXVII.

Victor Hugo and Capital Punishment.—" Le Dernier Jour d'un Condamné."—"Claude Gueux."—The Verses that Saved Barbès' Life.—Louis Philippe's Recognition.—Speech in the Constituent Assembly.—Trial of Charles Hugo.—Defence by his Father.—Protests from Jersey.—A Letter to Lord Palmerston.—John Brown and America.—Debate of the Genevan Republic.—" Pour un Soldat."

OF all the causes of which Victor Hugo was the champion, that of the abolition of capital punishment is without dispute the one to which he devoted himself with the greatest energy.

As far back as 1829 he had published " Le Dernier Jour d'un Condamné," which, being anonymous, was supposed by not a few of the reviewers to be the work either of an Englishman or an American. Written in consequence of an execution that had taken place on the Grève, it contains a description of all the physical suffering, and an analysis of all the mental torture, that a condemned man is likely to undergo in the course of the few hours preceding his execution. This thrilling appeal was eagerly read at the time, and in 1832 a preface was added which contained the following passage:

"It is the author's aim and design that posterity should recognize in his work *not* a mere special pleading for any one particular criminal, which is always easy and always transitory, but a general and permanent appeal in behalf of all the accused, alike of the present and of the future. Its great point is the right of humanity urged upon society. It comes face to face with the question of life and death denuded of all the equivocations of the bar, brought boldly out into the light of day, and placed where it must perforce be seen in its true and terrible colors—not at the tribunal, but at the scaffold; not in the presence of the judge, but under the hands of the executioner."

Nothing could be more eloquent than the plea in favor of the total abrogation of the penalty; and never has Victor Hugo been brought within view of a scaffold without raising his voice in defence of the inviolability of human life.

In 1834 he wrote " Claude Gueux," the history of one of those peculiar though not infrequent cases of murder under extenuating circumstances, where the victim is less interesting than the murderer. It came out originally in the *Revue de Paris*, of which M. Buloz had the management at the time. Two years previously the poet had interceded in vain for the unhappy hero who, after all, was executed. The story is terrible, and concludes with a soul-stirring reproof to the members of the Chamber, bidding them to take to pieces the old lame scale of penalties, and to remodel it afresh.

"There are," he said, "too many heads cut off every year in France. You profess to be anxious to economize; be economical in this. Pay schoolmasters instead of executioners. Many a man has become a highwayman who, under proper guidance and better teaching, would have proved an excellent citizen. Consider this head before you proceed to decapitation; cultivate it, weed it, dress it, fertilize it, illumine it, utilize it; you can do far better with it than cut it off."

He deemed the penalty so unworthy of a civilized nation that he never lost an opportunity of delivering his protest against it. On the 13th of May, 1839, while he was at the theatre witnessing the performance of " La Esmeralda," the report reached him that Barbès had been sentenced, and was condemned to be executed for the part he had taken in an insurrection. He hurried off to the greenroom, seized a sheet of paper, and in allusion to the recent death of the little Princess Mary and the recent birth of the Comte de Paris, he wrote a few lines, and sent them immediately to Louis Philippe:

"Oh, by thy child that is gone, fled away like a dove !
Oh, by the prince that is born and claims your sweet love !
The tomb and the cradle their messages send ;
Be gracious ! show mercy ! and pardon extend."

The king, who had resisted the entreaties of the duke and duchess, yielded to the petition of the poet. He wrote to him, " I, for my part, accede to your request; it only remains to obtain the assent of the ministry."

That assent was secured, and Barbès' life was spared.

This incident has been recorded by Victor Hugo in the seventh volume of "Les Misérables." Barbès sent him a letter of thankful acknowledgment:

"In my hour of danger I am proud to find myself protected by a kindly ray of your light. I could not die while you were my defender. I have not had the chance of showing myself worthy of being shielded by you, but each one has his own fate, and they were not all heroes whom Achilles saved.

"And now that I am writing, let me give you, in the name of France and of our holy cause, a thousand thanks for the great book that you have written. I believe that no other land save the land of Joan of Arc and of the Revolution was capable of producing your spirit and your genius. Happy son! happy in having placed upon your mother's brow a new garland of glory.

"Yours, with deep affection,

"A. BARBÈS.

"La Haye, July 10, 1862."

In reply, Victor Hugo sent him a charming letter, which has been included in the biography written by Madame Hugo.

The unremitted attacks which he made upon the scaffold did much to procure him the esteem of Louis Philippe, who was himself most strongly opposed to capital punishment. One day, when the poet had been summoned to the Tuileries, the king said to him:

"M. Hugo, I shall create you a peer of France. The title, which is the highest that our political order can confer, is ostensibly given you in recognition of your literary talent; but I wish you to understand that it is my especial desire that you should be rewarded for your noble efforts towards the abolition of the punishment of death."

In 1848, as a representative in the Assembly, he continued his agitation. Ascending the tribune, he exclaimed:

"Capital punishment is the peculiar and undeviating sign of barbarism. Where capital punishment is frequent, barbarism prevails; where it is rare, civilization predominates. At the head of the preamble of your constitution you write, 'In the sight of God,' and yet you proceed at once to rob God of what is essentially his own prerogative, the power of life and death. I mount this tribune to say one thing, which I believe to be

unanswerable. I say that after the 2d of February the people had conceived a grand idea. They had burned the throne; they longed to burn the scaffold. I grieve that those who acted then on the people's behalf did not rise to the greatness of the people's heart. In the first article of the constitution for which you are voting, you have carried out the people's foremost thought—you have overturned the throne. Now go on and do more—carry out their second thought, and overturn the scaffold!"

But the motion was lost.

Again, in 1849, Victor Hugo made a vigorous attempt to procure pardon for the men who had been condemned to death in the Brea affair; but the attempt was fruitless.

In 1851 Charles Hugo was brought to trial because he had written an article in L'Événement against the execution of Montcharmont, which had just taken place under horrible circumstances. The poet asked and obtained permission to defend his son.

Charles Hugo's writing that had given offence was to this effect:

"Four days ago in the public square of a French town, the law—that is to say, the divine and wholesome power of society—took a wretched creature by the neck, by the arms and legs, and having torn the hair from his head, and the skin from his body, dragged him howling and struggling to the scaffold. There, in the presence of a terrified and awe-struck crowd, the law continued for a whole hour to wrestle with crime."

Large and eager was the audience that assembled to hear the poet's defence of the accused.

"Gentlemen of the jury," he said, "you will understand me when I say that if there is any guilty party in this case, that guilty party is not my son, but myself. Myself, I say, because for the last twenty-five years I have been the open opponent of irrevocable penalties in every form, and because I have publicly taken every opportunity of asserting the inviolability of human life.

"This crime of defending the inviolability of life, if it be a crime, has been mine over and over again. Long before it was committed by my son, it was committed by myself with design, with premeditation, with persistency.

"Yes, I declare that all my life I have strenuously and consistently opposed this remnant of savage codes, this ancient and intelligent rule of retaliation, this vindictive law of blood for blood. And what I have done in the past I will do while I have breath in my body for the future. What I have done as a writer I shall continue to do as a legislator; and this I avow as it were before Christ, the greatest of all victims of capital punishment; this I declare in the very presence of that cross to which, eighteen centuries ago, for the eternal instruction of the world, human law nailed the law that was divine.

"And now, when a single cry escapes a young man's lips, a cry of anguish coming from his soul—a cry of horror, nay, a cry of common humanity—you would punish him for that cry! In the face of all the terrible events that have transpired, you would say to the guillotine, ' You are right,' and to pity, blessed, sacred pity, you would say, ' You are wrong.'

CHARLES HUGO.

"And you, my son, are honored in being deemed worthy to fight, if not to suffer, in the holy cause of truth. From this day forward you enter upon the manly life of our time; you take your place in the struggle for the true and the just. As yet you are but a soldier in the rank and file of democratic sentiment; but you may well be proud to stand, though it be in the dock, where Béranger and Lamennais have stood before you. Stand firm, then, my son, in your convictions; stand firm in your belief in progress; stand firm in your faith in the future, in your abhorrence of irrevocable penalties, in your execration of the scaffold! And if you require a thought to strengthen you, remember that you are only arraigned at the bar at which Lesurques has been arraigned before!"

The sensation caused by the speech was very great, and many hands were outstretched towards the orator. The attorney-general replied, and M. Crémieux spoke eloquently in behalf of the editor of *L'Événement.* The jury gave their verdict.

The character of that verdict and the view that was taken of it may be understood by a few extracts from the newspapers of the time.

On the same evening the following appeared in *La Presse:*

"CONDEMNATION OF CHARLES HUGO.

"'Only on rare occasions is the scaffold now erected in our public squares, and then only as a spectacle of which justice is ashamed.'—LÉON FAUCHER, 1836.

"This day, the 11th of June, 1851, Charles Hugo, who was defended by his father, Victor Hugo, has been sentenced to six months' imprisonment, because, under the Republic, he has written precisely what the above extract shows that Léon Faucher wrote under the Monarchy.

"'M. L. N. BONAPARTE, *President of the Republic.*
"'M. ROUHER, *Minister of Justice.*
"'M. LÉON FAUCHER, *Minister of the Interior.'*

"A tomb wants nothing but a date.
"Liberty in France exists no more.
"If I were to say all I felt during the trial from which I have just returned, I should be sent to join Nefftzer of *La Presse* and Charles Hugo of *L'Événement* inside a prison.

"However, I hold my tongue. I may have another part to play than the part of defendant. The time may come when I shall have to act as judge. I am silent now.
"ÉMILE DE GIRARDIN,
"*Representative of the People.*"

The article in the *National* was much in the same strain:

"Our surmises were incorrect. The Court of Assizes has just sentenced M. Charles Hugo to six months' imprisonment and a fine of 500 francs. We must respect the judgment, though it surprises us and grieves us. We are sure that it will be received with sorrow by the whole of the press.

"M. Charles Hugo is the youngest of the editors of *L'Événement,* he fights under the banner of the Republic with the generous and passionate ardor that enthusiastic convictions ever impart; and although in his criticism of a penalty prescribed by our law he has employed language so strong that it has entailed condemnation, yet no one can doubt the loyalty of his intentions, or question the end that he desired to attain.

"M. Victor Hugo pleaded his son's cause with wonderful eloquence, and his defence will rank among his finest efforts, both for the loftiness of its sentiments and the brilliancy of its style. That eloquence, however, was foiled by the verdict of the jury; and although it is our rule never to protest against the decision of justice, we may be permitted to offer to *L'Événement* an expression of sympathy, assured that our sentiments are only in accordance with those of all republicans towards a journal that serves the cause of democracy with so much talent and courage.
"THÉOD. PELLOQUET."

To these might be added the notices in *Le Siècle, Le Charivari, La Gazette de France, La République,* and *Le Messager de l'Assemblée,* which were all very much in the same strain.

It might well be supposed that the republicans who thus protested against the guillotine at the risk of their liberty would no longer be called drinkers of blood; nevertheless, the accusation continued to be laid to their charge. The populace, however, greeted Victor Hugo with loud applause as he left the court, and cheered him all the way to his carriage.

Nor did the poet, throughout his years of exile, ever discontinue his pleading for the condemned; and it has been remarked that it was touching to see how the opponents of the guillotine turned to the rocks of Jersey and Guernsey to seek co-operation from the hand that had already shaken the scaffold and will ultimately overturn it.

Before Victor Hugo left Jersey, sentence

of death had, in 1854, been pronounced in Guernsey upon a criminal named Tapner. He had murdered a woman, and Victor Hugo sent a memorandum to the Guernsey people, stating that the magistrates must be allowed the credit of doing their duty according to the text of the code that they were bound to follow, and that they had simply discharged their obligations; at the same time, they were called upon to beware—they were practising retaliation. "Thou hast shed blood, and thine own blood shall be shed," in the estimate of human law was a righteous demand, but in the view of the divine law was altogether odious and intolerable. He begged the people to restrain themselves orderly within all legal bounds, but to keep up a peaceful agitation on the matter upon the popular mind and conscience.

Three years before this, in 1851, a Jersey man, named Fouquet, had shot another man. Independent juries had condemned the murderer to death ; but while the execution was pending a great meeting had been held, at which the Frenchman spoke with great effect; a petition was signed, and the queen commuted the sentence to transportation for life. Fouquet subsequently manifested so sincere a repentance that the governor of the jail in which he was confined urged a further remission of sentence. Mindful of this instance, Victor Hugo was now desirous that a similar course should be adopted in the case of Tapner. He did not deny that the man's crime demanded a long and solemn humiliation, and that his chastisement should be severe; but he asked what good they expected by driving a post into the ground, passing a rope round a man's neck, and wringing his life out of him, and whether they supposed that such a proceeding would set everything to rights.

The address created no little sensation. Meetings were held, a petition was forwarded to the queen. Three several respites were granted, and it began to be believed that the execution would not take place, when suddenly it transpired that M. Walewski, the French ambassador, had had an interview with Lord Palmerston, and two days afterwards an order arrived for Tapner to be hanged.

Victor Hugo shortly afterwards wrote to Lord Palmerston, reminding him that three pardons had been granted in Jersey during the space of eight years, and asking why something of the same grace should not be displayed towards the people of Guernsey. The circumstances of Tapner's execution were exceedingly revolting, the operation having lasted more than twelve minutes ; and after describing the horrible details the poet continued his remonstrance to the English Home Secretary in a strain the style of which the following extracts may serve as specimens:

"Both you and I occupy a sphere that is infinitely small. I am only an outlaw; you are merely a minister. I am ashes; you are dust. What do you care about capital punishment? For you to take a man's life is as easy as to drink a glass of water. But keep your nonchalance for the earth; do not offer it to eternity! Do not trifle over these unseen mysteries. I am nearer to them than you are! *Exul sicut mortuus;* and so I speak to you from the sepulchre. . . .

"What do you care? A man is hanged, and there is a rope to be rolled up, a gallows to take down, and a corpse to bury. And so something has been accomplished! But take care: that rope, that gallows, that corpse, all belong to eternity. By the ordinance of society the murderer becomes the murdered; this is a terrible thought. From the beam of the gallows the thing that departs is an immortal soul; is not this an awful consideration? . . .

"Yes; it is all keeping up the way of the past. Tunis keeps up the stake; the Czar maintains the knout; the Pope perpetuates the garrote; Asia and America have their slave-markets; France holds to the guillotine; and England still erects the gallows. But, believe me, all these are doomed to disappear. . . .

"And we have a message to deliver. You call yourselves the ministers of justice and the preservers of right; you call us anarchists, demagogues, and drinkers of blood. But I say we have something to tell you. We declare that human liberty is supreme, human intellect is holy, human life is sacred; nay, the human soul is divine!

"And now go on with your hanging!"

Nor did Victor Hugo's exertions end here. In 1859 an execution, if not more terrible, certainly more unjustifiable, than most, took place in America, that of John Brown, a man of property, and one of the purest characters in the New World.

The sufferings of the negro slaves in the Southern States had long excited Brown's sympathy, and he had satisfied himself that the fraternity inculcated by the Gospel ought to exist in something more than name. His life had been devoted to the abolition of slavery. As a white man he had braved every risk to procure the emancipation of the man of color, and, to use the expression of his widow, "his great heart suffered with the sufferings of the slaves."

In addition to his public spirit, he had well-nigh every virtue of private life. In his struggles with the advocates of slavery he had lost two sons. He was ill-supported by the poor degraded and demoralized creatures in whose behalf he labored, and was at last worsted in a final engagement, which cost the lives of two more of his children. Covered with wounds, he was seized and dragged before an improvised tribunal of Virginian slave-owners, all thirsting with a savage desire for vengeance. His blood trickled over the mattress on which he was lying, and his prosecutors stood awaiting some sign of moral weakness; but he replied with the utmost calmness to all the questions that were put to him, and received the sentence of death with a smile.

It was reported in England that a respite had been granted. Immediately Victor Hugo put in his word. He addressed to the American Republic a petition full of tender eloquence, urging that all men are brethren, and concluding with one of those impassioned appeals for mercy which none can write so well. The letter made a deep sensation.

"Beware," he said, "lest, even from a political point of view, the execution of John Brown prove an irreparable error that may shake the whole American democracy. From a moral standpoint it looks as though a portion of the light of humanity is being eclipsed, and the distinction between justice and injustice is being obscured. The day seems to have dawned when Liberty assassinates Deliverance!

"For myself, I know that I am but an atom; but yet I have a human conscience, and, urged by that, I kneel before the banner of the Stars and Stripes and implore the illustrious republic of America to preserve the sanctity of the universal moral law; I plead with it to save the threatened life of this John Brown; to take down the scaffold, and not to permit before its very eyes, I might almost say by its own fault, the perpetration of a crime odious as the first sad fratricide. Ay, let America be aware that more terrible

than Cain slaying Abel would be Washington killing Spartacus."

The Northern States were roused; various manifestations took place in the towns, and religious services were held. But the State of Virginia accomplished its crime, and Brown was led to the gallows by Wilkes Booth, the future assassin of President Lincoln.

For the American martyr Victor Hugo suggested the epitaph—

"Pro Christo, sicut Christus."

The prophecy he had delivered did not wait long for its accomplishment. In two years the American Union became out of joint, and the atrocious war between North and South had broken out. The blood of John Brown had not been shed without entailing its consequences.

Again, in another quarter, Victor Hugo laid himself out to promulgate his views. In 1862, when the republic of Geneva was revising its Constitution, and its Constituent Assembly had carried a motion for the retention of capital punishment, which only awaited the ratification of the people, a number of the advanced republicans wrote to the poet, as a known advocate of the abolition of the barbarity, and entreated his intervention.

"You ask my aid," he promptly replied; "I am at your service. The question is of capital punishment. I can only wonder when this gloomy rock of Sisyphus will cease to come rolling down on human society? When shall we begin to substitute Instruction for Penalty?

"Retaliation: eye for eye, and tooth for tooth: this seems to be about the sum and substance of our penal code. When will Vengeance cease to impose upon us by palming herself off on our judgments as righteous Prosecution? When will Felony leave off boasting to be proper State Business? It is just the same as when Fratricide puts on epaulets and calls itself War.

"What right has man to make God a judge before his own time? If a man be a believer, how can he cast an immortal soul into eternity? If he be an infidel, how can he cast a living being into annihilation?"

After the publication of this letter, the people of Geneva, in spite of the opposition of the Catholic party, carried their measure for the abolition of the punishment of death, so that for once Victor Hugo rejoiced in having gained his cause.

Some time afterwards he again raised his voice in behalf of a woman named Rosalie Doise, who had been falsely accused of parricide, and, notwithstanding her innocence, had been condemned to hard labor for life.

In 1867 he received the following letter from a Portuguese nobleman:

"Humanity has scored a splendid victory. Your voice, ever to be heard where there is a great principle to defend or a grand idea to be advanced, has reached us here; it has

JOHN BROWN.

In 1865 he supported the Central Italian Committee for the abolition of capital punishment.

In 1866 he entered a protest against Bradley's execution in Jersey.

spoken to our hearts; it has become among us a reality. Both Chambers of our Parliament have recorded their votes that capital punishment shall be erased from our statute-book."

Don Luiz, the young king of Portugal, had

14

signed the bill just before starting for the Paris Exhibition.

The victory was regarded by Victor Hugo as a certain triumph of civilization, and a noble stride in the progress of humanity.

Subsequently to this, when Bazaine was condemned to death, he was not executed, whence it was concluded that capital punishment was done away with in the army. According to Victor Hugo's view, the court-martial, by first declaring Bazaine, as a murderer of his country, to be worthy of death, and then deciding that he should not die, gave its judgment to the effect that henceforth neither treason nor desertion, nor parricide nor matricide (for murder of one's country is equivalent to murder of one's mother), should be punishable by death, and he held that the conclusion was logical enough. And it was owing to this argument that in 1875 a court-martial spared the life of a soldier named Blanc, who had been condemned to be shot at Aix. It was the pamphlet "Pour un Soldat" that saved the culprit's life.

On several different occasions M. Thiers granted various commutations of punishment entirely through Victor Hugo's intervention.

It has been the poet's intention to issue a work entitled "Le Dossier de la Peine de Mort;" for such a book he would only have to collect the materials that are already prepared. We have here already summarized the principal points that it would embrace.

CHAPTER XXVIII.

The People of Jersey Atone for the Past.—A Marriage.—Births.—Tour in Zealand.—*Incognito* of No Avail.—From Antwerp to Middelburg.—Dutch Hospitality.—An Ovation.—Return to Belgium.—"Les Chansons des Rues et des Bois."—Victor Hugo a Musician.—"Les Travailleurs de la Mer."—"L'Homme qui Rit."

BEFORE long the period of exile was to come to an end. It only remains for us to mention the chief incidents of that epoch in the poet's life.

In the place that he had first chosen as his asylum, he was to receive an acknowledgment of his uncompromising fidelity to the service of liberty. On the 18th of May, 1860, the walls were placarded with the announcement that Victor Hugo had arrived in Jersey. He had, in fact, returned for a single day at the request of about 500 of the inhabitants, who had invited him back to the island from which he had been expelled, in order that he might make a speech in behalf of the subscription that was being raised to assist Garibaldi in the liberation of Italy.

It was not in Victor Hugo's nature to refuse to mount any platform that was reared in support of liberty. In the presence of an immense audience, that was thrilled by every word he uttered, he gave a vivid picture of Italy in her thraldom. It was a proud return for the outlaw to make to those who had driven him from their shores, to plead among them the sacred cause of freedom and independence.

With all his poetic power of prophecy he solemnly avowed his conviction that the hour was drawing nigh when, thanks to Garibaldi, and to the assistance of France and England, Italy would rise from her death-slumber, and wake to life again, a great and glorious nation. Never is it likely that Italy will forget this intervention, nor be unmindful of the blood of France that was spilled in vindicating her rights.

On this occasion the attitude of the people of Jersey was greatly to their credit. The people had been deceived, and they now had a welcome to offer to the man whom they felt that all along they would have done well to protect. In doing what they could to acknowledge the error of the past, they did well.

New domestic pleasures were now awaiting the exile. In 1866 his son Charles, in Brussels, married a graceful girl, Jules Simon's ward, and in the following year Victor Hugo became a grandfather. He greeted his little grandson's birth in a characteristic letter:

"HAUTEVILLE HOUSE, *April 8, 1867*.

"GEORGES,—Be born to duty, grow up for liberty, live for progress, die in light!

"Bear in thy veins the gentleness of thy mother, the nobleness of thy father. Be good, be brave, be just, be honorable! With thy grandmother's kiss, receive thy grandfather's blessing."

But the little infant was not destined to live long in the land of his father's banishment. He died when he was just a year old. Fate, however, alternately cruel and gentle, was reserving consolation for the poet's old-age. Another Georges was born, not to blot out the remembrance of the first-born, but to grow up in his place; and in course of time a sister, little Jeanne, was added to the family. These two young folks are now the grandsire's joy and pride. They have inspired the composition of one of the most touching of his works, a book of which we shall have to speak hereafter.

Shortly after his son's marriage Victor Hugo made a tour in Zealand, which has been described with much grace and pleasant wit in a book written by Charles Hugo, but published anonymously under the title "Victor Hugo en Zélande."

While certain journals announced that the poet was in Paris and others reported him to be in Geneva, he was really on a pleasure excursion in Zealand with his two sons and a party of friends. He had started with the intention of preserving a strict *incognito*, as he was anxious to avoid the ceremonious receptions which he was aware his renown might cause to be given him; and nowhere, he thought, could he travel in greater privacy than in Zealand. But on arriving at Antwerp, where they intended to embark, he was recognized by the chambermaid of the hotel, who communicated her discovery, so that it came to the ears of the captain of the steamer. He accordingly treated his passengers with much consideration ; and when the *Telegraaf* arrived at its destination they found a comfortable carriage awaiting them, placed at their own disposal. *Incognito,* of course, was henceforth out of the question; and, as Charles Hugo puts it, Victor Hugo had come to discover Zealand, but Zealand had discovered him instead.

Although the various ovations on the route were somewhat irksome, the trip, on the whole, was enjoyable. The poet was delighted with everything he saw, being especially struck by the cleanliness of the towns. At every stage of his journey from Antwerp to Middelburg, hospitality was pressed upon him, and the principal residents vied with each other in soliciting the honor of entertaining so renowned a guest.

The tourists received an unexpected addition to their party through meeting accidentally at a hotel with a brother of Stevens the painter, and they met with a touching incident at Zierkzee. On alighting from his *char-à-bancs,* Victor Hugo found himself surrounded by all the municipal authorities; and two little girls, dressed in white, came forward and presented him with splendid bouquets.

Many agreeable circumstances enlivened the journey, and the travellers found a variety of things to interest them. The quaint architecture particularly attracted Victor Hugo's attention, and nothing delighted him more than to ascend to the top of the high towers that are of frequent occurrence. On one of these occasions some workmen who were engaged at the basement followed him to the summit, a height of 278 feet, to offer him their greetings.

So wearisome did the public homage become that Charles Hugo quite pitied his father, calling him the "Jean Valjean of glory." At one town after another the inhabitants made a point of putting on their best clothes and decorating their houses with banners; and, on finally quitting Dordrecht to return, the steamship, the *Telegraaf,* at a given signal was enveloped in a cloud of colored bunting, surmounted by the flag of France,

the captain saying that they could not do less than treat him as if he were a king.

Of all the homage he received, none gratified him so much as what was offered by the simple and the poor; and he came across several ministers who told him that they should be ready to read some parts of "Les Misérables" from their pulpits, and that they had actually put it into the hands of their school-children.

After his return from Zealand, Victor Hugo spent the summer in Belgium, in the pretty-valley of Chaudfontaine, where he put the finishing touch to several of the later works of his exile.

Of these we may here make a brief notice. "Les Chansons des Rues et des Bois" had appeared in 1865. The barrenness of the Muse of the Second Empire was quite deplorable, and it seemed time to the poet that his voice should be heard. After being the Benvenuto Cellini, the Juvenal, and the Orpheus of French literature, he would now come forward as a song-writer. Already he had exhibited his marvellous beauty of style. He had created and animated a new world ; he had given humanity new laws. He would now sing of things of comparatively less importance, *paulo minora ;* nevertheless, from the first page to the last of these harmonious strophes we find the poem of man's youth alternating with the poem of his wisdom.

The reception given to the "Chansons" at first was not altogether encouraging. The reviewers, always ready to gratify the ill-will of the emperor, made a point of pronouncing the book to be an inferior production; and, in spite of its attractive title, it did not meet with favor from the imperial Zoileans. But it may be said to be just what was wanting to complete the master's glory. He exhibits himself under a new aspect. In an infinite variety of verse he describes the living offspring of nature which is visible to poets alone, and he writes his melodies even as it were at the dictation of the woods and meadows themselves.

Without abandoning the traditional Pegasus, he has curbed it, and made it canter in the flowery fields of idyl; and all the poems are so arranged that their harmony may be fully grasped by any one who reads them in their orderly connection. Some of them are like flourishes of trumpets, some of them like whispers of love. For "Jeanne seule" and for others he describes "l'éternal petit Roman," introducing pictures of delightful freshness; he lingers over a bird's-nest and inhales the fragrance of the forest flower till he anticipates the time of peace, when wars shall be no more; he dwells upon the thought that the same nature which teaches youth to love teaches man to do his duty; and he en-

to say this of a man who never professed to have any musical bias at all, and in whose house Charles Monselet has observed that the complete works of Viennet were far more likely to be found than a pianoforte or any other musical instrument. It was Charles

FRENILLE

AN OVATION.

dows the noble oak with speech, and makes its mighty strength become the witness to the glory of Liberty, Equality, and Fraternity.

In every page of the book the author reveals himself as having the soul of a true musician, however paradoxical it may appear

Monselet, one of the most refined writers of our time, though not yet an Academician, who composed a good-humored parody upon Victor Hugo's production. He called it "Une Chansonette des Rues et des Bois," of which he says, "I did not put my name to

it, but I have never denied being the author."
It was he also who declared of Victor Hugo
that he was really a great musician, and that
he composed grand overtures, of which he
cites one as an example:

"Hark! how the bow now trembles in the leader's
hand,
Moves o'er the answering strings and stirs the
waiting band!
The orchestra below, concealed from curious eye,
Wakes at the bidding and clangs out shrill reply.
Just as in silent eve, whence th' unseen vineyard lies,
The laughter of grape-gatherers takes us by sur-
prise;
Then next the alto of the mellow flute ascends,
Like graceful capital in which a column ends;
Next, rising, falling, sweeping through the air
around,
The scales first fill,then empty,all the vase of sound."

These verses form a portion of a piece entitled " Que la Musique date du Seizième
Siècle," and Monselet asks whether it might
not be signed by Hérold or Rossini.

Victor Hugo's musical temperament indeed appears at every turn of his work.
Putting aside his dramatic poem of " La
Esmeralda," that was composed expressly for
the opera, do not " Ernani," " Rigoletto," and
" Lucrezia Borgia " mark him out as well-
nigh the first librettist of the century? He
has written romances that must be prized
as gems, and "Les Chansons des Rues et des
Bois" must be esteemed as a casket full of
them.   Certain couplets, too, introduced into
" Les Misérables " will occur to the reader.
Music must be allowed to be frequently in
his thoughts, and there are some of his
poems, the "Guitares," the " Autres Guitares," and some of the musical masses in the
" Chansons," of which it might be said that
Cherubini offers nothing better.

The poems were succeeded in 1866 by another important work, " Les Travailleurs de
la Mer." The author announced the completion of this in a letter published in the
newspapers.

" My desire in these volumes has been to
glorify work, will, devotion, and whatever
makes man great. I have made it a point to
demonstrate how the most insatiable abyss is
the human heart, and what escapes the sea
does not escape a woman."

And in the book itself he wrote:

" I dedicate this work to the rock of hospitality and liberty; to the corner of the old
Norman country inhabited by the noble little
people of the sea; to the Isle of Guernsey,
rugged yet gentle, my refuge for the present,
and probably my grave in the future!"

In this marvellous story it was his aim to
complete his study of the struggles of the
human race.   We are weighed down by a
triple ἀνάγκη—that is to say, by the fatal necessity of dogmas, of laws, and of circumstances.   In " Notre Dame de Paris " he has
denounced the first, in " Les Misérables " he
has depicted the second, and he here proceeds
to illustrate the third.   He does not now
bring forward the great agitations of history,
nor the events of contemporary revolution;
he gives a picture of the life of a seaboard
people, and within a wild and majestic framework places at once a drama and an idyl.

By its vigorous simplicity, by the severity
of its style, by the sombre coloring that pervades it, the book affords an admirable example of its author's power. As a lyrical
poet he haunts the realms of light; as a
dramatist he analyzes every sentiment of
woe; and like a gifted painter he reproduces the dazzling tints of the sea, the mysterious hues of the subterranean vaults, and
the movement of the boisterous waves. When
he describes the combat between man and
the brute forces of nature, he endows the in-
furiated elements with a soul, investing them
with the attributes of love, wrath, hypocrisy,
and hatred, just as though they were animate with human passions.

But although the more these pages are
studied the more they are to be admired, yet
they had their detractors; there were plenty
of critics to run them down, and they reproached the author for his power, though
this was only as if they found fault with an
eminence for making a man giddy,or as if they
reproved a rock for being rugged. The fault-
finders, moreover, discovered all kinds of
grievances. The language was too idiomatic;
the author had used terms that no French
dictionary warranted; nay, he had actually
employed Guernsey words that betrayed a
Celtic or Teutonic origin! The very character of such criticism is its own condemnation,and cannot be reprobated too severely.

Three years after this, Victor Hugo, in
1869, brought out another book which
proved equally successful.   He called it
"L'Homme qui Rit." This work abounds
with scenes of pathetic interest, but, like
everything else that the author produced, it
evoked a great deal of adverse criticism, not
a few writers professing that they were unable to comprehend it. But no criticism
availed to check its sale.

Parodies, of course, followed its appear-

THE EXILE'S ROCK IN GUERNSEY.
(From a Photograph by Auguste Vacquerie.)

ance. Some of these were written in a good-humored style, and bear their own witness to the impression that the original made; some, on the other hand, were rancorous and full of spleen.

The book is a singular mixture of the horrible and the graceful. Victor Hugo delights in antithesis; and here in his favorite way he joins moral beauty to physical de-formity, and moral ugliness to physical grace. Gwynplaine the mountebank, and Josiane the duchess, have become immortal types of character; and though detraction may do its worst, the love-passages of Déa will never be effaced from the memory of those who read them.

"L'Homme qui Rit" is another master-piece.

"L'HOMME QUI RIT."

CHAPTER XXIX.

Victor Hugo's Admiration of Shakespeare.—The Paris Exhibition of 1867.—"The Paris Guide."—The Reproduction of "Hernani."—"La Voix de Guernesey."—Letter to the Young Poets.—Literary Movement under the Second Empire.—*Le Rappel.*—Its Contributors.—A Manifesto.—Summary of the Works of the Exile.

AMONG Victor Hugo's other works we must not omit to reckon his magnificent essay upon Shakespeare, a review which is as fine a tribute as has ever been offered to the immortal English dramatist. He had already associated himself with the festivities that had been observed in honor of the great bard, and had contributed his own meed of homage.

In his study of Shakespeare he has manifested his veneration for the poet, who, like himself, had searched the depths of the human heart; and he calls attention to the faithful translation of the plays that had been made by his son.

The time was at hand when Victor Hugo's own dramas were to be the theme of general interest.

The exhibition of 1867 was made the occasion of the publication of a large work upon Paris called "The Paris Guide." A number of eminent writers took part in the compilation of the volume, and Victor Hugo was commissioned to write a preface, or rather a conspectus of the whole. He performed his task in his own elegant style, every line sparkling as it were with the brilliancy of a sky-rocket.

His contribution to the book made considerable sensation, but even this was soon outdone by a circumstance which procured him his proper honor, of which he had been defrauded so long. The first Empire had left literature in a state of absolute nudity, and the second had checked the magnificent flight it had taken since the restoration of 1830; but, though a man may originate a *coup d'état,* he may still be too weak to crush out genius.

While the emperor in 1867 was displaying the embellishments of the capital and the glories of the Exhibition to his innumerable visitors, he felt the demand that existed for the production of new dramas. The managers of the theatres were utterly at a loss;

there was absolutely nothing for them to bring out in the way of novelties. At the best houses the sterility was absolutely depressing, while at the second-rate theatres no resource seemed to be left but the repetition of the sensational melodramas, with their trap-door tricks, and the introduction of half-naked women singing obscene songs utterly void of wit. Many of these heterogeneous visitors, however, were quite capable of forming a just judgment in dramatic matters, and, conscious of this, the Minister of Fine Arts ventured to point out to the emperor that the world would be making remarks upon the decay, and would be asking what had become of the literary talent of the nation.

The Comédie Française had positively nothing in its repertory but what was universally known, and nothing modern offered itself for its acceptance that was likely to attract the crowd. In the midst of the perplexity Victor Hugo's name began to be timidly whispered, and after very considerable hesitation it was arranged that "Hernani" should be brought out at the Théâtre Français, and "Ruy Blas" at the Odéon.

A variety of circumstances that it would be tedious to relate long delayed the production of "Ruy Blas," but on the 20th of June "Hernani" was performed by a company worthy of the work; Delaunay took the part of Hernani, Bressant that of Don Carlos, Maubant that of Ruy Gomez, the rôle of Doña Sol being allotted to Mlle. Favart.

Immense interest was taken in the reproduction of the piece. More than 20,000 applications were made for places at the first performance. Great importance was attributed to the event; not only had the young men of letters (who of course knew all about the conflict of 1830) never had an opportunity hitherto of seeing the piece, but there was a great probability that politics would be dragged into the affair. It appeared quite likely that a demonstration would be made against the political principles of the exiled author, about whose genius there could be no dispute. It is said that every precaution was taken to maintain order, and even that a certain number of troops was kept ready to interfere in case of need.

The public, when admitted, consisted of several sections. There were numerous officials ready to make opposition to any political manifestation; and there were not a few of those who had been present at the riotous performances in 1830, and were now prepared to applaud with all the vehemence of defiance, and applaud they did. But there were none to contend against them; their old adversaries had disappeared, and in the new generation there was nobody who could want to hiss verses such as had never been written since the days of Corneille.

An eminent critic, M. Francisque Sarcey, who now admires Victor Hugo as much as he then depreciated him, after the first night's performance published a notice in which he pretended that the acclamations that greeted the piece had nothing voluntary in them, but were merely outbursts made at a preconcerted signal. And perhaps there was some ground for the suspicion, as on the opening night the house was to a very considerable extent filled with officials charged to maintain order. On the next night, however, there could be no mistake; the theatre was crowded with an independent audience; the vociferous applause was entirely genuine, and for eighty nights afterwards the assembly listened with an admiration almost amounting to awe, yielding the tribute of their homage in a measure ample enough to realize the author's most ambitious dreams.

A concourse of the young authors of the day, exulting in the grand success, lost no time in addressing the following letter to the poet:

"MASTER MOST DEAR AND MOST ILLUSTRIOUS,—We hail with enthusiastic delight the reproduction of 'Hernani.'

"The fresh triumph of the greatest of French poets fills us with transport. The night of the 20th of June is an era in our existence.

"Yet sorrow mingles with our joy. Your absence was felt by your associates of 1830; still more was it bewailed by us younger men, who never yet have shaken hands with the author of 'La Légende des Siècles.' At least, they cannot resist sending you this

tribute of their regard and unbounded admiration.
"Signed,
"SULLY PRUDHOMME, ARMAND SILVESTRE, FRANÇOIS COPPÉE, GEORGES LAFENESTRE, LÉON VALADE, LÉON DIERX, JEAN AICARD, PAUL VERLAINE, ALBERT MÉRAT, ANDRÉ THEURIET, ARMAND RENAUD, LOUIS XAVIER DE RICARD, H. CAZALI, ERNEST D'HERVILLY."

This letter, thus signed by names many of which have since become famous, was at the time a token of courage as well as a graceful tribute. It was forwarded to Brussels, whence the poet sent back his reply:

"DEAR POETS,—The literary revolution of 1830 was the corollary of the revolution of 1789; it is the specialty of our century. I am the humble soldier of the advance. I fight for revolution in every form, literary as well as social. Liberty is my principle, progress my law, the ideal my type.

"I ask you, my young brethren, to accept my acknowledgments.

"At my time of life, the end—that is to say, the infinite—seems very near. The approaching hour of departure from this world leaves little time for other than serious meditations. But while I am thus preparing to depart, your eloquent letter is very precious to me: it makes me dream of being among you, and the illusion bears to the reality the sweet resemblance of the sunset to the sunrise. You bid me welcome while I am making ready for a long farewell.

"Thanks: I am absent because it is my duty. My resolution is not to be shaken; but my heart is with you.

"I am proud to have my name encircled by yours, which are to me a crown of stars.
"VICTOR HUGO."

The performance of "Hernani" was not authorized for long. Not content with having banished the man, the Emperor Napoleon III. could not rest without trying to banish his sentiments. Only at the end of his reign, and that after much difficulty, was he induced to tolerate the representation of "Lucrèce Borgia" at the Porte-Saint-Martin. This performance was a great success for Marie Laurent, and drew forth from Georges Sand a striking letter to Victor Hugo, in which she said:

"I was present thirty-seven years ago at the first representation of 'Lucrèce,' and I shed tears of grief; with a heart full of joy I leave the performance of this day. I still hear the acclamations of the crowd as they shout 'Vive Victor Hugo!' as though you were really coming to hear them."

Another poem of Victor Hugo's appeared in 1867. It was issued under the title "La Voix de Guernesey," its object being to stigmatize the Mentana expedition, and to console Garibaldi under the defeat which he had sustained from the Pope and his ally Bonaparte. In an apostrophe to Pius IX. the poet addressed him in the language of stern severity:

"Ill-starred old man ! to thee the ravenous vultures owe
Their feast of skulls unearthed from scanty soil below!
Responsible art thou for ravens boding ill,
Thy gloomy visions now the open tombs fulfil.

"The mitrailleuse hast thou invited ; and now see
How that the dying owe their carnage all to thee !
Go, say thy mass; but first go wash thy crimson hand ;
Thus stained with blood, how canst thou at the altar stand ?"

It may easily be imagined how such language stirred up the wrath of the clerical press, especially when it is added that no less than seventeen translations of the poem, some of them in verse, appeared simultaneously in many languages. Garibaldi replied to Victor Hugo in some French verses which he called "Mentana," thousands of copies of which crossed the frontier and found their way to Paris. Imperial indignation was kindled, and not only was the performance of "Hernani" stopped, but a letter was sent to the poet in Guernsey:

"The manager of the imperial Théâtre de l'Odéon has the honor to inform M. Victor Hugo that the reproduction of 'Ruy Blas' is forbidden. CHILLY."

Victor Hugo at once replied, directing his answer not to the Théâtre de l'Odéon, but to the Tuileries:

"To M. Louis Bonaparte:

"Sir,—It is you that I hold responsible for the letter which I have just received signed 'Chilly.' VICTOR HUGO."

The document really reached its destination. Many letters despatched by the poet had not the same good-fortune; most of them were read upon passing the frontier, and not a few of them were confiscated. It was in vain that he availed himself of Art. 187 in the Penal Code, and wrote upon his envelopes "On private affairs only ;" the secret officers of the government did not hesitate to unseal and examine all his communications. Doubtless they thought that they had ample warrant for their proceedings; they were well aware that between him and his correspondents mutual pledges in behalf of liberty were continually being exchanged, and that the young men of the rising generation, in their aspirations for freedom, were being fortified and encouraged by the advice and counsel of the exile.

For himself, not unhappy in the present, and hopeful for the future, he waited on. He rejected the amnesty of 1859, and voluntarily remained in his expatriation; he held to the doctrine that the guilty have no right to offer pardon to the innocent, even as it is not the place of an executioner to provide a respite for a criminal. With still greater decision did he scorn the proffered amnesty of 1869: he had already placed his vow on record that he would never again visit the land which was "the resting-place of his ancestors and the birthplace of his love," until liberty had been restored to her; he had vowed that he must enter France in company with right, or he would not enter at all. To these vows he was never for a moment untrue.

Notwithstanding his compulsory absence from his country, his activity in political matters remained very considerable, and became still more so when *Le Rappel* was started on the 4th of May, 1869. It was the eve of the general election, and in order to continue the battle that had been commenced by Rochefort in *La Lanterne* it was considered necessary to establish a paper of sufficient power to be a telling organ with the democracy and to influence the popular vote. To render such an enterprise a success, it was indispensable that the services of men of tried courage and of known reputation should be secured. Just the men for the task were the old staff of *L'Événement*, and they were ready enough to undertake the responsibility and to fight to the very end. Thus it came about that the new journal was committed to Charles and François Hugo, Auguste Vacquerie, and Paul Meurice. They were subsequently joined by Rochefort, than whom no one had been more successful, by the brilliancy of his epigrams, in assaulting the outworks of the citadel of the Empire.

The characters of Charles and François Hugo have been already indicated, and we poet has rendered them the high praise they have deserved, professing himself proud of their friendship, their integrity, and their talent; he has dedicated verses to them,

PAUL MEURICE.

shall have further occasion to refer to their magnanimity; something, moreover, has been said of Victor Hugo's two faithful friends, Vacquerie and Meurice. Many a time the consoling them when assailed with slander, and encouraging them when called upon to submit to sacrifice. It has been through difficulty, but their way has led them to honor.

Paul Meurice is one of our great masters in the art of writing. All his works, his romances and his dramas, mark him out as a first-rate author; his ideas are as original as they are intellectual, while the united strength and simplicity of his style, the clearness and taste of his composition, his grace of manner and honesty of purpose, cannot fail to raise him to a high pedestal among the literary worthies of the century.

returned to Paris, and, without ceasing to be both poet and artist, devoted himself to the office of journalist, in which he has not many superiors. For ten years, day after day, he has produced articles, written upon the spur of the moment, that have invariably been remarkable for vigor and good-sense, inflexible in principle, and energetic in defence of

AUGUSTE VACQUERIE.

him to a high pedestal among the literary worthies of the century.

Auguste Vacquerie is also an original character, and his name, like that of his friend and brother-in-arms, is synonymous with talent, uprightness, and energy. He has faith in art and he has faith in the Republic, which nothing can shake. After having long been an exile by his own choice, he foresaw that the day of liberty was about to return; he

right. His work may well deserve the respect of posterity.

Under such an editorship as this, it was only to be expected that *Le Rappel* would prove an unprecedented success. Foreseeing the reception it would undoubtedly command, the imperial authorities forbade its sale in the public thoroughfares; but in spite of the prohibition it is said that 180,000 copies were printed, and that all the presses at the disposal of the journal were quite inadequate to meet the demands of the population, purchasers frequently fighting for the successive editions.

For those weary of servitude or worn out with degradation, *Le Rappel* beat the call of honor.

As a contribution to the opening number, Victor Hugo wrote a manifesto consisting of an address to the five co-editors:

"Le Rappel.

"It is a call. I love the word in every sense. It is the call to principle by conscience; the call to truth by philosophy; the call to duty by right; the call to the dead by reverence; the call to punishment by equity; the call to the past by history; the call to the future by logic; the call to action by courage; the call to idealism by thought; the call to science by experiment; the call to God in religion by the extirpation of idolatry; the call to the people's sovereignty by universal suffrage; the call to humanity by free education; the call to liberty by the awakening of France and by the stirring cry ' *Fiat jus !*'

"You say, this is our task! I say, this is your work!"

The circumstances of the poet did not permit him to take any share in the daily labor, but his heart was ever with those who continued the struggle, and who were reinforced by the assistance of Arthur Arnould, Jules Claretie, and by a pleiad of young authors of decided merit. The paper had to undergo repeated prosecutions, the detailed account of which would be superfluous, but it stood its ground triumphing over all opposition. It did a good work in enlightening the minds of many, especially of the young, and there are few who are not aware what good service was done by *Le Rappel* in hastening forward the day of justice to the nation.

In 1870, Napoleon had begun to feel the ground sensibly trembling under his feet, and devised the scheme of shoring up his tottering throne by a *plébiscite*. Consulted about this proposal for a *plébiscite*, Victor Hugo gave it a most outspoken negative, and proceeded to deliver his reasons in a vigorous article in the paper. He asked why the people should be invited to vote for the completion of a crime; he declared that the scheme should be treated with all the contempt it deserved, concluding what he wrote with this outburst of his indignation:

"While the author of the *coup d'état* wants to put a question to the people, we would ask him to put this question to himself: ' Ought I, Napoleon, to quit the Tuileries for the Conciergerie and to put myself at the disposal of justice?'

" ' Yes!'   Victor Hugo.".

Immediately the journal was prosecuted and the law-courts passed judgment against the author of the article. But these reverses were the harbinger of better days.

Perhaps we may be allowed to pause here awhile and make a general *résumé* of the poet's political action during the prolonged period of his exile. And this can hardly be given more completely than in the words in which Auguste Vacquerie has made his retrospect of the time:

"How far Victor Hugo has fulfilled his duty, and to what extent he has acted up to the spirit of the immortal verse

" 'Though only one remain, that one shall be myself,'

is universally known.

"From every quarter he received perpetual appeals. The bereaved sought him out to speak at the grave-side of the dear ones they had lost, and he delivered funeral orations over Jean Bousquet, Louise Julien, and Félix Bany; he was urged to use his pen in condemnation of the gallows, and he wrote remonstrances against the execution of Tapner and of Bradley, and he eulogized John Brown as the great deliverer of the blacks.

"By an emperor expatriated, for an emperor he entreated pardon — Juarez. He responded to the appeal of the people of Crete. He denounced the suppression of the revolt in Cuba as brutal, and he took up the petition of the three hundred women who had fled to New York for refuge. He was invited to Lausanne to preside at the Peace Congress. To him it was that Ireland turned with supplications that he would take up the defence of the convicted Fenians.

"Not one of these appeals did he reject.

"And this by no means represented all his work. Amid his labors he gave to an admiring world ' Napoléon le Petit,' ' Les Châtiments,' ' Les Contemplations,' ' La Légende des Siècles,' ' Les Chansons des Rues et des Bois,' ' Shakespeare,' ' Les Travailleurs de la Mer,' ' Les Misérables,' and ' L'Homme qui Rit.'

"One thing, too, there is worthy of all note. Throughout these nineteen years of incessant struggle, this duel with the Empire, this hand-to-hand conflict with tyranny in every shape, Victor Hugo remained uniformly calm and placid.

"Expelled from France for defending the rights of the people, driven from Brussels as the result of publishing 'Napoléon le Petit,' banished from Jersey because he had written 'Les Châtiments,' he nevertheless was as full of spirits in Guernsey, at last, as ever he had been in Paris.

"He lived among his family, finding in his wife a noble consoler of his exile, until she died, in 1868.

"Other sorrows came to overcloud the career of the illustrious poet, and he had ere long to shed more bitter tears of grief; but at length the hour for which he had been waiting—the hour of justice—drew near, and finally arrived."

CHAPTER XXX.

Return to France.—Distressing Journey.—Popular Ovation on Arrival. — The Siege.—A Cry for Peace.—
A Cry for War. — Public Performances. — Proceeds Purchasing Cannon. — Strange Diet. — Improvised
Verses.—Walks on the Ramparts.—Victor Hugo's Admiration of the People of Paris.

THE *plébiscite* was destined to lead France to Sedan. There had been a promise of "peace," but it had only led to war, and consequently to the dismemberment of the Empire—the result inevitable under such a government as that which dated from the 2d of December.

At the first news of the disaster of 1870 Victor Hugo left Hauteville House and hastened to Brussels, in order that he might be as near as possible to his country in the trying hour of her distress.

The capitulation of Sedan soon came, and with it the revolution of the 4th of September. On the 5th the poet re-entered France. On reaching Landrecies, the first scene that met his eyes was one of rout and disorder. Soldiers, faint and weary, and fugitives more than half starved, were holding out their hands for a morsel of bread. In the presence of the great disaster, whereby the whole French army seemed vanquished and dispersed, tears rolled down his cheeks, and his whole frame quivered with sobs. He bought up all the bread that could be procured, and distributed it among the famished troops.

His companion on this mournful journey was M. Jules Claretie, a man of good family, and a writer of no inconsiderable renown. It will be well for us to allow him to tell the story in his own touching words. He writes:

"On Monday, the 5th of September, the day after the fall of the Empire, Victor Hugo, then staying in the Place des Barricades in Brussels, presented himself at the railway booking-office, and, with an emotion in his voice that he in vain tried to suppress, asked for a ticket to Paris.

"I see him still. I had left the battle-field of Sedan and gone to Brussels, where I had spent the anxious day of the 4th in feverish suspense, rushing alternately to the post and telegraph offices. In the evening the news arrived that the Republic had been proclaimed in Paris. Immediately it was arranged that Victor Hugo should start on the following day. A voluntary exile from France since the amnesty, he had remained faithful to his vow, twice repeated, first in 'Les Châtiments,' then in his letter, 'When liberty returns, I will return.'

"France had now recovered herself, and it was no longer her liberty that was threatened, but her independence. Victor Hugo felt himself entitled to go back to Paris when Paris was besieged. It was my own privilege to accompany him on his journey, every detail of which has fastened itself upon my memory. The story of that day has become a page of history.

"Wearing a soft felt hat and carrying a small leather travelling-bag fastened across his shoulders by a strap, Victor Hugo, pale with excitement, looked instinctively at his watch as he pressed forward to get his ticket. It seemed as if he must be taking note of the precise moment when his exile was to come to an end.

"Truly a long time had passed (nineteen years!) since the day when he had been forced to leave Paris, which was overwhelmed by his genius, and to surrender everything that seemed to make up his life —his home, his books, his pictures, and his furniture; the day on which he had been torn from the pages he was writing, and of which the ink was not yet dry: yes, nineteen years had now elapsed.

"But it was all over! The time had come when once more he was to say, 'Here is France!'

"'A ticket for Paris!' he exclaimed, in a tone that seemed to me to ring like the note of a clarion.

"On the platform some faithful friends were waiting to see him off. One of these— the good Camille Berru, who has been described by Charles Hugo in 'Les Hommes de l'Exil'—was overpowered by grief because he was unable to accompany a man he loved so earnestly.

"The train started. Victor Hugo was

seated opposite to myself and M. Antoine Prévost. He gazed through the window, his eye fixed steadily on the horizon. He was manifestly watching for the moment when the frontier should be crossed, and once again his eyes should feast upon the meadows, the trees, the soil, the sky, of his own country. I shall never forget the expression that passed over his features. He was now sixty-eight. His head was whitened by his years of exile, but the glow of animation that was shed over his countenance as he first caught sight of a French soldier can never be obliterated from my recollection.

"This occurred at Landrecies. Making good their retreat from Mézières, on their way to Paris, the remnant of Vinoy's corps, poor harassed creatures, covered with dust and discolored with powder, pale with exertion and discouragement, were lying all along the road. Close behind them were the Uhlans. There was no alternative for them but flight if they would escape the disaster that had befallen the army at Sedan. Defeat was written in their faces, demoralization was evident in their attitude; they were dejected and dirty; they were like pebbles driven along by a hurricane. But what of that? Anyhow, they were soldiers of France; their uniform proclaimed their nationality; they wore the blue tunic and the red trousers, but, what was of infinitely greater consequence, they were carrying their colors back with them. Their defeat did not prevent them bringing back the tricolor safe and sound. Great tears rolled from Victor Hugo's eyes. He leaned from the carriage window, and, with a voice thrilling in its earnestness, he kept shouting, 'Vive la France! vive l'armée! vive la patrie!'

"Exhausted as they were with hunger and fatigue, the bewildered soldiers looked up. They scarcely comprehended what he said, but he continued his shouting, and it was almost like an order of quick-march to them all when they made out that they were being assured that they had done their duty, and that it was by no fault of theirs that they had sustained defeat.

"And so the train went on. The tears still lost themselves in Victor Hugo's snowy beard. He had lived in the proud illusion that France was invincible; he was a soldier's son, and could not conceive that the soldiers of his country were not pledged to glory. He had ever imagined them foremost and triumphant in the fight; but now his hopes were blighted, his anticipations had miscarried, and he could be heard sighing, 'Better, perhaps, never to have seen France again than to see her dismembered and divided, and reduced to what she was in the days of Louis XIII.'

"It is more than ten years since, but that hinders me not from still seeing those tears of the poet trickling as though they were drops from a wound in the depth of his heart!

"And may I not mention another incident of which I cannot be otherwise than proud? I gave him his first meal after he passed the frontier of his country on his homeward way. His arrival at Tergnier was expected; the refreshment-room was crowded; the *commissaire*, with a bow, told him that he needed no passport, and we made our way to the buffet, at which there was little enough to be had. Then it was that I solicited the honor of presenting him with the first meal of which he partook after this long estrangement from his country, he accepted my offer, and we made a hasty repast off new bread, cheese, and wine. During the meal, I saw him slip into his pocket a fragment of the bread which he had been eating as his earliest refreshment in his newly recovered country.

"'I have that piece of bread still,' he has more than once said to me, when speaking of that frugal entertainment; 'Madame Drouet takes care of it for me.'

"Except that morsel of bread, I think he took nothing more that day; sorrow had parched his throat.

"After we re-entered the train, the shades of evening began to gather, and for the rest of the journey Victor Hugo was thoughtful and silent. He broke the stillness by saying, 'I should like to enter our imperilled city on foot and alone, like an unknown traveller.'

"Charles Hugo was travelling with us, but at the Northern Railway-station François Hugo, Vacquerie, and Paul Meurice all rushed forward calling out, 'Vive Victor Hugo!'

"'Gently, gently!' cried a surgeon-major; 'we have some wounded men here,' and he pointed to some ambulance wagons that were smeared with blood. At a sign from Victor Hugo, his friends restrained their vociferations, but outside the station an enormous crowd was awaiting him, and no sooner was he recognized than he was triumphantly carried off.

15

"Through the midst of the vast populace I followed with my gaze. I looked with admiration on that man now advancing in years, but faithful still in vindicating right, and never now do I behold him greeted with the salutations of a grateful people without recalling the scene of that memorable night when, with weeping eye, he returned to see his country as she lay soiled and dishonored, and well-nigh dead!

"With reference to that day, Victor Hugo has written to me, saying, 'You are still young, but nevertheless to me you are an old friend; we have mutual recollections of my return to France.'"

To these pathetic reminiscences of Claretie we may add a few lines from Alphonse Daudet, who has chronicled the same event:

"He arrived just as the circle of investment was closing in around the city; he came by the last train, bringing with him the last breath of the air of freedom. He had come to be a guardian of Paris; and what an ovation was that which he received outside the station from those tumultuous throngs, already revolutionized, who were prepared to do great things, and were infinitely more rejoiced at the liberty they had regained than terrified by the cannon that were thundering against their ramparts! Never can we forget the spectacle as the carriage passed along the Rue Lafayette, Victor Hugo standing up, and being literally borne along by the teeming multitudes."

It was ten o'clock at night when the train arrived. The poet had chosen to reach his destination at this late hour, expecting that he should make his entry into the capital in quiet and unobserved privacy; but the crowds that filled the neighborhood of the station and the adjacent streets had waited for hours to give their welcome to the great citizen who had been so long the champion of their rights and liberty.

All Paris was eager not only to see but to hear Victor Hugo, who, in acknowledgment of his enthusiastic reception, delivered a short speech.

"Words fail me," he began, in a trembling voice, "and I am incapable of saying how much I am moved by the welcome which the generous people of Paris has pleased to extend me. Citizens, I have always said that when a Republic should return, I would return too. And here I am!

"There are two things that call me now. The first is the Republic; the other is danger. I am here to do my duty; and my duty is the same as yours. Upon every one of us there now rests the same obligation. We must defend Paris and save it!

"I thank you for your acclamations. But I attribute them all to your sense of the anguish that is rending all hearts, and to the peril that is threatening our land.

"I have but one thing to demand of you. I invite you to union. By union you will conquer. Subdue all ill-will. Check all resentment. Be united, and you shall be invincible. Rally round the Republic. Hold fast, brother to brother. Victory is in our own keeping. Fraternity is the saviour of liberty!"

Then, cheered continually along the whole route, he was conducted to No. 5 Avenue Frochot, the residence of his friend Paul Meurice, where he was to take up his abode. Here he again said a few words to the people, telling them that in that single hour they had compensated him for all his nineteen years of exile.

Throughout the siege the poet remained with Paul Meurice in an elegant suite of rooms on the ground-floor of a house that was enclosed by trees. At that time Madame Paul Meurice was alive.

No home could be kinder than that in which the poet was received. He needed warm and faithful friends. He had never anticipated that it would be his fate to come back and find that the imperial crime had been thus chastised by the invasion of a foreign foe.

To that country which he had ever loved so ardently, if he now brought nothing else, he brought noble advice. He came back to tell her how to resist and how to fight, and he was quite prepared to take his own share in her sufferings, her sorrows, and her struggles.

Enough for him to know that Paris was besieged, and that accordingly Paris was the proper place for him. In spite of the giant army of Prussia, France had regained her liberty, and he was not going to let France die now, except he were to die with her. His children and grandchildren were with him; they had scorned the Empire, but the sorrow of the land should now win their love. The young men of the second Empire might, if they pleased, escape beyond the frontier, and get out of the reach of the Prussian bombs; his own place was at the post of danger; his own breast should lie open as a target for the cannon that were levelled against the city of the world!

For some days after his return to France, the German army kept advancing by forced marches to invest the capital. It occurred to him to ask himself whether there was not yet time to interpose his voice between two was circulated in both the French and German newspapers.

"Germans!" he wrote, "he who now addresses you speaks as a friend. It is but three years ago, at the time of the Exhibition of 1867, that I sent you my good wishes, and bade you welcome to your city. Yes, I

MADAME PAUL MEURICE.

contending nations, of which the victorious kept saying to the vanquished, "We are not making war against you, but only against your emperor." Ought it not now to be that as the emperor had been set aside the strife should be brought to a close? And, under this conviction, he issued an appeal, which say *your* city; for Paris belongs not to us alone; it is yours as well as ours. You have, indeed, your capitals — Berlin, Dresden, Vienna, Munich, and Stuttgart; but Paris is your centre, and it is in Paris that men learn to live: it is the city of cities; it is the city of men. There has been an Athens, there has been a Rome; now there is a Paris, and Paris is a synonym for open hospitality.

"And now you will come back to us again, but you come back as enemies! Whence this dire misunderstanding? Why this invasion? What mean these savage efforts? What have we done?

"This war does not proceed from us. It was the Empire that willed the war; it was the Empire that prosecuted it. But now the Empire is dead, and a good thing too! We have nothing to do with its corpse; it is all the past; we are the future. The Empire was hatred, we are sympathy; that was treason, we are loyalty. The Empire was Capua, nay, it was Gomorrah; we are France. Our motto is 'Liberty, Equality, Fraternity;' on our banner we inscribe 'The United States of Europe.' Whence, then, this onslaught?

"Pause a while before you present to the world the spectacle of Germans becoming Vandals, and of barbarism decapitating civilization. Victory will not be for your honor.

"Persist, Germans, if you will; but remember you are warned. Paris will defend herself. I am an old man now, I shall not bear arms, but I am satisfied to be on the side of the people who are slain; I pity you who are on the side of the rulers who slay."

These were words of peace, but the German press only replied with cries of wrath and indignation. The manifesto was torn down and destroyed by the Prussian generals, and one of the newspapers declared that the proper place for the author was on the gibbet, "Hängt den Dichter an den Mast auf."

Meanwhile the enemy continued to advance. The last resource for Paris seemed to be to make a general levy, and to issue a peremptory call to arms. Victor Hugo raised the war-cry:

"Let every commune arouse itself! let every field take fire! let every forest be filled with a voice of thunder! Tocsin! tocsin! Let every house produce a soldier! let the faubourg become a regiment, the city become an army! The Prussians may be 800,000 strong, but you are forty millions! Stand up and blow upon them! Lille, Nantes, Tours, Bourges, Orléans, Dijon, Toulouse, Bayonne, gird up your loins! Lyons, take your rifles! Rouen, draw your sword! Marseilles, sing your hymn! Cities, cities, cities, make forests of pikes, mass together your bayonets, horse your cannon! Villages, bring out your pitchforks!

"What do you say? You have no powder? All a mistake; you have what you need. The Swiss peasants had but their hatchets; the Polish peasants had but their scythes; the Breton peasants had but their sticks; and yet they carried all before them. In a true cause everything helps. We are at home. The season will be ours; the north wind will be ours; the rain will be ours. War or disgrace! Where there's a will, there's a way! A bad gun is a good weapon if it be used with a brave heart; the stump of an old sword can do fine work if it be wielded by a valiant hand. The Spanish peasants did for Napoleon, let the peasants find a weapon now! Roll together your rocks, tear up your paving-stones, convert your ploughshares into axes, torment the invaders with the pebbles from the ground; the stones you fling in their faces shall be the soil of France itself!"

This ringing battle-cry was issued on the 17th of September. Its author was urged to go and promulgate it throughout the provinces, but he felt pledged to share the fate of Paris, and would not quit his post. On the whole the people acted very heroically, although in October some signs of disaffection appeared, and there was an attempt at a communist insurrection which was fortunately quelled.

Having thus first raised his voice in favor of peace by deprecating the advance of the Prussians, and having next encouraged a war that in his eyes was sanctified, inasmuch as so far from being an aggression it had no other object than to repel invasion, the poet felt himself constrained to address the people of Paris, and to urge upon them the imperative duty of concord.

"What you now owe to duty is to forget yourself," he said to every individual among them. He added:

"There must now be union. Without unity you cannot prevail. Your resentments, your grievances, your animosities, must all be cast to the winds, and disappear in presence of the cannon's roar. We must hold together so that we may fight together. Our merits must be deemed equal. Have any been outlaws? I know nothing about them. Have any been exiled? It is not for me to inquire. It is no time now for personalities; it is no time now for ambitions or reminiscences. The one common thought in which everything must now be merged must be the commonwealth."

Wise and patriotic as these counsels were, they were not universally received as they deserved; but the author of them remained steadfast in setting a bright example of courage and of equanimity.

In October a Parisian edition of "Les Châtiments" appeared; and the book thus became associated with the siege, playing its part during that terrible time. From the first issue, consisting of five thousand copies, the author received a profit of five hundred francs, which he at once contributed to the fund that had been started to procure cannon.

Very shortly after this the Literary Society proposed that some of the leading *artistes* of the city should combine to give a recitation of pieces taken from the book which, once proscribed, had now, by the re-establishment of the Republic, become a lawful publication. With the proceeds of the performance they begged their president to have a cannon cast for the national defence, and to allow it to be called by his own name. Victor Hugo replied that he was proud to accept their noble offer, but that he could not permit the gun to be named after himself, suggesting at the same time that it should be called "the Châteaudun," after the brave little town that, together with Strasburg, had attracted the admiration of Europe.

The recitation of "Les Châtiments" took place at the theatre of the Porte-Saint-Martin on the 5th of November. M. Jules Claretie made a noble speech on behalf of the society, recounting the history of the poet's exile, and pointing out how the sad predictions of his verses had all been fulfilled. It was with the nephew just as it had been with the uncle, that the Empire which professed that "*l'Empire c'est la paix*" had ended in invasion.

Recited as they were by the most gifted actors of the time, by Frédéric Lemaître, Coquelin, Marie Laurent, Lafontaine, and Berton, and accompanied by Pasdeloup's orchestra, the passages from "Les Châtiments" were rendered with a skill and received with an enthusiasm which none but an eye-witness could conceive.

The proceeds of the performance were 7500 francs; and the sensation was so great that the besieged population begged for a repetition of the entertainment, of which the success was still more complete. A third performance was given on the 17th of November, but on this occasion all the admittances were, by the poet's wish, perfectly free. M.

Tony Révillon delivered an address upon the work; between the pieces the actresses went round and made a collection in Prussian helmets that they handed about, and at the end a gilt laurel-wreath was thrown upon the stage, bearing the inscription,

> "For our Poet,
> who has labored to give peace of mind to the poor."

Altogether the amount thus realized exceeded 10,000 francs, and the Literary Society resolved that two cannon should be cast, one to be inscribed with the word "Châtiments," and the other with Victor Hugo's name. Both were also to bear the words "Société des Gens des Lettres." M. Dorian, the Minister of Public Works, acquiesced in the scheme. The guns cost about 7000 francs, and the rest of the money was applied to the relief of literary men who were thrown into distress by the war.

A further sum of 6000 francs, the proceeds of a performance of certain extracts from Victor Hugo's principal plays at the Porte-Saint-Martin, was appropriated to the ambulances.

But independently of these performances "Les Châtiments," as well as Victor Hugo's other works, became a kind of open property to the theatres, and by the author's permission were left at their disposal until January in the following year, when it was found impossible either to light or to warm the houses. It was a gracious act on the part of Victor Hugo, and it was owing to his generosity that several companies of infantry were kept provided with their necessary equipments.

Gambetta, not many days before he made his venturous ascent in the balloon, called upon the poet, desirous to acknowledge the services which he had endeavored to render to the Republic and to his country.

"For the public good," said Victor Hugo, "make use of me in any way you can. Distribute me as you would dispense water. My books are even as myself; they are all the property of France. With them, with me, do just as you think best."

There was scarcely any limitation to the range of the benefits which the poet by means of his works was now conferring. The stage-representations were multiplied in every direction. The needy and the sick, the widows and the orphans, none were forgotten; though Victor Hugo himself, who shunned public ovations, was never present at any of the performances.

To the very last the poet maintained his courage and kept up his hope. Alarmed though he might be, he was ever anxious to allay alarm in others, and in the severest hours of trial his cheerful demeanor never forsook him. From his pleasant quarters in Paul Meurice's house in the Avenue Frochot he made his way every morning to the Pavillon de Rohan, near the Rue de l'Échelle, where his family had found a retreat, and there he welcomed not only his personal friends, but many of the members of the Committee for National Defence. For the sake of example, they all put themselves under strict rule of rations, determining to partake of no more food than what was absolutely necessary.

To any of his colleagues whom Victor Hugo chanced to meet, he would say,

"Come and dine with me; I can give you a spread."

Of what the "spread" consisted, it may easily be imagined. There was hardly an animal of any kind that was not being utilized for food: horses, dogs, cats, and rats finding their way to table, and helping, as it was jocosely said, to make everybody's stomach a sort of Noah's Ark. But the Amphitryon kept up a good heart, laughed over his strange diet, seasoning the unsavory viands with a *bon-mot*, and making up for any deficiency of food by a store of good anecdotes. His *menu* furnished him continually with the theme for many amusing couplets that have been preserved by Madame Drouet, although the author has naturally considered them too trivial to allow them to be published. Horse-flesh was usually the material of the meals; and on one occasion, having partaken of a slice of some half-starved old hack that proved by no means easy of digestion, he wrote:

"My dinner for digestion far too heavy seems;
Horse in the stomach gives saddle in the dreams."

Nor was his jest always in verse. One evening, after Emmanuel Arago had been dining with him, he put on a very serious look and said to his guest,

"My dear friend, you know my opinion on capital punishment."

"Certainly," replied the statesman, assuming a very stern expression.

"I have to solicit your pardon for an individual who has been condemned to death."

"Oh, impossible, impossible! I do not know to whom you refer, but in critical times like these it is absolutely necessary for the sentence of the law to be strictly carried out."

"But permit me—" interposed the poet.

"Impossible!" repeated M. Arago; "I regret extremely that I cannot grant your request."

"Allow me to explain. The poor condemned mortal for whom I would plead is our dear friend Théophile Gautier's horse."

Amid general laughter the favor was granted, and the poor old animal was saved, at least for a time, from going to the shambles.

In M. Rivet's volume of anecdotes entitled "Victor Hugo chez lui," it is mentioned that towards the end of the winter, when the dearth began to be most severely felt, the idea began to be discussed of eating human flesh.

"Oh, of course," said Victor Hugo, "I should not object to be the victim to appease the hunger of my fellow-citizens," and he added the impromptu:

"Not my ashes to leave to my country I mean,
But myself, my own self, my very beefsteak!
And, ladies, you'll need but a morsel to take
To learn what a tender old creature I've been!"

The light-heartedness so peculiar to Frenchmen did much to enable them to endure their hard privations, and it was with a smile on their countenances that they swallowed the bread of which M. Magnin has never divulged the ingredients.

Every evening Victor Hugo, with sorrow at his heart, returned to his quarters, whence again during the night he would often go out and take long walks through the beleaguered city, composing, according to his wont, superb verses, many of which were ultimately to appear in "L'Année Terrible."

The sight of Paris in arms filled him with admiration. He would walk towards the ramparts where shells were falling, and, pursuing his meditations in the gloom, would be stopped from time to time by the sentinels, to whom he always responded with the cry "Vive la République!"

In reference to this terrible time he has often said:

"Never did city exhibit such fortitude. Not a soul gave way to despair, and courage increased in proportion as misery grew deeper. Not a crime was committed. Paris earned the admiration of the world. Her struggle was noble and she would not give in. Her women were as brave as her men. Surrendered and betrayed she was; but she was not conquered."

And the poet's voice ever trembles as he recounts the circumstances of that undeserved but not inglorious defeat.

PERFORMANCE AT THE THÉÂTRE FRANÇAIS.

[Sketch by Andrieux.]

CHAPTER XXXI.

ALTHOUGH he had refused to make any canvass, Victor Hugo obtained more than 4000 votes in the fifteenth arrondissement in the municipal election in Paris on the 5th of November, 1870; while at the general election of the 8th of February, 1871, that took place immediately after the signing of the armistice, he was chosen as representative for the department of the Seine, being second out of forty-three candidates with 214,169 votes.

The Assembly at first sat at Bordeaux, where he arrived on the 14th of February, just two days after Garibaldi had left. On the following day, at the conclusion of the first sitting, he was urged to address the people from a balcony overlooking the Grande Place. This he declined to do, saying that at so grave a crisis prudence was the better part of devotion. He thought it right to communicate with the people only through the Assembly, and held that it was from the tribune that he ought to make his choice between a desperate war and a still more desperate peace—between a despair coupled with glory and a despair linked with shame.

As the representative of Paris he sat in the ranks of the extreme Left. M. Grévy was the President of the Assembly. The first time that Victor Hugo spoke was on the 1st of March, when he delivered an energetic protest against the proposed preliminaries for peace. He said that Paris during her protracted struggle had been the admiration of the world; he declared that during five months of the Republic she had gained more honor than she had lost during nineteen years of the Empire; he professed that, though she was mutilated herself, she would never be a participator in the mutilation of France; and he maintained that if Alsace and Lorraine still wished to be French, it was good and equitable that they should remain so.

"In Strasburg," he explained, "in that glorious city that has now been overpowered by the Prussian artillery, there are two statues, one of Gutenberg, the other of Kleber; a voice within us bids us record our vow to Gutenberg that we will not quench the flame of civilization, and our vow to Kleber that we will not extinguish the light of the Republic."

Boisterous applause rose from the Left, and he concluded his speech by an eloquent appeal to "the universal Republic" and to Fraternity, which he asserted was his "vengeance," winding up by pronouncing in favor of continuing war as the only means of attaining an enduring peace.

But the treaty of peace was ratified.

The representatives of Alsace and Lorraine forthwith sent in their resignation to the Assembly; and a meeting of the radical Left was held on Thursday, the 12th of March, at which Victor Hugo announced his intention of submitting the following resolution to the Chamber:

"That the representatives of Alsace and Les Vosges retain their seats indefinitely, and that at every fresh election they shall be deemed duly elected."

In bringing forward his motion from the tribune, he declared that although from a German point of view Alsace and Lorraine might be dead, from that of the Assembly they were yet alive and in full vigor; therefore he demanded that there should be a distinct repudiation of the treaty, which, for his part, he ignored entirely as having no validity at all, inasmuch as it had been extorted by force.

Again he spoke to no effect. His words were not so effectual as his father's sword. The motion was rejected.

After the integrity of France had been thus disposed of by the ratification of the peace treaty, the Assembly proceeded to dispose of Paris, and came to the resolution that the Chamber should sit at Versailles. Victor Hugo made a vehement protest against what he called the decapitalization of the capital;

but once again the reactionary party prevailed and the Assembly went against him.

A few days after this a report was made upon the election of Algiers, where Garibaldi had been chosen as representative. It was proposed that the election should be declared null and void, whereupon Victor Hugo raised an earnest appeal. He said:

"France has passed through a tremendous ordeal; she has emerged bleeding and vanquished. Of all the powers of Europe, not

scribable tumult broke out in the Assembly; there was no insult too gross to be aimed at the orator; the Vicomte de Lorgeril rose and declared that M. Victor Hugo was not speaking French; and one deputy, the Abbé Jaffré, who had been returned at Morbihan, and was quite inexperienced in parliamentary forms, entirely misunderstood the cry of "À l'ordre, à l'ordre," that was being raised by the furious majority, and at the very top of his voice kept shouting "À mort, à mort."

GARIBALDI.

one has stirred itself to help the country which has ever been ready to take up the cause of Europe. Not one state, not one sovereign, has aroused itself on our behalf; nay, with a single exception, not one man. But *one* man there has been; and what has he had wherewith to aid us? Nothing but his sword. That sword of his had already delivered one nation, and he indulged the hope that it might contribute to the deliverance of another. And so he came; and so in our support he fought!"

At the delivery of these words an inde-

In the midst of the tumult Victor Hugo made himself heard; he said, calmly:

"Three weeks ago you declined to listen to Garibaldi; you now refuse to listen to me. Very good. I send in my resignation."

Satisfied in his own mind that he ought not to retain a place in a Chamber that appeared to him to be animated by a spirit more dangerous than the worst and most odious Chamber that had gone before it, he could only retire. He left the tribune, and, taking a pen from the hand of one of the reporters, he wrote a line signifying his resignation, and handed it to M. Grévy. Magnanimous as ever, the President of the Assembly (now President of the Republic) did everything in his power to induce the poet to reconsider his resolution, but no persuasion could move him; and after twenty-four hours' deliberation, during which M. Grévy pleaded with him most affectionately, he adhered to his resolve, and left the President no alternative but to announce that the Assembly was to lose the services of the distinguished representative of Paris.

Louis Blanc immediately rose. He beg-

devoted to humanity, and of humanity you are the first of apostles."

On the 13th of March, just as he was making his arrangements to return to Paris, Victor Hugo was about to join some friends at dinner at a restaurant, when he received the tidings of the sudden death of his son Charles, who had been seized with congestion of the brain in a cab as he was returning from an entertainment where he had been taking farewell of some of his friends.

It was a shock as trying as it was unexpected. After nineteen years of banishment,

CHARLES HUGO'S FUNERAL.

ged to express his extreme regret that a man to whom France was under so great an obligation should feel himself compelled to resign his seat in that Assembly; it was adding another drop of sorrow to the cup that was already over full; he grieved that a voice so powerful should be hushed just at an emergency when the country should be showing its gratitude to all its benefactors. He was seconded by M. Schœlcher.

Garibaldi himself wrote to Victor Hugo: "It needs no writing to show that we are of one accord; we understand each other; the deeds that you have done and the affection that I have borne for you make a bond of union between us. What you have testified for me at Bordeaux is a pledge of a life

after the loss of his true and loving wife, and after the bitter sufferings of the recent troubles of war and siege, the exile seemed to feel that he had returned to France to mingle a father's tears with those which he had shed as a patriot.

In deep distress, he had his son's body brought to Paris, resolved that it should be interred in the family vault at Père La Chaise, where the poet's father, mother, and brother Eugène were already lying. The funeral took place on the 18th, Victor Hugo himself, his surviving son François, Paul Meurice, Auguste Vacquerie, Paul Foucher, and some other friends following the hearse on foot. Without entering any church, the little procession went direct to the cemetery,

though, as the reporter to *Le Rappel* has related, it took up a remarkable contingent on
the way. In the Place de la Bastille, three
of the National Guard recognized Victor
Hugo, and, immediately taking their places
beside the hearse, marched along with lowered guns. As they proceeded a number of
their comrades joined them; and when the
cortége arrived at the burial-ground it included nearly a hundred soldiers, who had
voluntarily formed a guard of honor. Pa-
trolling detachments were then unusually
numerous, and on hearing whose funeral
was passing the men lowered their arms,
sounded their bugles, and beat their drums;
and even the guards on the barricades, not
in the direct line of thoroughfare, presented arms by way of salutation to the chief
mourner.

At the grave so great a crowd had collected that there was some little delay before
the bier could reach the vault. Two funeral
orations were delivered, one by Auguste
Vacquerie, the other by Louis Mie.

After speaking of the life of promise that
seemed to lie open before the son of their
venerable and sorrowing friend, M. Vacquerie proceeded to eulogize the principle of
right which the departed had learned to love
from his father, and which not even the
grave could annihilate, declaring that if he
could come back from the tomb it would be
only to commence afresh the struggle for
truth in which he had been arrested by the
hand of death.

M. Louis Mie spoke on behalf of the provincial press. Charles Hugo, he reminded
those who stood around him, had entered
the battle of life by advocating his father's
views as to the claims of humanity, and he
concluded by saying that while there had
been many sons who had detracted from
their father's honor, here was one whose
every action served to contribute something
of glory to a reputation to which already
nothing seemed wanting.

Notwithstanding the sympathy which was
so largely shown to him, Victor Hugo was
much overwhelmed by his grief, though his
ardent love for humanity inspired him with
strength to overcome it.

A few days after his son's funeral he
started for Brussels, where he had to go
through the formalities which his office as
executor and guardian of his grandchildren
entailed upon him. But his absence from
Paris did not make him cease to follow with

anxious interest the struggle that was going
on between the capital and Versailles. Raising his protest against the civil war, he
wrote:

" Hold, hold your hands ! your strife a bitter harvest
      yields ;
  Why spread the raging flame that devastates your
      fields ?
  When France looks face to face on France as foe,
  France murders all her honor, fills herself with woe ;
  Each victory sends the blight of mourning through
      the land
  When fellow-citizens in blood-red quarrel stand ;
  Each cannon-shot when Frenchmen Frenchmen
      strike,
  Is charged with death and fratricide and shame
      alike !"

And when he witnessed how the leaders of
the Commune, on the plea of retaliation,
plunged into every excess, he became indignant, and called on them to recollect how
nothing ought to be done outside the line of
honesty and justice. No sooner did he hear
of them cannonading the Colonne and the
Arc de Triomphe than his indignation waxed
still hotter, and he issued "Les deux Tro-
phées," in earnest hope that he might succeed in staying the ruthless hand of the de-
stroyers:

"Oh, has not France enough of slaughter seen ?
  Deluged with blood enough has France not been ?
          *   *   *   *   *
  Had it been Prussia's voice that bade you know
  That pillar and that archway down must go—
  'That brazen column stands too proud on high,
  That stately arch too much offends my eye—
  Down with them both !'
  How full of deadly fury you had turned !
  With what disdain you had her bidding spurned !
  With one accord to rescue them would haste ;
  Yet now by your own deed you lay them waste !"

Without hesitation, Victor Hugo condemned the Commune with the utmost vehemence of his nature. He wrote to *Le Rappel* that the city of science could not be
guided by ignorance, the city of light could
not be led by blindness. Ignorance generates
want of principle; blindness tends to brutality, and there was nothing less than brutality
in the affair of the hostages, which was an
abominable device of a few desperate madmen.

However, when the bloody days of May,
1871, were passed, and the insurrection was
quelled, Victor Hugo retained no animosity
against the men whose proceedings he had
so vehemently denounced; he not only protested against the decree of the Belgian government, which forbade the fugitives from
Paris to betake themselves to the country,

but he opened his own house to some of them as an asylum. He was still residing in Brussels, at 4 Rue des Barricades, and he maintained that his conscience impelled him to offer this retreat to those that needed it, satisfied that he was only acting in conformity with the principles that had ever guided him. Already he had written, years ago:

"Should e'er it chance to me to see my direst foe
   With bolts and dungeon threatened and by wrong
      distressed,
   My vengeful anger would I instantly forego;
   Nay, though it were the tyrant who myself op-
      pressed,
To find him safe asylum should be all my care,
Just as the Christ a vile Iscariot might spare."

He was ready to proclaim pardon for all; he would forgive the misguided who had been led astray by the terror of the political situation; he would forgive the Parisian workmen, who, failing to have confidence in M. Thiers, fancied that the Republic was in peril; he was anxious to extend protection to the defeated, and all this was only in accordance with what he had himself once said, that if Napoleon III. were in such a strait that he had to beg an asylum, he would give it him, and not a hair of his head should be hurt.

To little purpose, however, did Victor Hugo raise the plea for mercy. Two instances may be quoted to illustrate the vehemence of the fury of those who were opposed to him. One of these is somewhat ludicrous, the other verges on the tragical.

On the 22d of June, M. Xavier de Montépin, a writer of *feuilletons* as unwholesome as they were illiterate, wrote a letter to the President of the Society of Dramatic Authors, in which he submitted that the society would only be consulting their proper dignity by having the names of MM. Félix Pyat, Victor Hugo, Henri Rochefort, Paul Meurice, and all others who in any way made a compromise with the Commune, erased from the roll of their members. His way of recommending his proposal was droll enough.

"We shall thus," he writes, "be hollowing out an abyss between such men and ourselves."

The idea of M. Xavier de Montépin desiring to "hollow out an abyss" between himself and the author of "Hernani" and "Marion Delorme" was a fund of amusement to the society, who of course took no notice whatever of the letter; but the incident ought not to fail of being registered.

The more tragical illustration may be deferred to another chapter.

CHAPTER XXXII.

ON the 28th of April, Victor Hugo wrote from Brussels to Auguste Vacquerie and Paul Meurice on the subject of the events that were then transpiring in Paris. Without disputing that France had a perfect right to declare herself a commune if she would, he considered that she was bound to await a fitting opportunity.

"But why," he asked—"why break out into a conflict at such an hour as this? why rush into a civil war when a foreign war is scarcely at an end? How unseemly to treat Prussia to the spectacle of Frenchmen fighting like wild beasts in a circus, and that circus France itself!"

After censuring the insurrection as the result of an ignorant misunderstanding, he said that though he had been almost unconsciously a man of revolutions from his youth, always ready to accept great necessities, yet it had ever been under the condition that they should be the confirmation of principle, and not its convulsion. No one could have spoken with more prudence and moderation.

Meanwhile events thickened; the fatal days of May occurred, and many of the vanquished Communists sought refuge in Belgium.

The Belgian Minister of Foreign Affairs, questioned on the subject, pledged himself to do all in his power to prevent the country from being invaded by the Communists, whom he denounced as unworthy of the name of men, and such as ought to be arraigned at the bar of civilized nations. To this declaration, Victor Hugo made a reply which appeared in *L'Independance* of the 27th of May.

While accepting in large measure the principles of the Commune, he totally repudiated their acts, expressing his thorough detestation of their rule of hostages, **their** retaliations and their excesses; but he insisted that, **savage as** they had been, they ought not to be condemned without a trial. He said that although Belgium by law might refuse them an asylum, his own conscience could not approve that law. The Church of the Middle Ages had offered sanctuary even to parricides, and such sanctuary the fugitives should find at his home; it was his privilege to open his door if he would to his foe, and it ought to be Belgium's glory to be a place of refuge. England did not surrender the refugees, and why should Belgium be behindhand in magnanimity?

This brought about the tragical issue to which we have alluded.

On the very night after the publication of the article, he was about to retire to rest when there was a ringing of the house-bell. Opening his window on the first floor, he looked out and inquired who was there, and receiving the answer that it was Dombrowski, faithful to his promise that he would give an asylum to any that needed it he was about to descend to unbar the outer door, when a great stone struck the wall close by. Looking round again, he saw a group of men in the square, and, understanding only too well what they wanted, he called out to them that they were a set of ruffians, and hastily shut his window. At this moment, a huge fragment of paving-stone crashed through the window-pane close above his head and fell at his feet; while outside the shout was raised, "À bas Victor Hugo! à bas Jean Valjean! À mort Victor Hugo! à mort, à mort!"

The outcry brought Charles Hugo's widow running into the room with her two little children; and while the stones kept rattling through the window, the voices were distinctly heard crying out, "To the gallows! to the gallows! we will smash in his door!"

As the noise subsided, the startled inmates, thinking there was no further cause for alarm, went back to their rooms.

But half an hour afterwards the assault

was resumed. A large stone fell on Victor Hugo's bed. At the risk of her life, Madame Charles Hugo clambered over the roof of a conservatory, the glass breaking under her feet, and reached an adjoining house; but, though she did her utmost to attract attention, she could get no answer.

Once again the tumult ceased, and Victor Hugo was caressing the frightened children and carrying them back to their chamber, when another stone was hurled into the room and grazed the little girl's head.

The assailants, frustrated in their attempt to break in the door, next began to scale the house; but at that time of year there is no long duration of night, and two workmen passed by, who, seeing the commotion, hurried off to inform the police, upon whose approach the ruffians made off. Close at hand a heavy beam was found, which no doubt was being conveyed to the place with the intention of battering in the door.

It was a dastardly assault. So far from taking any measures to punish it forthwith, the government only issued an order, signed by the king and the minister of justice, to the effect that Victor Hugo must immediately quit the kingdom, and that, under the penalties of the law of 1865, he was forbidden to return.

In the Chamber, on the same day, the minister declared that Victor Hugo's letter must be regarded as a challenge, an outrage upon public morality, and an open defiance of the law; and consequently Victor Hugo, as a disturber of the public peace, must be ordered to quit the country.

In vain did M. Defuisseaux protest; in vain did he allege that the illustrious author of "Les Châtiments" was entitled to their sympathy; and that, so far from being disturbed by him, the public peace had been interrupted only by a few miscreants who were lost to all sense of justice or of honor. No one would listen. But the outrage, nevertheless, had the effect of making the government reflect, and they refrained from proceeding to proscribe every Communist indiscriminately; and, moreover, they took measures to have the agents in the disturbance of the 27th of May brought to justice. It was difficult, of course, so long after date, to procure much conclusive evidence, and the witnesses were few and hard to gather; there was, however, little room to doubt that M. Kervyn de Lettenhove, the son of the Minister of the Interior, had been one of the ringleaders in the dis-

graceful disturbance, and he was fined in the nominal sum of 100 francs.

Driven from Belgium, Victor Hugo made a tour through Luxembourg, going first to Vianden, where the news of his arrival soon spread. At this place one of the preachers from the pulpit denounced him as the assassin of the Archbishop of Paris, telling his congregation that the presence among them of such a man would be sure to bring a heavy visitation upon them. The sermon had a very unexpected effect. A musical society, known as "La Lyre," came out and serenaded the poet under his window, whence he thanked them with considerable emotion, as he had lately been far more accustomed to the tumult of passionate wrath than to any exhibition of sympathy. He said that this was the fifth time that he had visited the country; previously he had come, drawn by admiration of their wild and beautiful scenery; now he had been driven among them by a cruel blast, but their kind reception atoned for much of his trouble. He next made his way to London, where he remained some time.

Some time previously he had made a tour through the East of France, visiting the scenes of the recent war, and taking his grandchildren with him to show them the towns that had been bombarded by the Prussian shells.

Among other towns, he went to Thionville, where, in 1792, Châteaubriand had been wounded, and where, in 1814, Goethe had borne his part as an assailant. Here it was that General Hugo had made his haughty reply when summoned to surrender to the Baron of Hainault, and he asked to be shown the house where his father had resided at the time. The people at the hotel could not inform him, but advised him to apply to the mayor, who was very old and would probably recollect. On acquainting the mayor with his name, the venerable functionary started to his feet and exclaimed, "Ah, we wanted General Hugo, and Thionville again would have scorned to surrender to the Prussians!" The whole of the town council, on being informed that General Hugo's son was among them, rose to their feet and testified their respect.

It was sad to find that the portrait of the old soldier had not escaped the ravages of the shells; only a bit of the frame remained hanging to the wall. A Prussian sentinel marched to and fro outside the chamber.

A NIGHT ATTACK IN BRUSSELS.

One day, as the poet, while strolling in the suburbs, stopped to make a sketch, an old woman, who caught his name, came up to him and asked him whether he was the fine young man with whom years ago she had often danced at the town balls. He disclaimed all previous acquaintance with her, but on further conversation it turned out that she retained very clear recollections of his brother Abel, who had been in Thionville with his father.

We may be excused for introducing another little episode of this visit. The poet's grandson was crossing the court-yard of the hotel where they were staying, and a Prussian general, attracted by the child's handsome looks, held out his hand and said,

"Will you shake hands with me, little man?"

The child looked steadily at the officer for a moment, and then said, decidedly,

"No."

"Whose child is that?" the officer inquired.

"M. Victor Hugo's grandson," answered the nurse.

"Oh, then I understand," said the general; "you are quite right, little man!" and he smiled and walked away.

When Victor Hugo returned to Paris at the end of the year 1871, he did not resume his residence with Paul Meurice, from whom he had received such hospitality for six months before, but he rented apartments for himself at No. 66 Rue de la Rochefoucauld; in these, in consequence of being in mourning, he received hardly any company, and after about fifteen months he removed to No. 21 Rue de Clichy, where, interested in his grandchildren, and still devoted to the welfare of his country, he spent his days rejoicing in the return of peace.

CHAPTER XXXIII.

It **was while Victor** Hugo was travelling in Luxembourg that the elections of July 2, 1871, took place. They were seriously affected by occurring during a state of siege, **and** by the erasure of 140,000 names from **the roll** of electors. The absent poet obtained only 57,000 votes, but he wrote that he was more proud of them than he had been of the 214,000 which he had received in Paris in February.

On resigning his seat at Bordeaux, **he** had said, "In this Assembly there is a majority that will not allow an idea to be matured. It would not listen to Garibaldi; it has **not** listened to me. But mark me! on the very day that M. Thiers ceases to give it satisfaction, the Right will deal with him just in the same way that the Left has dealt with Garibaldi and myself; and nothing would surprise me less than his sending in his resignation. We are experiencing a repetition of 1815."

It was a prediction, like many others that Victor Hugo made, which was destined to be fulfilled. M. Thiers not only had to resign, **but** for a time it seemed very doubtful whether the monarchical party would not prevail. Only internal dissension prevented the re-establishment of a throne.

Ever zealous in the cause of liberty, Victor Hugo took advantage of every opportunity to intercede for all those who by court-martial had been sentenced to transportation or to death. He begged for the lives of Maroteau, Rossel, Ferré, Lullier, and Crémieux, declaring that political executions were only like a subterranean volcano, perpetuating the hidden dangers of civil war. But though he pleaded with unremitting earnestness, his appeal for clemency was of no avail, and all the answer he received was the bloody slaying of the hostages.

In December it was proposed to him, in view of the approaching supplementary elections, that he should accept the *mandat impératif.* This he could not do, because, according to his principles, conscience may

not take orders; but he endeavored to change the *mandat impératif* into a *mandat contractuel,* so that there might be a more open discussion between the elector and the elected. The amendment was accepted, but Victor Hugo only polled 95,900 votes, against 122,435, which were registered in favor of M. Vautrain; his defeat, no doubt, being in a great measure attributable to his posters, which were headed " Amnesty," and avowed that "there are times when society is alarmed and seeks assistance for the merciless."

His failure to secure his election did not **prevent him** from continuing to apply his **energies to** social questions; and although **he was** invited by the electors of Tours to **become** a candidate for the sixth arrondissement, **he** considered that for a time he could serve **the** Republic better by remaining out of the Assembly.

He published, **in** September, 1873, **a** poem which **he** called " La Libération **du** Territoire," and which was sold for the benefit of the people of Alsace and Lorraine. France at the time was getting up *fêtes* in honor of the Shah of Persia, the Asiatic potentate of whom it is affirmed that, having once conquered a city, he had the eyes of the principal inhabitants, to the weight of about thirty pounds, carried before him in trays; and this moved the indignant poet to ask whether it was well to be exhibiting the national army to such a man, even though he adorned his horse's tail with diamonds.

Only a short time afterwards he was called upon to sustain another trying blow. His only surviving son, François Victor, succumbed on the 26th of December to a painful illness that had confined him to his room for sixteen months. It seemed the overflowing of his cup of grief, and yet there were **men,** whose **names** had better not be mentioned, **who** jeered at the father's sorrow, **and openly** rejoiced over his loss.

Auguste Vacquerie inserted an **admirable** obituary notice in *Le Rappel,* claiming for

16

François the reputation of an historian rather than a journalist, and praising his kind and charming disposition. Long before the hour fixed for the funeral, a dense crowd assembled before the house. Shortly after noon the coffin was carried out, followed by Victor Hugo himself, who went on foot, accompanied by the widow of Charles Hugo, who

that Louis Blanc made a short oration, in which he eulogized the integrity and the industry of the deceased. Speaking of the father's sorrow, he said that it was consoled by the happy conviction that the separation of death is not perpetual. The poet believed his own words,

"The grave is life's prolonging, not its dreary end,"

FRANÇOIS VICTOR HUGO.

had been so patient in her devoted care to her brother-in-law during his illness that she was almost prostrate with weakness. A number of the most illustrious men in Paris joined the procession to the cemetery, where, the family grave being already full, the body was deposited in a temporary vault. The ceremony was performed in silence, except

and repudiated all idea of final severance. The eternity of God and the immortality of the soul are doctrines that strengthen a man in all his afflictions, and make him capable of living still so as to benefit humanity.

Victor Hugo wept bitterly as his friends led him away from the grave-side, and numbers around him kept shouting aloud, "Vive Victor Hugo! Vive la République!"

Two years later he was called upon to speak similar words of consolation to Louis Blanc, who had to consign Madame Louis Blanc to her grave; and he recalled the time when he had himself been chief mourner:

"What my friend performed for me two years ago is an office that I now discharge to him. The tender pressing of hand to hand at the brink of the open grave is a part of our mortal destiny; and destiny seems often to decree that the greatest souls should be most sorely tried: then it is they need the consolation of a sincere belief."

Such belief, it may confidently be affirmed, Victor Hugo possesses. He fails to recognize any intermediate agency between the soul and God, and, consequently, his conscience permits him to admit no human counsel in divine things; he repudiates all narrow dogmas and rejects all stern denunciations of eternal punishment. In launching forth his invectives against fanatics, monks, inquisitors, prelates, popes, and Jesuits, he is aware only of a desire to stand clear of superstition, and to represent God simply as he is—good and great, and worthy to be loved in his own glory. He holds that moral rectitude far transcends all religious ordinance. He had Lamennais for his confessor, but, like Lamennais, he left the bosom of the Roman Church, saying of himself:

"Yes, by education I was a Catholic, but that is all over and gone; still I hold my faith in the immortality of the soul. I am thankful to God for the years of mercy he has granted me, and, above all, I am thankful that he has permitted me to spend those years in useful labor."

It is beyond our sphere to comment upon this creed. With some differences, he holds the doctrines which were held by Voltaire, who never was the unbeliever which the priests whom he attacked desired to represent him. Like the author of "L'Essai sur les Mœurs," he has been exposed to the vituperations of the clergy, although he has not been uniformly hostile to Catholicism, inasmuch as he hailed the accession of Pius IX. to the popedom in 1846, believing that the new pope would invest the tiara with the best attributes of liberty—an anticipation which was falsified only too soon by the publication of the Encyclical.

From the period of his expulsion from Belgium until he entered the Senate, Victor Hugo kept himself incessantly occupied in the production of new works, all designed to further the cause that he had at heart. He wrote an admirable essay on the occasion of the Petrarch Centenary, and another on the Philadelphia Exhibition. He delivered funeral orations over Madame Paul Meurice, Edgar Quinet, Frédéric Lemaître the actor, and Georges Sand. He wrote to the Italian democrats; he pleaded the cause of the convict Simbozel. The days were not long enough for his work.

Day by day throughout the siege he had kept a register of the sad history, and this formed the basis of "L'Année Terrible," a poetical narrative which contains some of his noblest inspirations. He describes the catastrophe of Sedan, and sees how the glory of France was dimmed when the sword was surrendered into the stern conqueror's hand; he enumerates one fearful episode after another, denounces Germany as being answerable for the fratricidal war, and stigmatizes the invaders as plunderers. Apostrophizing the cannon that had been founded out of the proceeds of "Les Châtiments," he exclaims,

"... thou deadly weapon, offspring of my muse!
Put thou thy bronze into my bowed and wounded
    heart,
And let my soul its vengeance to thy bronze impart."

Every paragraph may be recognized as bearing the mark of being written on the spur of the moment, and as characterized by the alternate hopes and fears that each hour brought with it; but while he bewails his country's defeat and suffers with her agony, he foretells her coming resurrection.

All through his life Victor Hugo has cherished the vision of universal brotherhood, adapting the verses of "Patria" to an air of Beethoven's, deeming it a symbol of fraternal concord between France and Germany; but after Sedan he felt that he had no alternative but to encourage the national defence, convinced that to save Paris and France was the way to save civilization.

However, when the struggle was ended, and while many in their despondency were thinking it was all over with them, his was the first voice to cry, "Courage and hope!" The storm passed away, but it had left a deeper faith in his heart; he felt that the nation could not sink like lead, and so he made the strings of his lyre resound with the melodies of peace, and to pour forth the strains of promise that the day was not far distant when France would woo her sons to progress, and in the track of princes who were drunk with blood there should follow the dawn of justice and liberty. Contrasting the prosperity of the vanquished with the embarrassments of the conqueror, he adopted the language of prediction, asserting that France had only to be faithful to her mission, and France could not be annihilated.

Events have since proved that the poet was right.

"L'ANNÉE TERRIBLE."

CHAPTER XXXIV.

THE last romance published by Victor Hugo was "Quatre-vingt-treize." It appeared in 1874, and, like "Les Misérables," was translated at once into many languages. The tale of the year of blood is most strikingly told, the object of the book being to show how, from that sanguinary atmosphere and from that merciless strife, progress and humanity rose up and showed themselves triumphant.

As a second title the work was called "La Guerre Civile;" and La Vendée, as the last asylum of the royalist faith, is made the theatre of a dramatic history of which the scenes are relieved by charming descriptions of the country. The heroes of the book are impersonations of all the passions, the stoical virtue, the indomitable courage, the stern resistance, which characterized the men of the period.

There is a magnificent chapter which seems to bring into fresh life the Paris of '93; it represents the city in all its picturesqueness, seething and devoid of rest, while the account of the giant insurrection is entrancing in its interest and graced by passages of exquisite sentiment. The book received the most favorable criticism, although it was at last just as it had been at first, that the author's vocabulary was somewhat severely censured. It was in three volumes, and an anecdote is told about the first edition which may be worth repeating.

On the day of the first publication of the book, M. Escoffier, the editor of *Le Petit Journal*, was desirous to be the first to review it. *Le Petit Journal*, it should be said, was a paper which had done much to raise the moral standard of the people, and M. Escoffier, under the pseudonym of Thomas Grimm, had contributed a series of articles remarkable alike for their conciseness and for their strong sense. On this occasion he received a copy of the first volume at midday, followed two hours afterwards by a copy of the third volume, with a message

that he could not have the second volume until after five o'clock. Determined not to be baffled, M. Escoffier hurried off to the house of Paul Meurice, where he obtained an interview with Victor Hugo, and learned the full particulars about the missing volume in time to complete his review for the next morning.

As an instance of the poet's retentive memory, it may be mentioned that when M. Escoffier was introduced to him, although they had never met before, Victor Hugo said to him,

"I remember, M. Escoffier, being much struck with an observation of yours long ago; you observed that 'Les Girondins' had been the work of an epoch, and that 'Les Misérables' would probably be the work of a century."

It was more than eleven years since Escoffier had written this in a little Toulouse newspaper. Many similar instances have been related which demonstrate in how marked a degree Victor Hugo possesses the faculty of extraordinary memory.

After "Quatre-vingt-treize" there appeared in 1874 a touching pamphlet which the author called "Mes Fils," being a cry of hope which he associated with a tribute of affection to his own dead children. In 1875 a new edition was published of "Napoléon le Petit," the original of which had been issued in London in 1852.

This was followed by a work entitled "Actes et Paroles: avant, pendant, et depuis l'Exil," of which Victor Hugo has given his own description. He says about it:

"The trilogy is not mine, but the Emperor Napoleon's; he it is who has divided my life; to him the honor of it is due. That which is Bonaparte's we must render to Cæsar."

Each of the three volumes was devoted to a separate period of the exile, and from their pages have been drawn many of the incidents of the present work.

Commencing with an admonition to resist-

PETIT PAUL ("LA LÉGENDE DES SIÈCLES").

ance, the "Actes et Paroles" concludes with an exhortation to clemency; resistance to tyrants should not be deemed inconsistent with clemency to the vanquished.

Some time previously to this, the prolific author had issued his pamphlet "Pour un Soldat," a production which realized a double benefit, as not only did it contribute to the saving of the life of the poor soldier who had been condemned for a very venial crime, but the profits of the sale were applied to the relief of the sufferers in Alsace and Lorraine.

Next, in 1877, appeared the second part of "La Légende des Siècles," proving itself a worthy sequel to the first. Here, once again, the poet surveys the cycle of humanity from the days of Paradise to the future which he anticipates; he takes his themes alike from the legends of the heroic age of Greece and from the domains of actual history, and, after singing of the achievements of the great, he dedicates his lay to the little ones, and in a charming poem entitled "Petit Paul" he depicts with fascinating pathos all the tenderness and all the sorrows of childhood.

On the opening page of the book the author has inscribed a notice to the effect that the final series of "La Légende des Siècles" will be published if his life be spared to complete the task, but it has not yet appeared, although it is known to be almost finished.

At the date when the second series was published Victor Hugo was residing at No. 21 Rue de Clichy; circumstances having thus brought him back to the very street where he had passed some of his early years, and close to the school where he had learned to read. He shared the apartments on the fourth floor with Madame Charles Hugo, who, after remaining a widow several years, was married to M. Charles Lockroy, deputy for the Seine, and well known both as a politician and a man of letters. The third floor was occupied by Madame Drouet, the lady who had made such exertions on his behalf when he was proscribed in 1851, and who now placed her *salon* at his disposal for the reception of his friends.

This *salon*, decorated with furniture after the poet's own taste, may be said to have become historical, as having been associated with many of the learned men of the day; and the author of this volume may state that it has been at the receptions in this apartment that he has enjoyed the acquaintance of the great author, who once remarked to

him, with an expression of sadness, that the works which he had dreamed of writing were infinitely more numerous than those which he had ever found time to write.

The hand, no doubt, is too slow for the gigantic work that the poet conceives. And yet no moment is ever lost. Generally up with the sun, he writes until midday, and often until two o'clock. Then, after a light luncheon, he goes to the Senate, where during intervals of debate he despatches all his correspondence. He finds his recreation generally by taking a walk, although not unfrequently he will mount to the top of an omnibus just for the sake of finding himself in the society of the people with whom he has shown his boundless sympathy. At eight o'clock he dines, making it his habit to invite not only his nearest friends, but such as he thinks stand in need of encouragement, to join him and his grandchildren at their social meal.

At table Victor Hugo relaxes entirely from his seriousness. The powerful orator, the earnest pleader, becomes the charming and attractive host, full of anecdote, censuring whatever is vile, but ever ready to make merry over what is grotesque. Punctually at ten he adjourns to the *salon*, where, in the midst of a distinguished circle, he joins in the free flow of conversation. Always affable, he has not merely a cordial welcome for the renowned, but a word of kind animation for the humblest recruit in the literary army. No one can leave his company without feeling reassured and delighted.

On these occasions he makes a fine picture. Hale and vigorous in his appearance, precise and elegant in his attire, with unbowed head, and with thick white hair crowning his unfurrowed brow, he commands involuntary admiration. Round his face is a close white beard, which he has worn since the later period of his sojourn in Guernsey as a safeguard against sore throat, but he shows no token of infirmity. His countenance may be said to have in it something both of the lion and of the eagle, yet his voice is grave, and his manner singularly gentle.

The writer of this record of "Victor Hugo and his Time" cannot recall without the liveliest pleasure either the receptions in the *salon* or the various *tête-à-tête* interviews to which he has been admitted. He recollects how, on one occasion, the great master denounced to him the realistic character of many modern romances, regarding them as unwholesome and degraded, and how, on another occasion, he spoke with vehemence against the inconsistency of the Republic in admitting various creatures of the Empire to several public offices; but neither his literary convictions nor his political partialities ever really disturbed the calmness of his line of thought, and, as he states in the admirable letter which stands at the beginning of the present volume, his anger has never been vented upon anything except wrong.

As a general rule, his personal enemies do not give him much concern; but if a name that is specially odious should happen to be mentioned, he usually finds words to express his aversion. Thus on our incidentally alluding to Mérimée, he broke out,

"That man leaves an infamous memory behind him. He used his talent to declaim about what his heart was too barren to understand."

But such outbursts never seriously affect Victor Hugo's habitual serenity; his mind, like his books, would seem to be the simple unassuming expression of humanity. It is the love of humanity that has guided his genius, and his genius has made his works imperishable.

CHAPTER XXXV.

"L'Art d'être Grand-père."— Georges and Jeanne.—Romps, Tales, and Diversions.—"L'Histoire d'un Crime."

A BRIEF chapter must be devoted to Victor Hugo's love of children.

Some few months before the publication of the second series of "La Légende des Siècles" in 1877, the poet published a brilliant production, which he called "L'Art d'être Grand-père." It was a kind of sequel to the "Livre des Mères, ou Livre des Enfants," which consisted of a number of extracts selected from his works by his admirer, Hetzel, who, in introducing his book to the public, lauded Victor Hugo's peculiar faculty for describing the young, and declared that his reputation as the most sensitive and tender of authors stood unrivalled. The extracts are full of the merry songs of birds and the bright warblings of childhood, though at times they are tinged with sorrow too.

Ever considerate for the defenceless, Victor Hugo stands up for the rights of women and children. While Musset has dedicated his strophes to love as a passion, Hugo has regarded love as a sacred duty; he speaks directly to the maternal heart, and is constant in his endeavor to reinstate such as have fallen victims to misery or social laws. He is pathetic over an infant's cradle, he is delighted at childhood's prattle, and to him the fair-haired head of innocence is as full of interest as the glory of a man.

Thus beaming with affection for children in general, it is not in the least a matter of surprise that he should make his two grandchildren, Georges and Jeanne, the hero and heroine of "L'Art d'être Grand-père," a work into which he has thrown the fulness of his genius and the freshness of his love.

He has been taken to task about the title of the book, and told that there is no place for "art" in such a connection, but he has met the accusation with a smile; and when criticised for his tone of over-indulgence, he has replied:

"I own I want to have nothing to do with society. You say to me, 'All roses have thorns.' I say to you, 'You may pluck them off if you will;' for myself, I mean to inhale the fragrance of the rosebuds."

It has been suggested that the book might more appropriately be called the "*Pleasure* of Being a Grandfather;" but, remembering his own bereavements, and mindful of the sorrows of others, he felt that in many quarters the mention of "pleasure" might sound almost like a mockery.

He claimed the gratification of being indulgent as a right, agreeing entirely with M. Gaucher, who, in an article in the *Revue Politique et Littéraire*, remarks that "a father's duties are by no means light; he has to instruct, to correct, to chastise: but with the grandfather it is different; he is privileged to love and to spoil."

While the book abounds in many exquisite and gentle admonitions, it sparkles with the fun and sprightliness of child's play. While the poet inculcates kindness, obedience, and charity, he delights to tell how he has "plundered the housekeeper's jam-pots" for the gratification of his little pets, and how he was daring enough to distribute between them some dishes of strawberries that had been put ready for the after-dinner dessert, taking care, at the same time, to bid the children fetch in some houseless orphans that were crouching under the window, and make them share the dainty dishes with themselves.

Undaunted as he ever stood against the threats and persecutions of political opponents, he acknowledged that a child had ever the power to overcome him:

"Behold me by an infant now subdued!"

and avowed that he was not ashamed of any such humiliation, and sang of the pleasure he found in associating with the young, under the title of "Lætitia Rerum," making it his pleasant theme:

"My children, in the beauty of your eye
   The empyrean blue can I descry ;
   Your merry laughter like the springtime cheers,
   And like the morning dew-drops fall your tears !"

MATHA ("LA LÉGENDE DES SIÈCLES").
(*Drawn by J. P. Laurens.*)

And quite in accordance with what he wrote in his verse was his personal practice. Nothing could exceed his kindness, and no one ever took more pains to tell old tales and to invent new ones to awaken the interest of a juvenile audience.

Some of these tales were full of wonder, like "La Bonne Puce et le Roi Méchant," that had a very startling moral; some of the animal in a state of continual perplexity.

Nor was the grandfather-poet ever weary of devising little schemes to divert the young people, no one being more expert in balancing a fork on a decanter-stopper, or carving a pig out of a piece of bread, making lucifer-matches do duty for legs; nor was any one more interested in arranging juvenile en-

GEORGES AND JEANNE.
(" *L'Art d'être Grand-père.*")

them were pregnant with instruction, like that of the little dog who was transformed into a beautiful angel, because of its fidelity to a little girl; and some of them afforded infinite amusement, such as the tale of a donkey with the two long ears, one of which always heard "yes" and the other always heard "no," consequently keeping tertainments, especially at the season of the new year. It was at a Twelfth-night party that young Jeanne showed how early she had imbibed her grandfather's political opinions; in the midst of the "drawing of kings," which was the specialty of the occasion, getting weary of hearing such constant repetition of "Le roi! le roi!" she mounted on a chair, and began crying, "Vive la République!"

While they were quite young, his little grandchildren were allowed to bring their cat into the *salon* before dinner, when the diversion in the way of romping would be unlimited. The venerable gentleman whom they called their "papapa" would permit them to pull his fine white beard, and to roll themselves over him, laughing heartily as he called out,

"Ah! I see you know what a grandfather is made for: he is made to sit upon!"

As an illustration of his love for domestic joys, we may instance his definition of Paradise as "a place where children are always little and parents are always young." Young in his sympathies he has ever been; and it will be reckoned no serious betrayal of secret confidences to say that he has been known to carry off a pot of preserves to his little Jeanne when she has been shut up in disgrace, and that he has made a point of refusing to touch his fruit at dessert to show his grief at her having been naughty.

And all this love for the little ones is not in the least inconsistent with his detestation of the criminalities of the great. Under almost the same inspiration that produced the echoes of infantile prattle in the "Art of Being a Grandfather," he composed "The History of a Crime," a work which was issued on the eve of the elections of 1877, and of which he said,

"The need of this book is not only present, but urgent; therefore I publish it."

It was just the same intuition into the true principle of equity that made him stern towards the iniquity of tyrants, and tender towards the failings of the weak and the inexperience of the young.

CHAPTER XXXVI.

Victor Hugo's Creed.—Belief in the Immortality of the Soul.—Accusation **of Being an Atheist.**—" Le Pape."
—"Religions et Religion."—"La Pitié Suprême."—"L'Ane."

WE have already **said** that it is **not** our place to comment upon Victor Hugo's creed. What **that creed is** may be gathered alike from his philosophical works and from the explanations which he has himself **given in** relation **to** it.

He avows himself **a firm believer in the** immortality of the soul. A rationalist one day said to him, as is related by Madame de Girardin,

"So am I a believer to a certain extent; but surely the outcasts **of society can** have no faith in their own **immortality!"**

To which Victor Hugo replied,

"Perhaps they believe in it more than you do."

According to Arsène Houssaye, **the** poet has given a general exposition of his religious creed in something like the following terms:

"I am conscious **within** myself of the certainty of a future life. Just as, in a forest that is perpetually felled, young sprouts start up with renewed vigor, so my thoughts ever rise higher and higher towards the infinite; the earth affords me her generous **sap, but** the heaven irradiates me with the **light of** half-seen worlds. The **nearer I approach** my end, the clearer do **I hear the immortal** symphonies of worlds that call me to themselves. For half a century **I have been out**pouring my volumes of thought **in prose** and in verse, in history, philosophy, **drama,** romance, ode, and ballad, yet I appear **to** myself not to have said a thousandth **part of** what is within **me; and when I am laid in** the tomb I shall not reckon that **my life is** finished. The grave is not a *cul-de-sac*, it **is an** avenue; death is the sublime prolongation of life, not its dreary finish; it closes **on the** twilight, it opens in the dawn. **My work is** only begun; **I yearn** for it to become **higher** and nobler; **and this** craving **for** the infinite demonstrates that there is an infinity."

And in reply to the argument that those powers of his had been generated by Nature, the visible mother of **occult** forces, he **said,**

"There are no occult forces; occult force was chaos; luminous force is God. Man **is** a reduced copy of God, a duodecimo as it were of the gigantic folio; but still the same book. **Atom** as I am, **I can** still feel that I am divine, gifted with **divine** power because I can clear up the chaos that is within me. The books I write are worlds of themselves, **and I say** this without a particle **of** vanity, **no more** cherishing a feeling of **pride than a bird** that contributes its part to the **universal song. I am** nothing, a passing echo, an evanescent cloud; but let me only live **on** through my **future existences,** let me con**tinue** the work **I have** begun, **let** me sur**mount** the perils, the passions, the agonies, **that age** after age may be before me, and **who shall tell** whether I may not rise to have **a place in the** council-chamber of the ruler that controls all, and whom we own as God?"

The accusations of being an atheist he has met by drawing a satirical picture* of what he **conceives** to be the Catholic representa**tion of the** Deity, which he concludes by exclaiming, " Yes, priest, I am an unbeliever in such a God," and proceeds to describe the God whom he acknowledges to be the personification of the true, the just, and the beautiful; who neither constructs nor destroys religions; who is impalpable, but ev**erywhere to be felt;** who is supreme and

---

* "S'il **agit d'un** bonhomme à longue barbe blanche,
* * * * *
Dans la nuée, ayant un oiseau sur la tête,
À sa droite un archange, à sa gauche un prophète,
Entre ses bras son fils, pâle et percé de clous,
Un et triple, écoutant des harpes, dieu jaloux.
* * * * *
En colère et faisant la moue au genre humain,
Comme un Père Duchêne, un grand sabre à la main;
Dieu qui volontiers damne et rarement pardonne;
Qui, sur un passe-droit, consulte une madone;
Dieu qui, dans son ciel bleu, se donne le devoir
D'imiter nos défauts, et le luxe d'avoir
Des fléaux, comme on a des chiens, qui trouble
l'ordre,
Lâche sur nous Nemrod et Cyrus, nous fait mordre
Par Cambyse, et nous jette aux jambes Attila :
Prêtre, oui, je suis athée, à ce vieux bon Dieu-là."

"LE PAPE."

unchangeable, an eternal principle, our very conscience.

To develop this creed is the design of several of his later works. In "Le Pape" he depicts an ideal pastor making clemency the principle of his power, striving ever to be gentle and sympathizing with every phase of suffering, drawing around him the outcast and despised, repudiating infallibility, denouncing war, delivering the message of peace, and thus securing the divine benediction on himself. The book stirred up the indignation of the Catholics, and M. de Brigny issued a volume of poetry entitled "Pape contre Pape, ou le Pape de Victor Hugo et le Pape de l'Église." In reply to the storm that had been raised against him, Victor Hugo, in 1879, brought out "La Pitié suprême," the gist of which was to bespeak pardon and pity for such as were tyrants through their own ignorance and defective education. Like John Huss sighing "Poor man!" over the executioner who was kindling the stake, the poet here outpours his eager desire to rescue

"The hangman from his torture, and the tyrant from his throne."

Tolerance is the basis of Victor Hugo's creed, and this tolerance it was that inspired him to write his "Religions et Religion," which was published in 1880 with the notice prefixed:

"This book was commenced in 1870, and completed in 1880. The year 1870 gave infallibility to the papacy, and Sedan to the Empire. What is the year 1880 to bring forth?"

In this philosophical poem, the poet's thoughts turn much to the future; he professes his resolve to be free from subservience to superstition; the theme of the book is the delineation of what the religions of the world seem to be, and of what to his mind true religion ought to be; founded solely on morality; full of care for the rights, the duties, and the sorrows of humanity, and never losing sight of the immortality of the soul.

Prompted by his continued desire to overthrow pedantry and to replace it by knowledge, he has since published "L'Âne," where the ass prophesies like Balaam's, and holds forth against those whom the author would denounce as false teachers. He calls his ass "Patience," and, in the daring way that is characteristic of his genius, he makes the creature trample underfoot the musty libraries, the illegible manuscripts, and the worn-out folios that he maintains have too long stifled the progress of the human intellect.

Louis Ulbach has observed of the book that in its pages "the poet, at the climax of his life, dazzled though he is by the nearness of the dawn beyond, glances back at those whom he has left behind, addresses them with raillery keen enough to stimulate them, but not stern enough to discourage them, and from the standpoint of his serenity puts a fool's cap upon all false science, false wisdom, and false piety."

"HERNANI," ACT IV. SCENE IV.

CHAPTER XXXVII.

Revival of "Hernani."—Banquet in Celebration.—Revivals of "Ruy Blas," "Notre Dame de Paris," and "Les Misérables."—Saint-Victor on Victor Hugo's Vitality.—Banquet at the Hôtel Continental, February 26, 1880.—Victor Hugo's Speech.

ALTHOUGH Victor Hugo has outlived the hostility of adversaries, and now commands unbounded respect, persecution long continued to pursue him, and during the state of siege so long maintained by the Bordeaux Assembly all his dramas were prohibited, official instructions on this matter being enforced by military power. Sword in hand, General Ladmirault stopped the performance of "Le Roi s'Amuse," and it has not since appeared upon the stage; and another official had "Le Revenant" erased from the playbills, insisting that nothing of Victor Hugo's should be performed without a special license, such license to be renewed from evening to evening.

But in November, 1877, "Hernani" was revived by the Comédie Française, and was received with great enthusiasm. The actors and actresses proved themselves worthy of their task. Mlle. Sarah Bernhardt undertook the part originally filled by Mlle. Mars, and showed herself quite as successful as her popular predecessor.

As an acknowledgment of the talent she displayed, Victor Hugo sent the young *sociétaire* the following note:

"MADAM,—You were both great and charming. I am an old combatant, but at the moment when the enchanted people were applauding you I confess that I wept. The tear drawn forth by yourself is yours; I lay it at your feet."

"Hernani" attracted considerable crowds. After the hundredth performance, in conformity with custom, the poet gave a dinner, and about 200 guests, including the theatrical critics, many men of letters, and all the actors engaged in the play, met together at the Grand Hôtel to share the pleasure of a banquet, at which the great author himself presided. His deportment on the occasion could not fail to make a deep impression. Nothing in his manner betrayed the least symptom of vanity, though an expression of noble satisfaction rested on his countenance.

A rare cordiality reigned in the assembly. There were met together representatives of journals of the most antagonistic views, writers who fought obstinate battles in the daily press; but the poet, who, in spite of his seventy-five years, set them an example of youth, was a living type of Fraternity. Discord seemed banished from the midst, and one thought animated every heart; the presence of the great man they had met to honor appeared for the time not merely to realize the ideal of a republic of letters, but to exalt that republic above the level of human passion.

Similar entertainments were given both after the hundredth performance of "Ruy Blas" and the hundredth performance of "Notre Dame de Paris."

The romance of "Notre Dame de Paris" had been dramatized by François Hugo, and after this version had been revised by Paul Meurice it was performed at the "Théâtre des Nations," where, although Victor Hugo endeavored to screen himself from the public eye, he was recognized and received an enthusiastic ovation from two thousand spectators.

A welcome reception was accorded to the play founded upon "Les Misérables," which we have already mentioned.

But the noblest of all the *fêtes* that marked the revival of the poet's dramas was that which was celebrated at the Théâtre Français in 1880, in honor of the fiftieth anniversary of "Hernani," which was esteemed as "the golden wedding" of his genius and his glory. On the 25th of February, 1830, the first representation had been given amid the uproar of opposition; and now on the 25th of February, 1880, the company of the Comédie Française, with a glowing pride, performed the masterpiece of which it is scarcely an exaggeration to declare that it is the consummation of artistic beauty. On

THE "GOLDEN WEDDING" OF "HERNANI."

this occasion it was listened to with rapt attention by an audience that included the must illustrious men of the day; but no sooner did the curtain fall than there was an outburst of vehement applause.

In a few minutes the curtain rose again, and exposed to view a striking bust of Victor Hugo elevated on a pedestal profusely decorated with wreaths and palm-leaves. Behind it were grouped all the actors in the play and all the *sociétaires* of the theatre attired in the costumes of the poet's leading characters, while the back of the stage was thronged with ballet-dancers waving the gayest of banners. Sarah Bernhardt, in her character of Doña Sol, then stepped forward, and, holding a palm-branch in her hand, recited in her peculiarly harmonious and tender voice some appropriate verses composed by François Coppée. In her own enthusiasm she carried away the vast audience, and the applause thundered out louder than before.

M. Francisque Sarcey, one of the best-known dramatic critics, at this moment shouted,

"Rise!"

The whole house rose at once to their feet, and, following the bidding of their leader, made the air ring again with their vociferations.

"Ad multos annos! long live Victor Hugo!"

Overcome by his emotion, the poet had been obliged to retire.

And may we not hope that these aspirations will be fulfilled? It is Saint-Victor who has written of him:

"His old-age (if that august maturity which is ever green and untarnished can be called old-age) never asserts itself except by some outburst of rugged strength. Like his own Eviradnus,

"'He wearies not; years harden him.'

He is in his full vigor at the time of life when many great intellects have passed into their decline. His exceptional mind seems to call out an exceptional physique. Longevity may be predicted for him. At the close of the century the *carmen sæculare* may be chanted by the same voice as hailed its dawn."

Within a few days after the performance at the Théâtre Français, the Parisian press, anxious to testify its regard for the great dramatist and author, gave a banquet at the Hôtel Continental. All the *élite* of journalism were present. Victor Hugo himself presided.

After dinner M. Émile Augier, an author of considerable renown, proposed the toast of the evening, dwelling much on the marvellous vitality of the noble compositions of the poet.

"Time, O glorious master," he exclaimed, "takes no hold upon you; you know nothing of decline; you pass through every stage of life without diminishing your virility. For more than half a century your genius has covered the world with the unceasing flow of its tide. The resistance of the first period, the rebellion of the second, have melted away into universal admiration, and the last refractory spirits have yielded to your power. . . .

"When La Bruyère before the Académie hailed Bossuet as father of the Church, he was speaking the language of posterity, and it is posterity itself, thou noble master, that surrounds you here, and hails you as our father."

The entire assembly rose, and the room echoed with the name of "Father." It was the grateful and affectionate homage of sons rendered to the genius that overflowed with the love of humanity.

M. Delaunay then spoke a few words on behalf of M. Émile Perrin, who was unable to be present, and expressed a hope that the assembly would co-operate in soliciting from Victor Hugo another new dramatic work.

The suggestion was greeted with prolonged cheering, which became more vehement still when Sarah Bernhardt came forward and embraced the poet with manifest enthusiasm.

After a short speech from M. Francisque Sarcey, who acknowledged that he had once been one of the refractory spirits alluded to by Émile Augier, Sarah Bernhardt again recited François Coppée's verses, and the audience subsided into the silence of expectation.

Victor Hugo rose, and though ever and again his words faltered with emotion, he read his address of thanks with a full clear voice:

"I cannot, nor would I, say more than a few words.

"Before me I see the press of France. The worthies who represent it here have endeavored to prove its sovereign concord, and to demonstrate its indestructible unity. You have assembled to grasp the hand of an old campaigner who began life with the century and lives with it still. I am deeply touched. I tender you all my thanks.

. "All the noble words that we have just been hearing only add to my emotion.

"There are dates that seem to be periodically repeated with marked significance.

The 26th of February, 1802, was my birthday; in 1830 it was the time of the first appearance of 'Hernani;' and this again is the 26th of February, 1880. Fifty years ago, I who now am here speaking to you was hated, hooted, slandered, cursed. To-day, to-day . . . but the date is enough.

"Gentlemen, the French press is one of the mistresses of the human intellect; it has its daily task, and that task is gigantic. In every minute of every hour it has its influence upon every portion of the civilized world; its struggles, its disputes, its wrath, resolve themselves into progress, harmony, and peace. In its premeditations it aims at truth; from its polemics it flashes forth light.

"I propose as my toast, 'The prosperity of the French press, the institution that fosters such noble designs and renders such noble services.'"

The shouts of "Vive Victor Hugo!" broke out with tremendous peals of applause, which only died away as the company adjourned to the *salon*, which had been elaborately decorated with flowers for the occasion.

"That evening," wrote Aurélien Scholl next day, "was one of the finest spectacles imaginable." It was the triumph of the conqueror and the trophies of the victory were the immortal characters of Esmeralda, Quasimodo, Doña Sol, Didier, Ruy Blas, and César de Bazan.

DON CÉSAR DE BAZAN ("RUY BLAS").

CHAPTER XXXVIII.

Victor Hugo as a Draughtsman.—His First Effort.—His Subsequent Progress.—His Admiration of Albert
Dürer.—Album Published by Castel.—Letter of Victor Hugo to Castel.—New-year's Gifts.—Caricatures.
—Victor Hugo's Handwriting.—M. Jules Claretie's Observation.—Destination of Manuscripts.

THE sketches that have been introduced into various pages of this work will have given already some idea of Victor Hugo's style of drawing, but more special notice is demanded of his singular power as a draughtsman.

In an article published in *L'Art* in 1875 M. Ph. Burty has referred to the first drawing of this "child of genius," the rude figure of the bird within the egg-shell, to which we have alluded; but there is nothing to show that Victor Hugo in his youth occupied himself much with drawing. Of course, like other boys at school, he was taught to draw, but manifestly the pen had more charms for him than the pencil. There was nothing at that time to indicate the power that he would subsequently develop. He says of himself:

"The first time that I took a sketch from nature was after I had reached man's estate. I was making an excursion in the environs of Paris, travelling with a lady in a diligence. In a village near Meulan, if I remember right, the vehicle stayed to change horses. I alighted, and as we happened to be near the church I went inside, and was so much struck by the graceful beauty of the apse that I made an attempt to copy some of the details. My hat served for an easel. I had only about ten minutes at my disposal, but when I was summoned back I had so far finished my sketch that it was a very fair souvenir of the place. Then for the first time I realized how beneficially copying from nature might be combined with my literary pursuits. The lady travelling with me asked me whether I intended to be an artist, and we laughed together at the suggestion; but the incident was a happy circumstance for me, and I have ever since delighted in sketching architectural peculiarities of fabrics that remain in the original design and have not been 'improved' by modern handling. Architecture is often a witness to the climate of a district: a gabled roof tells of the preva-lence of rain; a flat roof, of sunshine; and a roof weighted heavily with stones, of wind."

But though drawing never became Victor Hugo's occupation, it grew more and more to be his recreation. By perpetually scribbling designs, either to employ his leisure moments, to fix some impression on his memory, or to amuse children, the desultory draughtsman trained himself into a striking artist. He is a visionary served by a hand that is singularly obedient, and that reproduces a conception much as the key-board of an instrument becomes the interpreter of the mind of a musician. M. Méaulle, who has engraved the illustrations given in this volume, not inaptly designates his style as the "hedge-school" style, implying that it is of a character that he has picked up promiscuously and by himself.

He has never had recourse to any patient and systematic teaching. Often as a mere relaxation for a weary mind he will scratch down a few random lines; soon they will bear the outline of a cloud; below the cloud a turret will appear, then a castle will reveal itself, and the scene will begin to be transformed into a ruin in a landscape dark as Walpurgis, dimly mingled with light and shade. For these vagaries anything will serve for a starting-point, and a chance blot of ink will soon be subject to the most startling metamorphoses, art coming in to finish what fancy has begun.

"My inkstand," he says, "is generally my palette; if I want a lighter shade, a glass of water is my only requisite, though a few drops of coffee are occasionally very useful."

So skilful, however, is his hand that, in spite of the simplicity of his material, he has produced much upon which the most illustrious artists have lavished their unqualified praise.

Almost all his drawings are commentaries upon his thoughts. Unlike Hoffmann, who used his pencil to assist his fancy, Victor Hugo employs it to develop his poems and to illustrate his own literary creations. In a word, he has the faculty which M. Thiers has described as " common alike to a painter and an author, the artistic imagination that may be characterized as the imagination of design."

It is impossible to make any direct comparison between Victor Hugo's drawings and those of any other artist, though we know from his own statement which of the old masters he admires most, since he has apostrophized Albert Dürer as his model,

"O Dürer, master mine, painter old and pensive!"

Many of his compositions attest his admiration for the banks of the Rhine, with their castles and ruins, and their recollection seems continually to haunt him. He has a loving veneration for the Middle Ages, which in a marvellous manner he has, as it were, recalled to life; he takes an evident delight in the dilapidated fabrics, the crumbling ceilings and the broken mullions, deprecating from his very soul all modern attempts to restore them.

Théophile Gautier has no hesitation in associating Victor Hugo with the masters of the romantic school. "M. Hugo," he writes, "is not only a poet, he is a painter, and a painter whom Louis Boulanger, C. Roqueplan, or Paul Huet would not refuse to own as a brother in art. Whenever he travels he makes sketches of everything that strikes his eye. The outline of a hill, a break in the horizon, an old belfry—any of these will suffice for a subject of a rough drawing, which the same evening will see worked up wellnigh to the finish of an engraving, and the object of unbounded surprise even to the most accomplished artists."

Many of his early drawings were collected into an album by Castel, the publisher, who received from him the following letter :

"HAUTEVILLE HOUSE, October, 1862.

"MY DEAR M. CASTEL,—You say that you have obtained possession of a number of my old scraps, collected from the margins of my manuscripts, and that you wish to publish them, and, moreover, that M. Paul Chenay offers to produce fac-similes of them. And now you ask for my consent. I can only say that I am very much afraid, in spite of all M. Chenay's talent, that these scrawls, clumsily put on paper by a literary man preoccupied by his work, will cease to have any claim to be considered drawings the very moment they assert their pretensions.

Nevertheless, as you insist upon it, I suppose I must yield to your request."

And after explaining that the proceeds of the sale would be devoted to his work among poor children, he adds:

"I should never have imagined that these scraps of mine would have attracted the attention of such a connoisseur as yourself. But do as you please with them; I abandon them to their fate; and, whatever criticism may decide upon them elsewhere, I feel sure that my poor dear little children will think them very good."

A preface was written for the album by Théophile Gautier, and it sold very well. Another and more valuable album has been for some time in preparation, the text of which was intended to be from the hand of the lamented Paul de Saint-Victor, and an edition of " Les Travailleurs de la Mer," with illustrations by the master himself, is to appear before long.

Victor Hugo does not confine himself to drawing old buildings, but has made many landscapes. M. Auguste Vacquerie possesses a number of land and sea pieces bearing the poet's own signature, some of them having been given him as presents; others he has received in exchange for mediæval caskets, which Victor Hugo delights in collecting; and a few of them he has won in games at draughts. From the sale in the Rue de La Tour d'Auvergne he procured a very remarkable sepia drawing. It was executed between 1848 and 1851, and represents Paris by moonlight.

Many more of his productions still remain at Hauteville House. Moreover, it has been his habit for some years past to send a watercolor drawing on New-year's-day to some of his more intimate friends. That which was received by Saint-Victor in 1868 represented a burnt-down village, devastated by bombs, stained with blood—a conspicuous object in it being a child's empty cradle; it has the inscription written below " Organisation Militaire."

M. Burty likewise has a drawing entitled " L'Éclair," which he received from the exile with a characteristic message:

"My drawings, or what are called so, are somewhat wild. If this one is too difficult for you to engrave, select another. In my undisciplined way, I use the feather of my pen as much as its point."

Madame Lockroy and Madame Drouet also

are in possession of keepsakes of this kind, and in Paul Meurice's study is a large sepia drawing representing a strong fortified city. This was done during the siege.

Many a time has Victor Hugo been a model to his artist friends. Painters and sculptors have vied with each other in reproducing his noble and powerful head, and it is interesting to trace from their labors the gradual change that has marked the character of his striking features.

M. Aglaüs Bouvenne has edited a curious catalogue of the portraits and caricatures of Victor Hugo from 1827 to 1879. The caricatures are about a hundred in number, and, undoubtedly, some of them are very humorous. Those by Daumier are irreverent enough; but the general run of them, particularly the later ones, imply as much of veneration as of satire. The caricaturists, indeed, may be said to have paused before the conviction of his greatness; Victor Hugo, for his part, was always ready to concede to them every reasonable license.

Akin to the subject of his drawing, although of somewhat inferior interest, is that of the poet's handwriting, to which a brief space may be here devoted.

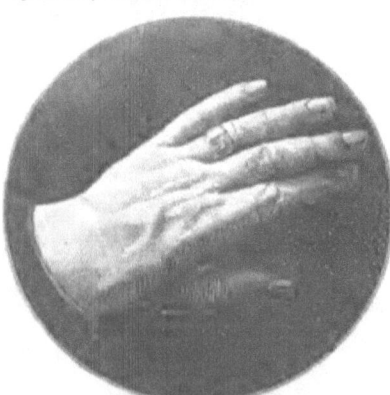

VICTOR HUGO'S HAND.
(From a Photograph by Auguste Vacquerie.)

This writing has undergone a considerable change. In his younger days it was very small and close, but by degrees it has become decidedly larger, as we ourselves have had the opportunity of judging from the perusal of many of his manuscripts, of which it is

said M. Jules Claretie intends publishing a description.

In reply to Michelet, who suggested that books might be printed just as they were written, with all the erasures exhibited, so that the various phases of the author's mind might be seen in the handwriting, M. Claretie says:

"Victor Hugo's manuscripts might serve as a model of the '*autographe imprimé*' of which Michelet dreamed. They exhibit the poet as he really was, writing down his inspirations upon any scrap of paper that came to hand, thus immortalizing the green placard on which he jotted down the poem in 'Les Feuilles d'Automne' which begins,

" O mes lettres d'amour, de vertu, de jeunesse !"

a poem which will endure for centuries to come.

"Under the hands of the great poet, what was mere waste paper, designed to be thrown away, has become worthy of perpetual preservation.

"As a great favor, I have been allowed to peruse these precious documents, and I find that they contain many readings that are as curious as they are interesting. Paul Meurice has specified many of these. Victor Hugo may be said to be here seen *en déshabillé*, but his genius loses nothing thereby. To judge from the manuscript of 'Les Orientales,' it is evident that the lines were composed while he was out walking, and written down immediately on his return. Nothing is easier for me than to imagine how he would come in from his walk, and, ascertaining that dinner was not on the table, would make use of the minutes while the cook was dishing up the soup, to write down upon some loose scrap of paper that was ready at hand verses wonderful as 'La Captive' and 'Lazzara.' He writes on anything and everything."

Since 1840 he has been in the habit of using small folio paper, which he has purchased for himself in the ordinary way; and which is not, as has been reported, the gift of a generous and admiring stationer. He still continues to write with quill pens, and his handwriting remains firm and well formed. Very few erasures are found in his work. By his will he has bequeathed all his manuscripts to the Bibliothèque Nationale, where they will be preserved, and will form a treasure of priceless value.

CHAPTER XXXIX.

Retirement from Senatorial Life.— Re-elected in 1876.— Recent Political Sentiments.— Speech at Château d'Eau.— Conversation at Home.— Anticipations for the Future.

ALTHOUGH Victor Hugo was repeatedly solicited to stand for election to the Assembly, we have already recorded how he remained aloof from political life. In 1873, the Lyons electors urged him to come forward, but he declined, because he was unwilling to do anything to compromise the cause of the amnesty, and considered that he could best serve the Republic by merging his own individuality. When he was selected as a delegate of the Paris municipal council for the senatorial elections, he issued an address to the French communes, calling upon them to consolidate a government which should make all men brethren.

On the 5th of February, 1876, he was elected senator for the Seine at the second ballot, being fourth out of five candidates. He took his seat with the extreme Left, and at the first sitting brought forward a motion for a full amnesty for the condemned Communists. The motion was rejected; the time for pardon had not yet arrived.

As a senator he took part most conscientiously in every serious debate, giving his vote upon every question that was at all important. His recent political opinions are the result of patient observation and long experience.

In order to give a just view of his present sentiments in political matters, we may be permitted first to give a *résumé* of a speech which he delivered not long since at Château d'Eau on behalf of the Workmen's Congress at Marseilles; and to follow this by an account of his view of the political situation, as he has himself expressed it in the course of private conversation.

"For four hundred years," he said, "the human race has not made a step but what has left its plain vestige behind. We enter now upon great centuries. The sixteenth century will be known as the age of painters, the seventeenth will be termed the age of writers, the eighteenth the age of philos-

ophers, the nineteenth the age of apostles and prophets. To satisfy the nineteenth century, it is necessary to be the painter of the sixteenth, the writer of the seventeenth, the philosopher of the eighteenth; and it is also necessary, like Louis Blanc, to have the innate and holy love of humanity which constitutes an apostolate, and opens up a prophetic vista into the future. In the twentieth century war will be dead, the scaffold will be dead, animosity will be dead, royalty will be dead, and dogmas will be dead; but Man will live. For all there will be but one country—that country the whole earth; for all there will be but one hope—that hope the whole heaven.

"All hail, then, to that noble twentieth century which shall own our children, and which our children shall inherit!

"The great question of the day is the question of labor. The political question is solved. The Republic is made, and nothing can unmake it. The social question remains; terrible as it is, it is quite simple; it is a question between those who have, and those who have not. The latter of these two classes must disappear, and for this there is work enough. Think a moment! man is beginning to be master of the earth. If you want to cut through an isthmus, you have Lesseps; if you want to create a sea, you have Roudaire. Look you; there is a people and there is a world; and yet the people have no inheritance, and the world is a desert. Give them to each other, and you make them happy at once. Astonish the universe by heroic deeds that are better than wars. Does the world want conquering? No, it is yours already; it is the property of civilization; it is already waiting for you; no one disputes your title!

"Go on, then, and colonize. If you require a sea, make it; and the sea will beget navigation, and navigation will bring cities into being. Only find the man that really wants a plot of land, and then say to him,

'Take it; the land is yours; take it, and cultivate it.'

"These plains around you are magnificent; they are worthy to be French, because they have been Roman. They have relapsed into barbarism, and next into savagery Do away with them. Restore Africa to Europe; and, by the same stroke, restore to one common life the four mother-nations—Greece, Italy, Spain, and France. Make the Mediterranean once more the centre of history. Add England to the fourfold fraternity of nations; associate Shakespeare with Homer.

"Meanwhile, be prepared for resistance. Deeds mighty as these must provoke opposition. Isthmuses severed, seas transported, Africa made habitable, these are undertakings that can only be commenced in the face of sarcasm and ridicule. All this must be expected. It is a novel experiment; and sometimes those who make the worst mistakes are those who ought to be the least mistaken. Forty-five years ago, M. Thiers declared that the railway would be a mere toy between Paris and Saint-Germain; another distinguished man, M. Pouillet, confidently predicted that the apparatus of the electric telegraph would be consigned to a cabinet of curiosities. And yet these two playthings have changed the course of the world.

"Have faith, then; and let us realize our equality as citizens, our fraternity as men, our liberty in intellectual power. Let us love not only those who love us, but those who love us not. Let us learn to wish to benefit all men. Then everything will be changed; truth will reveal itself; the beautiful will arise; the supreme law will be fulfilled, and the world shall enter upon a perpetual *fête* day. I say, therefore, have faith!

"Look down at your feet, and you see the insect moving in the grass; look upwards, and you will see the star resplendent in the firmament; yet what are they doing? They are both at their work: the insect is doing its work upon the ground, and the star is doing its work in the sky. It is an infinite distance that separates them, and yet while it separates unites. They follow their law. And why should not their law be ours? Man, too, has to submit to universal force, and inasmuch as he submits in body and in soul, he submits doubly. His hand grasps the earth, but his soul embraces heaven; like the insect, he is a thing of dust, but like the star he partakes of the empyrean. He

labors and he thinks. Labor is life, and thought is light!"

Such sentiments as these, it may well be imagined, were received, when they were delivered, with unbounded admiration, and are quoted to illustrate the poet's glowing aspirations for the future.

And in his own house Victor Hugo has just the same fascinating way of setting forth the opinions that he entertains. The present writer, having one day asked him what he thought of the existing condition of things in France, had the pleasure of hearing him confirm the views of the foregoing speech, and dwell upon the prospect which he believes is before his country.

Of course, it is impossible to reproduce the charm of the poet's language, but the tenor of his thoughts may be faithfully represented in the following summary:

According to his view, the Republic as it now exists is an acceptable Republic, and M. Jules Grévy, its president, is animated by intentions that are upright and praiseworthy. Although there is no close intimacy between the two men, they regard one another with respect and sympathy.

The poet holds that we are now in possession of a *bourgeoise* Republic, which is not an ideal one, but which will undergo a slow but gradual transformation. Its present stage is indispensable, because for a form of government that shall be capable of being brought to perfection it is essential to attach to it all who have hitherto had any share in directing public affairs; and the actual head of the State is a man of such rectitude of judgment and honesty of purpose that he may well inspire the completest confidence.

To this assertion Victor Hugo added the remark that he did not consider it the place of men of his time of life to take the lead in public matters. He regards himself and his contemporaries as having been pioneers and monitors, whose advice is worth obtaining, because they have gained their knowledge by experience, having lived through the struggles of the past; but whose theories cannot be put into practice by themselves. They are old, and the reins of government should be placed in the hands of men of a younger generation. They belong to the nineteenth century; the future solution of the social question belongs to the twentieth.

That solution, he declares, will be found in nothing less than the universal spread of instruction; it will follow the formation of new schools where salutary knowledge shall be imparted. Hitherto the teaching has been positively bad, as is demonstrated by the fact that a father, upon mature reflection, always has to say to his son, "Forget what I have made you learn." The great aim in instruction should be unity and truth. For this, in due time, the suitable lesson-books will be forthcoming. These will replace the manuals of the present century, although the present century is already in advance, having taken a stride, and made a beginning in illuminating humanity. By educating the child, you endow the man, and thenceforward, after that is brought about, you may proceed to exercise severe repression upon any one who resists what is right, because you have already trained him so that he cannot plead ignorance in his own behalf.

And are we to expect a Utopia, he asks, as soon as this endowment of knowledge is conferred? Certainly not. When we think of the progress of science and of the immense forces of nature, of those mighty currents that have hitherto remained unutilized in the vast tide, now despised, but hereafter to be brought into service, we become convinced that human efforts have been expended to no purpose. A great step has been already made; and when the time shall arrive that it is no longer requisite for man thus to throw away his time and strength, what will then be wanted to make him happy as man may be? He will require land to cultivate.

Then, too, it will be possible to say, "You require land; take the land! here is what will be for your advantage!" Distance no longer will be an obstacle; prolific continents, such as the whole interior of Africa, are destined erelong to be conquered by civilization.

Moreover, in the course of the coming century, frontiers, so to speak, will have disappeared, for the idea of fraternity is making its way throughout the world. Here the land is the monopoly of the few; far away it is owned by none. He who possesses none in the land of his birth must not hesitate to depart and become a proprietor in a country that no longer seems distant. The whole earth belongs to all men.

None are so unhappy as the idle; none so dissatisfied as those who persist in doing nothing for themselves; but these, thanks to salutary teaching, will gradually become fewer and fewer. A goodly future is dawning. It is impossible that the labors of centuries should forever remain unproductive.

In this way, only in his own unrivalled manner, he pours out his belief in the future of humanity; and if there be those who regard Victor Hugo's creed as blind credulity, and are disposed to treat his aspirations as visionary delusions, we can only say of such that they are themselves the losers. It is a bright creed and an encouraging, and is based upon the prospect of emancipation, uprightness, and coming happiness.

CHAPTER XL.

Present Residence of the Poet.—Domestic Habits.—Economy of Time.—*Fête* of February 27, 1881.—Procession of Children.—Address of Corporations.—Speech in Reply.—Illumination of Theatres.—The Poet's Continued Work.—Works yet to Appear.—Conclusion.

SINCE 1878 the poet has resided at No. 130 Avenue d'Eylau, at one end of Passy, near the Bois de Boulogne, in a part that is not yet completely built over, and which is in such a transition state that it can be called neither town nor country. His house is semi-detached, and adjoins that which is occupied by M. and Mme. Lockroy and Georges and Jeanne. There is a communication between the two residences, so that he may literally be said to be under the same roof as his belongings.

Throughout the neighborhood his house is familiarly described as "the house with the great veranda;" this veranda being glazed, and thus affording a shelter from the rain for any passers-by. The house is three stories high, and the study is on the first floor, where the poet lives in what may be said to be almost a bower, looking out on one side in the direction of the avenue, and on the other towards a pleasant garden, with a lawn surrounded by flowers and shaded by noble trees. From a small fountain a little stream trickles down, in which Jeanne's white ducks are constantly paddling about. A flight of steps leads down to the garden, and at the top of the steps is a glazed corridor leading into the *salon*. At the end of the corridor is the fine bust of Victor Hugo executed by his friend David, and in the library is an admirable portrait painted by Bonnat. The apartments are decorated with some rare and valuable tapestry, and the furniture throughout is highly elaborate.

Except there is a party of children, the number of guests that he entertains at his table never exceeds twelve, and his abode is still the resort of all of any repute in literature, science, art, or politics. These limited daily gatherings are now his sole recreation; he no longer dines out, but his own invitations are given with singular impartiality and the most cordial spirit. Sometimes it is Gambetta and sometimes it is Rochefort that arrives to partake of his hospitality;

and ladies are always found at his table, as, according to his judgment, a dinner from which ladies are excluded loses all its charm.

As a host he is, as we have observed, always delightful; his reminiscences extend from the beginning of the century, his manners are polished, and to the courtly dignity of a French peer he unites the affability of a kind and genial companion. His advancing age seems to bring him no depression; he speaks calmly of the short time that remains to him, and talks of the wide projects which his brain has yet to conceive. In this respect he is unlike Lamartine; he makes no attempt to ignore his age, and makes no apology for wearing spectacles.

Victor Hugo has never given up his habit of early rising; he nearly always quits his bed at five o'clock, remaining in his bedroom, which has become his favorite place of study, as being more quiet and retired than any other apartment. His bed is perfectly horizontal, and he uses neither bolster nor pillow. Among these minor details, we may mention that he has never accustomed himself to the use of an overcoat, and has never carried an umbrella; the absence of these precautions has resulted in more than one severe cold, and it is only within the last few years that he has yielded to the advice of an eminent physician, and abandoned the cold bath which it was his habit to take every morning. He has never been a smoker.

After dinner he still retains his habit of receiving his friends in the *salon*, and as the visitors arrive, more serious conversation is generally laid aside for lighter topics. In the midst of the social enjoyment of the evening a philosophic friend, thinking to carry on an argument that had been commenced at the dinner-table, asked him,

What, then, do you think is a proper definition of *wrong?*"

"Why," said the poet, "I think it would be 'wrong' to speak of 'wrong' now, when

VICTOR HUGO'S GARDEN IN THE AVENUE D'EYLAU.

we ought to be enjoying the society of the ladies."

His cheerfulness is perpetual. He has not, however, the same strain put upon his social powers as he had in the Rue de Clichy. His

Altogether he has much to which he must attend, notwithstanding that he has ceased to open for himself the numerous letters which pour in day after day, and has learned to rely upon the assistance of his

VICTOR HUGO IN HIS STUDY.
(A Sketch from Nature by M. Régamey.)

residence is not so central, and he has no visitors after midnight; consequently, he retires earlier. In 1878 he found an acceptable respite from all receptions in a few weeks' visit to Guernsey.

secretary, Richard Lesclide, and Madame Drouet. In this way, only matters of real importance are brought to his personal notice.

His age, with relation to his pursuits, more

THE SALON IN THE AVENUE D'EYLAU.

than justifies the remark that he is accustomed to make with a smile,

"I have no longer any time to waste."

Our task is done. By the aid of such material as has come within our reach, we have endeavored to present a faithful portrait. But

"A poet is a world shut up within a man,"

and Victor Hugo alone could portray Victor Hugo. He advances in years like the sturdy oak; or rather, perhaps we might say, he is like one of those stately tropical trees which, though bearing the weight of centuries, sends forth robust branches and giant foliage, gathers creepers round its bark, spreads its shade and diffuses its sweetness far around, thus uniting strength with grace, and compelling the tribute of admiration.

This marvellous existence has not yet reached its limit.

As an introduction to this history we gave a record of the *fête* at Besançon, the city of the poet's birth, and it appears to be an appropriate denouement to our work to relate the circumstances of the *fête* that was celebrated in his honor in Paris on the 27th of February, 1881.

A few days before Victor Hugo's birthday, M. Bazire made a proposition in *Le Beaumarchais* that the people of Paris should be invited to celebrate the occasion by paying their respects to him at his house.

M. Jeannin, the editor of *Le Beaumarchais*, readily entered into the scheme, and very quickly, through his exertions, not only the capital, but the nation at large, began to devise what form the tribute of homage should assume. A committee was forthwith formed, and deputations hastened up from every quarter. Representatives came from London, Vienna, Pesth, and Brussels; and flowers, scarce as they were at that season of the year, were contributed with boundless profusion.

The *fête* was fixed for the following Sunday, the 27th.

On the Saturday evening previous, Victor Hugo's *salon* was crowded with an unusual number of his friends, and M. Jules Ferry, the President of the Council, accompanied by his secretary, M. Rambaud, arrived with a magnificent Sèvres vase, which he presented to the poet, making a brief and appropriate speech in the name of the government of the French Republic.

By ten o'clock next morning a long line of people in holiday attire began to make their way to the Avenue d'Eylau, which was hung with flags. Platforms were erected along it, and Victor Hugo's house was decorated so profusely both inside and out with the flowers that had been sent for the purpose that it had the aspect of a vast bower. One of the most exquisite of the wreaths was contributed by the Comédie Française, and was surrounded with banners emblazoned with the names of the great author's dramas. A procession was formed of little girls tastefully attired, and bearing a banner inscribed "L'Art d'être Grand-père," with which they entered the *salon*, where they were received with the greatest delight by the venerable man and his two grandchildren. One of the girls recited some verses that had been composed by M. Catulle Mendès, upon which Victor Hugo embraced her affectionately, saying, "In embracing one of you, I embrace you all." After this they all retired into the street, where they were joined by an immense number of the children of various schools, and Victor Hugo showed himself at the window while the youthful multitude made the air ring again with their merry voices.

Immediately after this, the hero of the day received an address which was delivered by M. Dommartin in the name of the Belgian press; and shortly before noon the municipal *cortège* left the Place de l'Arc de Triomphe, which was the general rendezvous for the many corporations that were to file before the house. Standing at his window, he made them a brief speech. He said:

"It is not in my own name, for I am nothing, but in the name of every one who possesses life or reason, or love, or hope, or power of thought, that I give my greeting this day to Paris. It is Paris that I hail with my heart and soul. From time to time history has set upon certain cities a mark that is unique. And during 4000 years there have been three cities that may claim to be signalized as the headquarters of civilization. There have been Athens and Rome, and now there is Paris. What Athens was to Grecian antiquity, and what Rome was to Roman antiquity, such is Paris to Europe, to America— nay, to the whole civilized globe. Who speaks to Paris speaks to the world; he speaks *urbi et orbi*.

"And what am I but a humble wayfarer among you all? I have only my own share

THE POET'S HOUSE ON FEBRUARY 27, 1881.

18

in your lot; and as one of yourselves, in the name of all the cities of Europe and America, from Athens to New York, from London to Moscow, I salute and extol, as I love, the sacred city of Paris!"

While this address was being delivered the whole of the procession kept in motion.

of their land. It would take long to enumerate the elements of that marvellous crowd assembled to pay their tribute of respect to the bard of humanity; there were representatives of every class—students from the halls of arts and sciences, and deputations from all the great Lycées, many of them car-

THE CHILDREN'S GREETING.

Hail was falling, and it was bitterly cold. Yet no one seemed to regard the weather. The poet stood bareheaded at the window, his grandchildren beside him, and the whole concourse defiled past the house. There were not less than half a million people who thus thronged to pay their homage to the poet whom they honored as the glory

rying wreaths of flowers as they marched along.

One great stream flowed towards the Trocadéro, where a performance had been arranged of portions of the poet's plays, the proceeds of which were devoted to the poor. For this the leading *artistes* of the day had volunteered their services. M. Louis Blanc made a speech, recounting the incomparable services which the noble poet had rendered to their national literature. M. Coquelin also recited some laudatory verses that had been specially composed by Théodore de Banville.

All through the hours of the performance the crowd kept passing along before the poet's window, and it was not until it was quite dusk that he could retire to his *salon*, which by that time was full of friends who had come to congratulate him on his proud enjoyment. In the course of the evening he said to some ladies,

"I feel as if I were only twenty to-day."

Messages from every quarter throughout the length and breadth of France were pouring in all day, and many provincial towns had their own *fête* in recognition of the national rejoicing.

All the theatres were illuminated in the evening, and many verses were recited to celebrate the poet's honor.

Such are some of the principal details of the festival which was observed to testify the universal admiration of one whom Émile Augier has worthily called "the father of literature." His name has been adopted in the street nomenclature of various towns, and the Place d'Eylau is now the Place Victor Hugo, and has since been marked by the erection of his statue.

And Victor Hugo's labors are not ended yet. No ovation so satisfies him as to induce him to lay aside his work. His youth asserts itself as perpetual, his strength of intellect still demonstrates itself to be prodigious. Since the *fête* of 1881 the appearance of "Les Quatre Vents de l'Esprit" has again borne witness to his magic power, and other surprises are still in reserve: already completed, though not yet published, are "Toute la Lyre," two volumes of poetry; "La Vision du Dante," "La Fin de Satan;" and the third part of "La Légende des Siècles." Besides these, there are "Torquemada," a poetical drama in five acts; "L'Épée," also in verse; and two comedies, "La Grand'-mère" and "La Forêt Mouillée." Not that the list of his unpublished works is thus complete, for, at his own request, we have inspected his long accumulating hoard of manuscripts, and have found many which hereafter will see the light.

And what more is to be added? We must append the praise that all his writings have been devoted to the cause of humanity. The multitude and variety of his works yield their testimony to his unparalleled industry; but it is the glory of them all that they are faithful witnesses to his belief in right, his horror of meanness, his contempt of injustice, his truth, his integrity, and his courage.

As his mind became emancipated from its early trammels, his genius soared aloft like an eagle in its flight. Fate has allotted him his share of suffering; but every storm that has passed over him has only left him more calm and gentle. The course of time seems reluctant to touch his venerable head, and there are those who venture to indulge the hope that he may survive to preside over the centenary of the Revolution of 1789.

His old-age is full of honor. He has lived long enough to witness his own apotheosis; already he enjoys the glory of immortality, even though he has not ended his mortal days.

THE END.

BY VICTOR HUGO.

Ninety-Three.

Ninety-Three. A Novel. By Victor Hugo, Author of "Toilers of the Sea," "Les Misérables," &c. Translated by Frank Lee Benedict. 8vo, Paper, 25 cents; 12mo, Cloth, $1 75.

The types in "Ninety-Three" are many and grand. They remind us of Jean Valjean, of Enjolras, of that legion of august and legendary characters which he has created. Gauvain is the staunch, ardent Republican of the Danton cast, seeking in clemency and union, rather than in repression and inflexibility, the means of marshalling Republican France under one banner. Lantenac is a magnificent embodiment of the last Bretons. Cimourdain is the true incarnation in Revolution of what Lantenac is in Royalism. Sergeant Radoub gives a capital idea of the dare-devil Parisians of the Revolutionary time—rough, good-natured, and brave to foolhardiness—who made head against the coalescent armies of Europe.—*Athenæum*, London.

Beautiful sayings, true and noble thoughts, inexpressibly tender sentiments, are just as abun-

dant. We need not refer to them; they will be discovered and made much of, as they deserve to be. This work is written with no abatement of the vigor of his manhood: it is full of invention, artistic cunning, and a wafting wind that is not to be resisted. Hugo has but to lay his finger on children to make them adorable, and such a *voyage autour de la chambre* as the three little ones perform in the library of the tower of the Tourgue, when the storming of the château is in preparation and the shadow of a terrible destiny hangs over them, could only have been imagined by this poet of children and powerful disposer of extreme and vivid contrasts.—*Pall Mall Budget*, London.

Its purpose is high, and is served by novel researches into the history of the Revolution.—*Academy*, London.

The Toilers of the Sea.

The Toilers of the Sea. A Novel. By Victor Hugo, Author of "Les Misérables." 8vo, Paper, 50 cents; or, with Two Illustrations by Gustave Doré, 8vo, Cloth, $1 50.

In laying down the "Toilers of the Sea," after reaching its last page, we feel as though we were rising from an involuntary detention in a dreamland to which the author could alone admit us. Standing, as it does, above its predecessors in

reality, and therefore in interest, no power of prophecy is needed to assert that the "Toilers of the Sea" will be more widely read and more highly thought of than even "Les Misérables" or "Notre Dame de Paris."—*London Review*.

Victor Hugo's History of a Crime.

The History of a Crime: the Testimony of an Eye-Witness. By Victor Hugo. Illustrated. 8vo, Paper. Parts I. and II., each 25 cents; Complete in one Number, 4to, Paper, 10 cents.

A magnificent piece of writing.—*Examiner*, London.

Tells the story of the *coup d'état* with wonderful power. It is Hugo at his best.—*Independent*, N. Y.

In this work Victor Hugo has outdone himself, and he has given the world what it seems only reasonable to call the greatest of even his

writings. * * * Although the world is tolerably familiar with the crime of which he here tells the story, it reads here in Hugo's compact, eloquent, vivid pages like a revelation of something. * * * The book, with its fulness of detail and wonderful eloquence, is a most important contribution to modern history. * * * No novel can compare with it.—*Atlantic Monthly*, Boston.

Published by HARPER & BROTHERS, New York.

☞ Harper & Brothers *will send any of the above works by mail, postage prepaid, to any part of the United States, on receipt of the price.*

www.ingramcontent.com/pod-product-compliance
Lightning Source LLC
Chambersburg PA
CBHW020340030726
47496CB00007B/1961